Theories
of
Attitude Change

THE CENTURY PSYCHOLOGY SERIES

Richard M. Elliott, Gardner Lindzey,
and Kenneth MacCorquodale

Editors

CHESTER A. INSKO

The University of North Carolina

Theories

of

Attitude Change

APPLETON-CENTURY-CROFTS

Division of Meredith Publishing Company

New York

677-1

Library of Congress Card Number: 67-24334

PRINTED IN THE UNITED STATES OF AMERICA
E 47748

PREFACE

The recent proliferation of attitude change research has created an obvious need for a single systematic presentation of this material. There are at least two possible ways to systematize or organize the attitude change literature—in terms of theories or in terms of problems. An organization based on problems would obviously be the best way of presenting the research on a particular issue but would not allow for a very coherent presentation of any theory, such as dissonance theory, which has implications regarding many different issues. An organization in terms of theories, on the other hand, does allow for an adequate presentation of the theories as well as a reasonably adequate presentation of research on any given issue. For that reason the book has been organized in terms of theories. Admittedly, such an organization does create difficulties with specific research issues which are relevant to more than one theory, such as communicator discrepancy.

In describing the research it would have been very easy to summarize and comment upon a group of experiments without going into any of the details of procedure, statistical tests, etc. Indeed many readers may strongly wish that such an approach had been taken. Certainly this would have made the book more entertaining and readable. While such an approach may be of value in some contexts, it was not followed here for two reasons. First, due to methodological problems and conflicting findings it is frequently very difficult to summarize lucidly and accurately the findings on any given research topic. Second, unless the reader is already familiar with the research in a given area it is extremely difficult for him to understand and accept evidence provided by a given experiment or group of experiments. Thus, considerable time has been spent describing the procedural details of experiment after experiment. This approach has resulted in a reference book or handbook rather than in an orthodox textbook, although the book is suitable for use in advanced undergraduate classes as well as in graduate classes.

While the book does include most of the existing theories, some theories have not been presented because they are only secondarily concerned with attitude change or because they have not attracted much attention. An attempt has been made to present the theories with which attitude change psychologists are most directly concerned.

Systematic search of the literature stopped in 1965, although some

1966 material has been included. At the time a particular chapter was revised, any readily available 1966 material was also included. One of the most frustrating tasks in connection with this book has been keeping abreast of the current literature.

Whatever merit this book has results in part from the assistance obtained from a number of people who read and made suggestions regarding various chapters in the manuscript. I gratefully acknowledge the able assistance of John Schopler, Irving L. Janis, Ronald C. Dillehay, William J. McGuire, Charles E. Osgood, Milton Rokeach, Theodore M. Newcomb, Milton J. Rosenberg, Jack Brehm, and Irving Sarnoff. Last of all, I am sincerely grateful for the many hours spent by my wife, Verla, in arguing about suggested changes in the manuscript.

C. A. I.

CONTENTS

Theories
of
Attitude Change

1

Introduction

How are attitudes changed? This vital question is of practical importance to people who are concerned with such things as advertising, propaganda, and education. Furthermore, it is a centuries-old question that has played a key part in such disciplines as oratory, homiletics, and rhetoric. It is only within the recent past, however, that problems of attitude change have been studied through controlled experimentation. There were some early experimental studies of attitude change during the 1920's and 1930's, but the most important fountainhead of contemporary research on attitude change is Carl Hovland's work, first with some colleagues in the Information and Education Division of the War Department during World War II (Hovland, Lumsdaine, and Sheffield, 1949) and, second, with some colleagues in the Yale Communication Research Program (Hovland, Janis, and Kelley, 1953). The Yale Communication Research Program eventually resulted in a series of volumes that set the stage for much of the subsequent empirical and theoretical work in the field (Hovland, Mandell, Campbell, Brock, Luchins, Cohen, McGuire, Janis, Feierabend, and Anderson, 1957; Janis, Hovland, Field, Linton, Graham, Cohen, Rife, Abelson, Lesser, and King, 1959; Rosenberg, Hovland, McGuire, Abelson, and Brehm, 1960; Sherif and Hovland, 1961).

Despite some theoretical speculation utilizing reinforcement and judgmental concepts, most of Hovland's work was oriented toward empirical problems rather than theoretical issues. Hovland, nonetheless, had a healthy respect for theory and explicitly avoided "action oriented" research for what he considered "theory oriented" research. Hovland, Janis, and Kelley (1953), in fact, favorably quote Lewin's reported statement, "Nothing is so practical as a good theory."

Since Hovland's time an increasingly large amount of the published research has been explicitly related to stated theoretical orientations. Also, the number of attitude change theories, many of them developed or contributed to by people who were associated with Hovland, has grown markedly in the last few years. For these reasons, the present volume will attempt to organize the literature in the field of attitude change within a framework of relevant theories.

Each chapter, except for the first and final ones, is divided into three basic parts: theory, research, and evaluation. The theory sections contain nonevaluative descriptions of the theories. The research sections are typically divided into a number of subsections relating to certain research areas which bear directly or indirectly on the theories. These subsections contain fairly exhaustive descriptions of the relevant research together with some comment on this research. Finally, the evaluation sections contain evaluations of the theories, both from the standpoint of clarity and internal consistency, and from the standpoint of the empirical findings described in the research section.

THE CONCEPT OF ATTITUDE

Various definitions of attitude have been advanced; here are a few examples. "*An attitude is a mental and neural state of readiness, organized through experience, exerting a directive or dynamic influence upon the individual's response to all objects and situations with which it is related*" (Allport, 1935, p. 810). "Attitude is primarily a way of being 'set' toward or against certain things" (Murphy, Murphy, and Newcomb, 1937, p. 889). An attitude is a "relatively stable affective response to an object" (Rosenberg, 1956, p. 367). Another view states that an attitude is a "tendency or disposition to evaluate an object or the symbol of that object in a certain way" (Katz and Stotland, 1959, p. 428). Allport's definition implies that attitudes refer to a very general "state of readiness." Murphy, Murphy, and Newcomb, however, restrict the state of readiness or "set" to reactions "toward or against" certain objects. Their phrase "toward or against" implies evaluation, pro or con. The two remaining more recent definitions focus on the affective tendency to favorably or unfavorably evaluate objects and entirely discard the notion that any overt behavior is implied. The most common contemporary usage seems to follow this example, thus regarding the evaluative dimension as the single defining dimension for attitudes.

This does not mean, though, that overt behavior is not a function of attitudes, however complex and devious the function may be. Nor does it mean that opinions bear no functional relationship to attitudes. (Opinions are typically regarded as nonevaluative beliefs or cognitions about some aspect of reality.) The fact, for example, that the college professor has a positive attitude toward academic freedom may mean that he believes the restraint of academic freedom would lead to the debasement of educational standards and that he might, in appropriate circumstances, sign petitions and make speeches supporting academic freedom. The study of attitude change is thus to some extent bound up with the study of both opinion change and overt behavior change.

GENERAL METHODOLOGICAL CONSIDERATIONS

This book will focus primarily upon experimental approaches to attitude change. By an experimental approach is meant a procedure in which the experimenter manipulates the independent variable. There will be no discussion of the survey research literature or of the literature on individual differences. Both of these approaches involve the observation and correlation, but not the manipulation, of variables. However, some attention will be paid to the literature in which individual differences are observed in conjunction with experimental manipulations.

The experimental study of attitude change involves certain general methodological considerations that can most appropriately be discussed in this chapter. These considerations relate to choice of experimental design, demand characteristics, and experimenter bias.

Choice of Experimental Design

The most popular experimental design in the field of attitude change is the before-after design. This design involves one experimental and one control group. The experimental group receives a pretest, an experimental manipulation, and then a posttest. The control group receives the pretest and posttest without the intervening experimental manipulation. Subjects are either randomly assigned to the two groups or matched on some prearranged basis. The results are typically analyzed by comparing the difference between the pretest and posttest in the experimental group with the comparable difference in the control group. The results, however, can be more elegantly analyzed by comparing the posttest scores for the two groups after the analysis of covariance has been used to eliminate that portion of the variance which is attributable to the pretests.

In a discussion of the before-after design Solomon (1949) points out that it is far from perfect. The main difficulty relates to the possibility of an interaction between the pretest and the experimental manipulation. Whatever difference there is between the experimental and control groups may be due to the experimental manipulation or it may be due to an interaction between the experimental manipulation and the pretest. In an attitude change study, for example, the pretest may commit the subjects to their initial positions and make the experimental communication less persuasive, or the pretest may sensitize subjects to the issue and make the experimental communication more persuasive. In agreement with

Solomon, Campbell (1957) states that "strictly speaking" the before-after design, which he refers to as a "pretest-posttest control group design," offers "no basis for generalization to the unpretested population" (p. 302). Campbell gives examples of two studies, one in which a pretest made subjects more responsive to a persuasive manipulation and one in which a pretest made subjects less responsive to a persuasive manipulation.

Solomon's main solution to the problem of a possible pretest × manipulation interaction lies in the use of a design involving four groups. This design, which has come to be known as the Solomon four-group design, is presented in Table 1–1. Solomon recommends adding two con-

TABLE 1–1. *The Solomon Four-Group Design Shown as Including Both Before-After and After-Only Designs*

		Pretest	*Manipulation*	*Posttest*
Before-after Design	Experimental Group	yes	yes	yes
	Control Group I	yes	no	yes
After-only Design	Control Group II	no	yes	yes
	Control Group III	no	no	yes

SOURCE: Adapted from Solomon, 1949, p. 147.

trol groups to the traditional before-after design. These two groups are a second control group which receives an experimental manipulation and a posttest, and a third control group which receives just a posttest. The missing pretest scores for the second and third control groups can be estimated on the basis of the pretest means for the experimental and first control groups. This allows for the computation of before-after scores for all four groups. The before-after scores for the four groups could then be put in an analysis of variance design which would yield information regarding the effect of the pretest, the experimental manipulation, and the pretest × manipulation interaction.

Campbell (1957) maintains that Solomon's recommendation regarding the estimation of pretest scores for the second and third control groups on the basis of the pretest scores for the experimental and first control groups is "inelegant." This procedure restricts degrees of freedom and violates assumptions of independence upon which the tests of significance are based. Campbell points out that an alternative mode of analysis, not entailing these difficulties, involves an analysis of variance of just the posttest scores for the four groups. This procedure also allows for the assessment of the pretest × manipulation interaction.

Three studies (Hicks and Spaner, 1962; Lana, 1959a, 1959b) have used Campbell's procedure for assessing the pretest × manipulation interaction in an attitude change setting, and all of them have obtained negative results. In these studies one independent variable was the presence or absence of a pretest and the other was the presence or absence of a persuasive manipulation. Lana (1959b) found that a provivisection communication had a significant effect but not the pretest nor the pretest × communication interaction. At the time of the study the vivisection issue was an unfamiliar one for Lana's subjects. In a second study Lana (1959a) used an issue, ethnic prejudice, that was of somewhat greater concern and interest to his border-state subjects. The communication was a mental health film. Once again the results indicated that the persuasive communication had a significant effect, but that the pretest and pretest × communication interaction did not. Hicks and Spaner's (1962) study dealt with improved attitudes toward the mentally ill following exposure to a mental hospital environment. The results of this study indicated that the exposure manipulation and pretest had significant effects, but that the pretest × exposure interaction did not. A main pretest effect is, of course, adequately controlled with the ordinary before-after design. All three studies thus failed to find any effect that would invalidate a before-after design. This obviously means that a study is not necessarily invalid simply because it employs a before-after design. We really, however, need more information about the circumstances under which a pretest × persuasive manipulation interaction might or might not occur. Satisfactory and thorough evaluation of attitude change research based on before-after designs cannot be achieved until such information is possessed.

As an alternative to the above designs Campbell (1957) recommends what he calls a "posttest-only control group design," commonly referred to as an after-only design. The design involves two randomly selected groups of subjects, one of which receives a manipulation and then a posttest, and one of which receives only the posttest. As Table 1–1 makes evident, the after-only design is really the second and third control groups of the Solomon four-group design. The effect of the manipulation is assessed through the comparison of the posttest scores for the two groups. This design has the advantage of controlling for everything that the before-after design does and, in addition, not creating the opportunity for a pretest interaction to occur. Campbell convincingly argues that the simplicity of the after-only design is one of its additional strong points. Because the design requires so little cooperation from the subjects, it can be potentially useful in nonlaboratory research as, for example, studies involving different types of door-to-door appeals or direct-mail campaigns.

In view of the after-only design's obvious advantages, one can wonder why it has not been used more frequently in attitude change research. There are at least two reasons. First, many psychologists undoubtedly feel more confident of actually having produced attitude change if they can directly measure the shift from before to after the persuasive manipulation. Any assessment of attitude change just by the comparison of the posttest scores in two groups, one of which was and one of which was not exposed to the manipulation, seems indirect and devious. After all, how can you be sure that the two groups were comparable in the first place? Campbell, however, points out that if the groups were initially randomly constituted, then appropriate tests of significance allow us to legitimately draw conclusions from the results. Second, many psychologists are undoubtedly more concerned about reducing error variance than eliminating the possibility of a pretest interaction. By subtracting the pretest scores from the posttest scores or, more elegantly, by doing an analysis of covariance, the difference in scores attributable to the initial difference between individuals is eliminated. There are indeed situations in which the initial difference between individuals is so large that the effectiveness of a persuasive communication can only be detected if this difference is controlled. Rather than use a before-after design, however, an alternative solution is to increase the sample size to a point at which the small difference between the two groups in the after-only design becomes statistically reliable. In some situations, though, this may be impossible or impractical. Thus, the before-after design may be the only possible solution. If we knew more about the circumstances in which pretest interactions occur we would be in a better position to evaluate this solution. Unfortunately we do not.

Demand Characteristics

The second general methodological problem relates to demand characteristics. Demand characteristics are considered by Orne (1962) to be the "totality of cues which convey an experimental hypothesis to the subject" (p. 779). By cues are meant "the rumors of campus scuttlebutt about the research, the information conveyed during the original solicitation, the person of the experimenter, and the setting of the laboratory, as well as all explicit and implicit communication during the experiment proper" (p. 779). Orne maintains that subjects engage in a kind of problem-solving behavior in which they seek to ascertain the purpose of the experiment and respond in a manner which will support the hypothesis. Such problem-solving behavior is, of course, guided by demand characteristics. The most effective demand characteristics are those that convey the experimental hypothesis in an inobvious way. If the purpose of the experiment is too obvious the subjects may become "fully conscious of the expectations of the experimenter" and consequently "lean over backwards to be honest" (p. 780).

One way of checking into demand characteristics is through the use of a postexperimental interview. Orne (1962) argues, however, that considerable self-discipline is necessary in order to use this technique effectively. For example, in an Asch-type conformity experiment there is a tendency to ask the subjects, " 'You didn't realize that the other fellows were confederates, did you?' " (p. 780); whereas Orne recommends the use of an open-ended technique which starts with very general questions and ends with very specific ones. He maintains that if the interviewer refuses to accept "I don't know" responses, then very few subjects will be found who have not developed definite hypotheses.

Orne states two general objections to his open-ended postexperimental inquiry. One is that the subject may be aware of the experimental hypothesis because he has observed the effect in himself, and the other is that the interview procedure itself has demand characteristics. To handle the first objection he recommends the use of a preexperimental inquiry. Control subjects are first told what is actually done in the experiment and then asked what they think is the purpose of the experiment. Since these subjects themselves have not actually responded to any of the experimental manipulations, any awareness cannot be due to their having observed effects in themselves. This is an interesting technique, but it definitely has limitations. Many experiments may be far too complex to adequately describe and explain. A better procedure might be to have control subjects observe experimental subjects who are actually involved in the experiment. Even this technique, however, would be of little value if the experiment involved a covert activity such as reading.

Orne really has no answer for the objection that postexperimental inquiries themselves contain demand characteristics. By asking increasingly pointed questions, the experimenter undoubtedly will suggest the correct answers, particularly to those subjects who have shown the hypothesized effects. Socrates, after all, was able to use questioning as a method of teaching. The whole problem of the assessment of demand characteristics thus turns out to be an exceedingly complicated one.

Orne has attempted to document his case concerning demand characteristics with some studies purporting to show that hypnotic subjects act in a manner consistent with role-playing expectations (Orne, 1959; Orne and Evans, 1965), but his most convincing evidence comes from a study of demand characteristics in sensory deprivation research (Orne and Schiebe, 1964).

Sensory deprivation research has found evidence for the deterioration of personality, as indexed through decrements in such things as mirror-tracing accuracy, word recognition, size constancy, and logical deduction, following prolonged periods in which the senses are partially deprived of stimulation. In Orne and Schiebe's experiment, male college students were recruited and paid for participating in a study of "meaning deprivation" at one of the psychiatric hospitals in the Boston area. The subjects were tested individually in one of two conditions, experimental and control. In the experimental condition an attempt was made to create an atmosphere of seriousness and importance. Each subject was greeted by an experimenter in a white laboratory coat who conducted a medical history interview. During the interview a plainly labeled "Emergency Tray" containing drugs and instruments was in full view. Following the interview and a brief description of the experiment, the subjects filled out a release form exempting the hospital from all legal responsibility, took a number of simple motor and cognitive tests, and then were left in the "isolation chamber" for 4 hours. The isolation chamber was actually a comfortably furnished room complete with ice water and a sandwich. Subjects were instructed that if at any time they needed to get out of the room they were to push a red button conspicuously labeled "Emergency Alarm." They were also informed that they would be watched through a one-way mirror and that they should verbalize whatever experiences they were having while in the room. After leaving the room the subjects were given the motor and cognitive tests for a second time. Control subjects were treated in a much less serious and formal manner. The experimenter did not wear a white coat or conduct a medical history interview. Furthermore, there was no emergency tray or panic button and the subjects were, in fact, told that they were control subjects in a sensory deprivation experiment. In other respects, however, the control subjects were treated identically with the experimental ones.

Before-after changes on the various motor and cognitive tasks indicated an overall significantly greater decrement for the experimental subjects than for the control subjects. Furthermore, on the basis of the experimenter's impressions and the subjects' reports the experimental subjects showed significantly more sensory deprivation symptoms. Both in the subjects' spontaneous statements and in a postexperimental interview, various perceptual aberrations were reported. Orne and Schiebe (1964) give the following examples: " 'the walls of the room are starting to waver'; 'the objects on the desk are becoming animated and moving about'; 'the lighting in the room is growing gradually dimmer and yellower' " (pp. 9–10). They report that these perceptual aberrations were, with one exception, neither upsetting nor compelling. The one exception was an experimental subject who pressed the panic button due to "disorganization of senses."

Orne and Schiebe's experiment obviously is a very dramatic demonstration of the role that can be played by demand characteristics. While most attitude change research typically does not involve such a blatant manipulation or manifestation of demand cues, there is certainly the possibility that even far less numerous and obvious demand cues will have an effect upon the subject's behavior.

Orne (1962) believes that a subject's behavior is determined by two sets of variables, experimental variables and demand characteristics. This statement, however, is obviously oversimplified. It does not even allow for error variance. Aside from this general matter, however, it is possible that subjects may adopt many sets other than that of responding in a manner supportive of the experimental hypothesis. Rosenberg (1965b), for example, has proposed that subjects may respond in a manner that will make them appear adjusted and mature to the omniscient psychologist who is conducting the experiment. He argues that subjects react to an experiment with "evaluation apprehension" due to their belief that psychologists have the ability to assess people's emotional adequacy or adjustment. The evaluation apprehension leads to a kind of behavior which the subjects believe will make them appear mature and healthy. It is apparent that this evaluation apprehension set is quite different from the demand characteristics set. It is also interesting to note that in many persuasion experiments the two sets could conceivably produce opposite results. In an Asch-type conformity experiment, for example, if a subject responds in accordance with the demand characteristics set he will be influenced, but if he responds in accordance with the evaluation apprehension set he will remain independent. This, of course, assumes that subjects place a higher value upon individualism than conformity, a relatively safe assumption in our culture.

In addition to the demand characteristics set and evaluation apprehension set there are numerous other sets that subjects may adopt. Many experimenters encounter individuals who have adopted what appear to be negativistic sets. These uncooperative individuals resent the necessity of participating in experiments or even of filling out questionnaires. Another set is that of task orientation. Subjects may become thoroughly engrossed in tasks given them by the experimenter and think of little else. This set is, of course, the ideal one for the experimental psychologist who is concerned about generalizing his results beyond the laboratory setting. In actuality, all of these sets probably operate from time to time in various experimental settings. It may be possible, however, to manipulate or control the experimental situation in such a way as to magnify or reduce any particular set. Certainly this is a matter in need of study. From our present vantage point, however, it seems likely that the prevalence of the demand characteristics set can be reduced by using children rather than adults for subjects, after-only rather than before-after designs, the same subjects in no more than one experimental condition, and only cover stories that have been adequately pretested.

Experimenter Bias

Closely related to the problem of demand characteristics is the problem of experimenter bias, recently emphasized by Rosenthal (1963). Rosenthal contends that a good deal of our research evidence may be suspect because of experimenter bias. By experimenter bias he does not necessarily mean out-and-out cheating, but more subtle, perhaps even unconscious, biasing effects. He lists a number of miscellaneous sources of experimenter bias such as the experimenter's expectations, the experimenter's motivation, early data returns, computational errors, and verbal conditioning. If the experimenter expects to obtain certain results and further is motivated to see that such results are obtained, prophecy may be self-fulfilling. Early data returns, of course, may be the origin of the expectations, and such things as computational errors and verbal conditioning may be the actual mechanisms by which the expectations are fulfilled.

The procedure that Rosenthal has used to document his speculation is illustrated in an experiment reported by Rosenthal and Fode (1963). Initially a large group of judges looked at pictures of faces and judged on a scale ranging from +10 to −10 the extent to which the individuals involved had been experiencing success or failure. On the basis of the ratings, 10 experimental pictures were selected that had ratings close to zero and that in fact averaged zero. In the actual experiment, psychology majors from an undergraduate course in experimental psychology were used as experimenters, and students from an introductory course in psychology were used as subjects. The experimenters were told that their task was to see whether they could replicate "well-established" findings as "students in physics labs are expected to do" (p. 494). They were further told: "You will be paid at the rate of $1.00 per hour for your time. If your results come out properly—as expected—you will be paid $2.00 instead of $1.00" (p. 507). The experimenters were led to believe that the proper or well-established findings were ratings averaging either +5 or −5 for the 10 above-mentioned pictures. The results indicated that the experimenters who were biased in a positive direction obtained a mean rating of +4.05 and the experimenters who were biased in a negative direction obtained a mean rating of −0.95, a highly significant difference.

These results are rather convincing. In further research, however, Rosenthal has not always obtained results which are consistent with the above findings. In a review of his research Rosenthal (1964) discusses some of the ambiguities. He also refers to and discusses research reported by other investigators which failed to find evidence for experimenter bias. In commenting on this research he states, "Indeed, there may be a large array of tasks which will prove relatively resistant to effects of experimenter expectancies. What sort of tasks are more or less resistant is a question deserving further research" (p. 104). This statement seems to reflect a shift from a belief expressed in an earlier statement, "In view of the wide variety of E, S, and context domains sampled, we may conclude that experimenter outcome-orientation bias is both a fairly general and a fairly robust phenomenon" (1963, p. 271). In any event, Rosenthal certainly cannot maintain that experimenter bias is a completely general phenomenon; if this were the case then we could regard his own experimental results as being a product of experimenter bias and hence disregard them. On the other hand, it is a reasonably safe assumption that experimenter bias does occur in some situations. The problem then, as Rosenthal himself is aware, is one of ascertaining the means whereby experimenter bias can be controlled or eliminated.

While our knowledge of experimenter bias is obviously incomplete, it is possible to make a number of recommendations which may help us to reduce or detect its presence. First, whenever possible, experiments should be set up in such a way that the experimenter cannot differentially reinforce expected and unexpected responses through words or gestures. For example, Rosenthal could have had his subjects write down their judgments of each picture rather than call them out to the experimenter. Such a procedure would eliminate the mediation of bias through verbal conditioning. Rosenthal, Fode, Vikan-Kline, and Persinger (1964) present some evidence indicating that verbal conditioning is not the mediator of bias in the picture judging situation, but it is still possible that in some situations verbal conditioning may be the mediator of bias. Second, it is probably advisable to mechanize as many of the procedures as is practical and meaningful. Machines such as counters and tape recorders are completely impartial. Third, a higher value should be placed upon replication. Some psychologists seem almost to believe that it is a waste of time to replicate someone else's work. Successful replication, however, is a way of guarding against experimenter bias, particularly if the second experimenter does not happen to believe in the previous results. Fourth, whenever possible it is probably advisable to institute the so-called "double-blind" procedure in which neither subjects nor experimenters know which subjects are in experimental conditions and which are in control conditions. Last of all, psychologists need to be made more strongly aware of ethical considerations. Anyone who believes that the business of science is unrelated to values is sadly mistaken. Without values and ethical standards no scientific edifice could ever be erected.

2

Hovland, Janis, and Kelley's

Reinforcement Theory

THEORY

The reinforcement theory of attitude change has received greatest emphasis from the work of Hovland and his associates in the Yale Communication Research Program. The theory as set forth by Hovland, Janis, and Kelley (1953) draws mainly upon the principles of learning developed by Hull (1943) and is adapted to complex forms of social behavior by Miller and Dollard (1941) and by Doob (1947). The essence of the theory is that attitude change results from learning produced through reinforcement.

Attitude Change as Mediated by Opinion Change

Hovland, Janis, and Kelley maintain that one of the main ways in which persuasive communications give rise to attitude change is through the production of a related opinion change. Opinions are beliefs such as interpretations, expectations, and anticipations. Attitudes are implicit responses oriented toward approaching or avoiding, reacting favorably or unfavorably toward, an object or symbol. Both "opinion" and "attitude" are regarded as intervening variables between which there is a high degree of mutual interaction. According to Hovland, Janis, and Kelley, the most important interaction is the change in attitude that follows the change in opinion. A change in opinion about a politician's motives, for example, may result in a change of attitude toward the politician. Opinions, like other habits, tend to persist unless the individual undergoes some new learning experience. Exposure to a persuasive communication which induces the individual to accept a new opinion constitutes a learning experience in which a new habit is acquired.

The "Learning" of New Opinions

Hovland, Janis, and Kelley state that there are common principles which apply equally to the learning of new opinions and various verbal and motor skills. They maintain, however, that the type and conditions of learning are quite different in the case of opinions. For example, the material to be learned in a persuasive communication is typically a single conclusion or proposition, while the material to be learned in a scientific lecture is typically a whole series of propositions.

What is the process by which new opinions are learned? The persuasive communication is regarded as a compound stimulus which raises a question and suggests an answer. Suppose a communication advocates that "smoking is harmful to health." The communication implicitly if not explicitly raises the question, Is smoking harmful to health? and at the same time suggests an answer, Yes.

When exposed to a persuasive communication the individual is assumed to react with two distinct responses: to think of his own answer to the question, and the answer suggested by the communication. Merely memorizing or learning the answer or conclusion suggested by the communication, however, will not result in opinion change. The acceptance of the new opinion is contingent upon the incentives that are offered in the communication. These incentives may take the form of arguments or reasons supporting the opinion or conclusion, or other expected rewards or punishments that follow upon the acceptance of the new opinion.

Attention, Comprehension, and Acceptance

Three important variables in the acquisition of new opinions are attention, comprehension, and acceptance. Before an individual can be persuaded by a communication it is obviously necessary that he first attend to it. A communication, for example, which deals with an unfamiliar and uninteresting topic may not be very persuasive because of a lack of attention. Even if a communication is attended to, however, it may not be persuasive if the individual is incapable of comprehending or assimilating the new information. The principles of learning concerned with attention and comprehension are assumed to operate in persuasion in the same manner as they operate in ordinary instruction. Hence, many of the hypotheses which relate to effective instruction will also relate to effective persuasion. Instruction differs crucially from persuasion in that acceptance is usually taken for granted in the classroom situation. Usually the student has initial expectations that the teacher will be correct in his or her conclusions.

Assuming that attention to and comprehension of a communication have occurred, persuasion will depend upon acceptance. The occurrence of acceptance in turn is dependent upon incentives. The persuasive communications may provide incentives in the form of arguments or reasons why the advocated point of view should be accepted, or the persuasive communication may arouse expectations of phenomena that are reinforcing (incentives) or that in the past have been associated with reinforcement.

Hovland, Janis, and Kelley do not attempt to catalog all of the expectations that may conceivably affect acceptance, but they do single out three as being of major importance. First, there is the expectation of being right or wrong. In the past, being right has usually been associated with various types of rewarding circumstances. Thus, since experts are thought of as usually being right, and since the expectation of being right has been associated with reinforcement, conclusions advocated by expert sources will, other things being equal, be more readily accepted than conclusions advocated by nonexpert sources. The second type of expectation affecting the acceptance of an advocated conclusion is the expectation of manipulative intent. Being influenced by someone who had something to gain has in the past been associated with nonreinforcing exploitation of some sort. Thus a communication coming from an untrustworthy source is not likely to be accepted, because it arouses the expectation of manipulative intent which has been associated with nonreinforcement. The third and final type of expectation mentioned is the expectation of social approval or disapproval. Social approval is seen as rewarding; thus anything in a communication which indicates that the acceptance of the advocated conclusion will lead to social approval should facilitate the acceptance of this conclusion. Since prestigious individuals may be seen as indicators of the social climate, conclusions advocated by these individuals may arouse the expectation of reinforcing social approval and thus produce acceptance or agreement.

The Persistence of Opinions

The persistence of an opinion over time is dependent on the retention of both the informational content of the persuasive communication and the incentives for acceptance. Thus, if an individual remembers none of the arguments contained in the communication or if he is no longer motivated to accept what was said, the opinion will not persist. Even if there is perfect retention of these matters, however, the long-range effectiveness of a persuasive communication will depend on the sustained resistance it can present to subsequent interfering conclusions coming from competing communications.

RESEARCH

Reward for Counterattitudinal Advocacy

Counterattitudinal advocacy occurs when an individual argues for a point of view different from his own. Such behavior may occur, for example, in a debate. A reinforcement orientation would lead one to expect that the individual who is rewarded for engaging in counterattitudinal advocacy would more likely be influenced by his own arguments than an individual who is not so rewarded. A number of experiments have investigated this matter.

Scott (1957) found that subjects who were reinforced by group approval for expressing an attitude opposite from their own showed a change in the direction of the expressed attitude. Students in 29 general psychology discussion sections were administered questionnaires to assess their attitudes toward three controversial issues: universal military training, night hours for women students, and de-emphasis of football. Four individuals, two definitely in favor of one of the above issues and two definitely opposed, were selected from each class and asked to support the point of view opposite to their own in a debate. Only one of the three issues was debated in each class; but every issue was debated in some class. At the conclusion of the debate the class members rated the performance of each of the debaters. The experimenter, however, falsified the scores so that half of the time the pros won (or were reinforced), and half of the time the cons won (or were reinforced). After the report of the ratings the class and the debaters took the attitude questionnaire "to see if the debaters had been able to influence class opinion."

The results indicated that on a 7-point scale the "winners" changed 1.25 points in the direction in which they had argued, and the "losers" changed 0.17 points in the opposite direction from which they had argued. The difference between winners and losers is significant. Scott offers two possible interpretations of his results. One interpretation is that the attitude change was produced through reinforcement of the verbal behavior, the contact with the opposite position in and of itself having no effect. The other interpretation is that the contact with the opposing arguments produced a change in attitude which was either reinforced or extinguished depending upon whether or not the individual considered himself to have won or lost the debate. Scott regards the second interpretation as somewhat more plausible.

Scott (1959) substantiated his earlier findings with different operations and, in addition, attempted to demonstrate the reinforcement effect upon neutral as well as extreme attitudes. In this experiment subjects debated for cash prizes before a group of three judges. Some of the subjects argued against their own point of view, some argued for their own point of view, and some argued for a point of view that simply deviated in one direction or the other from their neutral positions. Using a before-after design Scott found that for all groups combined, attitude change for the randomly assigned winners, 1.67 (on a 7-point scale), was significantly greater than change for the losers, 0.15, or the controls, 0.24. (Ten days later the winners' change score, 1.20, was still significantly different from the control group change score.) The subjects who argued against their own point of view changed 2.77, those who argued from a neutral position changed 1.47, and those who argued for their own point of view changed 0.63. These data are deceptive, however, inasmuch as those subjects who argued against their own point of view had the most room for change (in the direction of reinforcement), and those subjects who argued for their own point of view had the least room for change. Relative to the amount of change possible the three groups changed 55 percent, 49 percent, and 63 percent, respectively. Scott correctly points out that it is impossible to tell from this type of data whether reinforcement for advocating a position different from one's own is any more productive of attitude change than is reinforcement for advocating one's own position.

Bostrom, Vlandis, and Rosenbaum (1961) found that students who were given A's for their counterattitudinal essays showed more attitude change than students who were given D's. In a regular classroom setting students wrote counterattitudinal essays on one of two assigned topics, legalized gambling or socialized medicine. The following day the instructor returned the essays either with or without grades. The students were randomly divided into three groups so that one third received A's, one third received D's, and one third did not receive any grade. The latter students were told that the instructor had not had sufficient time to grade their essays. Immediately after returning the essays an attitude questionnaire was administered. Before-after change scores indicated that the students given A's changed 11:76 (on a 45-point scale), the students given no grades changed 7.11, and the students given D's changed 5.85. Every difference is significant except for the one between the mean change for the subjects given no grade (7.11) and the mean change for the subjects given D's (5.85). A comparison of attitude change between the topic on which essays were written and the topic on which essays were not written indicated significantly more change on the counterattitudinal topic.

Wallace (1966) investigated the effect of role reward and content reward on attitude change following counterattitudinal advocacy. Naive subjects engaged in a counterattitudinal debate with an experimental accomplice in the presence of two other accomplices. The debated issue was capital punishment. At the conclusion of the debate the two observers rated the debaters on two evaluative scales. One scale was concerned with the content of the speeches and the other with the manner in which the speeches were delivered. In a content reward condition the naive subjects were told that the observers considered the actual arguments they presented in the debate to be extremely powerful and persuasive but the manner in which the speeches were presented was comparable to that expected of the average college student. In a role reward condition the naive subjects were told that the manner in which their speeches were presented was superior but the content of the speeches was comparable to that expected from the average college student. In a neutral condition the naive subjects were not rewarded for either the content of their speeches or the manner in which the speeches were presented. Similar neutral feedback was given to the subjects' opponent in all three conditions.

Before-after change scores indicated that reward had the expected effect upon attitude change and, furthermore, that the reward effect was mainly due to the superior persuasive impact of the role reward condition. An additional finding was that the subjects who argued against capital punishment were more influenced than the subjects who argued for capital punishment.

Wallace interprets the superior persuasive impact of the role reward condition as being due to the greater dissonance (inconsistency) produced between behavior and attitude in this condition. Supposedly role reward produced more information regarding actual behavior than did content reward and thus more attitude change as a consequence of attempts to reduce the inconsistency between behavior and attitude. It is also possible, however, that role reward was simply more hedonically satisfying than content reward. Without further data it is impossible to say which explanation is correct.

Comment. The above research rather convincingly demonstrates that reward for counterattitudinal advocacy does have an effect on attitude change. Wallace (1966), however, has raised an important matter relating to whether or not this is a genuine reinforcement effect or an inconsistency reduction effect. Does reward for counterattitudinal advocacy directly produce attitude change or simply provide behavioral information that creates an inconsistent or dissonant relation between attitudes and behavior? Until this question is answered the above research can not be taken as unequivocally supporting a reinforcement point of view.

It is interesting to apply Wallace's (1966) distinction between role and content reward to Bostrom, Vlandis, and Rosenbaum's (1961) essay writing situation. Role reward for written counterattitudinal advocacy would certainly seem to involve quite different things from role reward for oral counterattitudinal advocacy. The difference, in fact, is so great there is some question as to whether Wallace's results could be replicated with written counterattitudinal advocacy. Role reward for written counterattitudinal advocacy would have to involve references to grammar, organization, punctuation, and other such matters that would not be too relevant to the subject's actual behavior, sincerity, and so forth. In any event, the problem is important enough to warrant empirical investigation.

Verbal Reinforcement

We now turn to a consideration of a number of studies which have investigated the effect of verbal reinforcement upon attitude formation and change. Attitudinal verbal reinforcement occurs when a subject encounters some expression of agreement with or approval for his repeated opinion and attitude statements.

Hildum and Brown (1956) demonstrated the effect of verbal reinforcement on responses to an opinion interview. Subjects were contacted by telephone and asked a series of 15 redundant questions concerning their opinions about the Harvard philosophy of general education. Half of the subjects were reinforced for expressing opinions indicating pro attitudes and half were reinforced for expressing con attitudes. Reinforcement was delivered by the experimenter saying "good" for half of the subjects and "mm-hmm" for half. This gave four conditions in all. The results indicated that "good" was an effective reinforcer in producing more pro or con interview responses but that "mm-hmm" was not. Of the subjects willing to guess at the experimenter's attitude, all but one said that he favored general education. A replication of the entire experiment gave similar results.

Ekman (1958) studied the verbal and nonverbal reinforcement of opinion responses indicating a negative attitude toward capital punishment. The verbal reinforcement was the statement "Good," and the nonverbal reinforcement was a head nod, smile, and slight movement forward. Female subjects were individually read a 63-item questionnaire relating to the use of capital punishment. Reinforcement of anti-capital punishment responses was delivered only on the last 42 items. Ninety-seven of the 187 subjects expressed extremely pro or anti attitudes on the first 21 items and were eliminated. The results indicated that the mean number of anti-capital punishment responses increased as a result of both types of reinforcement. The verbal and nonverbal reinforcements did not differ significantly in their effectiveness. A questionnaire administered after the conditioning indicated that the subjects receiving verbal reinforcement were better able to identify the reinforcement contingency than those who received nonverbal reinforcement. No attempt was made to relate awareness to amount of conditioning. Two difficulties with this experiment are the lack of a nonreinforcement control group and the elimination of over half of the initially tested subjects.

Krasner, Knowles, and Ullmann (1965) report a study in which a variety of reinforcement procedures ("mm-hmm," "good," smiling, head-nodding, etc.) were collectively successful in producing opinion responses favorable but not in producing opinion responses unfavorable to medical science. The subjects were mothers of children attending two nursery schools, and the experimenter was introduced as a physiological psychologist who was a member of the "British Medical Research Council." All subjects responded by agreeing or disagreeing to 54 statements concerned with medical science. One group of subjects was reinforced for responses indicating a favorable attitude, one group for responses indicating a negative attitude, and one group served as a nonreinforced control. The results indicated that reinforcement for favorable responses had a significant effect but reinforcement for unfavorable responses did not. The failure of the reinforcement for responses indicating an unfavorable attitude toward medical science is possibly attributable to the fact that the experimenter himself was identified with medical science.

Krasner, Knowles, and Ullmann also had their subjects squeeze a dynamometer before and after responding to the 54 medical science statements. They had initially thought that reinforcement for a favorable attitude toward medical science would produce a greater effort than reinforcement for an unfavorable attitude or no reinforcement at all. This expectation was not confirmed. Although before-after changes in dynamometer responses were correlated with extent of conditioning in the favorable reinforcement group, there were no significant differences among the various treatment groups.

Singer (1961) studied the generalization of reinforced prodemocratic responses. Subjects initially made agree or disagree responses to a lengthened version of the F scale. (The F scale is an instrument for assessing antidemocratic, fascistic, authoritarian attitude.) Experimental subjects were reinforced with "good" and "right" for responses indicating a prodemocratic attitude and control subjects were not reinforced for any responses. After finishing with the F scale all subjects responded to the E or Ethnocentrism scale without any reinforcement. Half of the subjects in the experimental and control groups responded orally to the E-scale items as they were presented by the experimenter, and half responded in writing to the E-scale items while the experimenter was absent from the room. The results indicated that reinforcement had a significant effect upon the F-scale responses and this effect generalized to the E-scale responses when made orally in the presence of the experimenter. There was significant generalization to the first 10 of the 30 *E*-scale items when responded to in the absence of the experimenter but there was no significant effect over all 30 items. Singer also reports that an assessment of the extent to which the subjects were aware of the reinforcement contingency revealed a nonsignificant tendency for the more aware subjects to make more prodemocratic responses.

Insko (*1965*) presented evidence consistent with the assertion that verbal reinforcement produces a genuine effect upon attitude and not just a temporary modification of responses in an interview situation. Students in an introductory psychology course at the University of Hawaii were contacted by telephone and reinforced with "good" for agreement or disagreement with a series of opinion statements relating to the creation of a Springtime Aloha Week. (Aloha Week is a festival in Hawaii that normally occurs every Fall.) The reinforcing was done by a number of male assistants who were in no way connected with the course. Approximately 1 week later the instructor passed out a "Local Issues Questionnaire" in class. Two-thirds of the way through this questionnaire was an item measuring attitude toward the creation of a Springtime Aloha Week. It was found that verbal reinforcement produced an effect on the telephone responses that carried over to the attitude questionnaire. From a strictly operational point of view the experiment demonstrates response generality as a result of verbal reinforcement.

Maccoby, Maccoby, Romney, and Adams (*1961*) studied the reinforcing effect of agreement-expressing conversation in a nonlaboratory setting. Experimental communications advocating later toilet training were administered to a group of women 2 weeks after and immediately before a questionnaire assessment of opinion. The women were later interviewed and asked about their opinions and conversations. Among the subjects influenced by the communications it was found that the new opinions were maintained to a greater extent by those subjects who talked with individuals agreeing with the new opinion than by those who talked to individuals disagreeing with the new opinion or by those who did not discuss the matter at all. Among the subjects initially not influenced by the communications, conversations appeared to have no influence. The effect of conversation apparently was not to produce additional or delayed opinion change but to prevent "backsliding." It is not apparent from the data why reinforcing conversations did not produce, but simply maintained, opinion change.

Calvin (*1962*) attempted to use social reinforcement to alter the color of clothes worn by female college students. If it is assumed that a change in the color of clothing worn to school reflects a change in preference or attitude, then the Calvin study is relevant to the present discussion. Twenty-four students at Hollins College served as experimenters while the remaining 550 students served as subjects. First a count was made of the number of students in the school dining hall who wore blue clothes. Then the experimenters reinforced every student they met dressed in blue with such expressions as, "My that is a nice looking sweater" or "That coat certainly is attractive." During the 13-day period of reinforcement and some time afterwards, counts were periodically made of the number of students wearing blue. With the cessation of reinforcement for blue, a periodic count of the number of students wearing red was carried out along with the continued count of the number of students wearing blue. Two days after the cessation of the blue reinforcement, red reinforcement was begun and continued for 20 days. The results are to some extent ambiguous. Before reinforcement 25 percent of the subjects wore blue. After reinforcement for blue the percentage rose to 37 percent and stayed at an average of 38 percent during reinforcement. After the cessation of reinforcement for blue and before the beginning of the reinforcement for red the number of students wearing blue dropped to 27 percent. During the next period when red was reinforced the percentage wearing blue unexpectedly rose to 35 percent. The percentage of students wearing red before reinforcement averaged 12 percent. After the beginning of reinforcement the percentage wearing red increased to 22 percent and then dropped to 18 percent. Without the aid of an equivalent nonreinforced control group, as Calvin points out, the data cannot be interpreted unambiguously. The fact, however, that reinforcement of both red and blue produced statistically significant effects is some further evidence that verbal operant conditioning may, in fact, produce attitude change. Calvin (1962) speculates that the increased number of subjects wearing blue with the beginning of reinforcement for red may be due to the fact that "a person previously reinforced for blue—when reinforced for red—may have been 'reminded' of previous blue reinforcements" (p. 15). That something like this did happen seems very plausible.

Mitnick and McGinnies (1958) present some evidence indicating that discussion with a group of similarly ethnocentric individuals modifies the amount of prejudice change produced through exposure to a persuasive film. On the basis of scores on the E or Ethnocentrism scale, high school students were divided into three groups differing in degree of ethnocentrism. Within each of the ethnocentrism groups the students were further subdivided into two experimental groups and one control group. Both experimental groups were exposed to a film which persuasively treated prejudice as a communicable disease. The experimental groups differed in that one of them had a passively directed discussion of the film immediately after exposure to the film and one did not. The discussion groups were always homogeneous with respect to ethnocentrism. At the end of the experimental treatment both groups filled out the E scale for the second time. The control group filled out the E scale a second time without either being exposed to the film or engaging in a discussion. One month later all groups filled out the E scale for a third time.

An analysis of variance of the before to immediately after change scores revealed no significant effect for ethnocentrism, but showed significant effects for experimental treatments and the interaction between treatments and ethnocentrism. The treatment effect indicates that the film-only and film-discussion treatments both produced significantly greater prejudice reduction than occurred in the control group. The interaction indicates, in agreement with expectations, that for the high ethnocentric subjects greater prejudice reduction occurred in the film-only than in the film-discussion group, and for the low ethnocentric subjects greater prejudice reduction occurred in the film-discussion than in the film-only group. A further analysis of the data by t test, however, revealed that only the effect for the high ethnocentric subjects was significant. This means that when these subjects discussed the film with other like-minded individuals its persuasive effect was dissipated, but when the low ethnocentric subjects discussed the film with other like-minded individuals its persuasive effect was not increased. An analysis of variance of the before to 1 month after change scores indicated that only the experimental treatment effect was still significant. The nonsignificance of the treatments × ethnocentrism interaction in this analysis means that the reinforcing effect of discussing the film with similarly minded individuals was fairly temporary. An examination of the discussion transcripts showed that the subjects did find a good deal of expressed agreement from individuals of similar ethnocentrism. There was no significant difference in attitude change, however, between the subjects who participated and those who did not participate in the discussion. This finding was interpreted as meaning that reinforcement of opinion change can occur without active verbal interchange.

Goldstein and McGinnies (1964) further demonstrated the reinforcing effect of group discussion. On the basis of an attitude questionnaire four-person groups were formed that differed in their attitudes toward the church. One member of each group who was selected to read a strongly antichurch essay to the other three subjects was always prochurch in attitude. The other three group members were all either prochurch, neutral toward the church, or antichurch. Following the reading of the essay the groups were directed to discuss it and then fill out the attitude questionnaire for the second time. Goldstein and McGinnies found that although none of the listeners significantly changed their attitudes, the speakers significantly changed in the antichurch direction. Further, the change in the speakers who interacted with neutral and antichurch groups was significantly greater than the change for the speakers who interacted with prochurch groups. Apparently the reinforcing effect of group discussion modified the effect of being forced to read the antichurch essay.

Levin (1961) demonstrated that with an extensive interviewing procedure one can find a relationship between awareness and ordinary verbal operant conditioning. Levin's study did not deal specifically with attitudes but his findings have obvious relevance to the verbal reinforcement of attitude. He used a sentence construction task developed by Taffel (1955). Subjects were presented with a series of cards each containing six pronouns ("I," "we," "you," "he," "she," "they") and a different past tense verb. They were instructed to construct a sentence using one of the pronouns and the verb. If they constructed a sentence using either "I" or "we," the experimenter said "Good." Immediately following the conditioning trials the subjects were interviewed concerning their awareness of the reinforcement contingency. The first four questions in the interview were approximately similar to those of other studies which had failed to find a relationship between awareness and conditioning. These questions inquired generally about how the subjects decided which words to use and what they thought was the purpose of the experiment. The remaining questions in the interview inquired more specifically whether they were aware of any occurrences during the interview and, if so, what such occurrences meant. On the basis of responses to the first four questions only 3 out of 60 experimental subjects were classified as aware of the reinforcement contingency, or the fact that a "good" followed sentences beginning with either "I" or "we." After elimination of these 3 subjects Levin found a significant increase in the number of "I"-"we" sentences, just as had previous investigators. On the basis of responses to the extended interview 16 additional subjects were classified as aware. When these subjects were eliminated Levin found no evidence for conditioning. These 16 subjects were the ones who accounted for the positive evidence in the previous analysis.

In a review Spielberger (1962) found ample empirical evidence for the association or correlation between awareness and conditioning. He states that the evidence simply does not support the point of view that reinforcement acts unconsciously and automatically, and, further, that awareness, as measured by an intensive interview, is an important variable in verbal conditioning.

Dulany (1962) has presented a theoretical network which breaks down awareness into three concepts: reinforcement hypothesis (awareness of the reinforcement contingency), behavioral hypothesis (awareness of what the experimenter wants the subject to say or do), and behavioral intention (intention to do what the experimenter wants the subject to do or say). These three concepts are all measured with a retrospective, structured interview. According to Dulany's theorizing it is the existence of behavioral intention that produces response selection resulting in verbal operant conditioning. Thus, since behavioral intention is dependent upon behavioral hypothesis and behavioral hypothesis upon reinforcement hypothesis, it is to be expected that behavioral intention will correlate most highly and reinforcement hypothesis least highly with verbal operant conditioning.

In an experiment using the Taffel (1955) procedure Dulany found that the correlations of behavioral intention, behavioral hypothesis, and reinforcement hypothesis with the conditioning of "I"-"we" sentences were +.71, +.57, and +.36 respectively. Although not required by the theory, the correlations are all significantly different from each other.

Comment. The research on the relationship between awareness and verbal reinforcement has raised considerable doubt as to the genuineness of the verbal reinforcement or conditioning phenomenon. There are a number of problems with this research, however. First, the fact that extended or very direct interview questions are necessary in order to obtain evidence of any appreciable amount of awareness suggests that the questions may be suggesting the correct answers. Socrates, after all, was able to teach simply by asking appropriate questions. Second, there is a problem as to the causal significance of the correlation between awareness and conditioning. Just because awareness is correlated with conditioning does not mean that awareness causes conditioning. It is at least possible that conditioning causes awareness or that subjects become aware because they observe the conditioning effect in themselves. And third, the research on awareness has failed to adequately distinguish between two quite separate issues. One issue has to do with whether or not awareness of the reinforcement contingency is necessary for conditioning to occur. The other issue has to do with whether or not awareness of the experimenter's hypothesis is necessary for conditioning to occur. Dulany (1962) refers to the first type of awareness as reinforcement hypothesis and something similar to the second type as behavioral hypothesis. Rather than combining the two types of awareness into one theoretical network, however, it is perhaps just as important to emphasize the distinction between the two. The first type of awareness raises an issue that has been of historical concern in the field of learning. The second type of awareness raises quite a different issue that has to do with whether or not verbal reinforcement is a genuine phenomenon or simply an artifact of demand characteristics of the laboratory situation. Successful attempts to verbally reinforce attitudes in nonlaboratory situations (e.g., Hildum and Brown, 1956; Insko, 1965) seemingly demonstrate that the verbal reinforcement phenomenon is not an artifact of the laboratory. Of course, it may be that only certain types of nonlaboratory social relations generate the appropriate type of group feeling or "nonlaboratory demand characteristics" to allow for successful verbal reinforcement. This, however, is certainly no justification for considering the verbal reinforcement phenomenon an artifact. Hopefully, future research will concentrate on specifying the social conditions that facilitate or hinder the verbal reinforcement effect.

In general, research indicates that verbal reinforcement can change attitudes. The data are not as consistent as they could be, but, by and large, reinforcements delivered either by experimenters or by other individuals of known attitudes seem to have attitudinal effects. An interesting theoretical issue concerns whether the attitudinal effects are a direct result of the reinforcement or due to inconsistency between attitude and the verbally reinforced overt responses. Perhaps reinforcement produces overt responses that are inconsistent with existing attitude, and attitude change occurs as a result of an attempt to reduce the inconsistency. This is also a matter in need of investigation.

Classical Conditioning

The next topic has to do with the modification of attitudes through classical conditioning. In some of this research the attitudinal or conditioned response is associated with the unconditioned stimulus or reinforcement over a number of trials, and in some of the research the association occurs just once. In none of the experiments, however, is reinforcement instrumentally dependent upon performance of the attitudinal response.

Staats and Staats (1957) present evidence indicating that attitudes toward nonsense syllables may be classically conditioned by associating them with adjectives of evaluative meaning. Nonsense syllables (CS words) were presented visually by a slide projector and at the same time nouns or adjectives (US words) were presented orally by the experimenter and immediately repeated by the subjects. Ostensibly the subjects' task was to learn to recognize both visual and auditory stimuli. The six nonsense syllables were: YOF, LAJ, XEH, WUH, GIW, and QUG. They were presented in a random order with 5-second exposures. On each presentation the nonsense syllables were paired with different words. The nonsense syllables XEH and YOF were always paired with adjectives of evaluative meaning. The other four nonsense syllables were paired with nouns of no evaluative meaning. In one condition XEH was paired with adjectives of positive evaluative meaning, e.g., "happy" and "valuable"; and YOF was paired with words of negative evaluative meaning, e.g., "bitter" and "ugly." In another condition XEH was paired with negative adjectives and YOF with positive adjectives. Each nonsense syllable was presented 18 times. After the conditioning phase was completed the subjects were asked to evaluate their feelings toward the nonsense syllables on a 7-point scale ranging from pleasant to unpleasant, and tested for recall of the words. They were also asked to state what they considered to be the purpose of the experiment and what they had thought about during the experiment. On the basis of this inquiry a few subjects who indicated awareness of the relationship between words and syllables were eliminated. The remaining subjects showed significant conditioning. The nonsense syllables associated with the pleasant adjectives were judged significantly more pleasant than the nonsense syllables associated with the unpleasant adjectives.

Staats and Staats (*1958*) utilized the same procedure as in their previous experiment to condition attitudes toward the national names "Dutch" and "Swedish." These national names were associated with evaluative adjectives, and the national names "German," "Italian," "French," and "Greek" were associated with words of no evaluative significance. Staats and Staats eliminated the subjects who reported being aware of the name-word relationship and found significant conditioning. The national names associated with the pleasant adjectives were judged more pleasant than the national names associated with the unpleasant adjectives.

In a second experiment exactly the same procedure was used except the CS names were "Harry," "Bill," "Tom," "Jim," "Ralph," and "Bob." Again, significant conditioning was found. Of the 93 subjects in both experiments, 17, slightly more than 18 percent, were eliminated because they reported awareness of the name-word contingency.

Staats, Staats, and Biggs (*1958*) report that they were able to condition evaluative meaning in two additional experiments. In one experiment the CS words were "red" and "yellow" and in another they were "unfair" and "awful." The data from nine subjects (12 percent of the total sample) who indicated some degree of awareness were excluded from the analysis. The results indicated that significant conditioning occurred in both experiments and furthermore that the amount of conditioning obtained in the two experiments does not differ despite the obvious evaluative meaning of the CS words in the second experiment.

Blandford and Sampson (*1964*) replicated the Staats and Staats (1957) study with the same nonsense syllables and evaluative adjectives. However, instead of the evaluations being made on a single bipolar, *pleasant-unpleasant* scale, a number of additional scales such as *like-dislike, beautiful-ugly, valuable-worthless, good-bad, nice-awful, colorful-colorless,* and *kind-cruel* were used. Blandford and Sampson found, as had Staats and Staats, that significant conditioning occurred.

In a second experiment the critical nonsense syllables were associated, not with evaluative adjectives, but with prestigious names, e.g., "Churchill," "Rickover," "Kennedy," "Lincoln," or nonprestigious names, e.g., "Stalin," "Hoffa," "Hitler," "Hiss." The noncritical nonsense syllables were associated with more neutral names. The names were classified as prestigious, nonprestigious, or neutral on the basis of ratings from another sample of students. Again Blandford and Sampson found significant evidence for conditioning. The results were interpreted as illustrating the induction of prestige suggestion through classical conditioning.

The subjects in both experiments were asked to indicate what they considered to be the purpose of the experiment. Blandford and Sampson state that 4 out of 80 subjects reported being aware of some aspect of the conditioning contingencies.

Staats, Staats, and Heard (1960) investigated the phenomenon of partial reinforcement. In this experiment the conditioned stimuli were nonsense syllables (YOF, XEH, LAJ, QUG). Two of the four nonsense syllables, YOF and XEH, were given zero percent, 50 percent, or 100 percent reinforcement for different groups of subjects. In all groups YOF was paired with words of positive evaluative meaning, and XEH was paired with words of negative evaluative meaning. The number of reinforcements in the 50 and 100 percent groups was kept constant by doubling the number of trials in the 50 percent group. Of the 76 subjects in the 50 and 100 percent reinforcement groups, 27 (36 percent) indicated some degree of awareness. (It is not stated whether the aware subjects were or were not eliminated from the subsequent analysis.) The extent of conditioning for each subject was determined by subtracting his *pleasant-unpleasant* rating for the nonsense syllable associated with the pleasant words, YOF, from his rating for the nonsense syllable associated with the unpleasant words, XEH. The results indicated that the rated pleasantness was significantly greater in the 100 than in the 50 percent group and in the 50 than in the zero percent group.

Das and Nanda (1963), two Indian investigators, adapted the sensory preconditioning paradigm to the study of attitudes. The procedure involved associating nonsense syllables first with the names of Indian aboriginal tribes and then with the adjectives "good" or "bad." The associating of the nonsense syllables (JAGAPA and KACHADA) with the aboriginal tribes (Ho and Munda) was accomplished by having the subjects repeat after the experimenter two pairs 30 times each. (Counterbalancing was employed so that some subjects were exposed to the pairs JAGAPA-Ho and KACHADA-Munda and others to the pairs JAGAPA-Munda and KACHADA-Ho.) In the second stage of the experiment one of the nonsense syllables was paired with "good" 85 percent of the time and "bad" 15 percent of the time and the other with "bad" 85 percent of the time and with "good" 15 percent of the time. (Counterbalancing of the nonsense syllables and adjectives was employed.) This association was accomplished by telling the subjects one of the nonsense syllables and asking them to guess the adjective that followed. In the third stage of the experiment the subjects rated the two tribes, Ho and Munda, on a *good-bad* rating scale and selected adjectives from a group of 20 favorable and unfavorable adjectives which they considered descriptive of the tribes. The results with regard to both the ratings and the selected adjectives indicated that the two tribes when paired with nonsense syllables which were paired with "good" were evaluated more favorably than when paired with nonsense syllables which were paired with "bad." The results were interpreted as demonstrating the generalization or transference of attitudes. No attempt to assess awareness was reported.

Cohen (1964) demonstrated that there is a relationship between awareness and the classical conditioning of attitudes. Using the Staats and Staats (1957) procedure Cohen found significant conditioning of attitudes toward nonsense syllables only when the aware subjects were left in the sample. The unaware subjects did not show significant conditioning. Awareness was assessed by an open-ended inquiry similar to the one used by Staats and Staats. The subjects were simply asked to state " 'anything you thought about the experiment, especially what you think the purpose of the experiment was, and anything you thought about during the experiment' " (Cohen, 1964, p. 374). The responses of the 97 subjects were rated as aware or unaware by three judges. All three judges agreed that 45 subjects were aware and that 23 were not. Of the remaining 29 subjects two judges believed that 14 and one judge that 9 were aware. Cohen classified any subject as aware if at least one judge considered him so. In view of the fact that careful interview procedures reveal an association between awareness and verbal operant conditioning, it is not too surprising that careful interview procedures find an association between awareness and the classical conditioning of attitudes.

Insko and Oakes (1966) present some data which they interpret as indicating that the Staats and Staats (1957) conditioning procedure produces not a change in affect but rather in symbolic reference to affect. Visually presented nonsense syllables were paired with aurally presented adjectives over a number of trials. The key nonsense syllable, YOF, was associated with adjectives of either positive or negative evaluative meaning and the remaining nonsense syllables were associated with adjectives of neutral evaluative meaning. Four variables were manipulated in the experiment: percentage of trials on which YOF was associated with adjectives of evaluative meaning (50 or 100), number of extinction trials (0, 15, or 30), type of reinforcement (YOF associated with adjectives of positive evaluative meaning or with adjectives of negative evaluative meaning), and presence or absence of an intertrial activity (color naming). All of these variables involved between-subject comparisons. The color naming manipulation was included in order to see if direct interference with the subjects' hypothesizing behavior and awareness would produce an indirect reduction in the conditioning effect. Conditioning was assessed by having the subjects rate YOF on a number of evaluative semantic differential scales. Awareness of the reinforcement contingency was assessed through a number of questions which became increasingly specific during the course of the interview. The initial question inquired indirectly whether anything was noticed about the words that were pronounced, and one of the last questions asked directly if YOF was associated with words of pleasant (or, in the appropriate condition, unpleasant) evaluative meaning. Responses to the questions were coded so that the earlier in the interview the subjects verbalized the reinforcement contingency, the greater the degree of awareness. Finally, awareness of the demand characteristics of the experimental situation was assessed through a question which asked if the subjects felt they were supposed to rate the nonsense syllables in any particular way.

The semantic differential ratings of YOF indicated that the association with adjectives of either positive or negative meaning had an effect and also that this effect was reduced by color naming. The extinction and percentage of reinforcement manipulations produced nothing of significance. The effect of color naming on the evaluative ratings of YOF was paralleled by a similar reduction in awareness of the reinforcement contingency and demand characteristics. On the assumption that color naming directly interferes with awareness and not with conditioning, these results indicate that awareness had a causal influence on the supposed conditioning effect.

The data were also analyzed by examining just the subjects who were unaware of the reinforcement contingency and just the subjects who were unaware of the demand characteristics. The subjects who were unaware of the reinforcement contingency showed no significant conditioning effect, but the subjects who were unaware of the demand characteristics did. Taken at face value these results indicate that while there is no conditioning without awareness of the reinforcement contingency, the obtained conditioning effect is still, at least to some extent, a genuine effect capable of being generalized to nonlaboratory situations. This does not mean that awareness of the demand characteristics does not have some causal influence; it just means that such awareness cannot account for all of the variance.

One of the more puzzling findings relates to the failure to obtain extinction. Insko and Oakes interpret this failure as being due to the type of conditioning change produced by the Staats and Staats procedure. If the procedure produced a change in the affect or feeling directed at YOF, then extinction should have occurred. If, on the other hand, the procedure produced a change in the symbolic evaluative meaning of YOF, then it is more understandable why extinction did not occur. Insko and Oakes base their case on the often quoted statement that "a theory is not refuted by evidence but by a new theory." In terms of the present situation the argument is that an evaluative concept is not refuted by disconfirming adjectives (like those that occurred during extinction) but by a new concept. Since the adjectives presented during extinction suggested no new concept, the old concept of pleasant or unpleasant evaluative meaning, like an old theory, was maintained.

Previous research in this conditioning tradition had not distinguished between the direct conditioning of affect and the conditioning of symbolic reference to affect. The distinction, however, may prove to be an important one. Insko and Oakes argue that a conditioning procedure which uses single adjectives for unconditioned stimuli is not likely to produce a genuine affective change in the conditioned stimulus, but that a procedure which uses nonsymbolic unconditioned stimuli, such as food, may indeed produce a conditioning of affect. Before affect can be conditioned it must be aroused, and it seems unlikely that single evaluative adjectives arouse any great amount of affect.

Razran (1940) used nonsymbolic reinforcers to classically condition the evaluation of sociopolitical slogans such as "America for Americans," and "Workers of the World, Unite." The slogans were first rated for personal approval, social effectiveness, and literary value, and then divided into two sets. One set of slogans was always presented while the subjects were enjoying a free lunch and the other while they were required to inhale a number of putrid odors.[1] A number of nonexperimental slogans were added to each session. After five to eight conditioning sessions the slogans were again rated. Razran found that the slogans previously associated with lunch showed an increase in rated personal approval, literary value, and, to a lesser extent, social effectiveness, whereas the slogans previously associated with the putrid odors showed a decrease in rated literary value, personal approval, and to some slight extent in social effectiveness. Razran claims that these before-after changes were not a matter of conscious memory, since the subjects' knowledge of which slogans were combined with reinforcement and which with nonreinforcement was little above chance.

Did Razran's experiment produce a change in affect, symbolic reference to affect, or both? On the basis of the reported data it is impossible to say.

Razran (1938) also used this lunchroom technique to increase the judged character, beauty, intelligence, and other traits of a number of large pictures of college girls to which were attached minority group names. Razran's two studies are the first that attempted to modify attitudes through a classical conditioning procedure.

Stagner and Britton (1949) attempted to negatively condition the attitudes of male subjects toward Colombians and Bolivians. In con-

---

[1] Razran neither describes the procedure used in presenting his slogans nor presents the data that he obtained.

nection with a number of nonpsychology courses, attitudes toward several national groups were measured. Sometime later in a psychology laboratory approximately half of the subjects were negatively conditioned toward Bolivia and half toward Colombia. Two conditioning procedures were used with both groups of subjects. The first involved receiving a painful but not severe electric shock every time "Bolivia" or "Colombia" appeared on a memory drum. The subjects were supposedly trying to learn the following serial list: Siam, Atlantic, Liberty, Window, Pancreas, Albania, Antartica, Confidence, Cabbage, Thyroid (Bolivia or Colombia), Sahara, Research, Gun, Cortex, Siberia, Caribbean, Charity, Table, Corpuscles. Occasional shocks were also given after the words "Window" and "Gun." The second procedure was a word-odor association test in which the subjects attempted to associate certain words, including either "Bolivia" or "Colombia," with the names of certain odors which were smelled on each trial. The key words were associated with a very unpleasant odor. Approximately 2 weeks after the conditioning procedures the attitude measures were again administered in the nonpsychology classes. A control group took the before and after tests without the intervening conditioning. The results indicated that neither of the experimental groups shifted significantly in their attitude toward either of the national groups. The control group, however, showed significant positive shifts for both national groups. The difference in shift between the experimental and control groups was significant. The positive shift in the control group was attributed to the flow of "Good Neighbor" propaganda that resulted from the bombing of Pearl Harbor. The attack on Pearl Harbor occurred between the administration of the before and after tests. Thus the failure of a positive shift to result in the experimental groups was attributed to the conditioning procedure. The finding that neither experimental group changed its attitude toward either Bolivians or Colombians when it was aversively conditioned toward only one of these nationalities was attributed to the fact that, as revealed through subject interviews, there was very little differentiation between South American nations. In the interviews the subjects also reported that they had seen no connection between the conditioning procedures and the before or after tests.

Janis, Kaye, and Kirschner (1965) report some evidence that eating free food while reading communications facilitates persuasion. In a supposed test for reading preferences, individually tested subjects were asked to read four persuasive communications and then evaluate them. The communications argued for the occurrence of future events within specific times, as, for example, the replacement of two-dimensional movies by three-dimensional movies within 3 years and satisfactory progress in the search for a cancer cure within 25 years. There were two experimental conditions in the experiment, food and no-food. In the food condition the subjects were offered peanuts and soft drinks by an experimenter who had already started eating when they arrived. In the no-food condition neither the subjects nor the experimenter had any food. The experimenter told the subjects in both conditions that he agreed with some of the communications and did not agree with others.

Before-after change scores indicated more influence in the food condition than in the no-food condition. The effect is significant for three of the communications and nonsignificant for one. No overall test of significance is reported. Janis, Kaye, and Kirschner state that their results agree with Razran's (1940) findings concerning the effect of free food. They are reluctant to interpret their results as being due to conditioning, however, in view of the fact that a favorable attitude toward the donor of the food may be a more adequate explanation. Informal postexperimental interviews apparently indicated that the experimenter was regarded more favorably in the food than in the no-food condition.

Dabbs and Janis (1965) investigated the effect of contiguity versus noncontiguity of food with exposure to persuasive communications and positive versus negative endorsement of the communications by an experimenter. The conditioning interpretation predicts that food will facilitate persuasion only if it is contiguous with or immediately follows exposure to persuasive arguments. An alternative interpretation suggested by Janis, Kaye, and Kirschner (1965), however, suggests that the donation of free food will lead to acceptance of persuasive arguments only if the donor is perceived as endorsing the arguments.

The experiment involved two independent variables: contiguity versus noncontiguity of food with exposure to two persuasive communications and positive versus negative endorsement of the communications by an experimenter. Different subjects were tested in each of the four conditions generated by these two variables. The endorsement variable was manipulated by having the experimenter inform the subjects that he personally agreed or disagreed with the two written communications. One communication argued that Hollywood is steadily improving the quality of its movies and the other advocated more severe treatment of juvenile delinquents. The contiguity variable was manipulated by providing food either during an initial 15-minute period in which the subjects rated their liking or disliking for 10 paintings, or during a later 15-minute period in which the subjects first silently read the two persuasive communications and then rated five political slogans for their adequacy and effectiveness. The food (a choice of soft drinks, mixed nuts, potato chips, and corn chips) was introduced with the statement that later the experimenter would be working with people who were extremely hungry, but for now he wanted to obtain some preliminary comparative data for subjects who were not particularly hungry. (Responses from a final interview indicated that the subjects accepted this rationale without any suspicions.) Immediately after rating the political slogans the subjects indicated their agreement with each of the two persuasive communications.

An analysis of variance of the after-only scores indicated that neither contiguity nor endorsement had significant effects. Dabbs and Janis (1965) did find, however, that there was significantly more agreement with the two communications in the positive-endorsement-contiguity condition than in the remaining three conditions. These results were interpreted as indicating that the consumption of food "*induces a momentary mood of compliance toward the donor that is strongest at the time the food is being consumed but that decreases in strength rapidly after the food has been consumed*" (p. 141). Dabbs and Janis further interpret Janis, Kaye, and Kirschner's (1965) results as possibly indicating that the subjects thought the experimenter implicitly endorsed the persuasive communications to which they were exposed.

The ratings of the paintings and slogans provide further data on the conditioning of attitudes and opinions. Comparing the ratings obtained contiguously with food and the ratings obtained noncontiguously with food revealed nonsignificant differences for both paintings and slogans. As Dabbs and Janis point out, these results disagree with those obtained by Razran (1938, 1940).

McGuire (*1957*) demonstrated that a communication which presents desirable information before undesirable information is more persuasive than a communication which presents information in the reverse order. According to McGuire this information sequence effect is produced by attention and comprehension responses. The communication which places highly desirable information first reinforces or conditions the attention and comprehension responses so that they have a tendency to continue even when the communication becomes less desirable. On the other hand, the communication which places less desirable information first establishes an avoidance reaction by negatively reinforcing the attention to and comprehension of the less desirable information. This avoidance reaction has a tendency to continue even after the information becomes more desirable.

In McGuire's experiment a questionnaire was administered to the subjects 1 week before and immediately after the persuasive communication. The questionnaire contained statements regarding college life, such as federal aid to supply free textbooks and scheduling of 7 A.M. classes to ease the classroom shortage. Each statement was rated both according to its likelihood of occurrence and its desirability. On the basis of these ratings four high desirability and four low desirability items were selected. The communication consisted of the written replies to a series of questions concerning the above items asked of a fictitious university president, "Dr. Harold Wilson." All of Dr. Wilson's eight replies were plausible, factual arguments that the events in question were likely to occur. Each subject received only four of the eight replies. For half of the subjects the replies were presented in an H-L order (high desirability-low desirability), and for half they were in an L-H order (low desirability-high desirability).

McGuire used analysis of covariance to correct the opinion scores in the second questionnaire on the basis of the responses to the initial questionnaire. The corrected opinion scores for the H-L and the L-H groups differed significantly across all items. As predicted, the H-L groups showed the most opinion change. The second questionnaire, which was administered immediately after the communication, contained some multiple-choice items designed to measure the comprehension of the communication. If persuasion is mediated by attention and comprehension, then the H-L group should have retained more of the content of the communication than the L-H group. McGuire found that the groups differed in the predicted direction at the .06 level of significance.

Comment. Our survey of the literature concerned with the classical conditioning of attitude and opinion has revealed several different experimental approaches. Some research has used symbolic reinforcement and some has used more primitive reinforcement such as food or unpleasant odors. Some research has paired the reinforcement with the to-be-conditioned response over a number of discrete trials and some has not. And some research has used persuasive communications and some has not. In view of these numerous differences between experiments it would be unwise to argue that the different experiments lend each other much mutual support. From the present vantage point it does appear as if classical conditioning is relevant to attitude and opinion change, but the evidence is far from confirmatory.

Fear Arousing Communications

Now we turn to a consideration of a number of studies that have dealt with the effect of fear arousing communications. These studies deal with a particular subvariety of reinforcement. The escape from or avoidance of fear is theoretically reinforcing.

Research on this problem is more difficult than research on many other attitude change problems for two reasons. First, the arousal of fear is not always easy to accomplish, and, second, the strong and weak fear arousing communications must be equated on every dimension besides that of fear arousal. Research that failed on one or the other of these two counts (Goldstein, 1957, 1959; Leventhal and Niles, 1964, 1965; Moltz and Thistlethwaite, 1955) will not be considered below.

Janis and Feshbach (*1953*) presented high school students with slide-illustrated lectures on the cause and prevention of tooth decay. Three forms of the lecture were prepared containing essentially the same factual information but differing in the amount of fear arousing material. The strong fear appeal emphasized the painful consequences of tooth decay, diseased gums, etc., that could result from improper dental hygiene. This communication was accompanied by a series of slides realistically portraying tooth decay and mouth infections. The moderate fear appeal described the dangers of tooth decay in a milder, less personalized manner. The slides accompanying this communication showed less severe cases of oral pathology. The weak fear appeal replaced the fear arousing information with information on the growth and functions of the teeth. The accompanying slides were pictures of healthy teeth and X rays of cavities. All of the communications were approximately 15 minutes in length.

A week before the communications were presented to three separate classes the subjects were given a questionnaire to ascertain how much and in what way they were currently brushing their teeth. A different questionnaire administered immediately after the presentation of the communications revealed that the communications had the desired differentially fear producing results and that there was no difference in the retention of the material from the three communications. A follow-up questionnaire administered a week after the presentation of the communications revealed that the strong fear arousing communication produced the least reported change in toothbrushing practice and the weak fear arousing communication the most. It was also found that an attack against one of the major assertions of the communications (the importance of using the proper kind of toothbrush) was most successful in the group that had heard the strong fear arousing communication and least successful in the group that had heard the weak fear arousing communication. Janis and Feshbach interpreted the results as indicating that strong emotion prevented the subjects from recalling the content of the communications when brushing their teeth. The evocation of emotional reactions might be an effective way of prompting immediate action such as donating money or volunteering for a task, but when the communication contains no reassurance or immediate way of obtaining reassurance then the emotional reaction may lead either to an avoidance of thinking about the content of the communication or to a minimization of the importance of the communication. Hovland, Janis, and Kelley (1953) amplify the above interpretation by stating that a fear arousing communication leads to the acquisition of a learned fear or avoidance drive. If the fear drive is reduced by the appropriate reassurances the resulting reinforcement will lead to opinion or attitude change. If, however, the learned fear drive is not reduced by reassurances there is no reinforcement and consequently no attitude or opinion change.

Janis and Terwilliger (1962) performed an experiment in which they obtained some evidence in support of the defensive resistance hypothesis. The weak threat communication was a series of 15 paragraph-statements by medical authorities which indicated that heavy smoking causes a serious type of cancer that can be avoided by smoking less. The strong threat communication consisted of the same 15 paragraphs plus 7 additional paragraphs which elaborated on the seriousness of lung cancer. These 7 additional paragraphs were interspersed among the 15 mildly threatening ones. The subjects, student and adult volunteers most of whom were smokers, read either the weak or the strong threat communication, one paragraph at a time. After each paragraph they verbalized their associations which were recorded by a concealed tape recorder. While giving associations each subject wore earphones which delivered white noise of sufficient intensity to mask the sound of his or her voice. Before and after being exposed to either the weak or strong threat communications the subjects were asked to verbalize their ideas while they thought of themselves smoking a cigarette. A content analysis of the before-after material indicated that the strong threat communication was possibly less influential than the weak threat communication in changing attitudes toward smoking ($p < .09$). A content analysis of the associations made during the communications indicated that the strong threat communication did indeed produce more fear or expressions of affective disturbance than did the weak threat communication. It was further found that the strong threat group made significantly more explicit rejection associations to the 15 mildly threatening paragraphs than did the weak threat group. Since the high threat group made more rejection statements and manifested less attitude change, Janis and Terwilliger concluded that they had produced evidence in support of the hypothesis that a strong threat communication arouses defensive resistance to the arguments, conclusions, and recommendations contained in the communication. No attempt was made to relate defensive rejection and attitude change on an individual or within-group basis.

Haefner (1956) reports that both strong fear arousing and strong guilt arousing communications are less persuasive than weak fear and guilt arousing communications. The topic of the communications was the destructive capabilities of hydrogen weapons and the advisability of international agreement concerning the cessation of atomic testing. Two of the communications were designed to evoke fear in either a strong or a mild degree by referring to the dangers of nuclear war, and two of the communications were designed to elicit guilt in either a strong or a mild degree by reference to Hiroshima, Nagasaki, and the dangers of fallout from recent U.S. testing. All of the communications contained the same information concerning atomic weapons and the same reassuring recommendations concerning the advisability of cessation of testing through international agreement. An affective response measure administered before and after the presentation of the two communications indicated that the four groups of subjects, members of fraternities at the University of Rochester, differed in the expected manner in aroused guilt and fear. An information measure indicated that the guilt arousal groups retained more of the content of the communications than did the fear arousal groups, but that there was no difference in retention between the strongly and mildly aroused groups. Before-after changes in attitude toward the value of an internationally inspected ban on atomic testing were reported, as predicted, to be greater in the moderately aroused groups. After reanalyzing Haefner's data, however, Leventhal and Niles (1965) point out that while the above statement is true for guilt, it is not true for fear. Moderate guilt was more influential than strong guilt, but moderate fear was not more influential than strong fear.

Berkowitz and Cottingham (*1960*) theorized that two additional factors have to be considered in the conceptualization of strong and weak fear arousing communications: the interest value or attention-getting quality of the weak fear appeal, and the relevance of the material in the strong fear appeal. To the extent that a weak fear appeal is uninteresting it will have little if any effect and thus will not be more persuasive than a strong fear appeal. The effect of the strong fear appeal, on the other hand, will depend upon relevance; the greater the relevance of the material, the greater the defensive avoidance and the less the attitude change.

In the first of two experiments, Berkowitz and Cottingham obtained before-after measures of attitudes toward the use of seat belts from one control group and two experimental groups. Between the before and after measures, one of the experimental groups was presented with a strong fear arousing communication advocating the use of seat belts and the other a weak fear arousing communication. Relevance was operationally defined as high or low according to the frequency with which the subjects rode in cars. The results indicated that, while the subjects in the strong fear condition admitted to significantly greater tension, there were no overall attitude change differences among experimental and control groups. It was found, however, that, as predicted, the low relevance subjects changed more than the high relevance subjects in the strong fear condition.

In order to test the interpretation that the lack of difference between strong and weak fear conditions in the above study was due to a lack of interest in the weak fear communication, Berkowitz and Cottingham replicated the experiment with an expanded postquestionnaire. This postquestionnaire indicated, in fact, that significantly more of the subjects regarded the weak fear communication as uninteresting. With

regard to attitude change it was again found that the weak fear communication did not produce significantly more change than occurred
in the control group, and presumably the strong fear communication
did not produce significantly more change than occurred in either the
control or weak fear conditions, although this is not explicitly stated.
A comparison of the high and low relevance subjects again revealed that
in the strong fear condition the low relevance subjects changed the most.
The data from the two experiments were taken as support for the two
initially stated hypotheses with regard to the interest value and relevance of threatening communications.

   DeWolfe and Governale (1964) report some evidence which they
interpret as being consistent with a thesis advanced by Janis and Feshbach (1954) to the effect that if a persuasive communication contains
reassuring recommendations as to how threat can be averted, fear can
be expected to facilitate attitude change. DeWolfe and Governale's evidence was obtained from a study of two groups of student nurses, one
of which was given a 6-week training session nursing tuberculosis patients (experimental group) and one of which was not (control group).
Both groups of nurses were rated on fear of tuberculosis and adoption
of an ideal attitude toward the nursing of tuberculosis patients at the
beginning, middle, and end of the 6-week period. During the 6-week
period the experimental nurses were continuously both formally and
informally exposed to fear averting information. They also presumably
obtained reassurance through identification with more experienced and
less fearful staff members. Thus the obtaining of reassurance was supposedly, in some fashion or other, bound up with the adoption of a
more ideal attitude toward the nursing of tuberculosis patients. The
ideal attitude was determined on the basis of Q sorts on the nurse-
patient relationship obtained from two nursing educators and two head
nurses, all of whom had long experience in the treatment of tuberculosis
patients.

   The results indicated that there was a significant decrease in fear
and a significant increase in attitude change only in the experimental
subjects. Furthermore, the changes in fear and attitude were significantly
greater for the experimental than the control subjects. The level of fear
on the first day was significantly correlated with attitude change in
the experimental group (+.411) but not in the control group (−.024).

   Insko, Arkoff, and Insko (1965) qualified the Janis and Feshbach
(1953) interpretation of the differential persuasiveness of strong and
weak fear arousing communications by hypothesizing that weak fear
arousing communications will be more persuasive when directed at currently ongoing activity (punishment), while strong fear arousing communications will be more persuasive when directed at the precluding
of possible future activity (avoidance). This would mean, for example,

that potential smokers would be more influenced by a strong fear arousing communication pointing to the detrimental effects of smoking, while
actual smokers would be more influenced by a weak fear arousing communication. As a partial test of this hypothesis, nonsmoking seventh-
grade students were presented with either strong or weak fear arousing
communications which pointed to the detrimental effects of smoking.
There were two dependent variables: opinion about future smoking behavior and opinion about the effect of smoking upon health. The first
of these dependent variables was measured by summing the responses
to a number of questions such as "Will you ever try smoking cigarettes?"
and "Will you become a regular smoker?" Similarly, the second dependent variable was measured by summing the responses to a number
of questions such as "Do you believe that smoking causes lung cancer?"
and "Do you believe that smokers die earlier than nonsmokers?" Before-after change scores revealed that the strong fear arousing communication produced significantly more advocated change in opinion
about future smoking behavior than did the weak fear arousing communication, but that the two communications did not differ in changing
opinion about the effects of smoking upon health. Furthermore, the
difference between the strong and weak fear arousing communications
was significantly greater for opinion about future smoking behavior than
for opinion about effect of smoking upon health. These results were
interpreted as indicating that nondefensive fear reduction acted so as
to produce change differences between the communications for the
former but not the latter opinion. Fear avoidance should produce a
change in opinion about future smoking behavior but not in opinion
about effect of smoking upon health.

It was further found that after a week the change score differences
between the arousal conditions decreased. This was due to increasing
change in the weak fear condition and decreasing change in the strong
fear condition, and was interpreted as resulting from possible interaction among the subjects in the two conditions. A further study is obviously called for in which the subjects from the strong and weak
arousal conditions are segregated over time.

Rosenblatt (1965) reports data from an experiment indicating that
a strong fear arousing communication is more effective than a weak
fear arousing communication in convincing people that they should *not*
have tuberculosis chest X-ray examinations. College students read written communications on the topic of tuberculosis chest X rays supposedly
in order to evaluate the communications' "readability, interest value,
and other characteristics." The experiment involved two independent
variables: amount of opinion change advocated and level of fear. Amount
of opinion change advocated was manipulated by having the communication recommended either that no one should ever get a chest X ray or that

only the people exposed to tuberculosis should do so. Level of fear (strong or weak) was manipulated in the standard manner. A check into the adequacy of the fear manipulation indicated that the strong fear condition produced more worry and fright than did the weak fear condition. An after-only assessment of opinion regarding the advisability of getting chest X rays indicated that level of fear had a significant effect but that amount of change advocated did not. Strong fear produced significantly more change than did weak fear.

Rosenblatt's experiment, like Insko, Arkoff, and Insko's (1965), dealt with an avoidance topic; i.e., the communications in both experiments advocated that the subjects avoid some activity (smoking, getting X rays). Both experiments agreed in finding that acceptance of the avoidance recommendation was facilitated by strong fear.

Leventhal, Singer, and Jones (1965) investigated the effect of fear and specificity of recommendation upon the intention to obtain and the actual obtaining of tetanus inoculations. Yale seniors were individually exposed to written persuasive communications concerning the advisability of obtaining tetanus inoculations. Two independent variables were manipulated: fear (strong or weak) and specificity of recommendation (high or low). The specificity of recommendation variable concerned the extent to which subjects were informed of the procedure of obtaining inoculations, the times at which inoculations were available, the location of the University Health Service, and so forth. A check into the adequacy of the fear manipulation indicated that the strong fear communication was indeed more fear arousing than the weak fear communication.

The results indicated that, both for subjects who had and who had not had inoculations within the last 2 years, strong fear was more effective than low fear in producing reported determination to obtain inoculations and perceived importance of inoculations. The specificity of recommendation had no effect on either of these two dependent variables. With regard to actually getting the shots, however, only the specificity of recommendation variable had a significant effect. During the 4- to 6-week period following the experiment, 9 of the 59 subjects obtained shots. Of these 9 subjects, 4 were in the high-fear-specific condition, 4 in the low-fear-specific condition, 1 in the low-fear-nonspecific condition, and none in the high-fear-nonspecific condition. Due to the fact, however, that no shots were obtained by a control group of 60 subjects who were only exposed to the specific information, it was concluded that some degree of fear arousal is necessary in order to instigate shot taking.

These results seemingly indicate that specificity of recommendation does not interact with level of fear and thus can offer no explanation of the finding that strong fear is sometimes more and sometimes less effective than weak fear. To the extent that specificity of recommendation is similar to Janis and Feshbach's (1953) notion of reassurance, the evidence does not support the hypothesis that strong fear arousing communications will be least effective only when there is not some immediate reassurance as to how the fear can be reduced. Of course, it may be that reassurance or specificity of recommendation is an important interactive variable only in situations where other factors conspire to produce exceedingly strong defensive reactions against strong fear arousing communications.

Another thing that should be pointed out about this experiment is that the communication topic, the obtaining of inoculations, is neither a punishment nor an avoidance issue. The subjects were not told to stop doing something they were doing (punishment) or not do something they were not doing (avoidance), but rather to do something they had or had not done. All the subjects (those who had and those who had not been inoculated) were told to obtain inoculations.

Comment. Some of the above research indicates that strong fear arousing communications are less persuasive than weak (Janis and Feshbach, 1953; Janis and Terwilliger, 1962) and some that strong fear arousing communications are more persuasive than weak (DeWolfe and Governale, 1964; Insko, Arkoff, and Insko, 1965; Leventhal, Singer, and Jones, 1965; Rosenblatt, 1965). Such inconsistency, of course, suggests that one or more interactive variables are of crucial importance. The problem then is one of specifying those variables.

One approach to the problem is to assume that, in general, strong fear arousing communications will be most persuasive unless the fear produces counteracting defensive reactions.[2] Viewed in this manner the problem becomes one of specifying the variables or circumstances which are likely to facilitate or hinder defensiveness. One suggestion is Insko, Arkoff, and Insko's (1965) notion that, relative to weak fear arousing communications, strong fear arousing communications are more likely to arouse defensive reaction in punishment situations than in avoidance situations. Two studies that involved avoidance situations (Insko, Arkoff, and Insko, 1965; Rosenblatt, 1965) found strong fear more persuasive than weak, as would be expected; and two studies that involved punishment situations (Haefner, 1956; Janis and Terwilliger, 1962) found either strong fear less effective or no difference between strong and weak fear. However, the additional study which found strong fear less effective than weak (Janis and Feshbach, 1953) involved both a punishment situation and another type of situation which is neither punishment nor avoidance. Subjects were punished for incorrect dental hygiene and, in addition, directed to use correct dental hygiene. Furthermore, the Leventhal,

---

[2] Without defensive reactions, strong fear arousing communications would benefit from their superior attention-getting and motivating qualities.

Singer, and Jones study (1965) cannot be classified as either punishment or avoidance. All of this ambiguity does not create a large amount of confidence in the formulation. It still may be the case, however, that whether one is dealing with a punishment or avoidance situation will have at least some influence on the extent to which strong fear arousing communications evoke defensive reactions.

An additional matter that may have an effect on the relative persuasive impacts of strong and weak fear arousing communications is source credibility. Aronson, Turner, and Carlsmith (1963) have argued that two alternative responses to a persuasive communication are conformity to the communicator's point of view and disparagement of the communicator. Conformity and disparagement are alternative responses; if one tends to occur, the other will not tend to occur. Aronson, Turner, and Carlsmith further argue that a highly credible source is more difficult to disparage than a mildly credible source. This means, of course, that as source credibility increases, conformity increases and disparagement decreases. This theorizing is relevant to the problem of fear arousing communications because of the apparent similarity between disparagement and defensiveness. Disparagement involves lowering the credibility and worth of a communicator and his arguments, and defensiveness may, at least to some extent, involve the same sort of thing. In any event, there is an obvious similarity between lowering the worth of a communicator and his arguments, and defensively deciding that a communicator and his arguments are not worth thinking about. Thus, defensive reactions to strong fear arousing communications will be more difficult if the communication and its source have high credibility. The defensive reactions evoked by strong fear arousing communications in certain situations may be magnified or reduced according to the credibility of the communication and communicator. It should be emphasized that source credibility, in the present context, refers both to the credibility of the communicator and to the credibility of the communication. Rosenblatt (1965) argues, on the basis of some unpublished data, that the strong threats used in Janis and Feshbach's (1953) dental hygiene study are inherently less believable (credible) than are the weak threats. This at least suggests that strong fear arousing communications on some issues may be more readily disparaged than strong fear arousing communications on other issues. Furthermore, with changes in the informational environment there may be changes in the ease with which strong fear arousing communications on any given issue may be disparaged. For example, before the causal link between smoking and lung cancer was generally accepted, a strong fear arousing communication on the topic would probably have evoked much more disparagement and/or defensiveness than would be evoked today. Unfortunately, this sort of thing makes hypothesis testing rather difficult.

Another consideration that may have an effect on the extent to which strong fear arousing communications evoke defensive reactions is simply the amount of fear involved. It may be that defensive reactions occur only in response to extremely high levels of fear. This would mean that fear is curvilinearly related to persuasion, with moderate fear being more persuasive than either high or low fear. Unfortunately, what little evidence there is does not support this hypothesis. To date, the only experimental study which had more than two levels of fear is Janis and Feshbach's (1953), and they found a relation between fear and persuasion that is at least approximately linear. It still may be the case, however, that exact level of fear in interaction with other variables will have some predictive power.

A final matter concerned with defensive reactions evoked by fear arousing communications relates to individual differences. This whole research area may be one in which individual differences are exceedingly important. Goldstein (1959), for example, has argued that only some individuals will react defensively to strong fear arousing communications. He makes a basic distinction between two types of individuals, copers and avoiders. Copers attempt to handle fear and anxiety in a nondefensive manner and avoiders in a defensive manner. Goldstein thus believes that copers will be more influenced by strong fear arousing communications and avoiders will be more influenced by weak fear arousing communications. This is a matter that should be looked into.

Unfortunately, our knowledge about the relative persuasive effects of strong and weak fear arousing communications is still fairly primitive. Because of the topic's great practical importance, however, we can hope that future work will make significant advances.

Source Credibility

Another area of research that is relevant to the reinforcement theory of attitude change is that of source credibility. Hovland, Janis, and Kelley (1953) maintain that, since receiving information from credible sources has, for most everyone, been associated with reinforcement, conclusions advocated by credible sources will be more readily accepted than conclusions advocated by noncredible sources. The discussion of source credibility will be limited to experiments in which the credible and noncredible sources are linked to persuasive communications of some length and not just to single assertions, because it is this former type of situation that was of principal concern to Hovland and his associates.[3]

Hovland and Weiss (1951) demonstrated that a communication represented as coming from a high credibility source is more persuasive

---

[3] The latter "prestige suggestion" literature is discussed in Chapter 6.

than the same communication represented as coming from a low credibility source. Four communications, each administered to two different groups, were used. The communications were concerned with the advisability of selling antihistamines without a prescription, whether or not the steel industry was to blame for the then current steel shortage, the future of the movie industry with the advent of TV, and the practicality of building an atomic powered submarine. The communications were represented as coming from a high or a low credibility source for different groups of subjects. For example, the high credibility source for the atomic submarine communication was Oppenheimer, and the low credibility source was *Pravda*. Opinion questionnaires were administered before, immediately after, and a month after the presentation of the communications. The before questionnaire revealed that the four high credibility sources were judged to be trustworthy by 81 to 95 percent of the subjects, and the four low credibility sources were judged to be trustworthy by 1 to 21 percent. The difference between the opinion scores of the before and immediately after questionnaires indicated that significantly more (16.4 percent) of the subjects were influenced by the high credibility than by the low credibility sources. Four weeks later, however, this difference had disappeared. The number of subjects influenced by the high credibility source had decreased, and the number of subjects influenced by the low credibility source had increased. The difference in the direction of change for the two groups was highly significant. This increase in the influence of the low credibility source over time was called the "sleeper effect." Recall, both of the content of the communications and of the sources of the communications, was not significantly different for the high and low credibility source groups either immediately after or 4 weeks after the presentation of the communications.[4] Furthermore, the subjects who showed the sleeper effect did not show inferior recall of the source. Hovland and Weiss speculated that the sleeper effect may be due to the failure of the subjects over time to spontaneously associate the source with the content of a communication.

Kelman and Hovland (1953) tested the hypothesis that the sleeper effect is due to a dissociation of source and content over time. The communication, which advocated a more lenient treatment of juvenile delinquents, was attributed to either a high credibility source (a judge in a juvenile court who was also the author of several authoritative books on juvenile delinquency), a low credibility source (a dope peddler out on bail), or a neutral source. The taped communication was presented in

---

[4] The comparison of source recall after 4 weeks for the high and low credibility groups was not explicitly made by Hovland and Weiss. Computations on the basis of reported data, however, indicate that source recall for the two groups is essentially the same.

the context of a supposedly real, educational radio program. An opinion measure taken immediately after the communication indicated that the subjects exposed to the high, neutral, and low credibility sources differed significantly in the expected direction. Three weeks later the opinion questionnaire was readministered. Half of the subjects filled out the questionnaire after being exposed to that part of the previously presented tape recordings which introduced the source of the communication, and half of the subjects filled out the questionnaire without any prior "reinstatement" manipulation. The results indicated that the sleeper effect was evident without reinstatement but was dissipated by reinstatement. Relative to the nonreinstatement conditions, reinstatement of the high credibility source increased agreement with the communication, and reinstatement of the low credibility source decreased agreement with the communication. Furthermore, an analysis of those subjects in the nonreinstatement groups who remembered more of the details about the sources indicated that they did not continue to be influenced by the sources to a greater extent than did the subjects who remembered less about them. Within the low credibility group, in fact, the subjects who remembered the source the best were most inclined to show the sleeper effect. Kelman and Hovland thus produced evidence that the sleeper effect is due to a tendency to dissociate the source and content and not to any simple tendency to forget the source of a communication.

Watts and McGuire (*1964*) failed to find unequivocal evidence for a sleeper effect. Subjects read four different persuasive communications spaced over a 6-week interval. Immediately after exposure to the last communication, opinion and retention measures for all four communication topics were taken. These topics were: "Puerto Rico should be admitted to the Union as the 51st state," "Courts should deal more leniently with juvenile delinquents," "The Secretary of State should be elected by the people, not appointed by the President," "The State Sales tax should be abolished" (p. 235). The communications dealing with each of the four topics were rotated among the four time intervals. For half of the subjects the communications were represented as coming from high credibility sources and for half from low credibility sources. For example, with regard to the sales tax issue the high credibility source was a "Presidential Council for the study of the sales tax," and the low credibility source "a defense argument by a man convicted of sales tax fraud" (p. 235).

Watts and McGuire found that with regard to opinion change the main effect of source credibility as well as the interaction between source credibility and time were both significant at only the .10 level. (Although Watts and McGuire do not discuss the matter, the results look a little better if one is willing to take advantage of the direction of the predictions and thus lower the obtained significance levels from .10 to .05.)

Initially the high credibility sources were more persuasive than the low credibility sources, but the differences between sources dissipated over time. This dissipation resulted from a more rapid decay for the high than for the low credibility sources and may be due, in part, as Watts and McGuire suggest, to a regression effect. Hovland and Weiss (1951) and Kelman and Hovland (1953) found that the dissipation of the differences between source conditions over time was due to decreasing change in the high credibility source condition and, in disagreement with Watts and McGuire, to increasing change in the low credibility source condition. Consistent with Hovland and Weiss, and Kelman and Hovland, however, Watts and McGuire did find that the dissipation in opinion change over time was no more rapid for the subjects who could as opposed to those who could not recall the sources.

Hovland and Mandell (1952) failed to find that a high credibility source is significantly more influential than a low credibility source. The topic of the communication, devaluation of currency, was represented as coming from either an economist or an importer who would stand to gain from the devaluation. The communicators thus differed in trustworthiness if not in expertness. There were two communications: a communication in which the conclusion that U.S. currency should be devaluated was explicitly drawn, and one in which the conclusion that U.S. currency should be devaluated was not explicitly drawn. Hovland and Mandell found that while the explicit drawing of the conclusion caused a significantly greater number of people to change than the failure to explicitly draw the conclusion, the trustworthiness of the communicators did not produce a significant effect. The difference in favor of the trustworthy communicator is 7.2 percent with the conclusion drawn by the communicator and 4.9 percent with the conclusion not drawn by the communicator. These values, although in the predicted direction, are still far from being significant ($p < .23$ and $p < .33$ respectively). This failure to produce a significant effect was not due to an inadequate manipulation of the independent variable because significantly more of the subjects felt that the trustworthy, as opposed to the untrustworthy, communicator did a "good job" and was "fair and honest" in presenting the facts.

It is possible that the lack of significant results can be attributed to the fact that the sources differed in trustworthiness rather than in expertness, although some of Hovland and Weiss's (1951) sources, as for example, *Pravda* and Oppenheimer, appear to differ as much in trustworthiness as in expertness. It is more probable that the influence of source credibility (expertness or trustworthiness) may be greater with some types of persuasive communications than with others. One possibility is that the influence of source credibility upon persuasion is inversely proportional to the logical soundness of the communication.

A less persuasive effect may be produced by a source when associated with a communication which lucidly develops a flawless logical argument than by the same source when associated with a communication which presents arguments involving more unproven assumptions or logical gaps. Unfortunately, it is not known for certain whether the communications of Hovland and Mandell (1952) were any more logical than those of Hovland and Weiss (1951), Kelman and Hovland (1953), and Watts and McGuire (1964). Inasmuch, however, as the Hovland and Mandell communications were designed so that the audience should be able to deduce the conclusion from the presented evidence even if the conclusion was not explicitly stated, it is reasonable to suppose the communications involved a high order of logical imperativeness.

Choo (1964) presented subjects with a 6-page written communication advocating essentially no causal relationship between smoking and lung cancer. The communication was represented as coming from either "Dr. W. C. Hueper, Head of the Environmental Cancer Section of the National Cancer Institute, Public Health Service" (high credibility source) or "Mr. J. P. Richards, Director of Tobacco Industry Public Relations Committee" (low credibility source). Ratings obtained previous to the administration of the communication indicated that the "Public Health Service" and the "Director of Tobacco Public Relations Committee" were considered approximately equal in knowledge of the facts, but that the former was considered more trustworthy than the latter. Choo found that the high credibility source produced more before-after change than the low credibility source, and that the subjects who considered the communication more highly discrepant from their own positions were more influenced than the subjects who considered the communication less highly discrepant. An analysis of variance revealed no significant interaction between credibility and subject differences in perceived communication discrepancy. A check on the success of the source credibility manipulation indicated that the high credibility source was considered more trustworthy than the low credibility source.

Aronson and Golden (1962) investigated the effect of objectively relevant and irrelevant aspects of communicator credibility upon attitude change toward the value of arithmetic. Four different groups of sixth-grade school children were exposed to four different communication sources: a white engineer (high relevant and high irrelevant credibility), a Negro engineer (high relevant and low irrelevant credibility), a white dishwasher (low relevant and high irrelevant credibility), a Negro dishwasher (low relevant and low irrelevant credibility). In all four groups the communication on the virtue of arithmetic was the same taped material. The communication source was present in every case, but did not speak, supposedly because of hoarseness. The after scores, adjusted by analysis of covariance for the before variance, revealed that the relevant engineer-dishwasher variable was significantly effective but the irrelevant Negro-white variable was not. Ratings of sincerity in the communicators revealed no differences among the four groups, but ratings of intelligence indicated that the engineers were perceived as more intelligent than the dishwashers. There was no difference in the perceived intelligence of the Negro and white communicators. A breakdown of the subjects into prejudiced and unprejudiced on the basis of questionnaire responses indicated that the prejudiced subjects were less influenced by the Negro communicator than were the unprejudiced subjects. There was, however, no difference in the intelligence and sincerity ratings of the prejudiced and unprejudiced in any of the four groups. These results were taken as indicating that the prejudiced and unprejudiced subjects responded on the basis of objectively irrelevant cues.

It is, of course, possible that the subjects perceived the Negro communicator as more or less "good" along some other nonmeasured but still relevant dimension. Other possible relevant dimensions such as trustworthiness, honesty, competence, however, seem to be closely related to either sincerity or intelligence. Perhaps the subjects responded on the basis of liking-disliking, an irrelevant dimension.

Comment. In view of the high degree of consistency in this source credibility literature we can safely generalize that a high credibility source will be more influential than a low credibility source.[5] Being able to state this generalization, however, does not mean that we really understand source credibility. What is it that makes a source credible and how does source credibility operate? These are questions for which research has provided no ready answers. The Aronson and Golden (1962) experiment on the differences between objectively relevant and irrelevant aspects of credibility makes it quite evident that we are really just beginning to study source credibility. Perhaps some help could be obtained from a consideration of the social power literature (Schopler, 1965).

One possible approach to source credibility is in terms of interactive variables. If we knew more about the variables with which source credibility interacts, we would undoubtedly understand more about source credibility itself. We have discussed the literature on the interaction between source credibility and amount of time after communication presentation. There is also some literature on the interaction between source credibility and communicator-communicatee discrepancy (Aronson, Turner, and Carlsmith, 1963; Bergin, 1962; Bochner and Insko, in press) that is discussed in Chapter 3. This literature seemingly demonstrates the greatest superiority of the high credibility source when the communicator advocates a position that is moderately to extremely dis-

---

[5] This literature is so consistent that we have not even bothered to discuss all of it.

crepant from that of the communicatee. In an experiment discussed in Chapter 13, Kelman (1958) presents evidence for interactions between the basis for a source's credibility (attraction, expertness, or means control power) and the salience or surveillance of the source when opinion regarding the issue in question is measured. Other interactions undoubtedly relate to the type of communication with which a highly credible source is linked. Certainly not all high credibility sources will be equally influential when associated with the same communications. Some sources may be considered expert only when discussing certain issues and some sources may be considered trustworthy only when advocating certain points of view.

Primacy versus Recency

Is the greater persuasive effect more likely to be produced by the first or the second of two opposing communications successively presented to a communicatee? According to convention the case in which the initial communication has the greater effect is called one of primacy, and the case in which the final communication has the greater persuasive effect is called one of recency.

The history of research on the primacy-recency issue is a long one. In 1925 Lund gave various subjects different written communications in support of one side of a controversial issue (e.g., the advisability of a protective tariff), and then presented communications on the other side of the same issue. Using a before-after design Lund found that more opinion change was obtained after the first communication; i.e., primacy was obtained. Lund maintained that his results supported a "Law of Primacy." Using a similar before-after design Knower (1936) obtained the same results. Cromwell (1950), however, found significant results in the direction of recency for one set of opposed communications and neither primacy nor recency for another.

Hovland and Mandell (1957) did a whole series of experiments using various procedures and various controversial issues. The general conclusion arising from this research program is that there is no universal law either of primacy or recency. Hovland (1957) pointed out, however, that none of the foregoing experiments really investigated the relative effects upon attitude change of a *first* as opposed to a subsequent communication, because the communications were always concerned with well-known issues about which the subjects had undoubtedly received much prior information. He also speculated "that the nearer one comes to achieving primacy in the sense of the first presentation of unfamiliar material, the more apt one is to obtain primacy effects" (p. 139).

As several people have pointed out, the notion that primacy will occur when there is a lack of familiarity is consistent with a set interpretation. According to the set interpretation the first of two opposing communications produces a set or context for the interpretation of the second communication, thus resulting in a primacy effect. Furthermore, the first communication will be able to establish a stronger set if the issue in dispute is a completely unfamiliar one.

Lana (*1961*) experimentally investigated the effect of familiarity upon primacy-recency. A preliminary questionnaire demonstrated that the topic of the communications, vivisection, was completely unfamiliar to 95 percent of the subjects. The 85 subjects were divided into three groups, one of which received a long familiarization talk and discussion on vivisection, one a short familiarization talk with no discussion on vivisection, and one neither a talk nor a discussion. After 12 days, each of these groups was divided into two subgroups, one of which received the communications in a pro-con sequence and the other in a con-pro sequence. A before-after measure of attitude toward vivisection indicated that with greatest familiarization significant primacy was obtained, with intermediate familiarization nonsignificant primacy was obtained, and with no familiarization significant recency was found. These results are exactly opposite to what Hovland expected and to what would be expected on the basis of the set interpretation.

Thomas, Webb, and Tweedie (*1961*), in a similar experiment, used persuasive communications concerning the advisability of using a new anticancer serum routinely in medical practice. In two replications of the experiment they did not obtain significant order results in either the familiar or the unfamiliar conditions. In discussing their results Thomas, Webb, and Tweedie point out that it may be important to distinguish between familiarity with the topic of a communication and familiarity with the attitudes aroused by the topic.

Insko (*1962*), utilizing an after-only design, also failed to find significant primacy or recency in either familiar or unfamiliar conditions. The communications, which were either both one-sided, both two-sided, or one one-sided and one two-sided,[6] were concerned with the guilt or innocence of a defendant in a supposedly real bigamy trial. There is, thus, reason to doubt that familiarization has any uniform, simple effect upon primacy-recency.

Lana (*1963a*) investigated the effect of topic controversy upon primacy-recency. He states that according to the set interpretation a

[6] The above statement regarding nonsignificant order effects in the situation in which one communication was one-sided and one two-sided is based on statistical comparisons not presented in the published article. Although inexactly referred to as primacy-recency differences in the article, the comparisons that were made between one- and two-sided communications were concerned with the relative effectiveness of one- and two-sided communications when in either first or second position.

topic of low controversy is more likely to produce a set from the presentation of the first communication and thus result in a primacy effect. The matter is not made explicitly clear, but there may be two reasons for the prediction. First, relative to high controversy, low controversy implies less familiarity. Second, relative to high controversy, low controversy implies a more noncritical attitude that should facilitate the formation of a set on the basis of the first communication. Lana, however, postulated that increasing controversy, like increasing familiarity (Lana, 1961), would produce increasing primacy.

From controversy ratings of 13 topics Lana selected 1 high controversy topic (nuclear weapons) and 1 low controversy topic (Picasso). Independent groups of college students were presented with either the high or low controversy topics in either a pro-con or con-pro order. The experiment was also replicated on a sample of high school subjects. Before-after change scores revealed that for the college sample the high controversy topic resulted in a nonsignificant primacy effect and the low controversy topic in absolutely no order effect whatsoever. For the high school sample the high controversy topic resulted in nonsignificant recency and the low controversy topic in nonsignificant primacy. An analysis of covariance revealed a significant controversy × order interaction for the college sample only. This interaction indicates that the high controversy topic resulted in significantly more primacy than the low controversy topic. These data, then, do not support the set interpretation and give rather inconsistent support to Lana's hypothesis that primacy is to be expected when the communications are controversial. It is, of course, very probable that Lana's communications differ along many dimensions other than that of controversialism.

Lana and Rosnow (*1963*) failed to replicate Lana's (1963a) results regarding topic controversialism and also report some inconclusive results regarding the obviousness of the pretest. Subjects were orally exposed to communications relating to either a high controversy topic (nuclear weapons) or a medium controversy topic (public censorship) in either a pro-con or con-pro order. The groups were further subdivided in terms of whether the pretest was hidden (buried among a number of related questions) or not hidden (given all by itself). An analysis of covariance revealed no significant interaction with order; that is, neither controversy nor obviousness of pretest had a significant effect upon primacy-recency. The one significant order result was a primacy effect for the medium-controversy-hidden-pretest subgroups.

These results would appear to put an end to the matter. Lana and Rosnow, however, seemingly hold out the hope that controversy interacts with the obviousness of the pretest so as to have an effect upon order. Despite the fact that the triple-order interaction between controversy, obviousness of the pretest, and order is not significant in their experiment, a significant primacy effect was still obtained with medium controversy and a hidden pretest.

Why should the obviousness of the pretest have an effect upon primacy-recency? If the pretest establishes a set which the first communication rearouses, then the impact of the first communication and of primacy is minimized. If, on the other hand, the pretest is sufficiently hidden so that it does not create a preliminary set (or if there is no pretest or if the pretest occurs long enough before the communications), the impact of the first communication is not minimized by an interfering set. The set interpretation thus predicts that primacy will be minimized with high familiarity, high controversy, and an obvious pretest.

Lana (*1964a*) reports some further evidence on the effect of the pretest. In an incomplete factorial design some groups were given an immediate pretest, some a pretest 12 days before the presentation of the communications, some no pretest, some an immediate posttest, and some a posttest 12 days after the presentation of the communications. The communications were pro and con arguments concerning Nikita Khrushchev as man and leader. Lana found significant primacy in the groups with no pretest and an immediate posttest, significant primacy in the groups with a pretest 12 days before and a posttest 12 days after the communications, and nonsignificant primacy in the groups with a pretest 12 days before and a posttest immediately after the communications. The remaining groups, which all had immediate pretests, yielded either no order effect or nonsignificant recency. No overall comparison of the immediate pretest groups with the remaining groups is reported.

Lana points out that these results fit the set interpretation, discussed above. If it can be assumed that the topic in the present experiment, Nikita Khrushchev as man and leader, is low enough in controversialism, then Lana's argument may carry some weight. One difficulty, however, is the fact that the topic is seemingly of moderate familiarity.

Almost all of the experiments in this area have used before-after designs. Since before-after designs involve pretests, this means that most of the previous studies are of ambiguous relevance to the set hypothesis. There are, however, a few studies (Insko, 1962; Miller and Campbell, 1959) which used after-only designs and thus no pretests. In the conditions comparable to the ones of present concern, these studies found no order effects. The communications in these studies were built around jury trial situations. Lana implies, but does not state, that this would mean a high degree of controversialism. The set hypothesis, as currently interpreted, predicts a primacy effect with low controversialism, low familiarity, and no or a hidden pretest. All of this implies that the set hypothesis is "down but not out."

Lana (*1963b*) reports an additional primacy-recency study that is concerned with the effect of the communication media and interest in the communication topic. Subjects read or listened to taped communications presented in either a pro-con or con-pro order. Ten days earlier the subjects had indicated their degree of interest in the communication topic (integration), and thus were evenly divided into two groups differing in level of interest. Integration had been judged as a highly controversial topic by a group of comparable subjects.

An analysis of covariance of the results indicated that the media × order, and the media × interest × order interactions are both significant. The first interaction means that more overall primacy was obtained with the taped than the read communications. The second interaction means that the primacy-recency differences between interest groups varied according to the media of presentation. For the subjects manifesting the higher interest, reading resulted in primacy and listening in recency; and for the subjects manifesting the lower interest, reading resulted in recency and listening in primacy. Order effects are apparently the outcome of complex interactions among a number of unlikely variables. Conceivably these results could be related to the set interpretation, if enough assumptions were made. Lana, however, does not discuss the matter.

Anderson and Hovland (*1957*) and *Anderson* (*1959*) formalized mathematically a "linear operator" theory that, in the simplest case, predicts recency effects. This theory is based on the assumption that the amount of change produced by a persuasive communication is an increasing function of the amount of change advocated (communicator-communicatee discrepancy). The second or last communication should thus have the advantage because the first communication increases the distance between the subject and the second communication.[7] This argument holds, however, only for the situation in which the first communication does not result in too great a reduction in susceptibility to the second communication. Such reduced susceptibility could, for example, be produced by a strong commitment to the position of the first communication. If the reduction in susceptibility is too great, a primacy effect is expected. Anderson and Hovland (1957) and Anderson (1959), however, do not specify the conditions which would produce such a reduced susceptibility and in general seem to assume the simpler case in which susceptibility is not reduced. In a rather elaborate experiment using jury trial testimony Anderson found empirical support for the recency prediction.

The key assumption of the linear operator theory is that the greater the amount of change advocated, the greater the amount obtained. Evidence reviewed in Chapter 3, however, indicates that, at least in many circumstances, there is a curvilinear relationship between the amount

[7] As Anderson is aware, this statement applies to the situation in which the two communications advocate positions on either side of the subject's position.

of change advocated and the amount obtained. With increasing discrepancy between the communication and subject there is increasing attitude change only to a certain point. Beyond this point the curve levels off and then begins to drop so that increasing discrepancy produces decreasing change. This makes matters considerably more complicated for the theory, although conceivably some adaptation could be made. If it were the case that the greater the amount of change advocated the less the amount obtained, primacy would seemingly be expected. The first communication would have the advantage because it would be closer to the subject's position than the second, opposing communication. This, of course, assumes that the first communication does not increase susceptibility to the second communication, a fairly plausible assumption.

Miller and Campbell (1959) made some predictions, derived from the Ebbinghaus forgetting curve, about the circumstances under which primacy and recency effects may be expected. Underwood (1948) had previously shown that for verbal learning the relative superiority in the retention of the second of two lists decreases as the time between learning and testing becomes greater. This result follows in a straightforward manner from the nature of the Ebbinghaus curve. With a long enough time interval the forgetting curves for both lists reach asymptote and recency is not found. Miller and Campbell's view of the implication of the Ebbinghaus curve as it applies to two competing communications is presented in Figure 2–1. These curves are drawn on the assumption of no interaction between communications and an initial primacy advantage for the first communication. They do not comment on the first assumption and they justify the second assumption simply by the statement that previous studies had frequently found an initial primacy advantage.

The curves in Figure 2–1 represent four separate conditions: condition 1, the successive presentation of two communications with a measure of opinion directly following the second communication; condition 2, the successive presentation of two communications with a measure of opinion a week after the second communication; condition 3, the presentation of two communications a week apart with a measure of opinion directly following the second communication; condition 4, the presentation of two communications a week apart with a measure of opinion a week after the second communication.

On the basis of these curves Miller and Campbell made five predictions. Stated in terms of the relative magnitude of the recency-primacy effects for the various conditions these predictions are: $3 > 4$, $3 > 1$, $3 > 2$, $1 > 2$, and $4 > 2$. Since the specific curve parameters are not known, predictions as to whether primacy or recency would occur at any point were not made. However, assuming the curves reach asymptote in approximately the time indicated in Figure 2–1, one would expect

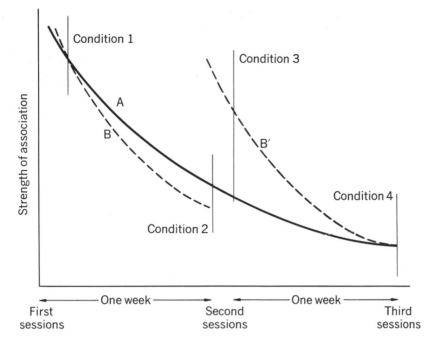

FIGURE 2-1. Hypothetical forgetting curves for two competing communications with an added primacy effect; the primacy effect is represented by the higher initial starting point and final asymptote of Curve A in comparison with Curve B or B'. The initial communication is represented by Curve A, and the second by either Curve B or B'. (Miller and Campbell, 1959, p. 2)

neither primacy nor recency to occur in conditions 1 and 4, primacy in condition 2, and recency in condition 3.

In their experiment Miller and Campbell used a tape recording of an edited transcript of a lawsuit as their communication source. The testimony of the witnesses for the plaintiff was called the pro communication, and the testimony of the witnesses for the defense was called the con communication. The two communications were equal in length and in number of points made. A 9-point rating scale enabled the subjects to express the degree to which they thought either the plaintiff or the defendant responsible for an accident. High values indicated agreement with the con point of view. A multiple-choice test was used to measure the amount of information retained from both pro and con communications. Duplicating each of the four conditions in a pro-con and a con-pro order gave eight experimental groups. Each group was measured only once.

Since agreement with the con position means a high score, whenever the con-pro sequence results in a higher score than the pro-con sequence, a primacy effect has been obtained. The five predictions were all confirmed $(1.67 > -.11, 1.67 > .06, 1.61 > -2.11, .06 > -2.11,$ and $-.11 > -2.11$ respectively). Also the guesses about the curve parameters were fairly accurate. Neither primacy nor recency was obtained in conditions 1 and 4, primacy was obtained in condition 2, and recency in condition 3.

These results are interesting, but a look at the data concerning retention reveals that Miller and Campbell's theory has some rather basic shortcomings. Treating the retention data in a fashion directly parallel to the foregoing treatment of the opinion measures revealed that four of the relationships among the experimental conditions were as predicted, but that one was not; condition 1 did not show more recency than condition 2. Furthermore, condition 2 showed neither primacy nor recency (not primacy, as did opinion), and condition 4 showed recency (rather than neither primacy nor recency, as did opinion). Finally, the average within-groups correlation between the opinion scores and recall scores was $-.10$, nonsignificantly different from zero.

Thomas, Webb, and Tweedie (1961) attempted to test the Miller and Campbell (1959) prediction that primacy may be obtained under conditions of delayed measurement. Using persuasive communications concerned with the advisability of utilizing an anticancer serum in medical practice they failed to obtain significant results in either a familiarity or a nonfamiliarity condition. These results, taken with Miller and Campbell's failure to obtain recency in retention under similar conditions, imply that delayed opinion measurement after two contiguously presented communications will not reliably produce a primacy effect.

Insko (1964) tested the Miller and Campbell theory with one communication presented either immediately, 2 days, 1 week, or 2 weeks after the other, and the measurements taken either immediately, 2 days, or 1 week after the second communication. The communications were the prosecution and defense in a supposedly real bigamy trial, and the subjects were told that the experiment was concerned with jury deliberation. According to an after-only design the communications were presented in the two possible orders (prosecution-defense or defense-prosecution) and the opinion and retention were measured just once. Opinion was measured with a 9-point rating scale and retention with a straight recall test (unlike the multiple-choice recognition test used by Miller and Campbell).

The results with regard to opinion are presented graphically in Figure 2–2. From this figure it can be seen that in the immediate measurement conditions, the longer the time interval between the two communications the greater the recency effect. Furthermore, delayed measurement in all of the conditions with a time interval between the communications revealed a decreased recency effect. These two major

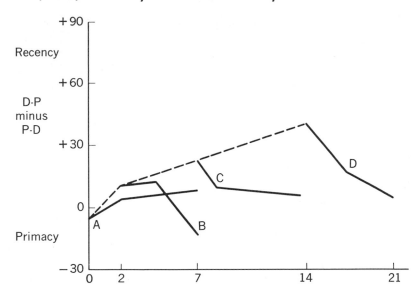

FIGURE 2-2. Recency and primacy in persuasion as a function of the time between communications (dotted line) and the time between the second communication and the measures (solid line). Point A refers to the delayed measurement
conditions with no time between communications; Point B, to the delayed measurement conditions with 2 days between communications; Point C, to the delayed
measurement conditions with 7 days between communications; and Point D, to the
delayed measurement conditions with 14 days between communications. (Insko,
1964, p. 386)

findings are in agreement with Miller and Campbell's theory. However,
in agreement with the results of Thomas, Webb, and Tweedie (1961),
delayed measurement in the conditions in which the two communications
occurred in immediate succession did not produce primacy or even an
increasing trend in that direction. Since this postulated primacy effect is
not an integral or necessary part of Miller and Campbell's theory, however, its disconfirmation does not disturb the remainder of the analyses
relating opinion to retention effects.

The recall results were roughly similar to those for opinion. The
longer the time interval between the communications, the greater the
recency effect on retention measured immediately after the second communication; and the longer the time elapsed from this second communication to the time that retention was measured, the less the recency effect.
Also, delayed measurement in the conditions in which there was no time
interval between the two communications did not indicate a consistently
increasing primacy effect. In general, however, the time intervals seemed
to have a much more marked and significant effect upon recall than

opinion. The zero order correlation between the two dependent variables, recall and opinion, was +.24 ($p < .01$), and the average within-cell correlation between the same two variables was +.10 (ns). This average within-cell correlation is more encouraging than Miller and Campbell's average within-cell correlation of −.10, but still is of trivial magnitude.

Hovland, Janis, and Kelley (1953) theorize that opinion change is mediated by three factors: attention, comprehension or learning, and acceptance. Miller and Campbell's theory assumes that opinion is a function of retention and thus focuses upon the comprehension or learning factor. If Miller and Campbell's theory is correct one would expect that changes in opinion over time should parallel those in retention, and measures of opinion should correlate positively with those of retention. Both Miller and Campbell, and Insko found that changes in opinion over time roughly parallel those in retention, but that, when the effect of time is held constant, by taking the average within-cell correlation, there appears to be no significant relationship between opinion and retention. These results make it appear as if retention does not mediate the effect of time upon opinion, but that time independently affects both opinion and retention. The issue obviously is a complicated one.

Watts and McGuire (1964) systematically investigated the relationship between opinion and retention over time. Subjects read four different communications spaced over a 6-week interval. Immediately after exposure to the last communication, opinion and retention measures for all four communication topics were taken for the first and only time. The topics were: "Puerto Rico should be admitted to the Union as the 51st State"; "Courts should deal more leniently with juvenile delinquents"; "The Secretary of State should be elected by the people, not appointed by the President"; "The State Sales tax should be abolished" (p. 235). The communications dealing with each of the four topics were rotated among the four time intervals. For half of the subjects the communications were represented as coming from high credibility sources and for half from low credibility sources. Opinion was measured by four 15-point agree-disagree scales and retention by a series of increasingly demanding tests. The first retention test required the subjects to recall the topics of each of the four communications. The second test reinstated the topics and required the subjects to designate whether a pro or con stand was taken on each. The third test reinstated the topics and stands and required the subjects to select the sources from a list of four for each communication. The final test was a multiple-choice assessment of retention for the three specific arguments contained in each communication.

Combining the data for the four communications revealed an overall decay rate for opinion that was linear. The decay rates for the four retention curves, on the other hand, were all negatively accelerated like the characteristic forgetting curve for ordinary verbal learning. Watts and McGuire interpret the differing shapes of the retention and opinion functions as indicating that the persistence of opinion change is only partially dependent on communication retention. Further analysis of the data revealed that opinion was directly related over time to retention of both the side taken and the specific arguments used in the communications. Opinion was positively related to recall of the communication topic after an interval of 1 week but negatively related after an interval of 6 weeks. Opinion was positively related to recall of the high credibility source but not of the low credibility source over all time intervals. Only, then, in the case of retention of the side taken and of the specific arguments used is there clear evidence for a simple functional dependence between opinion and retention.

Watts and McGuire's data do give some support to the assumption of Miller and Campbell's (1959) theory that opinion is a function of retention. Retention, however, as Watts and McGuire have made clear, is a complex matter, and further theoretical specification in this direction is called for.

Schultz (*1963a*) failed to find an increase in recency as a result of a 2-week time interval interpolated between opposing communications dealing with the amount of time and money that should be devoted to cancer research in the next 5 years. Using a before-after design Schultz manipulated three independent variables: order of communications (pro-con or con-pro), time between communications (none or 2 weeks), and awareness of manipulative intent (strongly aware, moderately aware, or not aware). The strongly aware subjects were told that the experiment was concerned with changing their attitudes toward cancer research and that there was no doubt that their attitudes would be changed. The moderately aware group was told that the experiment was concerned with the attitudes of college students toward cancer research and that there was some chance that their attitudes might be influenced by the procedure. The not-aware group was given no awareness instructions. The results were as follows: the strongly aware groups showed nonsignificant and trivial primacy in both the immediate and 2-week conditions; the moderately aware group showed nonsignificant but sizeable primacy in the immediate condition and significant primacy in the 2-week condition; the not-aware group showed significant and approximately equal recency in both the immediate and 2-week conditions. An analysis of variance revealed that order and the order × awareness interaction are both significant. The main effect for order indicates that more recency than primacy was obtained, and the interaction indicates that recency was obtained in the not-aware conditions and primacy in the aware conditions.

Schultz's not-aware condition is, of course, most directly related to the previous research on primacy-recency. Why is it that in the not-aware condition Schultz failed to obtain more recency with an interval between communications? Both Miller and Campbell (1959) and Insko (1964) found such an effect. These studies, however, did not find either significant recency or primacy in the immediate conditions. Thus there was plenty of room for any recency effect, due to interpolated time, to become evident. Schultz obtained recency in the immediate conditions, so the time variable *may* have been fighting some sort of ceiling effect. If this speculation is correct then the problem becomes one not of explaining why increasing time failed to produce increasing recency but why there was a recency effect in the immediate condition. The literature related to this problem is blatantly contradictory. We simply do not know what the conditions are that determine whether primacy or recency will result in a situation with no time interval between communications.[8]

Comment. It has been some time since Hovland and Mandell (1957) decided that there is no universal law of primacy or of recency. The assertion, however, seems to be as true now as it did then. Taken at face value, the existing body of research appears highly inconsistent. Order effects apparently are the resultant of interactions between a rather large number of variables. *Some* experimental evidence exists indicating that the following variables affect primacy-recency: familiarity with the topic (Lana, 1961); degree of controversy about the topic (Lana, 1963a); interest in the topic (Lana, 1963b); media of presentation (Lana, 1963b); presence or absence of a pretest (Lana, 1964a); awareness of manipulative intent (Schultz, 1963a); time between communications (Insko, 1964; Miller and Campbell, 1959); time between second communication and measurement (Insko, 1964; Miller and Campbell, 1959). If all of these variables do have an effect upon primacy-recency, and, furthermore, interact with each other in various ways, then the seeming inconsistency in the existing literature is more understandable.

We have discussed three theories relating to order effects: set theory, linear operator theory, and what may be called forgetting theory. As a result of considerable empirical evidence, set theory or the set hypothesis has been successively revised by Lana and others so that it now implies that a primacy effect is most likely with low familiarity, low controversy, and no pretest. Although there is not much empirical evidence to support such a generalization, we cannot at the present time completely rule it out. It is interesting to note that with low familiarity, low controversy, and no pretest the persuasion situation begins to at least approximate the impression formation situation made famous by Asch (1946). Asch found

_____

[8] In a separate article Schultz (1963b) presents a theoretical account of primacy-recency that differs from any described above. For a discussion see Lana (1964b).

that if subjects are asked to form an impression of a stimulus person described by a series of adjectives, the first adjectives in the list have a more marked effect than the later adjectives. Asch interprets his results as being due to the context (or set) established by the first adjectives, and thus he may be considered one of the originators of the set interpretation. One of the problems with this point of view, however, is that it does not clarify under what conditions either recency or no order effect will be obtained. Supposedly primacy will not be obtained when there is high controversy, high familiarity, or an obvious pretest. A lack of primacy, though, can mean either no order effect or recency.

Anderson's linear operator theory is an interesting formulation that might conceivably be of some predictive power, particularly if it were modified so as to take account of the shape of the communicator-communicatee discrepancy function and if it incorporated some statements as to when a change in susceptibility to the second communication occurs. Recent work on the theory, however, has been in the context of impression formation rather than persuasion (e.g., Anderson, 1965b).

Finally, Miller and Campbell's forgetting theory is a promising formulation that may have considerable value for situations in which time intervals are interpolated between the opposing communications or between the second communication and measurement. Correlational results obtained by Insko (1964) and by Miller and Campbell (1959) themselves, however, call into question the basic assumption that opinion is a positive function of retention, and Schultz (1963a) failed to confirm the basic prediction that increasing time between the two communications should produce increasing recency. All of this implies that Miller and Campbell's formulation is far from adequate. We still appear to be a long way from a completely accurate conception of primacy-recency effects.

EVALUATION

In evaluating the reinforcement theory of attitude change as stated by Hovland, Janis, and Kelley (1953) it should be borne in mind that the theory was intended only as a preliminary statement or "an initial framework for subsequent theory building" (p. 17). However, even an initial framework has strong and weak points which may be evaluated.

One of the major weak points of the reinforcement theory of attitude change is also a weak point of the reinforcement theory of learning. This is the lack of success in stating connotatively rather than just denotatively what a reinforcing stimulus is. It is possible to point to certain stimuli, such as food pellets, which on the basis of casual observation or controlled experimentation appear to act as reinforcers or response strengtheners and infer that they will also act as reinforcers with other organisms in other situations. It is evident, as Meehl (1950) has pointed out, that this does not involve any circular logic. The reinforcement exponent, however, is still left in a rather unsatisfactory theoretical state of affairs. What is it about a reinforcing stimulus that makes it reinforcing? In the literature reviewed in this chapter the following have been considered positive reinforcers: hearing desirable information, winning a debate, getting an A on an essay, eating a free lunch, hearing words of positive evaluative meaning such as "happy" or "good," hearing expressed agreement for one's new opinion in casual conversation, hearing someone say "good" after the expression of an opinion, and receiving a compliment about the attractiveness of one's clothing. The only reinforcer in this list that sounds like a Hullian drive reducer is the consumption of the free lunch and consequent reduction of the hunger drive. All of the reinforcers possibly involve positive affect, although the amount of affect associated with hearing words like "happy" would seem to be extremely small. One could argue that the word "reinforcer" ought to be reserved for those stimuli that involve or evoke at least some degree of positive affect or reduction of negative affect, but most behavioristic reinforcement theorists are not so inclined. In any event, until some satisfactory theoretical statement of the nature of reinforcement is given, reinforcement theory will remain a rather primitive theory no matter how mathematically elegant it may be.

Attention, comprehension, and acceptance are obviously key concepts in the theoretical statement of Hovland, Janis, and Kelley. Despite this fact, however, the relationship between these concepts has not been thoroughly worked out. Both the existing research evidence and the theoretical statement are vague and inconclusive about the relationship between comprehension and acceptance, for example. It may be that in some situations comprehension is both necessary and sufficient for acceptance, and in others comprehension is only necessary for acceptance. Further, in some situations only a minimal amount of comprehension may be necessary in order for there to be some effect upon acceptance, and in other situations a maximal amount of comprehension may be necessary. A thorough theoretical statement of the nature of these various situations needs to be made.

What about the relationship between attention and acceptance? While attention may be in many cases a necessary prerequisite for acceptance, the possibility remains that many attitudes or opinions may be acquired or accepted incidentally without the aid of explicit attention. If so, how do such attitudes or opinions differ from those acquired through a process of attention? Are they more or less resistant to change? Furthermore, it is obvious that attention is not an all or none phenomenon but varies in degree. This, in turn, raises a question about the effect of varying amounts of attention to a persuasive communication.

Hovland, Janis, and Kelley assert that one of the main ways in which persuasive communications give rise to attitude change is through the production of related opinion change. Attitude change through the mediation of opinion change is thus one of the key links of the theory. In spite of this fact, however, very little is said about the manner of and reason for this occurrence. Does a changed opinion result in a changed attitude because of the logical or quasi-logical relationship existing between the opinion and attitude, or for some other reason? If it is asserted that opinion-mediated attitude change is a result of quasi-logical considerations, then to what extent is a strictly reinforcement interpretation being forsaken for a consistency point of view?

One of the least convincing aspects of reinforcement theory has to do with the explanation of how a persuasive communication supplies reinforcement for acceptance of an advocated point of view. It can be asserted that such acceptance is dependent upon the communication's arousing expectations of possible future reinforcements as a consequence of conformity to the recommended point of view, but, in general, this is not very convincing. Possibly such a consideration may be relevant in some situations, but many persuasive communications do not obviously appear to dangle any great incentives before the nose of the communicatee. It also may be maintained, as Hovland, Janis, and Kelley do, that the arguments in the communications inherently supply reinforcement for accepting the recommended point of view. This also, however, is simply not very convincing without further elaboration.

There are thus many unsolved problems relating to the reinforcement theory of attitude change. As was stated above, however, it should be borne in mind that the theoretical statement of Hovland, Janis, and Kelley (1953) was intended only as "an initial framework for subsequent theory building" (p. 17). As such, it has served well to help guide Hovland and his associates into various productive research areas. Research areas such as those concerned with the effects upon attitude change of reinforcement, fear, source credibility, and communication order *are* related, however tangentially, to the theoretical framework. Further, the concepts of attention, comprehension, and acceptance are of obvious theoretical importance. What is needed is for the theory to be expanded and made more specific to the attitude change situation. The "initial framework" as it stands may have outlasted much of its initial usefulness.

3

Sherif and Hovland's

Assimilation-Contrast Theory

A judgmental theory of attitude change is an attempt to either directly or analogically apply some of the principles of judgment to the phenomenon of attitude change. There are two varieties of judgmental theory: adaptation-level theory and what, for lack of a better name, can be called assimilation-contrast theory. Assimilation-contrast theory was developed by Sherif and Hovland (1961) and Hovland, Harvey, and Sherif (1957); adaptation-level theory was developed by Helson (1959, 1964). This chapter will be devoted to assimilation-contrast theory and Chapter 4 to adaptation-level theory.

THEORY

Assimilation-contrast theory, as developed by Sherif and Hovland, utilizes such concepts as the formation of reference scales, anchors, contrast, assimilation, and latitudes of acceptance and rejection.

Formation of Reference Scales

When repeatedly presented with a number of stimuli, individuals tend to form reference scales that allow for the relative placement of these stimuli along one or more dimensions. Sherif and Hovland discuss three types of laboratory demonstrations of reference scale formation: scale formation on the basis of a well-graded stimulus series having an explicit standard within it, scale formation on the basis of a well-graded stimulus series without an explicit standard, and scale formation with neither a well-graded stimulus series nor an explicit standard. Scale formation on the basis of a well-graded stimulus series having an explicit standard is illustrated by experiments using the method of constant stimuli. In judgments of weight, for example, the subject on each trial is presented with a standard stimulus of a designated weight and one of a series of variable or comparison stimuli. The subject's task is to judge the weight of the comparison stimulus on the basis of the known weight of the standard stimulus. Such weight judgments are found to be fairly accurate, particularly near the center of the stimulus series in the vicinity of the standard stimulus. The closer the subject's reference scale is to the standard stimulus the greater the degree of accuracy and the less the variability.

Scale formation on the basis of a well-graded stimulus series without an explicit standard is illustrated by studies using the method of single stimuli. The subject is presented with a series of stimuli, as for example weights, one at a time without a standard stimulus. The subject may be told to assign numbers "1" through "6" to the stimuli with "1" designating the lightest and "6" the heaviest. Initially the subjects experience difficulty in making the judgments, but after encountering the two extreme stimuli a reference scale develops that allows for the categorization of the stimuli with some degree of confidence and accuracy. Judgments near the extremes of the reference scale, unlike those in the method of constant stimuli, are found to be more accurate and stable. The end stimuli appear to act as reference points.

Reference scale formation with neither a well-graded stimulus series nor an explicit standard is illustrated by research on the autokinetic phenomenon (Sherif, 1935b). Judgments of the illusory perceived movement of a small light in an otherwise completely dark room appear to eventually become more or less stabilized with a characteristic range and modal value; i.e., a reference scale of perceived autokinetic movement develops. Furthermore, a common reference scale is formed when individuals first make their judgments in the group situation, but still occurs even if individuals have previously formed idiosyncratic reference scales by making judgments alone.

Sherif and Hovland assert that many social stimuli do not exist along a well-ordered dimension or set of dimensions, but will nonetheless result in reference scale formation just as does autokinetic movement. Furthermore, since the social stimuli lack objective standards and do not exist in a well-ordered series, the resultant reference scales, like those formed in the group autokinetic situation, will be partially due to social influence. Exposing members of society to the social stimuli of political events, for example, has resulted in the formation of a somewhat socially shared conservatism-liberalism reference scale.

Anchors

Stimuli which exert a relatively large influence upon the determination of judgment, such as end points in a series of stimuli or standard stimuli, are called anchors. The effect of anchors upon judgment is illustrated in an experiment by Rogers (1941). In Rogers' experiment subjects judged the inclination of lines, using categories ranging from 1 to 6. The subjects were told to assign the number "1" to the smallest slope and the number "6" to the greatest. In the early sessions subjects made judgments based on the variation of the stimuli in the series. Rogers then presented an anchoring stimulus before each judgment, with the statement that this angle of inclination was to constitute category 6. The anchor's angle of inclination was made increasingly greater than that of the stimuli of the series, but remained constant for any single series. The results indicated that as the angle was increased there was a shift in judgment toward the lower categories (1, 2, and 3) so that with the remotest anchors the upper categories (4 and 5) dropped completely out of use.

Anchors can be either external or internal. Rogers' experiment was concerned with external anchors; an experiment by Hunt and Volkman (1937) illustrates the effect of an internal anchor. Subjects were presented with a series of colored papers and asked to judge the pleasantness of these papers by assigning the lowest category to the least pleasant and the highest to the most pleasant. When the subjects were asked to "think of the most pleasant color you can" and assign it to the highest category, it was found that the judgments shifted away from this internal anchor and toward the unpleasant end of the scale. The effect of a less experimental internal anchor is illustrated by an experiment of Perloe (1960) which compares the judgments of high status individuals (Yale students) and average status individuals (individuals contacted in a nationwide survey) with regard to the prestige of various occupations. It was found that the Yale students displaced the prestige of occupations at the middle and lower ranks away from their own actual or anticipated high status positions.

Anchors are directly related to the phenomenon of attitude change because an attitude or opinion is regarded as an internal anchor and a persuasive communication as an external anchor. Thus the influence situation, from the standpoint of assimilation-contrast theory, involves a confrontation of the discrepancy between two anchors. The discussion of the results of this confrontation takes us directly to the concepts of contrast and assimilation.

Contrast and Assimilation

Contrast is a shift in judgment away from an anchor, and assimilation is a shift in judgment toward an anchor. Contrast results from the placement of an anchor at a relatively extreme position beyond either end of a series of stimuli, and assimilation results from the placement of an anchor at either end or slightly beyond either end of a series of stimuli. The range of possible anchor locations which will produce an assimilation effect is thus much narrower than the range of possible anchor locations which will produce a contrast effect. Furthermore, the range of assimilation is much narrower for well-defined continua than for less well-defined continua. Assimilation and contrast are illustrated by a series of three similar weight-judgment experiments reported by Sherif, Taub, and Hovland (1958). In one of the experiments the anchors were located increasingly below the stimuli for successive sets of judgments, and in the two other experiments the anchors were located increasingly above the stimuli for successive sets of judgments. In all of the experiments it was found that anchors located at the end of the range of stimuli produced assimilation effects. Assimilation effects produced by anchors immediately beyond the range of stimuli were found only in the two experiments with the light anchors, possibly because the discrepancies between the anchors and the stimuli were somewhat less in these experiments. In all three experiments, increasingly extreme anchors produced increasingly extreme contrast effects.

Thus according to assimilation-contrast theory, a primary factor affecting the influence of a persuasive communication upon attitude and opinion change is the degree of discrepancy between the position of the communication (external anchor) and the recipient's attitude or opinion (internal anchor). If the communication advocates a position that is not too discrepant from that held by the communication recipient, assimilation will result; i.e., the individual will perceive the communication as advocating a less extreme position, will favorably evaluate the communication, and will be strongly influenced. If the communication advocates a position that is highly discrepant from that held by the communication recipient, contrast will result; i.e., the individual will perceive the communication as advocating a more extreme position, will unfavorably evaluate the communication, and will be either minimally positively influenced or negatively influenced.[1] These assimilation and contrast effects are also conceived of as being affected by the degree of ambiguity in the exact position of the communication.

The above account, however, is oversimplified. According to Sherif and Hovland the important discrepancy is not the discrepancy between communication and attitude or opinion but between communication and latitude of acceptance.

---

[1] It is not explicitly stated how the perception, evaluation, and influence effects are directly causally related.

Definition of Latitudes of Acceptance and Rejection

Sherif and Hovland conceive of the individual's stand on a social issue not as a single point but as a range of related acceptable positions or as a latitude of acceptance. The latitude of acceptance is operationally defined in terms of the range of Thurstone-type scale statements that are considered acceptable (including the one most acceptable). The latitude of rejection consists of all of those points of view that the individual finds unacceptable or, in operational terms, the range of items that are considered objectionable (including the one most objectionable). Between the latitudes of acceptance and rejection is the latitude of neutrality. Latitudes of acceptance and rejection theoretically vary in width according to the individual's degree of ego-involvement or personal concern with the object of the attitude. With high ego-involvement the latitude of acceptance will be narrow and the latitude of rejection wide, and with low ego-involvement the opposite.

If a persuasive communication advocates a point of view falling within an individual's latitude of acceptance, assimilation will tend to occur. If a communication advocates a point of view falling within an individual's latitude of rejection, contrast will tend to occur. At the transition point between the latitudes of acceptance and rejection neither assimilation nor contrast will occur. All of this implies that a communication dealing with a topic of low ego-involvement is more likely to be persuasive than is a communication dealing with a topic of high ego-involvement. This follows because the individual's latitude of acceptance is wider in the case of low ego-involvement topics.

As long as a communication remains within an individual's latitude of acceptance, the greater the degree of communication discrepancy, the greater the degree of influence. When a communication passes into the latitude of rejection, however, the degree of influence will steadily decrease and may eventually become negative. This means that for issues of low ego-involvement there is a large range in which it will be the case that the greater the amount of change advocated the greater the amount obtained. For issues of high ego-involvement, on the other hand, it will more likely be the case that the greater the amount of change advocated the less the amount that is obtained. In general, however, a curvilinear relationship is expected between communication discrepancy and attitude change.[2]

---

[2] At no place do Sherif and Hovland explicitly state that a curvilinear relationship is expected. The curvilinear hypothesis flows so obviously from their theoretical concepts, however, that it seems very reasonable to include it as part of the theory. In his doctoral dissertation done under Hovland's direction, Freedman (1964) presents the curvilinear hypothesis as an integral part of assimilation-contrast theory.

RESEARCH

There are four areas of research that are relevant to assimilation-contrast theory: effect of discrepancy between communication and communication recipient upon attitude change, effect of discrepancy between communication and recipient upon perceived communication location, latitudes of acceptance and rejection, and effect of judge's attitude upon the placement of Thurstone scale items. Since the latter topic, however, is not directly related to attitude change or necessary prerequisites for attitude change, discussion will be limited to the former three topics.

Effect of Discrepancy Between Communication and Recipient Upon Attitude Change

We will first consider those studies dealing with the effect of discrepancy between communication and communication recipient upon attitude change.

There is a logical problem with discrepancy research that has to do with the relation of the amount of change obtained to the amount possible. It is impossible for subjects slightly discrepant from a communication to exhibit as much change as a subject moderately or extremely discrepant from the same communication. This does not mean that slightly discrepant subjects cannot in some circumstances exhibit more change than moderately or extremely discrepant subjects; it just means that any finding which indicates that greater discrepancy produces greater change may be due to a ceiling effect in the amount of change possible or measurable.

All of the early research and some of the later research on the discrepancy problem has confounded communication discrepancy with the initial positions of the subjects. This research has used a design in which the subjects' initial positions are measured and then a persuasive communication presented. The further the distance between the initial position of any one subject and the position of the communication, the greater the discrepancy. Thus communication discrepancy is not manipulated independently of initial position. This can be called a between-subjects procedure. An alternative design that does not confound communication discrepancy with initial position is to experimentally vary communication discrepancy. This involves, first, constructing a number of communications each arguing for different positions on the discrepancy dimension and, second, presenting one of each of the communications to different groups of subjects with the same initial positions. This can be called a between-communications procedure.

There are two specifiable problems with the between-subjects procedure. First, as Hovland (1959) has pointed out, there is the problem of regression toward the mean. If the communication is located near the mean of the initial positions, then regression toward the mean would guarantee that the more discrepant individuals would change the most. Similarly, if the communication is located at an extreme position, the more discrepant individuals would again change the most. In this latter case the regression and persuasion effects would summate for the individuals most discrepant from the communication and negate each other for the individuals least discrepant from the communication. The net result would be that greater change would go with greater discrepancy. This difficulty can be met to some extent with a control group not receiving a communication.

The second specifiable problem has to do with the fact that individuals occupying more extreme positions are considered to be more ego-involved with their positions (Sherif and Hovland, 1961) and are known to be more certain of their positions (Cantril, 1946; Suchman, 1950). Reasoning on the basis of this knowledge leads one to expect that a communication occupying a neutral position will influence the least discrepant individuals more than the most discrepant individuals. This problem cannot be handled with a control group. In both the experimental and control groups, discrepancy is confounded with certainty. This certainty effect may, in some circumstances, negate the regression effect discussed above, but there is no way of knowing for sure. Obviously, solid knowledge about the discrepancy problem can be obtained only from an experimental design that does not confound communication discrepancy and the subject's initial position.[3]

Using the between-subjects procedure or the procedure which confounds discrepancy and initial position, some studies found that the greater the discrepancy the greater the change (Chen, 1933; Cohen, 1959; Ewing, 1942; French, 1956; Gorfein, 1963; Sims, 1938); some found that the greater the discrepancy the less the change (Cohen, 1959; Hovland, Harvey, and Sherif, 1957;[4] Sherif and Hovland, 1961, pp. 155–167); and some found a curvilinear relationship between discrepancy and change (Carlson, 1956; Weiss, 1961; Whittaker, 1963[5]).

The studies which did not confound discrepancy and initial position will be discussed in more detail below.

[3] This statement does not imply that the subject's initial position is of no theoretical importance. It is quite possible that the form of the discrepancy function will vary with the location of the subject's initial position.

[4] Since this study presented data that may be analyzed by examining differences between communications as well as differences between initial positions, it will be discussed further below.

[5] Whittaker reports two experiments which confound discrepancy and initial position, and one which does not.

Goldberg (1954) had male subjects judge the intelligence of male Negroes on an IQ scale ranging from 50 to 150 by looking at bust-size photographs taken from a high school yearbook. The initial judgments were made privately but in the presence of other subjects. An experimental group of subjects made second judgments after the experimenter individually informed them of the mean group judgments. These bogus group judgments differed by 10, 30, or 50 from the subjects' initial judgments. A control group simply judged the pictures a second time, without the intervening influence manipulation.

Goldberg reports that 25 percent of the subjects perceived that the rather transparent manipulation of influence was in fact an attempt at influence. He does not say whether these subjects are included or excluded from the reported data. In any event, the data that are reported indicate that the experimental group changed more than the control group and that the greater the discrepancy between the initial opinion and the influence, the greater the amount of change. An additional finding is that the variance of opinion change appears to increase markedly as discrepancy and mean opinion change increase. This is possibly because the number of subjects who are minimally influenced steadily increases as discrepancy increases. This would seem to indicate that if the discrepancy becomes large enough, mean opinion change would level off and drop for increasingly extreme discrepancies. According to Sherif and Hovland's assimilation-contrast theory, even for issues of low ego-involvement such as Goldberg's, an individual's latitude of acceptance may not extend indefinitely. With increasingly extreme influence attempts the latitude of neutrality between the latitudes of acceptance and rejection may be crossed and the amount of influence fall off. In view of the obtained correlation between means and variances it is at least possible that such would have been the case in Goldberg's experiment had the amount of discrepancy been greater.

Hovland and Pritzker (1957) administered a questionnaire which measured opinion on a 7-point scale on 12 uninvolving issues such as whether married women or single women are better teachers. A month later the questionnaire was readministered with the opinions of various authoritative groups indicated for each item. These bogus authoritative opinions were manipulated for each subject individually so that they differed from his previous opinions by one step for some items, two steps for some, and four steps for others. For each of the possible responses to each opinion item on the initial questionnaire, one third of the subjects were given an authoritative opinion one step removed, one third an authoritative opinion two steps removed, and one third an authoritative opinion four steps removed. This assured that the amount of advocated change was completely independent of the overall initial opinion. The results indicated that the greater the amount of advocated change the greater the amount obtained. When the amount of change obtained was expressed as a percentage of the amount possible, it was found that with slight discrepancy the average amount of change is 88 percent of that advocated, with moderate discrepancy 62 percent, and with marked discrepancy 58 percent.

Rosenbaum and Franc (*1960*) carried out an experiment using the same issues and essentially the same method as that of Hovland and Pritzker (1957). The two experiments differed in that the source of influence for Rosenbaum and Franc's experiment was "a professional person's own position" on each of the opinion items while for Hovland and Pritzker it was any of a number of sources which the subjects themselves considered authoritative. The results for the two experiments agreed in showing that the greater the discrepancy between the subject's opinion and the influence, the greater the amount of change.

Tuddenham (*1958a, 1958b*) investigated the discrepancy problem by using a special apparatus to study the effect of group influence upon individual judgment. Five subjects at a time sat at separate panels and threw switches to indicate their judgments of materials shown on a screen in front of them. All of the judgments (visual comparisons, general information, and opinion) called for the selection of nine alternatives. Panel lights successively lighted on all panels either as the result of the subjects' making their judgments or as the result of the experimenter's supplying bogus judgments. The subjects were given 74 trials, among which were 30 critical trials in which a bogus norm was supplied. On these critical trials the subjects always believed themselves to be responding last.

Although the differences are significant for females only, Tuddenham found that the bogus norm located at the 99th percentile of a control group's responses resulted in greater mean influence than did a bogus norm located at the 95th percentile. There was also a consistent increase in the standard deviation from the less extreme to the more extreme bogus norm for both sexes. (No statistical tests for this particular comparison were reported.)

Helson, Blake, and Mouton (*1958a*) used a simulated group technique to investigate the discrepancy problem. Subjects were given earphones and a microphone so that they could hear and interact with other group members supposedly located in other rooms. Actually the subjects, who were individually tested, were exposed to a tape recording of people talking. The conversational episodes were separated by time intervals of sufficient duration to allow the naive subjects to become involved in the "interaction." The subjects were instructed to give agreement-disagreement responses to opinion statements concerning war and peace. The opinion statements had been so selected that on a 7-point, agreement-disagreement scale the modal control group response was either 7 or 1.

The judgments given by the simulated group differed by either 0, 2, 4, or 6 steps from these modal control group responses. Helson, Blake, and Mouton found that the greater the discrepancy the greater the number of individuals influenced by the simulated group. The percentage of subjects giving responses different from the modal response of the control group are 13.89, 22.78, 45.56, and 55.14 for 0, 2, 4, and 6 degrees of discrepancy, respectively. As Helson, Blake, and Mouton point out, there is some tendency for the rate of influence to decrease at the higher discrepancies.

Hovland, Harvey, and Sherif (1957) used a before-after design to study the reactions of various groups to communications dealing with the consumption of alcoholic beverages. The study was carried out prior to a statewide vote on prohibition. The subjects were either drys, moderately wets (unselected subjects), or wets, and the communications were either wet, moderately wet, or dry. The wet communication was presented to dry and moderately wet subjects, the dry communication to wet and moderately wet subjects, and the moderately wet communication to dry subjects. Unfortunately the experiment was designed with the idea of comparing the attitude change of subjects with differing initial positions. Analyzed in this way the results indicate that the wet communication produced significantly more change in the moderately wet subjects than in the dry subjects, the dry communication produced nonsignificantly more change in the moderately wet subjects than in the wet subjects, and the moderately wet communication produced small, nonsignificant change in the dry subjects. These results were interpreted as indicating that only the subjects fairly close to the communication were significantly influenced; that is, the greater the amount of change advocated the less the amount obtained. It is also possible, however, to make comparisons between groups of subjects with similar initial positions who were exposed to different communications. Dry subjects were exposed to either a moderately wet or a wet communication, and moderately wet subjects were exposed to either a wet or a dry communication. These comparisons also indicate that the greater the amount of change advocated the less the amount obtained, although no relevant tests of significance are reported.

Due to the fact that the topic of the communications was ego-involving, it can be maintained that these results are consistent with assimilation-contrast theory. Since ego-involvement theoretically restricts the latitude of acceptance and expands the latitude of rejection, communications at extreme discrepancies are likely to fall in the latitude of rejection and thus produce less change than communications at slight or moderate discrepancies.

Freedman (1964) used a concept formation task to investigate the effect of involvement and discrepancy upon opinion change. Subjects, high school and college students, initially attempted to solve a series of three concept formation tasks. The concept instances consisted of a rectangle containing figures that varied in shape (circle, triangle, or square), size (large or small), number of a particular size or shape (one, two, or three), and position (any of three). On each of the three tasks the subjects were presented with a series of eight instances, each labeled according to whether they did or did not exemplify the concept. After examining all eight instances the subjects indicated what they considered to be the concept, for example, a triangle in the second position. After completing the three concept formation tasks the subjects copied the concept for the first task on a separate sheet of paper and examined 16 new instances which were supposedly labeled according to whether they did or did not exemplify the same concept. Of these 16 new instances 5 were inconsistent with the initial concept, but all were consistent with a new concept. In a low discrepancy condition the two concepts shared three elements, in a moderate discrepancy condition, two elements, and in a high discrepancy condition, no elements. The subjects examined the 16 new instances and then indicated what they considered to be the concept. Approximately half of the subjects were told that the first part of this "intelligence test" was most important (high involvement) and half that the second part was most important (low involvement). Involvement was thus manipulated through a type of commitment.

The dependent variable was the rated change in the concept from the first to the second part of the test. The results indicated that in the low involvement conditions concept change was significantly linearly related to discrepancy, and that in the high involvement conditions concept change was significantly curvilinearly related to discrepancy. Neither the curvature in the low involvement conditions nor the linearity in the high involvement conditions was significant. Overall, there was more change with low than with high involvement, but no test of the interaction between involvement and discrepancy was reported. Since high involvement theoretically expands the latitude of rejection and contracts the latitude of acceptance, these results are roughly consistent with what one would expect on the basis of assimilation-contrast theory.

Fisher and Lubin (1958) studied the effect of influence discrepancy upon the numerosity judgments of paratroopers depicted in briefly shown photographs. In the initial warm-up period the subjects, who were tested two at a time, judged and discussed their judgments of five photographs. The judgments were written on small slips of paper and then exchanged. During the testing period each subject was given bogus information regarding the judgments of the other subject for two new photographs. For each of these two experimental photographs the subjects made and "exchanged" five judgments in succession. The bogus information indicated that the number of paratroopers guessed by the other subject was discrepant from the true number by either 0, 40, 160, 320, or 5100. The first experimental photograph actually contained 165 and the second 300 paratroopers.

Fisher and Lubin report that for the first photograph the *median* change from the first to the second judgment increased over the range of small and moderate discrepancies but appears to reach asymptote for the extreme discrepancies. (No substantiating tests of significance were reported, but the experiment was replicated twice on sizeable samples, so we may have some confidence in the results.) Since the distributions of influence scores at the extreme discrepancies have marked positive skewness, *mean* influence undoubtedly did not reach asymptote at the highest discrepancy levels used in this experiment. Inspection of graphed data appears to indicate a perfect or near perfect rank order correlation between discrepancy level and influence variability. *Median* change from the fourth to the fifth judgment for the first photograph appears, once again from inspection of graphed data, to be curvilinearly related to the amount of discrepancy. Such an effect would be predicted from assimilation-contrast theory on the basis of the increased commitment to or ego-involvement with the fourth judgment relative to the first. With increased commitment the extreme discrepancies are more likely to fall close to or within the latitude of rejection. With regard to change expressed as a percentage of the discrepancies, it was found that for both the difference between the first and second judgments and the difference between the third and fourth judgments, the greater the amount of discrepancy the less the amount of change. This finding agrees with that of Hovland and Pritzker (1957).

What about the data for the second photograph? Because of some results obtained by Fisher, Rubenstein, and Freeman (1956) indicating that intertrial influence is greater than intratrial influence, Fisher and Lubin (1958) expected that the greater the discrepancy for the first photograph the larger would be the first judgment for the second photograph. This expectation was confirmed. Subjects who had been resistant to influence on the first photograph anticipated the large judgments that were to come on the second photograph, and made large judgments before hearing the other subject's judgment.

Insko, Murashima, and Saiyadain (1966) obtained support for the curvilinear relation between influence and discrepancy in a numerosity judgment situation. Despite the fact that Fisher and Lubin (1958) had a very thorough manipulation of discrepancy they did not initially find a curvilinear relationship with influence as assessed through numerosity judgments. Insko, Murashima, and Saiyadain reasoned that a less ambiguous judgment stimulus than Fisher and Lubin's photograph of 165 paratroopers would more readily produce a curvilinear effect.

In the experiment small groups of subjects privately judged the number of figures contained in eight briefly shown posters after being exposed to the oral judgments of two "volunteers" on a different but similar set of eight posters. For any one group of subjects the figures varied in size, shape, color, and spatial distribution but not in number. The experiment involved two independent variables: stimulus ambiguity and discrepancy. Stimulus ambiguity was manipulated by using posters that contained either 30 or 50 figures. The standard deviation of the mean poster judgments for control subjects exposed to the 30-figure posters was found to be significantly less than the similar standard deviation for control subjects exposed to the 50-figure posters. Stimulus ambiguity was thus operationally indexed in terms of between-subject variability. Discrepancy was manipulated by having the two volunteers or stooges give judgments that for different groups of subjects differed from the control group means (25 for the 30-figure set and 38 for the 50-figure set) by 5, 35, 65, 95, 125, 155, and 185.

Six subjects (4.9 percent) were eliminated because they indicated on a postexperimental enquiry that the experiment was concerned with influence. The results for the remaining subjects indicate that influence was curvilinearly related to discrepancy in both the 30- and 50-figure conditions and that there was more overall influence in the more ambiguous 50-figure condition than in the less ambiguous 30-figure condition. It had also been predicted that the difference between the two influence curves would be greater at the moderately high discrepancies than at the slight discrepancies. This prediction was nonsignificantly supported.

Zimbardo (1960) tested two derivations of Festinger's (1957) theory of cognitive dissonance with regard to the discrepancy phenomenon. Dissonance arises from the psychological incompatibility of two or more cognitive elements (ideas, beliefs, etc.). According to Festinger, one way in which such dissonance arises is through the confrontation of an opinion contrary to one's own. The magnitude of the dissonance created by the expression of a contrary opinion will increase with (1) the extent of the discrepancy in opinion, and (2) the importance of, or involvement with, the cognitive elements of the situation. Since one of the main ways in which dissonance is reduced is through conformity, dissonance theory, according to Zimbardo, predicts that the greater the extent of the discrepancy and involvement the greater the attitude change.

By involvement Zimbardo means something different from what Sherif and Hovland (1961) mean. Sherif and Hovland operationalize ego-involvement on a given issue in terms of membership in a group that takes a definite stand on that issue. Zimbardo correctly points out that Sherif and Hovland's notion of ego-involvement seems to imply concern with a given issue because it is related to an individual's needs and values, and he thus calls involvement in this sense issue-involvement. Zimbardo calls concern with the consequences of one's responses or concern with the instrumental meaning of one's opinions response-involvement, and it is this latter type of involvement which he investigated experimentally.

In the experiment a before-after design was used in which pairs of girl friends privately gave their opinions about the locus of blame for a juvenile delinquent's crime, were exposed to bogus information regarding their friend's judgments, and then gave their opinions a second time. Discrepancy was manipulated by exposing the subjects to bogus opinions that were, on the average, either one or three steps discrepant on a 9-point scale. Response-involvement was manipulated by telling the subjects either that their judgments would give a good indication of their basic social values, personalities, and so forth, or that their judgments would not be an indication of their basic social values, personalities, etc. The results indicated that, as predicted, more opinion change was produced by high discrepancy and by high involvement. Since Sherif and Hovland's assimilation-contrast theory does not contain the variable of response-involvement, these results cannot be accounted for in terms of that theory.

Cohen (*1962a*) formulated and attempted to test an intriguing dissonance formulation of the boomerang effect, or change contrary to the direction of influence. According to Cohen, if a person is highly committed to a point of view and encounters a strong influence against it, he may reduce the resulting dissonance by bolstering his own point of view and consequently moving in the pro direction. The problem of committing subjects to their own point of view was solved by having pairs of subjects attempt to persuade each other. On the basis of a preliminary attitude questionnaire subjects were selected who were slightly against to fairly strongly against undergraduate coeducation at Yale. After being told that the experiment was a study of how well people can convince each other, the subjects were divided into pairs. All subjects were given an additional attitude scale and then misinformed that their partners were slightly in favor of coeducation at Yale. The subjects attempted to persuade their partners by writing essays opposed to coeducation, and then "exchanging" them. In fact, each subject was shown a fictitious essay favoring coeducation. After reading the essays the subjects gave their reactions by indicating their attitudes toward coeducation and were given bogus information regarding the identical reactions of their partners. Half of the subjects were informed that their partners had become slightly more favorable toward coeducation (small discrepancy) and half that their partners had become much more favorable toward coeducation (large discrepancy). All subjects believed that their partners were negatively influenced by having read the essays. Finally,

after being assured of the anonymity of their attitudes, the subjects
filled out an attitude questionnaire identical to the initial questionnaire
given before the experiment.

The before-after change from the first to the final measure indicated that the mean negative change in the large discrepancy condition
(−.67, boomerang) was significantly different from the mean positive
change in the small discrepancy condition (+1.13, conformity). There
was no test of whether the boomerang effect in the large discrepancy
condition was significantly different from zero. In terms of the percentage
of subjects who changed, however, Cohen does report that in the high
discrepancy condition significantly more subjects boomeranged (59 percent) than conformed (19 percent). The corresponding percentages in
the low discrepancy condition are 19 and 53. A chi-square test of all the
percentages in both high and low discrepancy conditions is significant.
When the subjects were split at the median according to how well they
liked their partners, a two-factor analysis of variance revealed an interaction between discrepancy and liking. This interaction means that the
difference between the boomerang of the high discrepancy condition
and the conformity of the low discrepancy condition is greater with high
than with low liking for the partners. Supposedly more dissonance was
created when liking for the partner was high than when it was low.

These results are very remarkable, particularly when one considers
the fact that the negative movement or boomerang was combating a
ceiling effect in terms of the amount of possible change. The one difficulty with the experimental design has to do with the problem of repeated measurement. Attitudes toward coeducation were measured four
times.

Aside from these matters, however, Cohen points out that there is
a theoretical difficulty in terms of a nondissonance explanation of the
findings. The boomerang effect may have resulted from the subjects'
desire to "get even" with their partners. The subjects were told that their
final attitude ratings would be anonymous, but they may have intended
to approach their partners after the experiment and show them that
they could be "just as unreasonable." This alternative explanation has
at least a degree of plausibility. Still another alternative explanation,
which Cohen does not mention, is in terms of assimilation-contrast theory.
If one assumes that the subjects were highly ego-involved with their
positions, the boomerang effect in the high discrepancy condition is
roughly predicted. The problem is that the theory does not specify how
much discrepancy and how much ego-involvement is necessary to produce such an effect.

Aronson, Turner, and Carlsmith (1963) tested some theorizing of
Festinger and Aronson (1960) regarding the interaction of communicator
credibility and communicator discrepancy. According to Festinger and

Aronson, when an individual is confronted by a discrepant communication, dissonance is created. Further, the more discrepant the communication the greater the dissonance. The resulting dissonance can theoretically be reduced in any of four ways: disparaging the communicator, conforming to the communicator's opinion, convincing the communicator to change his opinion, or seeking social support. In most laboratory experiments, however, the last two modes of dissonance reduction are unavailable. Since the communication is usually written or taped the communicator is not present, and the subjects are not allowed to interact with anyone inside the experimental setting. This leaves disparagement of the communicator and conformity to the communicator's opinion as the two available modes of dissonance reduction. Theoretically, both conformity and disparagement increase with the degree of discrepancy-produced dissonance. However, Festinger and Aronson argue that at extreme discrepancies disparagement will be increasingly preferred as a method of dissonance reduction. Thus Aronson, Turner, and Carlsmith maintain that unless a communicator is perfectly credible, i.e., incapable of being disparaged, there will be a curvilinear relationship between discrepancy and conformity.

One difficulty with this theorizing is that the reason why disparagement rather than conformity should be chosen as a means of dissonance reduction at the extreme discrepancies is not made explicitly clear. Aronson, Turner, and Carlsmith argue very plausibly that if at some extreme discrepancy the communicator is severely disparaged he is not likely to be very influential. However, this still does not explain why disparagement rather than conformity is chosen as a means of dissonance reduction. Some light may be thrown on the problem if it is assumed that increasing conformity with the communicator will produce increasing dissonance with other cognitive elements (beliefs, attitudes, etc.). If this dissonance builds up too much it may eventually eliminate conformity as a means of overall dissonance reduction. The dissonance created by the discrepant communication could be reduced by conformity, but other dissonance resulting from inconsistency between the newly acquired conformity cognition and other cognitions would be created. Thus at extreme discrepancies conformity may not occur because it would not produce a net reduction in dissonance.

Aronson, Turner, and Carlsmith's subjects, paid female volunteers, were asked to rank nine stanzas from obscure poems, all of which contained alliteration, and then to read a communication entitled "The Use of Alliteration in Poetry." For one third of the subjects the communication discussed the stanzas ranked eighth by the subjects as average, for one third as superior to all but two of the nine examples, and for one third as superior to all of the nine examples. Half of the subjects were told that the communication was written by T. S. Eliot (highly credible source), and half of the subjects were told that the communication was written by a student at Mississippi State Teachers College who was studying to become a high school English teacher (mildly credible source).

The results of the experiment are presented in Figure 3–1. The data were analyzed with multiple *t* tests and not with trend analysis or analysis of variance. The results appear to indicate that for the highly credible source the greater the discrepancy the greater the amount of change, but that for the mildly credible source there is a curvilinear

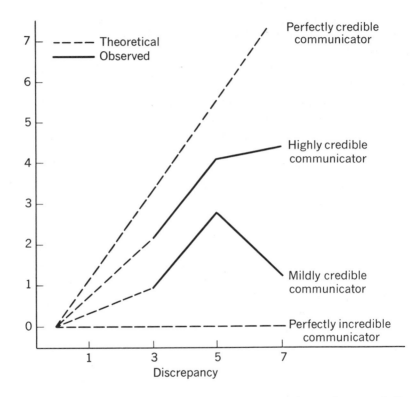

FIGURE 3-1. Opinion change as a function of credibility and extent of discrepancy—theoretical and observed curves. (From Aronson, Turner, and Carlsmith, 1963, p. 34)

relationship between discrepancy and change. For the high credibility source, however, the extreme discrepancy condition (7) is not significantly different from the moderate discrepancy condition (5). This indicates that the high credibility curve has reached asymptote at the highest discrepancy level.

In addition to measuring opinion change Aronson, Turner, and Carlsmith also attempted to measure disparagement of the communicator by having the subjects indicate their strength of agreement or disagreement with 14 evaluative statements about the essay and author. They found that at each discrepancy level the highly credible source was evaluated more highly than the mildly credible source, but that, contrary to prediction, there was no difference in evaluation between discrepancy levels. Thus while the opinion change data support the theory, the communicator disparagement data do not.

Can assimilation-contrast theory account for these results? Hovland (1959) does state that increasing discrepancy may lead to increasing change only when the communication is perceived as being credible, prestigeful, etc. However, this is just an educated guess. The prediction is not made to flow in any convincing way from analogies with the psychology of judgment. It conceivably could be argued that the latitude of acceptance increases with an increase in the credibility of the source, but this has neither been proposed nor demonstrated.

Bergin (*1962*) also reports some evidence relating discrepancy and communicator credibility. Subjects were exposed to information regarding their masculinity-femininity by either a high or low credibility source. Before and after the exposure the subjects indicated their latitudes of acceptance and rejection on a masculinity-femininity dimension. This was done by having the subjects rate themselves in terms of the most acceptable, acceptable, most objectionable, and objectionable degrees of masculinity-femininity. The high credibility source was a member of the staff of the Psychiatry Department of Stanford Medical Center who based his interpretations of the subjects' masculinity-femininity upon a battery of test information. The low credibility source was a high school freshman who did not have access to any test information. The masculinity-femininity information given to the subjects was at one of three levels of discrepancy (slight, moderate, and extreme). The slight discrepancy level was within the latitude of acceptance, at least 2 points away (on a 13-point scale) from the most acceptable rating. The moderate discrepancy level was within the latitude of rejection, at least 4 points away from the most acceptable rating. The extreme discrepancy level was the position rated most objectionable, at least 6 points away from the most acceptable rating.

The results in terms of the before-after change in the most acceptable ratings indicated that overall the high credibility source was significantly more effective than the low credibility source. Only at the slight discrepancy level was the effect nonsignificant. For the high credibility source the extreme discrepancy level was significantly higher than the slight discrepancy level and nonsignificantly higher than the moderate discrepancy level. The curve appears to have just about reached asymptote and is strikingly similar in appearance to Aronson, Turner, and Carlsmith's (1963) high credibility curve shown in Figure 3–1. The low credibility curve nonsignificantly but uniformly decreases over the three discrepancy levels. Only if the intermediate discrepancy levels are ignored is the interaction between credibility and discrepancy significant. Unfortunately no trend analyses were performed on the data. The fact that Bergin's low credibility curve nonsignificantly but uniformly decreases while Aronson, Turner, and Carlsmith's low credibility curve has a curvilinear form is probably attributable to the fact that Bergin's low credibility source is less credible and his issue more ego-involving than Aronson, Turner, and Carlsmith's. A high school freshman is probably less credible than a college student, and one's own degree of masculinity-femininity more ego-involving than the relative merits of various obscure poems.

Bergin also presents some evidence, obtained from a postexperimental interview, with regard to the sources' perceived ability to evaluate personalities. This information was intended as a validation of the source credibility manipulation, and, in fact, Bergin did find that the high credibility source was judged more expert than the low credibility source. More interesting, however, is the fact that judged expertness of the low credibility source declined significantly from the slight to the extreme discrepancy levels. This finding supports Aronson, Turner, and Carlsmith's (1963) prediction concerning the increased disparagement of the communicator at the extreme discrepancy levels.

Bergin discusses his results as being consistent with a dissonance formulation, as indeed they roughly are. It should be pointed out, however, that assimilation-contrast theory cannot account for these results. First of all, assimilation-contrast theory does not include the variable of source credibility and thus is unable to explain the differences between the credibility conditions. But more important is the fact that knowledge of the latitudes of acceptance and rejection was of no help in specifying the point of maximum influence. In the high credibility condition maximum influence occurred when the communication advocated the point previously rated as most objectionable, and in the low credibility condition maximum influence occurred when the communication advocated a point within the latitude of acceptance. The point of maximum influence is theoretically supposed to be somewhere between the latitudes of acceptance and rejection. Apparently it is not.

Bochner and Insko (1966) report some data from a study in which the discrepancy dimension was thoroughly explored from one end to the other. It is apparent that various investigators may obtain different results simply by focusing on different segments of the discrepancy dimension. If the relation between discrepancy and opinion change is in fact curvilinear, then a study which explores the slight discrepancies will find an increasing relationship between opinion change and discrepancy and a study which explores the extreme discrepancies will find a decreasing relationship between opinion change and discrepancy. Bochner and Insko picked a dimension which can be completely explored: number of hours of sleep the average young adult should get per night. Complete exploration is possible with this dimension because it has a finite ceiling, zero hours per night.

In the context of a reading comprehension test subjects were presented with a written communication that advocated either 8, 7, 6, 5, 4, 3, 2, 1, or 0 hours sleep per night. The communications were attributed to either a Nobel prize winning physiologist, a high credibility source, or to a YMCA director, a medium credibility source. Three dependent variables were assessed after exposure to one of the communications: opinion regarding sleep, source disparagement, and communication disparagement. Source disparagement was assessed by summing the responses to 7-point scales indicating the extent to which the communicator was "sincere," "competent," "trustworthy," etc. Communication disparagement was assessed by summing the responses to 7-point scales indicating the extent to which the communication "made sense," and was "reasonable," "logical," etc. Aronson, Turner, and Carlsmith's (1963) variable of communicator disparagement is a combination of both source disparagement and communication disparagement.

The results indicated that opinion change was linearly related to disparagement in the high credibility condition and curvilinearly related to discrepancy in the medium credibility condition. In the high credibility condition the opinion curve does have a marked drop at the most extreme discrepancy, zero hours per night, and the deviation from linearity is significant. The curvilinear component, however, is not significant. Thus, contrary to Bochner and Insko's initial supposition, a thorough exploration of a given discrepancy dimension will not necessarily result in a curvilinear relation between discrepancy and influence. It was further found that source credibility interacted significantly with discrepancy. This interaction was produced by a significant superiority of the high credibility source at the extreme discrepancies and a non-significant superiority of the medium credibility source at the moderate discrepancies. Theoretically the high credibility source should have been equal to or slightly superior to the medium credibility source at the moderate discrepancies and greatly superior to the medium credibility source at the extreme discrepancies. The reason for this is simply that relative to a medium credibility source, a high credibility source should be more resistant to the disparagement that supposedly occurs at the extreme discrepancies and produces a drop in the influence curve.

What about the other two dependent variables? The results indicate that communication disparagement increased linearly over discrepancy levels for both the high and medium credibility sources, and that source disparagement increased linearly for the medium credibility source and varied randomly for the high credibility source. Furthermore, the high and medium credibility conditions differed significantly in source disparagement but not in communication disparagement. Bochner and Insko interpreted this pattern of results as indicating that source disparagement is a more important determiner of the opinion curves than is communication disparagement. When source disparagement increases linearly, as it did in the medium credibility condition, the opinion curve is curvilinear; and when source disparagement varies randomly, as it did in the high credibility condition, the opinion curve is linear.

Further examination of the relation between disparagement and opinion in terms of the within-cell correlations across discrepancy levels created some doubt as to whether or not either type of disparagement is a sufficient explanation for a decreasing opinion curve. Theoretically the correlation between disparagement and opinion should become increasingly negative as the amount of discrepancy increases. This is due to the fact that increasing discrepancy eventually produces enough disparagement to result in decreasing opinion change. The pattern of within-cell correlations roughly corresponds to this expectation in the medium credibility condition but not in the high credibility condition. This is to some extent reasonable in view of the fact that only in the medium credibility condition is there a curvilinear relation between discrepancy and opinion. However, for the high credibility condition the correlations did not become more negative even at the extreme discrepancy level where opinion decreased.

While these results do not support Bochner and Insko's initial supposition with regard to the curvilinear relation between opinion and discrepancy, it is true that further research in this area should make an effort to thoroughly explore the discrepancy dimension. But how can this be done on issues without finite ceilings? For example, how could the dimension relating to the amount by which tuition should be increased at a given university be thoroughly explored? This dimension continues into infinity. Bochner and Insko argue that since dimensions without finite ceilings lack upper anchors, discrimination should become progressively poorer as discrepancy increases. An increase in tuition from $50 to $1050, for example, should appear more extreme than an increase from $1050 to $2050. If this is in fact the case, then there is a possible solution to the problem. The most extreme communication should be placed far enough along the dimension so that any possible further extreme communication would appear only trivially different. Location of this most extreme discrepancy level would, of course, be achieved through some sort of scaling procedure. This scaling procedure would also allow for a more adequate placement of communications along the entire length of the dimension.

Comment. From the present vantage point it appears as if dissonance theory does a better job of accounting for the discrepancy data than does assimilation-contrast theory. Under appropriate circumstances both theories predict a curvilinear relationship between discrepancy and influence. However, assimilation-contrast theory's prediction concerning the location of the curve inflection in the area between the latitudes of acceptance and rejection has not been supported (Bergin, 1962); nor is assimilation-contrast theory obviously capable of accounting for the apparent interaction of source credibility and discrepancy (Aronson, Turner, and Carlsmith, 1963; Bergin, 1962; Bochner and Insko, 1966). This does not mean that dissonance theory is able to handle all of the existing data. Bochner and Insko's (1966) correlational results, for example, make it appear as if disparagement is not a complete explanation for a decreasing influence curve. It just means that at present dissonance theory seems to fare somewhat better than does assimilation-contrast theory.

Most of the reviewed studies which used a design that does not confound discrepancy with initial position found that the greater the discrepancy the greater the change (Aronson, Turner, and Carlsmith, 1963; Bergin, 1962; Bochner and Insko, 1966; Fisher and Lubin, 1958; Freedman, 1964; Goldberg, 1954; Helson, Blake, and Mouton, 1958a; Hovland and Pritzker, 1957; Rosenbaum and Franc, 1960; Tuddenham, 1958b; Zimbardo, 1960); one study found that the greater the discrepancy the less the change (Cohen, 1962a); and four studies found a curvilinear relationship between discrepancy and change (Aronson, Turner, and Carlsmith, 1963; Bochner and Insko, 1966; Freedman, 1964; Insko, Murashima, and Saiyadain, 1966). It may be that for most uninvolving issues, assuming at least a moderately credible communicator, the relationship between discrepancy and influence is linear and not curvilinear. Additional research is needed in which the discrepancy dimension is more thoroughly explored.

The fact that discrepancy seems to interact with such variables as source credibility and ego-involvement may mean that it interacts with a large number of other variables. This is a matter that needs to be investigated. Communicator discrepancy appears to be an exceedingly important attitude change variable.

Effect of Discrepancy Between Communication and Recipient Upon Perceived Communication Location

Theoretically when a communication is located within the latitude of acceptance it will be assimilated toward the individual's position, and when a communication is located within the latitude of rejection it will be contrasted away from the individual's position. Thus the exact position of a communication on the discrepancy dimension will determine whether assimilation or contrast effects will occur in perceived communication location.

In the previous section it was pointed out that the effect of discrepancy upon attitude change could be studied by either of two procedures, a between-subjects procedure which confounds discrepancy with initial position and a between-communications procedure which manipulates discrepancy directly. These same two procedures are available for research on the effect of discrepancy upon perceived communication location. All of the research, however, has used the between-subjects procedure. The between-communications procedure involves constructing several communications of differing discrepancies and having subjects of the same positions judge the perceived communication locations on the discrepancy dimension. For example, suppose that subjects were presented with communications advocating 1, 2, 3, 4, 5, 6, 7, or 8 hours sleep per night and asked to judge how many hours sleep per night any one communication advocated. This example makes it apparent why such a procedure has not been used. Since the position of any single communication is perfectly clear there is not likely to be much distortion, at least along the hours of sleep dimension. If the experimenter switches from a discrepancy dimension with a physical counterpart to a purely psychological dimension, such as degree of isolationism, distortion is more likely. In this case, however, the experimenter is confronted with the problem of knowing the true position of any given communication. Without such information it is impossible to know whether or not distortion has in fact occurred. Such problems are undoubtedly part of the reason why research has concentrated on a between-subjects rather than a between-communications procedure.

The between-subjects procedure specifically involves comparing the perceived locations of a given communication by subjects who are either pro, neutral, or con. If a communication advocates a pro position, the pro subjects should theoretically perceive the communication as more pro than the neutral subjects (assimilation) and the con subjects should perceive the communication as more pro than the neutral subjects (contrast). If the communication advocates a neutral position the pro subjects should theoretically perceive the communication as more pro than the neutral subjects (assimilation) and the con subjects should perceive the communication as more con than the neutral subjects (assimilation). If the communication advocates a con position, the pro subjects should perceive the communication as more con than the neutral subjects (contrast) and the con subjects should perceive the communication as more con than the neutral subjects (assimilation).[6] The use of pro, neutral,

---

[6] This general statement assumes that the neutral part of the scale does not fall within the latitude of rejection for the pro and con subjects.

and con communications in this between-subjects procedure, of course, assumes that the experimenter is capable of grossly classifying communications as either pro, neutral, or con.

The between-subjects procedure does not involve the regression problem discussed in connection with attitude change because only one measure of perceived communication location is taken. However, it still is the case that the most discrepant individuals will be the ones most certain of their positions. This means, of course, that an unconfounded manipulation of discrepancy is not achieved. Furthermore, since the individuals at the extremes of one attitude dimension may be either more or less certain of their positions than the individuals at the extremes of another attitude dimension, results may not be generalizable across attitude dimensions. When individual differences are studied the degree of experimental control drops markedly.

Research in this area (Dillehay, 1965; Hovland, Harvey, and Sherif, 1957; Manis, 1960, 1961a, 1961b; Sherif and Hovland, 1961, pp. 151–153; Sherif, Sherif, and Nebergall, 1965, pp. 149–163; Weiss, 1961) has in general produced inconsistent results. Sometimes assimilation effects are obtained, sometimes contrast effects, and sometimes neither. Specification of the circumstances that will produce either of these three possibilities has furthermore not been convincingly achieved. In view of the lack of control involved in a between-subjects procedure, this state of affairs is not too surprising.

The situation is made yet more difficult for assimilation-contrast theory in view of the fact that alternative theoretical formulations meet with moderate success in accounting for at least some of the data. This is illustrated in an experiment of Dillehay's (1965).

Dillehay investigated the perception of a communication by a sample of middle-class housewives. The housewives, who were interviewed in their homes, took a semantic differential test of attitude toward fluoridation, were exposed to a communication moderately favorable to fluoridation, and then indicated the perceived position of the communication on a graphic scale. On the basis of the responses to the semantic differential the subjects were divided into three attitude classes: opposed to fluoridation, slightly favorable toward fluoridation, and highly favorable toward fluoridation. The results indicated a positive relationship between attitude toward fluoridation and perceived communication location; i.e., the housewives assimilated the communication toward their own positions.

If it is assumed, as Dillehay apparently did, that the communication lay within the latitudes of rejection for the housewives who were opposed to fluoridation, then assimilation-contrast theory predicts a contrast effect for these subjects. Taking a cue from Manis (1961a), Dillehay offers an explanation of his results in terms of dissonance aroused through hearing an opposing but persuasive communication. Theoretically this dissonance can be reduced by assimilating the communication toward one's own position. Dillehay argues that the psychophysical evidence upon which assimilation-contrast theory's predictions are based may be misleading in its simplicity. Disagreement and its accompanying unpleasantness do not occur in psychophysical experiments.

If this theorizing is correct, then a group of people with strong social support for their attitudes should experience little dissonance from being exposed to an opposing but persuasive communication, and thus should not show assimilation effects. Dillehay tested this prediction by collecting some additional data from a group of public health school nurses. These subjects were assumed to have strong social support for their favorable attitudes toward fluoridation. When subsamples of nurses and housewives who were similar in attitude and in familiarity with the fluoridation issues were compared, Dillehay found a significant difference. The subsample of housewives with favorable attitudes toward fluoridation judged the communication as more favorable toward fluoridation than did the nurses. This was interpreted to mean that, as predicted, the housewives showed more assimilation than did the nurses. Dillehay is, of course, aware that the sample of nurses and housewives differ in many unspecified ways. One obvious difference is that of education. A check on the relationship between education and judged communication location, however, revealed nothing of significance.

In general, assimilation-contrast theory does not fare too well in accounting for the data on perceived communication location. In fact, it looks as if a variant of dissonance theory can handle the existing data just as well as, if not better than, can assimilation-contrast theory.

Latitudes of Acceptance and Rejection

It was stated above that theoretically the latitudes of acceptance and rejection vary in size according to the degree of ego-involvement. With an increasing degree of ego-involvement the latitude of acceptance decreases and the latitude of rejection increases. This is an important assumption because it allows for the prediction that with high involvement (and consequently with a large latitude of rejection) decreasing influence with increasing communicator discrepancy is more likely and with low involvement (and consequently with a large latitude of acceptance) increasing influence with increasing discrepancy is more likely.

Hovland, Harvey, and Sherif (1957) collected the first data pertaining to the latitudes of acceptance and rejection in the previously mentioned study of attitudes toward prohibition. In the initial session the subjects were given a Thurstone-type scale consisting of nine statements and asked to indicate the statements which were most acceptable, acceptable, most objectionable, and objectionable. This procedure yielded latitudes of acceptance and rejection for each subject. The results indicated that subjects whose most acceptable positions were at the extreme ends of the scale tended to have smaller latitudes of acceptance and larger latitudes of rejection than did the subjects whose most acceptable positions were more intermediate. On the assumption that the most ego-involved subjects were the ones at the extreme ends of the scale, the result can be predicted on the basis of assimilation-contrast theory.

It is difficult to know, however, to what extent the above finding is genuine and to what extent it is an artifact. Individuals whose most acceptable position is at one end of the scale will of necessity only be able to find acceptable positions in the direction of the neutral part of the scale. Even for those individuals whose most acceptable position is near but not at the extreme end of the scale there still would be more available positions in the neutral direction. If the end statements of the attitude scale are only moderately extreme the problem would be much greater than if the end statements represented more extreme positions. Only if the end statements represented the most extreme positions conceivable could we be certain that anyone whose most acceptable position was at one end of the scale would not find a more extreme position acceptable.

An additional problem with this type of research design is that ego-involvement is not directly manipulated. The design involves looking at the differences between subjects and consequently has a very low degree of experimental control. Other investigators who have used this design (Sherif and Hovland, 1961, pp. 136–145; Sherif, Sherif, and Nebergall, 1965, pp. 26–52; Whittaker, 1963) have obtained results roughly comparable to those obtained by Hovland, Harvey, and Sherif.

Miller (1965) found that the experimental involvement of high school students in their attitudes toward the amount of mathematics and science in the high school curriculum had no effect on latitudes of acceptance or rejection. An elaborate manipulation was used to involve students either in their attitudes toward the amount of mathematics and science in the high school curriculum or in their attitudes toward fluoridation of public drinking water. The involvement manipulation contained four parts or aspects. First, the subjects were given information designed to increase the saliency of their attitudes by stressing the importance of the issue; second, social support was provided for their attitudes through reference to like-minded groups; third, the subjects were asked to provide reasons in support of their own attitudes; and fourth, the subjects committed themselves to distributing literature in support of their attitudes.

An after-assessment of the latitudes of acceptance and rejection on the curriculum issue revealed no difference between the group involved in the curriculum issue and the group involved in the fluoridation issue. This evidence is fairly damaging to assimilation-contrast theory if it can be established that the involvement manipulation was adequate. Two pieces of evidence suggest that it was. First, an after-assessment of attitude toward the curriculum issue obtained from various Likert items demonstrated that the involvement procedure did succeed in creating more extreme attitudes. Second, a before-after assessment revealed that a fluoridation communication presented to both groups was more persuasive in the group uninvolved on the fluoridation issue.

Comment. In evaluating the literature relating to latitudes of acceptance and rejection considerably more weight must be given to Miller's (1965) experimental study than to the other nonexperimental studies. In view of this fact it appears that the assumption or hypothesis that the latitudes of acceptance vary with the degree of ego-involvement is incorrect.

EVALUATION

The possibility of applying judgmental principles to the phenomenon of attitude change is an intriguing one, and Sherif and Hovland have made a laudable pioneer effort in this regard. With the benefit of hindsight, early efforts frequently appear naive. Without the pioneer, however, science would never mature to more enlightened conceptions.

From a point of view of internal consistency the theory is weak because there is no exact specification of the causal relationships between perceived communication location, communication evaluation, and attitude change. Supposedly all three of these variables are in some fashion a resultant of the discrepancy between communication and communication recipient. But what about the direct relationship between these variables? One guess is that perceived communication location causes communication evaluation which in turn causes attitude change. This, however, is never stated.

From the standpoint of the empirical evidence the theory is most effective in its predictions of attitude change. The most damaging research in this area is that of Bergin (1962). Bergin found that the asymptote of the influence curve is not in the neutral zone between the latitudes of acceptance and rejection. In addition, a dissonance theory formulation appears to do a better job than does assimilation-contrast theory in handling the existing data. This is partially because dissonance theory contains a number of crucial variables (source credibility, response involvement) that assimilation-contrast theory does not. With regard to perceived communication location, the literature is too inconsistent to allow for confident generalization. A variant of dissonance theory, however, does appear to do as well, if not better than, assimilation-contrast theory in handling these data. With regard to latitudes of acceptance and rejection, it seems on the basis of one experimental study (Miller, 1965) as if ego-involvement has no effect.

A consideration of all these matters leads to the conclusion that assimilation-contrast theory, at least in its present form, is not a serious contender in the field of attitude change. This does not mean that judgmental principles have no relevance to attitude change. It just means that such relevance has not been adequately demonstrated.

4

Helson's Adaptation-Level Theory

THEORY

Adaptation-level theory as developed by Helson (1959, 1964) is indigenous to the field of perception and has been elaborated most thoroughly with regard to perceptual phenomena. Helson, however, claims wide applicability for adaptation-level or AL theory and has shown no hesitancy about generalizing it to social behavior.

Bipolar Dimensions

One of the cornerstones of AL theory is the concept of dimension. According to Helson all stimuli can be dimensionalized or arranged in a meaningful order. He agrees with Woodworth (1938) that "Lines can be arranged in order of length, time intervals in the order of their duration, boxes in the order of their weight. . . . Historical personages can be arranged, roughly at least, in the order of their eminence" (p. 393). Helson qualifies Woodworth's statement, however, by noting that these dimensions are bipolar in nature. Thus weights, for example, are not conceived of as varying from readily liftable to unliftable, but from light, to neither light nor heavy, to heavy. All dimensions, whether they be good-bad, far-near, or large-small, are conceived of as being bipolar in nature; i.e., as ranging from those stimuli which evoke the response in question to its fullest extent, through those which will not evoke it at all, to those which will evoke an antagonistic response to its fullest extent.

Adaptation-Level

Presumably every dimension has a zone of transition from one extreme to the other. It is this zone of transition or neutral zone that Helson calls the adaptation-level. The adaptation-level is of crucial importance because other stimuli on the dimension are judged in relation to it. A good illustration of this is the classic example of the person who dips both hands into lukewarm water after having had one hand in cold water and the other in hot. The hand that was initially in the hot water feels cold and the hand that was initially in the cold water feels hot. The adaptation-level for the hand initially in the hot water was raised, and the adaptation-level for the hand initially in the cold water was lowered. Thus the lukewarm water feels cold for the hand with the high adaptation-level and hot for the hand with the low adaptation-level.

Focal, Contextual, and Residual Stimuli

The adaptation-level is dependent upon the interaction of three types of stimuli: focal, contextual, and residual. Focal stimuli are the stimuli in the series being judged, such as colors which are to be categorized according to their degree of pleasantness. Contextual stimuli are the out-of-series or background stimuli which are immediately present but not being judged. Residual stimuli, also called residual factors, are the residues of previous stimulation outside of the experimental setting.

How do all of these stimuli interact so as to produce the adaptation-level? According to Helson the adaptation-level is the weighted geometric mean of all stimuli affecting the organism. Geometric means give relatively greater weight to the smaller values. Thus, taking the geometric mean assures that stimuli of lesser magnitude will have a relatively greater effect than stimuli of larger magnitude in the determination of the adaptation-level. The stimulus values may be weighted for such factors as recency, frequency, position, vividness, and spacing of stimulation. Helson points out, however, that in some instances other properties such as beauty, prestige, "significance quality," and so forth must also be considered as weights. The necessity of using frequency as a weight is illustrated by the raising of the adaptation-level from 475 to 550 grams when, in a series of stimuli ranging between 400 and 600 grams, the 600-gram stimulus is presented twice as frequently as any other. Raising the adaptation-level assures that all of the stimuli will be relatively lighter and thus judged as lighter.

The contrast effect produced by an extreme anchoring stimulus can be predicted on the basis of a shifted level of adaptation. An extremely heavy anchoring stimulus will shift the level of adaptation upward so that all of the comparison stimuli will be judged relatively lighter or "contrasted" away from the anchor.

Application to Social Behavior

According to Helson, AL theory can be directly and not just analogically applied to social behavior. The critical problem is to determine how focal, contextual, and residual stimuli interact so as to produce social behavior. From this standpoint residual stimuli include such things as traits, beliefs, and attitudes (Helson, Blake, Mouton, and Olmstead, 1956). Level of group action defined in terms of the number of individuals taking positive, negative, or neutral stands on a given issue provides the background stimuli. Background and residual stimuli, along with key focal stimuli being judged, interact so as to modify the expression of attitude or the adjustment of the individual. Theoretically, with appropriate weighting of the stimuli all expressions of attitude can be accounted for.

RESEARCH

The research that Helson and his associates have carried out in the area of persuasion relates to conformity. On the assumption that conformity is the resultant of a changed adaptation-level, exposure to the behavior of other people should result in greater conformity. The behavior of other people is typically regarded by Helson and his associates as falling into the class of background stimuli.

A question can be raised concerning the extent to which exposure to the behavior of other people is most directly relevant to the subject's actual conformity behavior, as Helson and his associates imply, or to the subject's *expectations* of how other people behave. The behavior of other people exists on a dimension shared both by the subject's own behavior and his expectations regarding other people's behavior. But what is the most direct variable whose adaptation-level is affected through exposure to other people? Helson never discusses this question.

Aside from the above ambiguity, however, there is an even more serious problem. Much of the research carried out by Helson and his associates is concerned with the effect upon conformity of numerous variables, all of which involve different dimensions. When the behavior of the subject and of the model lie along the same dimension, matters are at least reasonably straightforward. When the effects upon conformity of other variables lying along different dimensions are brought into the picture, however, things become more ambiguous. It may be true, for example, that the ascendance-submission of the subjects will have a significant effect upon their conformity behavior, but conformity and ascendance lie along different dimensions. What is the adaptation-level obtained from combining two such different dimensions? The adaptation-level is conceived of as the neutral zone on *one* bipolar dimension. The theory, at least in its present form, cannot be meaningfully applied to variables involving different dimensions. Despite this fact numerous investigators have attempted to do just that.

In the research described below we will look first at the studies that have dealt with only one dimension and then at the studies which have dealt with more than one dimension.

Research Involving Single Dimensions

Blake, Rosenbaum, and Duryea (1955) had two graduate assistants contact other graduate students in the Psychology Department at the University of Texas to solicit funds for the purpose of buying a gift for a secretary who was leaving her position. The assistants each contacted 25 other graduate students who were all personally known to them. When the assistants made the contacts they incidentally exposed a clipboard which, in all but the standard control condition, listed the supposed previous donations. These donations averaged either 25 cents or 75 cents. In the standard condition no donations were listed on the clipboard. (The average donations were based on arithmetic means and not geometric means as adaptation-level theory requires.) The investigators found that the average donation in the 25-cent condition was 32 cents, in the 75-cent condition was 63 cents, and in the standard condition was 75 cents. All of the differences except the one between the 75-cent and standard condition are significant.

Rosenbaum and Blake (1955) found that the conformity of individuals to a request was significantly influenced by the previous conformity or lack of conformity to the same request by another individual, a stooge. In the experimental conditions, subjects were approached in the library at the University of Texas and asked to volunteer for an experiment immediately after the same request had been made of a stooge sitting next to them. For 15 of the experimental subjects the stooge conformed with the request and for 15 he did not conform. The control condition differed solely in that the stooge was not contacted prior to the encounter with the subjects. Rosenbaum and Blake found that the behavior of the stooge had a significant effect upon the behavior of the subjects. When the stooge conformed to the request the majority of the subjects conformed, and when the stooge did not conform the majority of the subjects did not conform. In the control conditions approximately equal numbers of subjects did and did not conform.

Ball (1953) investigated some of the factors affecting agreement or disagreement with opinion statements, specifically the statements in the Droba Attitude Toward War Scale (1931). For one group of subjects statements 1–19 were prefaced by "Most people think that" and statements 20–38 by "Only a few people think that," and for another group statements 1–19 were prefaced by "Only a few people think that" and statements 20–38 by "Most people think that." A control group received the statements without any prefaces. The subjects in all groups simply indicated their agreement or disagreement with each statement. The results indicated that the groups differed in the predicted direction on both the 1–19 set and the 20–38 set. The "most people think" preface significantly increased agreement over that obtained with the "only a few people think" preface. In both sets the agreement scores in the control groups were intermediate to those of the two experimental groups. A further interesting finding was that the difference between the two experimental groups was larger in the initially presented set (statements 1–19) than in the second set (statements 20–38). This was interpreted as meaning that residual stimulation from the first set produced an effect on the agreement-disagreement with statements in the second set.

Blake and Brehm (1954) used a simulated group procedure to study conformity. Subjects were taken one at a time into a dark room and told that other subjects were in the adjoining rooms. The subjects would supposedly be able to communicate with the aid of headsets and microphones. Actually the subjects, who were individually tested, were exposed to a tape recording. The voices on the tape recording were interspersed with time intervals of sufficient duration for the subject to get involved in the "interaction." Blake and Brehm compared autokinetic judgments given alone with autokinetic judgments given in the simulated group procedure and found that the simulated group procedure produced a significant amount of influence.

McConnell and Blake (1953) report an additional study in which it was found that subjects' autokinetic judgments given in a real group situation and in the simulated group situation did not differ significantly from each other but did differ significantly from the judgments of subjects tested in a noninfluence, alone situation. In the real group situation all but one of the participants were stooges who gave a standard set of judgments identical to those given in the simulated group situation.

Olmstead and Blake (1955) report the same general finding with regard to judgments of the number of clicks made by a metronome within a standard time interval. Judgments obtained in the simulated group and real group situations did not differ significantly from each other but both differed significantly from the judgments obtained from subjects in a noninfluence, alone situation.

Comment. These studies all agree with the commonsense expectation that a person's behavior is influenced by the behavior of other people. All of these studies are at least reasonably straightforward because in each study the independent variable and dependent variable share a common dimension. The following studies deal with the theoretically more ambiguous multidimensional situation.

Research Involving Several Dimensions

Rosenbaum (*1956*) repeated the Rosenbaum and Blake (1955) experiment with the addition of an intensity-of-request variable. Subjects were persons in the library at the University of Texas approached with either a strong, moderately strong, or weak request for assistance in an experiment immediately after a similar request was made of a stooge sitting next to them. The stooge either conformed or did not conform to the request. Regardless of whether the subjects did or did not conform, rating scale data on willingness or unwillingness to conform were obtained from them. The results for both dependent variables (actual conformity behavior and rating of willingness or unwillingness to conform) indicated that both independent variables (intensity of request and background behavior of the stooge) produced significant effects in the predicted direction. There was greater conformity when the stooge conformed and when the request was of strong intensity. Furthermore, the interaction between the two independent variables was not significant when tested with either of the dependent variables.

Rosenbaum conceived of the intensity-of-request stimuli as focal stimuli and the behavior of the stooge as background stimuli. According to adaptation-level theory the focal, background, and residual stimuli interact so as to produce the adaptation-level. All of the stimuli, however, are conceived of as varying along the same dimension. Thus, for example, brightness judgments are determined by the brightness of the immediate series of focal stimuli, the brightness of the background stimuli, and the brightness of the previously encountered or residual stimuli. Thus brightness is the common dimension that is of crucial theoretical importance. The problem with Rosenbaum's experiment concerns the specification of the common stimulus dimension relating the focal stimuli, background stimuli, and dependent variable. The focal stimuli vary along an intensity-of-request dimension, and the background stimuli and dependent variable lie along a conformity to request dimension. These dimensions obviously do not overlap. Thus Rosenbaum's results are not unambiguously relevant to adaptation-level theory, at least in its present form.

Freed, Chandler, Blake, and Mouton (*1955*) report an experiment which studied the reactions of people to a sign prohibiting entry into a university building. Pretesting produced three degrees of sign strength. Ranging from strongest to weakest these signs were: "Absolutely No Admittance—Use Another Entrance." "You Are Requested to Enter by Another Entrance," and "Absolutely No Admittance." Background conditions were varied by having the subject approach the entrance alone or preceded by a stooge who either violated or complied with the sign.

Both the background and sign variables produced significant effects in the predicted directions. The most violation occurred when the sign was weak and the stooge did not conform, and the least violation occurred when the sign was strong and the stooge did conform. Once again, however, it is evident that the stimulus dimension of sign strength is quite different from the stimulus dimension of conformity to the sign. This ambiguity is not discussed.

Lefkowitz, Blake, and Mouton (1955) studied some of the stimulus conditions relating to violation of traffic signals by pedestrians. Subjects either approached the street corners alone (control condition) or preceded by a stooge (experimental conditions). Two independent variables were manipulated: dress of the stooge (high status or low status), and behavior of the stooge (violation or nonviolation of the "wait" signal). The results indicated no difference between the control condition and the experimental condition in which the stooge conformed to the traffic signal. Ninety-nine percent of both the control subjects and the experimental subjects exposed to the conforming stooge conformed to the traffic signal. In the experimental condition in which the stooge violated the traffic signal, however, there were significantly more violations than in the control condition. Furthermore, the high status attire produced significantly more violations than did the low status attire.

Kimbrell and Blake (1958) studied some of the variables affecting the violation of a sign prohibiting the use of a water fountain. A naive subject and a stooge were asked to wait in the hall outside the experimental room until the experimenter called them. During the 3-minute waiting period the stooge either drank or did not drink from a water fountain over which a "Do not use" sign was hung. Previous to waiting in the hall the subject and stooge had either been given crackers treated with hot sauce, untreated crackers, or nothing. The results indicated that the greater the motivation to drink the greater the number of subjects who did drink; and the violation of the prohibition against drinking by the stooge produced a significant (by one-tailed test) increase in the number of subjects who also violated the prohibition. The interaction between these two variables is not significant.

Hain, Grahm, Mouton, and Blake (1956) studied some of the stimulus factors affecting petition-signing behavior. Male students walking by the Student Union at the University of Texas were asked to sign a petition requesting that the University officials place lights on a campus memorial fountain. The requests to sign the petition were of three strengths. For the strongest request the experimenter said, "Would you read and sign this petition, please?" While making the request a pencil was offered. For the intermediate request the experimenter said, "Would you read and sign this petition?" A pencil was available but not offered. For the weak request the experimenter said, "You don't want to sign this petition, do you?" No pencil was in sight. Background stimuli were varied by having a stooge either agree or not agree to sign the petition immediately before the naive subject was confronted. In a control condition no stooge was involved. The results indicated that the petition-signing behavior was significantly increased by the strength of the request and the conforming behavior of the stooge.

Helson, Blake, and Mouton (1958b) studied further some of the factors affecting petition-signing behavior. Subjects were presented with one of two entirely different petitions. One requested that floodlights be put on a university fountain and the other that soft drink dispensing machines be removed from university buildings. Pretesting had shown that in a standardization group 96 percent of the accosted students signed the first petition and only 15 percent signed the second. The experimental subjects were asked to sign one of the two petitions after a stooge agreed or refused to sign. The two independent variables manipulated in the experiment were: difference between petitions and conformity of the stooge. All of the subjects were accosted on the way to an experiment in which they were given a test of ascendance-submission (Allport and Allport, 1928).

Helson, Blake, and Mouton found that the two manipulated variables and the interaction between them were significant. The floodlight petition resulted in more signatures than the soft drink petition, and the conforming stooge resulted in more signatures than the nonconforming stooge. The significant interaction is due to the fact that by far the largest number of signatures was obtained from the combination of the floodlights petition with the conforming stooge. Further, the personality data, by and large, support the prediction that the subjects who signed the petition were more submissive than the individuals who did not.

Helson, Blake, Mouton, and Olmstead (1956) used the simulated group technique to influence agreement-disagreement responses to the statements in a Thurstone militarism scale. The experiment had three independent variables: background reports (strongly agree, neutral, and strongly disagree), residual subject type (ascendant, average, submissive), and type of statement (promilitaristic, neutral, antimilitaristic). The residual subject type was measured with an ascendance-submission test (Allport and Allport, 1928). The experiment involved a factorial design in which the three above independent variables were put together in all possible combinations. The results indicated that the simulated group had a significant influence upon all subjects, but that the submissive subjects were more influenced than the ascendant. It was further found that the subjects agreed more with the promilitaristic than with the antimilitaristic or neutral statements. These results were interpreted as supporting the social application of adaptation-level theory. It is obvious, however, that each of the independent variables involves a very different dimension. The background reports vary along the agreement-disagreement dimensions, the focal statements along the militarism-pacificism dimension, and the residual personality types along the as-cendance-submission dimension.

Mouton, Blake, and Olmstead (1956) studied some of the variables affecting susceptibility to simulated group influence concerning number of metronome clicks. They found that unanimous background judgments were more influential than nonunanimous background judgments and that subjects who gave their names before each judgment were influenced to a greater degree than subjects who did not give their names. A break-down of the latter finding according to ascendance-submission type re-vealed that significantly greater influence with lack of anonymity was evident only for submissive subjects. There was no overall significant difference between ascendant and submissive subjects in yielding to simulated group influence.

Blake, Helson, and Mouton (1957) investigated the influence of the simulated group upon numerical judgments of metronome clicks, agree-ments with attitude statements about war and peace, and reported solu-tions of arithmetic problems worked out with paper and pencil. The investigators found that subjects showed more complete conformity to the simulated group responses on the attitude task than on the metronome or arithmetic tasks. However, no significance tests were reported and the order of tasks was not varied for different subjects. Blake, Helson, and Mouton also found that the more difficult the arithmetic problems and the faster the speed of the metronome the greater the conformity to the simulated group. Once again, however, no significance tests were reported. The only reported significance tests had to do with the sig-nificant correlations bewteen conformity scores for the three tasks: metronome and attitude, +.59; metronome and arithmetic, +.51; and arithmetic and attitude, +.38.

Comment. This research is interesting, but nonetheless mostly ir-relevant from the standpoint of adaptation-level theory. Only the research in which the independent variable and dependent variable share a com-mon dimension can be understood in the context of the theory.

EVALUATION

Adaptation-level theory is highly respected in the field of percep-tion. Unfortunately, however, adaptation-level theory has not lived up to expectation in its application to social phenomena. The considerable evidence that Helson and his associates have amassed relating to con-formity is mostly irrelevant from the standpoint of adaptation-level theory.

This research is largely a matter of interesting confirmations of common-sense predictions. Helson and his associates, however, should not be criticized for testing commonsense predictions but rather for claiming this research as relevant to adaptation-level theory. Predictions relating to the effect upon conformity of such variables as the ascendance-submission of the subject, the motivation to conform, the status of a nonconforming stooge, and the strength of a request are all of commonsense and not of adaptation-level theory origin. The main problem, as previously pointed out, is the fact that these variables lie along different dimensions, each of which theoretically has its own adaptation level. How do all of these adaptation levels interact so as to affect the adaptation level of conformity behavior, the dependent variable? The theory has not been developed to handle such complex situations and hence can make no predictions. The only way in which other dimensions could be involved is as *ad hoc* weights or corrections. Such an approach, however, is theoretically barren; one could do just as well without the theory. If Helson and his associates had been content to deal with the modification of a subject's behavior just via similar behavior in a stooge they would have been on safer ground. The obvious fact that conformity is complexly determined apparently led them to investigate additional variables lying along other dimensions. Unfortunately it was not recognized that this necessitated revision or extension of the theory. To quote Helson,

At first sight it might appear that transfer of AL theory from study of sensory responses to social behavior is merely by way of analogy, but consideration of the studies dealing with such social acts as volunteering . . . , gift-giving . . . , and conformity to social pressures . . . shows that this is not the case. (1959, p. 602)

Until a somewhat more realistic appraisal of the situation is made, adaptation-level theory is not likely to be of significant value in the investigation of conformity behavior.

5

McGuire's Logical-Affective

Consistency Theory

THEORY

The theory to be presented in this chapter is one developed by William J. McGuire (1960a, 1960b, 1960c). McGuire has not given the theory a specific name, but for purposes of this discussion it can be called logical-affective consistency theory.

Two Postulates

Logical-affective consistency theory is based on two postulates. One, the cognitive consistency postulate, states that there is a tendency for an individual's beliefs or expectations to be related in a manner required by the rules of formal logic. The other, the wishful thinking postulate, states that there is a tendency for an individual's beliefs to be consistent with his desires or wishes. These two postulates together help to explain the relationships existing among any individual's beliefs.[1]

Belief System as Represented by Propositions

According to McGuire the individual's belief system is potentially reducible to a series of propositions to which the individual can assent or dissent. In actuality McGuire has worked with parts or aspects of the belief system as represented by a set of 48 propositions. The subjects rate the probability that each of the propositions is true on a 100-point

[1] McGuire briefly discusses other factors affecting relationships among beliefs, such as the tendency to commit logical fallacies, to compartmentalize beliefs, to be influenced by prestigeful communication sources, to distort judgments in the direction of assimilation or contrast, and so forth.

scale and the desirability of each of the propositions on a 5-point scale. Thus a measure of the strength of belief and amount of desirability is obtained. Although McGuire does not discuss the matter, presumably disbeliefs are indicated by propositions given a truth probability rating less than 50.

Socratic Effect

According to McGuire an individual's beliefs do not exist in a completely consistent relationship but are distorted by various tendencies such as that of wishful thinking. If, however, several inconsistent beliefs are elicited together, then the individual will become sensitized to the inconsistency and change his beliefs so that there is a greater degree of logical consistency. This latter change is a resultant of the above-mentioned tendency toward cognitive consistency. McGuire calls the whole process of movement toward a greater degree of logical consistency following the relatively simultaneous elicitation of inconsistent beliefs the Socratic effect. Presumably this effect can occur in the absence of awareness.

Logical Repercussions of Change

It follows from the cognitive consistency postulate that if a persuasive communication produces a change in a given belief then logically-related beliefs should also change so as to maintain logical consistency. This effect should occur even though the remote, logically-related beliefs are not mentioned in the communication. On the basis of a cognitive inertia assumption, however, this prediction is qualified somewhat. Due to the existence of cognitive inertia McGuire states that the amount of change in the remote beliefs will be less than that which is logically required for complete consistency. And furthermore, the effect on the remote beliefs will not occur all at once but gradually over time. Inertia results in less and slower change in the remote beliefs than in the target belief affected by the communication.

Logic and Probability

The above discussion implies quantitative degrees of logical consistency, and logical consistency is traditionally and commonly conceived of as qualitative or all or none (two beliefs if related are either consistent or inconsistent). The problem is rather ingeniously handled by combining aspects of formal logic and probability theory.

$$(a \cap b) \cup k \rightarrow c. \qquad (5\text{-}1)$$

This means that if a and b or k are true then c follows logically. The terms in the formula can be illustrated as follows:

a—Lowered tariffs will result in an economically stronger Europe.
b—Tariffs will be lowered within the next years.
k—Factors other than lowered tariffs are going to result in an economically stronger Europe within the next ten years.
c—Europe is going to become economically stronger within the next ten years

This logical expression is modified in terms of the additive and multiplicative laws of probability. According to the multiplicative law the probability that two independent events will occur is equal to the product of their separate probabilities. And according to the additive law the probability that either of two mutually exclusive events will occur is equal to the sum of their separate probabilities. By making several assumptions, such as the independence of a and b and the mutual exclusiveness of $(a \cap b)$ and k, McGuire (1960a, p. 105) is able to write the following equation:

$$p'(c) = p(a)p(b) + p(k). \qquad (5\text{-}2)$$

This means that the predicted probability of c being true is equal to the product of the probabilities of a and b being true plus the probability of k being true.

The p(k) Difficulty and the Change Equation

The major problem with Equation 5-2 is that of measuring $p(k)$, or the probability of all other statements or beliefs besides a and b that imply c. In terms of the example above, if the probability ratings of the a statement, "Lowered tariffs will result in an economically stronger Europe," and the b statement, "Tariffs will be lowered within the next ten years," are known, then it can be predicted that the conclusion, "Europe is going to become economically stronger within the next ten years," will be given a probability rating equal to or greater than the product of the separate probabilities of a and b. The probability rating given to c cannot be predicted exactly, however, because of the difficulty or impossibility of measuring $p(k)$.

McGuire (1960a) discusses three possible ways of measuring $p(k)$, none of which he considers to be entirely satisfactory. The first method is to exhaustively ascertain for any individual the probabilities of all beliefs logically related to a certain conclusion. The second is to have the individual rate the probability of the statement: "Even if a or b were not so, c would still be the case." And the third is to empirically determine $p(a)p(b)$ and $p(c)$ and then obtain $p(k)$ by subtraction. The first method is not feasible when there are very many premises from which a belief follows, the second possibly lacks psychological meaningfulness, and the third assumes a priori that a person's beliefs are internally consistent when this is usually what is being assessed.

The only satisfactory way around the $p(k)$ difficulty is in terms of predicted change. McGuire (1960a, p. 70) presents the following equation to describe the predicted change in the probability of the conclusion following upon a change in the probabilities of both a and b:

(3) $$\Delta'p(c) = \Delta p(a)p(b) + \Delta p(b)p(a) - \Delta p(a)\Delta p(b).$$ (5-3)

In this equation $p(a)$ and $p(b)$ refer to the initial beliefs before a change, $\Delta p(a)$ and $\Delta p(b)$ to the change in a and b, and $\Delta'p(c)$ to the predicted change in c. This equation allows for exact predictions concerning the amount of change necessary for logical consistency. If $p(a)$ is experimentally treated and $p(b)$ is untreated and thus shows only trivial change, the last two terms in Equation 5-3 [$\Delta p(b)p(a)$ and $\Delta p(a)\Delta p(b)$] vanish.

RESEARCH

McGuire (1960b), in his first experiment, had subjects rate the truth probability and desirability of 16 sets of 3 syllogistically related statements (48 statements altogether). The major premise, minor premise, and conclusions belonging to any one syllogism were randomly dispersed among the other statements. The questionnaires were administered on three separate occasions. Between the first and second occasions the subjects read a series of persuasive communications arguing for the truth of the minor premises. The third administration of the questionnaire came a week after reading these persuasive communications. Changes in the probability ratings between first and second (or between first and third) administrations measured the persuasive impact of the communications. The subjects were told that the experiment was a study of people's ability to understand controversial materials. After reading each communication they were required to take a comprehension test on the material in the communication. Any one subject received only 4 of the possible 16 persuasive communications. The subjects were high school and college students who had modal high school grade averages below the 30th percentile.

The rather complex results can be divided into two parts: Socratic effect results and logical repercussions of change results. The analysis of the probability ratings made in the no-communication situations provides the data for the examination of the postulated Socratic effect. The 16 syllogisms were divided into two sets according to the initial desirability ratings. One set of 8 syllogisms had conclusions rated relatively more desirable than the premises, and the other set of 8 syllogisms had conclusions rated relatively less desirable than the premises. The excess probability rating of the conclusions over the product of the premises was found to be 17.18 (on a 100-point scale) in the subset of syllogisms with highly desirable conclusions and 2.20 in the subset with relatively less desirable conclusions. The obtained significant difference between these means is consistent with the wishful thinking postulate. The Socratic effect hypothesis was tested by examining the change in the excess probability of the conclusions over the product of the premises from the first to the second session. If there is a shift toward greater mutual consistency this excess should decrease in the subset of syllogisms with relatively desirable conclusions and increase in the subset with relatively undesirable conclusions. The data indicated that this predicted shift occurred to a significant degree.

The second part of McGuire's results has to do with the logical repercussions of change. A comparison of the before-after differences in the communication and no-communication situations indicated that the persuasive communications had a large and significant effect upon the minor premises. In order to maintain logical consistency, a change in the minor premise should result in a change in the conclusion even though the conclusion is not mentioned in the persuasive communication. McGuire, in fact, found a significant before-after change in the conclusion in the direction of increased logical consistency. He also found, in accordance with the cognitive inertia assumption, that the before to immediately after change was significantly less than that needed for complete logical consistency. Furthermore, the 1-week interval between the immediately after measure and the third measure produced a significant loss in the probability of the minor premises toward which the communications had been previously directed, but a very small and nonsignificant loss in the probability of the logically related conclusions. The net result was greater logical consistency 1 week after the communication than immediately after, although the effect was not tested for statistical significance. McGuire interpreted these results as indicating that continued seepage of the delayed-action effect upon the conclusions was almost completely overcome by decay in the impact of the persuasive communication.

McGuire (1960c), in a second experiment, attempted to test some implications of Festinger's (1957) dissonance theory which appear to coincide with expectations based on logical-affective consistency theory. The experiment dealt with the differing effects of dissonance-increasing and dissonance-reducing communications. Both communications were directed at certain target opinions. If a persuasive change in the target opinion will produce additional logical inconsistency with related beliefs or opinions, then the communication is considered dissonance-increasing; and if a persuasive change in the target opinion will produce less logical inconsistency with related beliefs or opinions, then the communication is considered dissonance-reducing. Thus dissonance theory predicts that a dissonance-increasing communication will produce less change in the target opinion and more change in the logically related beliefs than a dissonance-reducing communication. Also, dissonance theory, as interpreted by McGuire, predicts that dissonance-reducing change will persist longer than dissonance-increasing change.

Purportedly to study the relationship between reading comprehension and the reader's beliefs regarding the material read, subjects were given a questionnaire containing 24 scrambled, syllogistic statements. In three separate sessions the probabilistic truth value of each statement was rated, and in the first session the desirability of each statement was also rated. In the second session the subjects received communications arguing for the truth of 4 of the 8 minor premises, took a reading comprehension test, and then rated the truth value of all of the statements. Different subjects received communications on different sets of 4 statements.

On the basis of the desirability ratings from the first session, the syllogisms were divided into two groups, syllogisms with premises relatively more desirable than the conclusions and syllogisms with premises relatively less desirable than the conclusions. McGuire argued that communications directed at minor premises from syllogisms with relatively desirable premises were dissonance-increasing and that communications directed at minor premises from syllogisms with relatively undesirable premises were dissonance-reducing. McGuire thus expected that the communications directed at the minor premises of the syllogisms with the relatively undesirable premises (the dissonance-reducing communications) would produce more change in the minor premises than the dissonance-increasing communications. This expectation was confirmed. It was also found, as predicted, that the dissonance-increasing communications produced significantly more change in the logically-related but unmentioned conclusions than did the dissonance-reducing communications. It was not found, however, that the dissonance-reducing changes were more persistent over time than the dissonance-increasing changes. McGuire interpreted this latter finding as indicating that the increased saliency of the tendency toward logical consistency produced by the communications gives way over time to an increased saliency of the wishful thinking tendency. This results in the dissonance-reducing changes being distorted back toward wishful thinking.

Dillehay, Insko, and Smith (*in press*) report two studies dealing with the Socratic effect and logical repercussions of induced change. Both studies used the same syllogisms, communications, and instructions as McGuire (1960b).

The first study, like McGuire's, utilized a before-after design but, unlike McGuire's, did not have a follow-up measure a week after the communications were presented. The study was carried out on two different populations, lower and upper division students at the University of California. Following McGuire's method, the syllogisms were divided into two sets according to whether the conclusions were rated relatively more or less desirable than their premises. A comparison of the difference between the two sets in the excess probability of the conclusions over the product of the probabilities of their premises revealed a significant difference for the lower division students only. For the lower division students the high desirability conclusions had relatively higher probabilities than the low desirability conclusions. For the upper division students there was a nonsignificant trend in the same direction. For neither student group, however, was there a significant Socratic effect. According to McGuire a before-after change in the direction of mutual consistency means that the excess probability of the conclusions over the product of their premises should increase for the syllogisms with relatively undesirable conclusions and decrease for the syllogisms with relatively desirable conclusions. This postulated Socratic effect was not significantly supported.

The results for the direct and indirect effects of the persuasive communications are more encouraging. The persuasive communications had a highly significant effect upon the minor premises toward which they were directed, and this effect carried over to the unmentioned but logically related conclusions. The change in the probability of the conclusions, in fact, was not significantly different from that required for complete logical consistency. This latter finding disagrees with McGuire's theorizing that, due to cognitive inertia, the obtained change in the conclusions should be significantly less than that required for logical consistency.

The second experiment utilized an after-only design and included a follow-up measure a week after the persuasive communications were presented. The subjects were upper division students at the University of California. The division of the syllogisms into two sets on the basis of the excess desirability of the conclusions over the premises did not result in a significant difference between the two sets in the excess probability of the conclusions over the premises. This result agrees with the previous finding for similar upper division students. There, furthermore, was no significant Socratic shift in the direction of greater mutual consistency. This result agrees with both the findings for lower division and upper division students in the previous study but disagrees with McGuire's (1960b) finding. It is likely that the initial degree of wishful thinking distortion was not large enough to allow for a significant shift back in the direction of logical consistency over the week interval. McGuire deliberately did his experiment on unintelligent subjects, and unintelligent subjects who have not had the benefit of several years in a stimulating university should and, in fact, did manifest a greater degree of wishful thinking distortion.

The results for the direct and indirect effects of the persuasive communications are consistent with McGuire's (1960b) findings. The persuasive communications had a significant effect upon the minor premises, and this effect carried over to the unmentioned but logically related conclusions.[2] Unlike the previous experiment, but in agreement with McGuire's findings, the change in the probability of the conclusions was significantly less than that required for complete logical consistency. This finding agrees with McGuire's cognitive inertia hypothesis. With regard to change a week after the communications, in agreement with McGuire's results, Dillehay, Insko, and Smith found significant loss in the probability of the minor premises and nonsignificant loss in the probability of the conclusions. The net result was significantly greater logical consistency 1 week after than immediately after exposure to the persuasive communications. McGuire does not report a test of significance for his analogous finding.

In discussing their results, Dillehay, Insko, and Smith make the suggestion that the change in the conclusions produced by communications directed at logically related minor premises may be due to the extralogical cognitive relatedness of the propositions.

If persuasion produces a change in acceptance of fact A about object X this change may influence other facts about the object, especially facts that have an experiential relationship to fact A or are "reasonably" related to A. What we are suggesting is that the process underlying the observed changes in McGuire's studies and ours may be due to a psychological process based on experience and/or judged reasonableness and not to valid logical structures among beliefs. (in press)

---

[2] Since the experiment involved an after-only design these results cannot be attributed to possible sensitization to logical implications resulting from the pretest.

This is certainly a matter that should be investigated further. Ideally, an investigator would find propositions that are related "reasonably" but not logically and then ascertain if change in one will produce change in the other. Such propositions, however, may be difficult to find. Reasonably related propositions may be propositions that are always logically related via other implicitly or explicitly held beliefs. Thus reasonableness may turn out to be a variant of logic.

EVALUATION

McGuire's logical-affective consistency theory has not received much attention, but it is nonetheless a very intriguing and promising formulation. The whole area of the *logical* relationships between opinions has received all too little attention from past and contemporary psychology. McGuire's idea of combining probability theory and logic may well open the door to many significant advances in the study of belief structure.

The theory as it stands, however, is rather incomplete. It needs to be generalized to cover the many logical relationships other than syllogistic ones which exist between opinions. McGuire (1960a) has briefly theorized about propositions related as consequents of the same antecedent in addition to propositions related as antecedent-consequent. However, no additional extensions have been made. It is only through further development of the theory that the implications of the logical consistency postulate can be adequately and fully tested.

The wishful thinking postulate is, of course, a statement of an old and widely accepted idea. New life could be put into this old idea, however, by theorizing more exactly about the type of logical relationships that wishful thinking is most likely to distort. For example, is it the case that the more remote the logical relationship between opinions the more likely wishful thinking is to distort this relationship? The theory seems to be pregnant with opportunity for further development.

It is apparent that there are a large number of variables, such as source credibility and communicator discrepancy, which are not explicitly accounted for in the context of the theory. If a theory is to make a claim for generality, it should, of course, attempt to incorporate all relevant variables. McGuire, however, apparently had no interest in generalizing or expanding the scope of his theory. The theory thus remains rather narrow in its applicability.

Turning to the small amount of empirical evidence pertaining to the theory, the findings of Dillehay, Insko, and Smith (in press) create some doubt about the existence of a Socratic effect. The failure to replicate McGuire's (1960b) findings may be due, however, to the lesser amount of wishful thinking distortion in Dillehay, Insko, and Smith's more intelligent subjects. Furthermore, the Socratic effect hypothesis is not really a necessary part of the remainder of logical-affective consistency theory. This is also true of the cognitive inertia hypothesis, the evidence with regard to which is rather inconsistent. The single most important, consistently replicated, finding has to do with the logical repercussions of change. Persuasive communications have effects that generalize to other logically related beliefs. This is the heart of the cognitive consistency postulate and is certainly a matter deserving further study.

The theory as it stands appears to present some promising leads about the nature of attitude change. It is unfortunate that logical-affective consistency theory has received so little attention while other more ambiguous and inexactly stated cognitive consistency theories have received far more attention.

6

Osgood and Tannenbaum's
Congruity Theory

THEORY

The congruity theory of attitude change, developed by Osgood and Tannenbaum (1955), is the first of a series of equilibrium theories that will be described in this and succeeding chapters.

Definition of Attitude

Osgood and Tannenbaum's concern with attitudes developed out of some work by Osgood (1952) and Osgood, Suci, and Tannenbaum (1958) on the measurement of meaning. In this work the initial step was to have subjects rate concepts such as "lady" on a series of 7-point bipolar scales. These so-called semantic differential scales consist simply of two antonymous adjectives such as *rough-smooth* or *beautiful-ugly* separated by seven spaces. In various studies such ratings were summed over subjects and concepts and the semantic differential scales were then intercorrelated. Finally, the correlation matrix was factor analyzed and a number of factors were extracted. In several such factor analytic studies it was found that the factor which accounted for the most variance was one loaded heavily on such scales as *good-bad, beautiful-ugly, sweet-sour, clean-dirty, tasty-distasteful, valuable-worthless, kind-cruel, pleasant-unpleasant*, etc. This factor was considered to be an evaluative factor, due to the favorable-unfavorable component that is common to all of the above scales.

Osgood and Tannenbaum consider the evaluative dimension to be an attitudinal dimension because of the obvious favorable-unfavorable or pro-con component. Thus, attitude is conceived of as being one of several dimensions in a space of total meaning. Attitude objects are located on a number of semantic dimensions such as active-passive or weak-strong, but it is the location on the pro-con dimension that defines the evaluative nature of the attitude involved. This means, of course, that two individuals with the same attitude toward the same object may differ widely in the nonattitudinal meaning associated with the object. For example, two people with equally negative attitudes toward Negroes may differ in that one individual considers Negroes to be weak and passive and the other, strong and active.

Tendency Toward Maximal Simplicity

Osgood and Tannenbaum assert that attitudes tend toward maximum simplicity. This means that attitudes move toward maximum polarization, either positive or negative. Osgood and Tannenbaum maintain that extreme, all-or-nothing judgments are simpler than more discriminating judgments. Extreme judgments have shorter latencies and are characteristic of emotional, immature, uneducated persons. It is simpler and easier to categorize an attitude object as all bad or all good than as part bad and part good.

The above discussion applies to attitudes considered singly. When two attitudes are associated via an assertion there is a movement toward equilibrium or congruity. This movement toward congruity of attitudes is another manifestation of the tendency toward simplicity.

Principle of Congruity

According to the principle of congruity, when two attitude objects of differing evaluation are linked with an assertion there is a tendency for the evaluations of each object to shift toward a point of equilibrium or congruity. For example, if Eisenhower praised Khrushchev there would be a tendency for Khrushchev to be evaluated more highly and Eisenhower less highly. If, on the other hand, Eisenhower praised democracy or Khrushchev praised Communism there would be no movement toward equilibrium because the associated attitude objects are equally positively or negatively evaluated.

Associative and Dissociative Assertions

In order for the principle of congruity to operate, two attitude objects must be linked via an assertion. Incompatible attitude objects, such as ancestor worship and fear of the dead, may exist in the same cognitive structure without stress because they are never associated.

Assertions are of two types, associative and dissociative. Associative assertions are illustrated by such statements as A is B, A likes B, A shakes hands with B, and A goes with B. Dissociative assertions are illustrated by such statements as A is not B, A dislikes B, A avoids B, and A criticizes B. The associative assertions associate A and B in some fashion or other, and the dissociative assertions dissociate A and B in some fashion or other. The distinction between the two types of assertions, however, is not precisely drawn. Furthermore, it is admitted that no exact definition of "assertion" has been formulated.

We realize that these examples do not provide a precise definition of "assertion." Although we are able to distinguish situations involving assertions (and hence dynamic interaction among sign-processes) from situations not involving assertions on an intuitive basis, so far we have not been able to make explicit the criteria on which we operate. (Osgood, Suci, and Tannenbaum, 1958, p. 202)

Pressure Toward Congruity

Attitude objects or objects of judgment are located on a 7-point evaluative semantic differential scale ranging from +3 to −3. If two objects of judgment differing in evaluation are linked by an assertion the result is pressure toward congruity. The total pressure toward congruity for a given object of judgment associated with another object of judgment is equal to the difference in evaluative scale units between the two objects of judgment; the sign of this pressure is positive when the direction of congruence is positive and negative when the direction of congruence is negative. The total pressure toward congruity for two objects of judgment linked with an associative assertion is stated mathematically as follows:

$$P_{oJ_1} = d_{oJ_2} - d_{oJ_1}, \tag{6-1}$$

$$P_{oJ_2} = d_{oJ_1} - d_{oJ_2}. \tag{6-2}$$

In these equations P_{oJ_1} symbolizes the total pressure toward congruity for the first object of judgment, P_{oJ_2} the total pressure toward congruity for the second object of judgment, d_{oJ_1} the evaluative scale position of the first object of judgment, and d_{oJ_2} the evaluative scale position of the second object of judgment.

The total pressure toward congruity for two objects of judgment linked with a dissociative assertion is formalized as follows:

$$P_{oJ_1} = - d_{oJ_2} - d_{oJ_1}, \tag{6-3}$$

$$P_{oJ_2} = - d_{oJ_1} - d_{oJ_2}. \tag{6-4}$$

The signs in Equations 6-1 through 6-4 simply give the direction of the pressure.

Change Equations

When two objects of judgment are associated with an assertion, the resulting pressure produces movement toward a point of equilibrium. Both objects of judgment, however, do not change equally in evaluation. The more polarized object of judgment (in either the positive or negative direction) changes proportionately less than the less polarized object of judgment; i.e., change is inversely proportional to the degree of polarization. This is stated mathematically as follows:

$$AC_{OJ_1} = \frac{|d_{OJ_2}|}{|d_{OJ_1}| + |d_{OJ_2}|} P_{OJ_1} \tag{6-5}$$

$$AC_{OJ_2} = \frac{|d_{OJ_1}|}{|d_{OJ_1}| + |d_{OJ_2}|} P_{OJ_2} \tag{6-6}$$

where AC_{OJ_1} symbolizes attitude change in the first object of judgment, AC_{OJ_2} attitude change in the second object of judgment, and P_{OJ_1} and P_{OJ_2} are defined in Equations 6-1 through 6-4.

A few hypothetical examples will make clear the application of these formulas. Suppose that Stevenson (+1) endorses Castro (−2); i.e., an associative assertion links Stevenson and Castro. The situation is pictured in scale I of Figure 6-1. If we designate Stevenson as the first

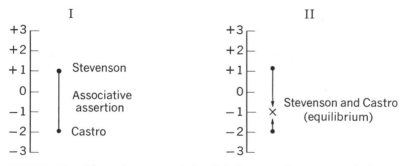

FIGURE 6-1. Effect of an associative link between Stevenson and Castro: (I) Original positions, (II) Equilibrium. (Adapted from Brown, 1962, p. 18)

object of judgment and Castro as the second object of judgment, then Equations 6-1 and 6-2 can be solved as follows:

$$P_{oJ_1} = d_{oJ_2} - d_{oJ_1}$$

$$P_{oJ_1} = -2 \; -(+1)$$

$$P_{oJ_1} = -3,$$

$$P_{oJ_2} = d_{oJ_1} - d_{oJ_2}$$

$$P_{oJ_2} = +1 \; -(-2)$$

$$P_{oJ_2} = +3.$$

The total pressure toward congruity for Stevenson is -3, and for Castro $+3$. This means that as a result of this associative linkage Stevenson will be evaluated less highly and Castro more highly. With the values obtained from Equations 6–1 and 6–2 it is now possible to solve Equations 6–5 and 6–6 for the predicted change.

$$AC_{oJ_1} = \frac{|d_{oJ_2}|}{|d_{oJ_1}| + |d_{oJ_2}|} \; P_{oJ_1}$$

$$AC_{oJ_1} = \frac{2}{1+2} \; (-3)$$

$$AC_{oJ_1} = -2,$$

$$AC_{oJ_2} = \frac{|d_{oJ_1}|}{|d_{oJ_1}| + |d_{oJ_2}|} \; P_{oJ_2}$$

$$AC_{oJ_2} = \frac{1}{1+2} \; (+3)$$

$$AC_{oJ_2} = +1.$$

Castro changes one unit in the positive direction, and Stevenson changes two units in the negative direction. The point of equilibrium for Stevenson and Castro, -1, is shown in scale II of Figure 6–1. You will notice that the less polarized object of movement, Stevenson, absorbed proportionately more of the change.

As a hypothetical example of a dissociative assertion, suppose that Stevenson condemns Castro. This situation is represented in scale I of Figure 6–2. If we continue to designate Stevenson as the first object of judgment and Castro as the second object of judgment, then the pressure toward congruity for each can be obtained with the aid of Equations 6–3 and 6–4 as follows:

$$P_{oJ_1} = - \; d_{oJ_2} - d_{oJ_1}$$

$$P_{oJ_1} = - \; (-2) - (+1)$$

$$P_{oJ_1} = +1,$$

$$P_{oJ_2} = - \, d_{oJ_1} - d_{oJ_2}$$

$$P_{oJ_2} = - \, (+1) - (-2)$$

$$P_{oJ_2} = +1.$$

The total pressure toward congruity for both Stevenson and Castro is +1. Substituting these values into Equations 6–5 and 6–6 the predicted change can be obtained as follows:

$$AC_{oJ_1} = \frac{|d_{oJ_2}|}{|d_{oJ_1}| + |d_{oJ_2}|} \, P_{oJ_1}$$

$$AC_{oJ_1} = \frac{2}{1 + 2} \, (+1)$$

$$AC_{oJ_1} = +\tfrac{2}{3},$$

$$AC_{oJ_2} = \frac{|d_{oJ_1}|}{|d_{oJ_1}| + |d_{oJ_2}|} \, P_{oJ_2}$$

$$AC_{oJ_2} = \frac{1}{1 + 2} \, (+1)$$

$$AC_{oJ_2} = +\tfrac{1}{3}.$$

The predicted change for Stevenson is $+\tfrac{2}{3}$ and for Castro $+\tfrac{1}{3}$. This boosts Stevenson to $+1\tfrac{2}{3}$ and Castro to $-1\tfrac{2}{3}$. The situation is illustrated in scale II of Figure 6–2. The theory has the rather paradoxical implication that a dissociative assertion between positive and negative objects of judgment results in the increased evaluation of both objects of judg-

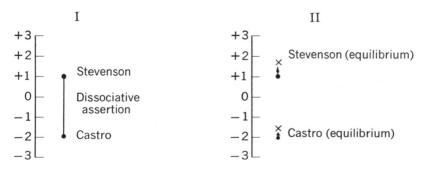

FIGURE 6-2.   Effect of a dissociative link between Stevenson and Castro: (1) Original positions, (2) Equilibrium. (Adapted from Brown, 1962, p. 21)

ment.[1] This situation holds, however, only for the case in which the positive object of judgment is least highly polarized. If the positive object of judgment is most highly polarized then a dissociative assertion results in the decreased evaluation of both objects of judgment. The theory also implies that a dissociative association between two positive objects of judgment results in the decreased evaluation of both, and that a dissociative association between two negative objects of judgment results in the increased evaluation of both.

Correction for Incredulity

When objects of judgment differing widely in evaluation are linked with an associative assertion, or when objects of judgment highly similar in evaluation are linked with a dissociative assertion, it may happen that the individual exposed to this information will become incredulous. Osgood and Tannenbaum illustrate this production of incredulity with examples in which a person or source makes assertions about a concept; for example, "Eisenhower (+3) praises Communism (−3)." They maintain that statements such as this one are more likely to arouse incredulity than ones in which the associatively linked source and concept are more congruent; for example, "Eisenhower (+3) praises Bulgarians (−1)."

What is done is to correct Equations 6–5 and 6–6 in terms of a number symbolized by i. This number always has the opposite sign of P and is defined in the following formula:

$$i = a(d_s{}^2 + b)(d_c{}^2 + d_c),   (6–7)$$

where the constants a and b are $\frac{1}{40}$ and 1 respectively, d_s is the attitude toward the source, and d_c the attitude toward the concept. The values for the constants allow i, or the correction for incredulity, to increase as the total pressure toward congruity or the absolute value of P increases.

Assertion Constant

According to the congruity model, change in both source and concept occurs as a result of linkage via an assertion. Common sense, however, seems to imply that the object of an assertion is more likely to be affected than is the source of the assertion. Osgood and Tannenbaum take this matter into account by adding a constant, the assertion constant, to the predicted change for the object of the assertion or the concept. The constant (±A) is positive for associative assertions and negative for

---

[1] This implication is modified by the assertion constant discussed below.

dissociative assertions and has been empirically determined by Osgood and Tannenbaum to be .17 in units of the 7-step semantic differential scale.

RESEARCH

Prestige Suggestion

Inasmuch as the area of research that has been traditionally labeled prestige suggestion is relevant to congruity theory, it will be briefly reviewed in this section. Research on prestige suggestion involves the study of the effectiveness of prestigious or nonprestigious sources in changing the evaluations of statements and objects. In this section there will be no attempt to cover all of the literature that might be considered relevant to this topic. For example, there will be no discussion of studies concerned with group influence or with the influence of prestigious sources on the acceptance of persuasive communications.

Farnsworth and Misumi (*1931*) attached the names of well-known painters (da Vinci, Rembrandt, Raphael, and Rubens) or of unknown painters (Doughty, Kensett, Dewing, and Smibert) to eight paintings that were judged for quality by two groups of subjects. The four paintings which had well-known names attached for one group of subjects had unknown names attached for the other group, and vice versa. For all eight paintings it was found that the attachment of a well-known name produced a more favorable rating than the attachment of an unknown name. However, for only three of the eight paintings was the effect large enough to be significant. No overall test of significance was reported.

Saadi and Farnsworth (*1934*) asked subjects to indicate, on a 5-point scale, their degree of agreement-disagreement with a series of 30 statements. Every statement was associated for some subjects with a best liked name, for some subjects with a least liked name, and for some subjects with no name. The best liked names (e.g., Lindbergh, Edison, Aristotle) and the least liked names (e.g., Capone, Sunday, Hearst) were selected on the basis of previously obtained student ratings. The only statement example reported is the following: "There is nothing sacred about the American constitution. If it doesn't serve its purpose, it should be changed as often as necessary" (p. 147).

The results of the experiment were not clear-cut. For 14 of the 30 statements the order of decreasing agreement was exactly as predicted: liked name, no name, disliked name. For eight of the statements the order of decreasing agreement was only partially as predicted: liked name, disliked name, no name. And for the remaining eight statements there were a number of orders in which either the no name or disliked name condition produced the most agreement. Saadi and Farnsworth indicate that possibly some of the unexpected results could be explained in terms of a differentiation between liking for the statement source and knowledge of the source's practical acquaintance with the subject matter of the statement. This is the first mention of the importance of differentiating between source prestige and source competence.

Sherif (*1935a*) investigated the effect of prestige suggestion upon the liking-disliking of prose passages. Subjects were presented with 16 short prose passages and asked to rank them in order of preference. Associated with each prose passage was the name of a different author. In actuality all of the passages were written by Robert Louis Stevenson. Sherif correlated the subjects' rankings of the passages with the previously obtained rankings of the authors. The subjects were divided into two groups according to whether they reported that they did or did not make special effort to overcome the influence of the authors' names. From a group of 33 Harvard subjects, 25 reported that they did not make an effort to overcome the influence of the authors. The average correlation for this group was +.45. The correlation for the remaining 8 subjects who reported the opposite was −.03. From a group of 19 Radcliffe subjects, 11 reported that they did not make any special effort to overcome the authors' influence. The average correlation for these subjects was +.53. The average correlation for the 8 remaining subjects was +.04.

Sherif replicated the above experiment with a variation which involved utilizing, for different groups of subjects, two different pairings of authors and passages to control for the intrinsic merit of the passages. Sherif reports that the average correlations for 22 Harvard students, 17 Radcliffe students, 10 extension course adults, and 8 school of education students who made no attempt to overcome the authors' influence were +.33, +.45, +.30, and +.31, respectively. The average correlation for 9 subjects who indicated that they attempted to ignore the authors was +.03.

In a similar study carried out with Turkish subjects, authors, and prose passages, the average correlation was +.45 for 67 males and +.47 for 39 females. Sherif states that the records of a "few" subjects who disregarded the authors were discarded. The correlation for these subjects is not reported.

Sherif's procedure of ignoring the data from some of his subjects obviously is open to criticism. All we can conclude on the basis of the reported results is that prestige suggestion appears to have some influence on the literary judgments of some people.

Lorge (*1936*), in a well-known experiment, presented evidence in support of the doctrine of prestige suggestion. The experiment involved three separate sessions. In the first session subjects indicated on a 5-point scale their respect for the political opinions of individuals such as Lenin, Jefferson, Marx, and Hoover. In the second session subjects rated on a 5-point scale their agreement with a series of 100 political or economic quotations and also guessed which of two individuals was actually the author of the quotation. In the third session the subjects again indicated their agreement with the quotations, which this time, however, had the correct authors indicated. The data were analyzed by ascertaining whether the change in authors from the second to the third session involved an increase, decrease, or no change in prestige. It was found that with increased prestige there was increased agreement, with decreased prestige there was decreased agreement, and with no change in prestige there was very minimal change in agreement ($+.034$). Furthermore, the greater the increase in prestige the greater the increase in agreement. For an increase of one scale unit the agreement change was $+.314$, for two scale units $+.557$, for three scale units $+.935$, and for four scale units $+.960$. The relationship for decreasing prestige was not quite as consistent. For a decrease of one scale unit the agreement change was $-.131$, for two scale units $-.171$, for three scale units $-.300$, and for four scale units $-.190$. One further aspect of the data is the fact that an increase in prestige produced more change in the agreement ratings than did a decrease in prestige. Although neither this nor the preceding findings are supported by tests of significance, Lorge does not hesitate to point out that the data as a whole are consistent with Thorndike's Law of Effect. According to Lorge, the increasing agreement produced by increasing author prestige resulted from the reward associated with agreeing with prestigious individuals. Furthermore, the fact that the increase in author prestige produced more change than the decrease in author prestige is consistent with Thorndike's truncated Law of Effect which states that only reward and not punishment is crucially important in producing learning.

Asch (1948) has pointed out a number of things about the Lorge experiment. For example, those subjects who, because of superior social knowledge, correctly identified the quotations in the second session of necessity contributed less to the study than did the other subjects. Furthermore, those quotations which, because of greater ambiguity or obscurity, made it more difficult to identify the correct authors, contributed more to the study than did the other, less ambiguous, quotations. Also, the greater change produced by the increase rather than the decrease in prestige can be attributed to the difference in the initial agreement ratings. More of the initial agreement ratings for the quotations which were later associated with less prestigious authors were at the extreme end of the scale. Asch argued that quotations which are clear-cut enough so as to be rated at one extreme end of a scale are probably going to show less change later on.

Duncker (*1938*) investigated the effect of prestige suggestion upon the food preferences of nursery school children ranging between 2 and 5 years in age. The children selected foodstuffs in order of preference from a low table. The foodstuffs (carrots, bananas, nuts, apples, bread, and grapes) were all presented in equal quantities. Duncker found that if the children were tested in pairs, the older child was more influential. When the older child made his choices first, 26 out of 28 of the choices were identical; when the younger child was first, 14 out of 24 were identical. These results, although not accompanied by tests of significance, were interpreted to mean that the older child was more influential because he was more prestigious. In a further variation Duncker found that when adult experimenters made choices before individual children made theirs, only 4 out of 17 of the choices were identical. Duncker interpreted these results as indicating that age differential alone is not sufficient to produce a prestige effect. A process of group formation and identification is necessary before imitation will occur.

In a third variation Duncker investigated the influence of the food preferences of heroes in a story upon the food preferences of the children. The children were told a short story in which two characters expressed a strong preference for one unfamiliar food and distaste for another. Then, on six different occasions throughout the next 15 days, the children actually tasted the foods and indicated which they liked best. The initial superior preference for the heroes' food steadily declined until the twelfth day when it was approximately equal to the preference of a control group which had not heard the story. On the twelfth day the children were reminded of the previously presented story and their preferences for the heroes' food markedly increased. None of these results, however, were accompanied by tests of significance.

Duncker presents an interesting theoretical account of prestige suggestion that anticipates some later developments. He mentions three ways in which a disliked or neutral object can become liked due to social suggestion. First of all, there is changed preference, not so much because the object is genuinely liked but because of the feeling of being in harmony with other peoples' expressed attitudes. Second, there is modification in the object of judgment either because the influence attempt provides a new meaning through modified context or because the influence attempt produces a favorable attitude toward discovering or emphasizing favorable object elements. Third, there is modification in the subject produced through repeated exposures. Repeatedly eating a disliked food may eventually produce a genuine liking for the food.

Duncker's point about the modification of the object produced

through the new contextual meaning provided by the influence anticipates Asch's (1948, 1952) elaboration of the same idea. According to
Duncker an object of judgment in association with a prestigious source
may have an entirely different meaning from the same object in association with a neutral or nonprestigious source. The food, as the food preferred by the heroes in the story, acquired new meaning and, thus, was
to some extent a changed object of judgment. Duncker (1938) states,
however, that "even in the story experiment, to say nothing of the group
experiments, the acquisition of such a (symbolic) meaning can hardly
have been more than a minor element of the social effect" (p. 505).

Asch, Block, and Hertzman (1938) investigated the phenomenon of
prestige suggestion with an after-only design. A control group ranked
10 political slogans in terms of five dimensions: intelligence of author,
ability to compel to action, social significance, personal inspiration, and
personal approval. An experimental group of 30 subjects was then given
a set of rankings for intelligence, correlating −1 with the median rankings of the control group, and asked to rank the statements in terms of
the remaining four dimensions. The experimental group was told that
the intelligence rankings were made by a group of the country's leading
psychologists. The results indicated that in 66 percent of the cases the
mean rank scores for the 10 slogans on each of the four dimensions shifted
away from the similar control group rankings in the direction of the bogus
standard (−1 intelligence rankings). No tests of significance were reported. Asch, Block, and Hertzman also indicate that there was only a
slight tendency for the intercorrelations between the four dimensions to
be lower in the experimental than in the control group. The results were
interpreted as implying that prestige suggestion generally produced in-
consequential or small effects.

Lewis (1941) investigated prestige suggestion using the same 10
political slogans and five dimensions of ranking as did Asch, Block, and
Hertzman (1938). A control group ranked the 10 slogans on the five
dimensions, and an experimental group was given the slogans with intelligence rankings that correlated +1 or −1 with those of the control group.
For half of the subjects the intelligence rankings were attributed to
Hoover and for half to Roosevelt. The subjects' task was to rank the
slogans on the remaining four dimensions. Lewis found that the correlations between the rankings of the mean experimental group on each
dimension and the rankings of the mean control group on the same
dimensions were mostly in the .80's and .90's with the +1 rankings and
were somewhat lower, particularly for Roosevelt, with the −1 rankings.
Since the majority of the subjects were of a liberal political persuasion,
it is understandable that Roosevelt should be more influential. Despite
the fact that no tests of significance were made, the results were interpreted as indicating that "under all experimental conditions mean rank-

ings remain substantially unchanged" (pp. 236–237). A further breakdown of the data was done in terms of the political affiliation of the
subjects. Once again some prestige suggestion effects were evident, particularly for the subjects of radical political affiliation when exposed to the
—1 Roosevelt rankings, but no tests of significance were reported.

The most interesting part of Lewis' results has to do with the
questionnaire responses obtained from the subjects at the conclusion of
the experiment. Lewis repeatedly found that the subjects reinterpreted
the meaning of the slogans so as to make more understandable the rankings that were attributed to either Hoover or Roosevelt. Here is an example: "Mr. Roosevelt's rankings of the slogans was intelligent since he
merely considered the intelligence of the author in putting across a point
(I think) and not the intelligence of the point put across" (p. 244).

The overall results were interpreted as indicating that suggestion
did not cause the subjects to change their judgments but simply operated
so as to redefine an ambiguous situation. The slogans acquired new meaning in the context of Roosevelt's or Hoover's rankings. Duncker (1938)
earlier made the same point without attributing as much theoretical importance to it.

Asch (1948, 1952) further amplified the Duncker thesis and made
a major theoretical point of view out of it. Asch presented subjects with
some of the political statements used by Lorge (1936) and had them
write paragraphs indicating what the statements meant. Some of the
statements were accompanied by prestigious authors and some by nonprestigious authors. This qualitative approach revealed that the differing
authors produced quite different interpretations. As an illustration consider the following statement: "I hold it that a little rebellion, now and
then, is a good thing, and is as necessary in the political world as storms
are in the physical" (Lorge, 1936, p. 391). When this statement was
attributed to Jefferson it seemed to imply a need for peaceful political
agitation. When, however, it was attributed to Lenin it seemed to be a
justification of the Russian Revolution. Similar differing interpretations
were found for the other statements for which Asch reports results.

Asch argues that Lorge's subjects were not influenced to change their
opinions by the prestigious or nonprestigious authors, but simply that the
authors changed the meanings of the statements with which they were
associated. A statement associated with a prestigious author was not the
same statement when associated with a nonprestigious author. Thus, we
have not attitude or opinion change, but meaning change.

Asch undoubtedly has made a contribution with this unique theoretical point of view. To what extent, however, it can be generalized
so as to cover all influence situations, as Asch seemingly would like to do,
is a highly debatable matter. Duncker (1938), who first made the point
about changed contextual meaning, doubted that it was anything more

than a partial explanation of the results in his food preference experiments. On the basis of Asch's and Lorge's studies we have evidence that the association of a particular author with a particular statement results both in a certain meaning and in a certain judgment. This correlation between meaning and judgment, however, is highly ambiguous as to its causal significance. Is it the case, as Asch maintains, that meaning causes judgment, or is it the case that judgment causes meaning, or that both causal sequences occur? If judgment causes meaning, then we have, as Krech and Crutchfield (1948) have pointed out, a kind of rationalization, and it is possible that in many influence situations something like this may occur. It is also at least as possible that influence causes both judgment and meaning and that judgment and meaning are not directly causally related. In any event, until Asch becomes somewhat more analytic in his investigations he will not succeed in demonstrating that a changed meaning context is the crucial determinant of a modification in judgment.[2]

Birch (*1945*) investigated the phenomenon of prestige suggestion by presenting subjects with a labeled or unlabeled paragraph statement that argued for increased civil liberty, socio-economic justice, and government regulation of industry. The paragraph was either labeled Communistic or Liberal or not labeled at all. The subjects indicated their agreement with the paragraph on a 6-point scale. The mean agreements with the paragraph in the Communist, unlabeled, and Liberal conditions were 3.6, 4.0, and 4.3 respectively. While neither of the labeled means differs significantly from the unlabeled mean, the labeled means, 3.6 and 4.3, do differ significantly from each other.

Michael, Rosenthal, and DeCamp (*1949*) asked subjects to rank poems or prose selections associated with certain authors in order of preference. The poems, prose selections, and authors had previously been separately ranked by the same subjects. The authors were associated with the selections so that the mean rank order of preferences for authors and selections correlated −1. Michael, Rosenthal, and DeCamp found little support for the doctrine of prestige suggestion. Small, inconsistent, and generally nonsignificant shifts occurred in the rerankings of the poems. A number of significant shifts did occur in the reranking of the prose selections, but the direction of shifts was only roughly in line with expectations based on the prestige of the associated authors. The picture was made still more complex by the fact that a control group which reranked the selections without the associated authors showed a large number of inconsistent but significant shifts.

Michael, Rosenthal, and DeCamp's procedure of associating selec-

---

[2] Rosenberg (1960a, 1960c) obtained some results, discussed in Chapter 9, which indicate that, at least in some circumstances, a change in judgment can cause a change in meaning.

tions and authors in a rank order of −1 guarantees that the greater the prestige of the authors the greater the initial lack of preference for the selections. Such confounding of author prestige with lack of preference for the authors' selections may account for the inconclusive results.

Hastorf and Piper (1951) investigated the effect of differing instructions at the time of the second administration of a test in a before-after investigation of prestige suggestion. Prestige suggestion is typically investigated by first measuring opinions or attitudes toward certain issues and then some time later remeasuring the same opinions or attitudes in the context of a prestige suggestion manipulation. The rationale for the second measure is usually vaguely stated and no mention is made of the first measure. Hastorf and Piper had three groups of subjects, one control and two experimental, which were obtained from a course in advertising at Dartmouth. All of the group responded on a 7-point, agree-disagree scale to 45 statements concerned with economics and education. One month later all groups filled out the same questionnaire a second time. At this time the two experimental groups were supplied with the bogus responses of "100 businessmen and educators here in the East." For 30 of the statements the bogus responses were 2 points discrepant from the previous mean group judgment, and for 15 they were identical with the previous mean group judgment. When the second questionnaire was administered the control group and one experimental group were given exactly the same instructions as previously. The other experimental group was told that they were to attempt to fill out the questionnaire in exactly the same way as previously, and that the investigator was interested in determining the magnitude of correlation between the first and second administrations. The results indicated that there was little difference between the two experimental groups. In the experimental group given the same instructions on both occasions 97 percent of the items shifted in the direction of the influence manipulations, and for 14 of the 30 items the shift was significant. In the other experimental group 93 percent of the items shifted in the direction of the influence, and for 13 of the 30 items the shift was significant. In the control group 40 percent of the items shifted in the direction of the nonpresent influence, and for 3 of the items the shift was significant. Although no overall tests of significance were made comparing the experimental groups, or the experimental groups with the control group, the results appear to lend support to the doctrine of prestige suggestion and to ease concern about the type of instructions used in the second session of the typical before-after design.

Cole (1954) exposed subjects to various influence attempts regarding the merit of four previously ranked abstract finger paintings. In one set of conditions the subjects were divided into small unstructured groups and asked to discuss the paintings. The groups were so constituted that each contained one sociometric star. With this simple procedure it was found that a nonsignificant 14 percent of the subjects raised their rankings of the paintings preferred by the stars. When, however, the stars were taken into the confidence of the experimenter and given a series of pseudorational arguments to support their rankings a significant 70 percent of the subjects were influenced. Although no significance test comparing the amount of influence in the two conditions was reported, the results were taken as indicating that prestige suggestion without bolstering rational arguments is ineffective. In another set of conditions the subjects were involved in a group discussion led either by a professor in the art department or by the experimenter. The art professor made clear what his preferences were and backed up these preferences with rational arguments. The experimenter, in the course of the group discussion he led, indicated several times the preferences of the art professor without any supporting arguments. The former procedure influenced a significant 70 percent of the subjects and the latter a nonsignificant 20 percent. Again, although no significance test comparing the two conditions was reported, the results were interpreted as indicating that prestige suggestion without the support of rational arguments is ineffective. Cole argues that his results indicate that the positive results from other prestige suggestion experiments may have been due in part to the implicit assumption that the prestigious sources could back up their judgments with rational arguments.

Das (1960) found that Indian subjects (incoming male students in the psychology department) were more responsive to body-sway suggestions when they came from the taped voice of the department head than from the taped voices of the laboratory assistant, attendant of the department, or an unidentified person. All the voices except the latter were identified before they made the suggestions. Cole's (1954) statement about prestige suggestion being effective because of the subject's implicit assumption that the prestigious sources could back up their assertions with rational arguments is an implausible explanation of these results.

Horowitz and Pastore (1955) presented subjects with a series of 10 statements paired with authors, some of whom were generally deemed of high esteem (Roosevelt) and some of whom were generally deemed of low esteem (Lenin). The subjects indicated on 9-point scales their degree of agreement-disagreement with the statements and their degree of respect-disrespect for the authors of the statements. The subjects also described what they thought were the authors' motives in making the statements. The motives were independently classified by judges as "praise-worthy," "condemnable," and "cannot-evaluate."

Although no tests of significance were reported, the results appear and were interpreted to indicate that the greater the esteem with which an author is held the greater the tendency to attribute good motives to what he said, and the less the esteem with which an author is held the greater the tendency to attribute bad motives to what he said. Also, the more the subjects agreed with a statement the greater the tendency to attribute good motives to the author, and the less the subjects agreed with a statement the greater the tendency to attribute bad motives to the author. These results were interpreted as indicating that the relation between a statement and an author is at least partially mediated by an attributed motive.

Pastore and Horowitz (1955) experimentally manipulated the motives attributed to prestigious or nonprestigious sources in making certain statements. Subjects were presented with 10 statements, each of which had either a positive or negative author and a positive or negative motive attached. With no apparent rationale each author's motive in making any given statement was simply described to the subjects. The results indicated both a greater acceptance of the statements when they were attributed to positive authors and a greater acceptance of the statements when the authors were described as having positive (praiseworthy) motives.

Goldberg and Iverson (1965) found that high status (prestige) people are more persuasive than low status people. Individually tested subjects initially filled out a 30-item questionnaire dealing with various aspects of health and nutrition and then listened to three taped communications dealing with the same topics. Each communication was relevant to a different group of the original 30 questionnaire items. After listening to each communication a stooge, who was supposedly another subject, indicated his responses to the relevant questionnaire items and the subject responded to these items for a second time. Half of the subjects were told that the stooge was a second-year medical student who had graduated from the university with honors (high status) and half were told that he was a hospital orderly who had not gone beyond his junior year in high school (low status). Before-after change scores indicated a significantly greater amount of influence for the high status stooge than the low status stooge.

Comment. The literature on prestige suggestion seems to indicate that prestigious sources can produce some influence in some situations. Exact specification of the situations or conditions under which prestige suggestion is effective, however, has not been achieved. Variables such as ambiguity of the statements, competence of the authors, and extent of initial statement disagreement have not been systematically explored. Further, little is known about the mechanisms producing the prestige suggestion effect. Does the prestige of the source act directly so as to produce a change in judgment or is this change mediated by imputed motives or modified contextual meaning? Hopefully, future studies will strive to provide answers to these questions rather than just attempting to demonstrate that prestige suggestion is or is not a genuine phenomenon.

Direct Tests of the Congruity Model

The doctrine of prestige suggestion implies that the linking of a source with a concept will change the evaluation of the concept. Congruity theory, however, implies that such a linkage will change both the evaluation of the source and the concept. The theory further makes exact mathematical predictions as to the extent of change in each. The present section describes the studies which have tested these predictions.

Osgood and Tannenbaum (*1955*) tested congruity theory with some data obtained from Tannenbaum's (1953, 1956) thesis. On the basis of a pretest Tannenbaum selected three sources (Labor Leaders, Chicago Tribune, Senator Robert Taft) and three concepts (Legalized Gambling, Abstract Art, Accelerated College Programs) toward which an approximately equal number of subjects held favorable, neutral, and unfavorable attitudes. A new group of subjects then rated these sources and concepts on the evaluative scales of the semantic differential. The subjects were told that the purpose of the study was to find out how college students feel about current issues and personalities and also to try out a new instrument in the assessment of these feelings. Five weeks later the same subjects were presented with reproductions of realistically written newspaper stories in which the sources made favorable or unfavorable assertions about the concepts. The materials were reproduced in standard newspaper type along with appropriate headlines. The subjects were told that the previous study (the before test) had shown the measuring instrument to be a useful one, and that now the experimenter wanted to see how it compared with a standard method in the field, the "Johnson technique." This technique involved reading a story and then writing its essence in 25 words or less. After writing out the story descriptions, the subjects marked the evaluative scales of the semantic differential supposedly for comparative purposes. On the basis of the scores from the before test, attitudes toward each source and concept were classified as either being positive, neutral, or negative. Change scores for each of the nine possible combinations of attitude toward source and concept were obtained by subtracting the before scores from the after scores. For each of the nine possible source-concept combinations, a comparison of the obtained changes with the predicted changes as corrected for incredulity revealed a fairly high degree of correspondence. All of the predicted directions of positive and negative changes were obtained, while predicted lack of change was substantiated through minimal obtained change. The predicted changes, however, were more accurate in magnitude for the sources than for the concepts. From these data Osgood and Tannenbaum obtained their assertion constant to correct for the fact that concept changes were generally larger than source changes. When the obtained data were corrected on the basis of the empirically obtained assertion constant, the correlation between obtained and predicted change for positive and negative assertions combined was +.91.

Osgood and Tannenbaum further analyzed the data by testing certain specific implications of the congruity model. One of these implications is that the more favorable the attitude toward the first object of judgment, the greater the effect of an associative assertion on raising attitude toward the second object of judgment and the greater the effect of a dissociative assertion upon lowering attitude toward the second object of judgment, whereas strongly unfavorable first objects of judgment have the opposite effect. Although the change scores, even after correction by the assertion constant, were less than the predicted ones, the trends were significant in the anticipated directions. Osgood and Tannenbaum (1955) state that the discrepancy between predicted and obtained change presumably results from the "limited effect of a single message" (p. 54). They state that the theory takes into account neither learning through successive assertions nor intensity of assertion and thus imply that an adequate theory ought to take into account these variables.

A second implication of the congruity model is that the association of a neutral object of judgment with a polarized object of judgment (plus or minus) should result in the neutral object of judgment changing more than the polarized object of judgment. In all eight instances in which a neutral object of judgment was associated with a polarized object of judgment in Tannenbaum's data, this prediction was upheld.

A third implication of the congruity model is that when an associative assertion links two objects of judgment of like sign, or a dissociative assertion links two objects of judgment of unlike sign, the more polarized object of judgment becomes less so. This implication includes the paradoxical situation in which a highly polarized object like Eisenhower (+3) becomes less polarized by praising less polarized objects like golf (+1) or denouncing less polarized objects like comic books (−1). It also includes the previously mentioned situation in which Castro (−2) becomes less negative by being denounced by Stevenson (+1). Of the 38 cases in which it was possible to test this prediction, 21 (55.3 percent) showed small changes in the predicted direction, 15 (39.5 percent) showed no change, and 2 (5.3 percent) changed in the opposite direction. The data are thus only mildly supportive of the theoretical implication. One possible difficulty has to do with regression toward the mean. The prediction states that highly polarized objects of judgment should change toward neutrality, i.e., in the direction of the mean. Thus the obtained results could be simple regression effects.

Stachowiak and Moss (1965) obtained evidence supporting the congruity predictions with regard to the direction of change but not with regard to the amount of change. After having evaluated "experimenter" and "Negro" along with a number of other concepts on an evaluative semantic differential, a group of male college students were individually exposed to an 11-minute oral communication favorable toward Negroes. The communication was delivered by the experimenter. At the conclusion of the presentation the subjects marked the evaluative semantic differential scales for a second time. Approximately 2 weeks later the subjects marked the scales for a third time.

The initial ratings of "experimenter" were quite positive and of "Negro" very slightly positive. Congruity theory thus predicts that on the second and third ratings "experimenter" (the source of the communication) should become less positive and "Negro" (the object of the communication) should become more positive. This prediction was upheld with regard to both the change from the first to the second rating and the change from the first to the third rating. Congruity theory also predicts that the least polarized object of judgment, "Negro," should change more than the most polarized object of judgment, "experimenter." This prediction was not upheld; "experimenter" changed more than did "Negro." Furthermore, the total amount of change for both objects of judgment was not sufficient to produce complete congruity. Stachowiak and Moss report that in a personal communication to them Osgood suggested that possibly the initial ratings of "Negro" were distorted so as to be more positive than was actually the case. This conceivably could account for the fact that the change in this concept was too small.

Kerrick (1958) studied the capability of the congruity model to predict concept change under the influence of both relevant and nonrelevant sources. She used a before-after design and presented source concept associations, as had Tannenbaum (1953), in the form of newspaper stories printed in newspaper type and set in newspaper column width. Semantic differential measures of attitude toward four concepts (protective tariffs for farm products, abstract art, flexible price supports, recognition of Red China) and four sources (Henry Wallace, Director of the Museum of Modern Art, U.S. Department of Agriculture, John Foster Dulles) were taken 2 weeks before and immediately after reading the newspaper stories. The sources and concepts were selected so that source 1 (Henry Wallace) was relevant to concept 1 (protective tariffs for farm products) but not relevant to concept 2 (abstract art), and source 2 was relevant to concept 2 but not to concept 1, etc. Two groups of 40 subjects each were used. In each group every subject received two relevant and two nonrelevant source-concept pairings or newspaper stories. Kerrick found that in the relevant situation two of the four sources and two of the four concepts showed significant change, while in the nonrelevant situation one source and one concept showed significant change. No overall test of significance comparing relevant and nonrelevant change was reported. Kerrick did report, however, that for all sources and for all concepts the congruity model predicted significantly better for the relevant than for the nonrelevant situations. Eighty-three percent of the total source shift was predicted in the relevant situation and 70.5 percent in the nonrelevant situation ($p < .01$). The corresponding percentages for the concept shifts are 97.5 in the relevant situation and 82.5 in the nonrelevant situation ($p < .1$.) Thus Kerrick has demonstrated that the congruity model is insufficient insofar as it does not include the variable of source relevancy.

Kerrick (*1961*) investigated the effects of differing instructional sets upon attitude change. Using newspaper stories to pair sources with concepts and a before-after design, as in the previous experiment, Kerrick, at the time of the after test, told one group of subjects that she was interested in finding out whether or not the newspaper stories had influenced their attitudes and another group that the after test was to provide a validity check on some of the semantic differential scales. The results indicated that the uninformed group changed in the advocated directions significantly more than did the informed group, and the informed group changed in the nonadvocated directions nonsignificantly more than did the uninformed group. Further, in six out of six instances (source and concept on three separate issues) the congruity predictions were in the correct direction for the uninformed group and in the incorrect direction for the informed group. Congruity theory, of course, makes no predictions for informed subjects.

Tannenbaum and Gengel (*1966*) demonstrated that a change in attitude toward a given concept will generalize so as to produce a change in attitude toward a source which previously made an assertion about that concept. Two weeks after subjects evaluated the concept "teaching machines" along with three sources, "Dr. George L. Maclay," "Dr. Walter E. Samuels," and "Dr. Kenneth W. Spence" on semantic differential scales, a group of college students was exposed to a message designed to create links between the sources and the concept. The message described a symposium at the American Psychological Association in which Dr. Maclay supported teaching machines, Dr. Samuels opposed teaching machines, and Dr. Spence, as moderator, remained neutral. Following this linking message the subjects were exposed to a communication ascribed to the U.S. Office of Education. For half of the subjects the communication favored teaching machines and for half the communication opposed teaching machines.

In order for congruity to be achieved a favorable change in attitude toward teaching machines should produce a favorable attitude toward the source with a positive linkage (Dr. Maclay) and an unfavorable change in attitude toward the source with a negative linkage (Dr. Samuels). An unfavorable change in attitude toward teaching machines, however, should produce an unfavorable change in attitude toward the source with positive linkage and a favorable change in attitude toward the source with negative linkage. The obtained results were as follows. For the subjects exposed to the communication favorable toward teaching machines the source with positive linkage changed 4.75, the source with neutral linkage 4.08, and the source with negative linkage 1.87. For the subjects exposed to the communication unfavorable toward teaching machines the source with positive linkage changed 1.44, the source with neutral linkage 3.59, and the source with negative linkage 3.61. The interaction between favorableness of the communication and type of linkage is significant, as predicted. The changes, however, were always in the positive direction. Theoretically, when a concept changes in the favorable direction a source with a negative linkage to that concept should change in a negative direction, and when a concept changes in an unfavorable direction a source with a positive linkage to that concept should change in a negative direction. These data indicate that this did not occur. An additional analysis of just those subjects within each communication condition who actually changed their attitudes toward teaching machines in the direction of the communication obtained somewhat more supportive results. For the subjects who changed their attitudes toward teaching machines in a favorable direction the source with positive linkage changed 5.49, the source with neutral linkage 3.98, and the source with negative linkage 1.16. For the subjects who changed their attitudes toward teaching machines in an unfavorable direction the source with positive linkage changed −.25, the source with neutral linkage 3.52, and the source with negative linkage 4.88. Tannenbaum and Gengel argue that the insignificant or small negative changes may have resulted from the linkage message creating a generally favorable impression of all the sources. The fact that the neutral source changed in a positive direction is consistent with this hypothesis. A control group which assessed attitude toward the sources before and immediately after the linkage message could have provided information on this matter.

Tannenbaum (1966) obtained evidence indicating that a change in attitude toward a given concept will generalize so as to produce a change in attitude toward a source which previously made an assertion about that concept and also to an additional concept about which the source has made an assertion. One week after subjects had rated the concepts "teaching machines" and "Spence learning theory" and the source "Prof.

Walter E. Samuels" on semantic differential scales, male high school students were exposed to one of four linking messages. One message described Samuels as being positive about both concepts, one as being negative about both concepts, one as being positive about teaching machines but negative about Spence learning theory, and one as being negative about teaching machines but positive about Spence learning theory. Half of the subjects in each of these four groups were then exposed to a communication favorable to teaching machines and half to a communication unfavorable to teaching machines.

Changes in attitudes toward teaching machines should theoretically generalize so as to affect attitude toward the source. For the subjects exposed to the communication favorable toward teaching machines positive linkage to this concept should produce positive change in the source and negative linkage should produce negative change in the source. For the subjects exposed to the communication unfavorable toward teaching machines positive linkage should produce negative change in the source and negative linkage should produce positive change in the source. This predicted pattern of results was obtained. The predicted negative changes, unlike in the Tannenbaum and Gengel (1966) experiment, were successfully obtained.

The predicted pattern of results with regard to change in the Spence learning theory concept are somewhat complex. If the generalized change in the source is positive, then attitude change toward Spence learning theory should be positive if the linkage is positive and negative if the linkage is negative. If the generalized change in the source is negative, then attitude change toward Spence learning theory should be negative if the linkage is positive and positive if the linkage is negative. This predicted pattern of results was significantly obtained.

These results are remarkable. Not only did attitude change generalize from a manipulated concept to a linked source, but also from the source to an additional linked concept. These findings provide strong support for congruity theory as well as for all balance or consistency formulations generally. The one puzzling matter has to do with why negative change in the sources was evidenced to a greater degree in the present experiment than in the Tannenbaum and Gengel (1966) experiment. Tannenbaum states that small changes in the persuasive communications, the use of a somewhat different experimental design, and the use of high school rather than college students as subjects may have produced the difference.

Kerrick (1959) studied the capability of the congruity model for predicting the evaluation of captioned news pictures on the basis of separate evaluations of the individual captions and news pictures. Subjects were presented with booklets containing five pictures alone, five captions alone, and five caption-picture combinations and asked to evaluate each on semantic differential scales. Two different forms of the booklet were prepared so that the caption-picture combinations could be varied. Kerrick (1959, p. 184) describes one of the pictures and the two different captions that were used as follows:

Picture 5 was a rear view of two small children, one with the arms around the other:
(C+) TWO-YEAR-OLD Donna Allen comforts her brother David, 4, as they watch firemen rescue their pet kitten from a tree.
(C−) TWO-YEAR-OLD Donna Allen comforts her brother David, 4, as they watch a Humane Officer carry away the broken body of their pet dog, Rumble. The dog was killed by a hit-and-run driver.

As can be seen from this example there was an attempt to make one of the captions positive in evaluation and one negative in evaluation. If a picture was associated with a positive caption in one booklet it was associated with a negative caption in the other.

Kerrick found that for three of the five pictures both the positive and negative captions produced significant changes in evaluation while for one picture only the positive caption produced a significant change. The remaining picture was not significantly changed by either the positive or negative captions. Of the 10 predicted shifts in evaluation 9 were in the directions predicted by the uncorrected congruity formulas. However, as Kerrick points out, this is not the whole story because of the fact that in three out of six cases in which the captions and pictures were on the same side of the scale the combinations were evaluated more extremely than either alone. Congruity theory predicts a point of resolution or equilibrium somewhere between the associated objects of judgment. Thus any such obtained summation effect is directly contrary to the theory.

Triandis and Fishbein (1963) investigated the adequacy of the congruity model to predict the evaluations of composite stimuli made up of four elements. Subjects rated, on a good-bad semantic differential scale, certain races, occupations, religions, and nationalities, and then certain combinations of all four of these characteristics represented as being individual persons. For example, the person might be described as white, bank manager, French, and of a certain religion. The Osgood and Tannenbaum formulas for predicting a point of equilibrium were expanded so as to include four and not just two judgment objects, and predictions were compared with those obtained from a type of summation formula developed by Fishbein (1961). According to the Fishbein formula, attitude toward the complex stimulus is a function of the algebraic sum of the attitudes toward the individual components with each attitude score multiplied by the belief, expressed in probabilistic terms, that the component is an actual part of the complex stimulus.

Symbolically the Fishbein formula (Triandis and Fishbein, 1963, p. 451) is stated as follows: [3]

$$A_o = \sum_{i=1}^{N} B_i\, a_i, \qquad\qquad (6\text{--}8)$$

where:

A = the attitude toward the stimulus
o = the complex stimulus
B_i = belief i about o
a_i = the evaluative aspect of B
N = the number of beliefs about o

Since in the present study there is little reason for the subjects to doubt that any of the four components actually characterized the experimentally represented stimulus individual, B_i was given a value of 1.

The subjects were 25 students from the University of Illinois and 25 students from the University of Athens. For both the American and Greek subjects it was found that the Fishbein predictions correlated significantly higher with the obtained good-bad evaluations than did the congruity predictions. The average correlation across both samples was $+.534$ for congruity theory and $+.651$ for Fishbein's theory ($p < .01$). Unfortunately the mean differences between the obtained and predicted judgments were not reported. Presumably the obtained scores exceeded those predicted by congruity theory, whereas this was not the case with the Fishbein predictions. It would be of interest, however, to know if the Fishbein predictions significantly exceeded the obtained scores. If all of the stimulus components were evaluated on the same side of the semantic differential scale (all positive or all negative), then the predicted composite evaluation would certainly be a very extreme one.

Anderson and Fishbein (*1965*) report a further study relating to the evaluation of an experimentally described stimulus person. In this study there was a comparison of the summation predictions with both the predictions of the extended version of the congruity formulas developed by Triandis and Fishbein (1963) and the predictions of a slightly different extension of the congruity formulas developed by Osgood (1963) himself. Some extension of the basic congruity formulas is necessary, of course, when predictions are made on the basis of more than just two associated objects of judgments. The results indicated that the obtained

---

[3] It is interesting to note the similarity between Formula 6–8 and Rosenberg's (1953, 1956) procedure of predicting attitude on the basis of the sum of the products of value and instrumentality ratings.

evaluations of the stimulus person correlated significantly better with predictions based on Fishbein's formula (+.66) than with correlations based on either of the two congruity formulas (+.38 and +.39).

Fishbein and Hunter (1964) report a study which investigated the effect of increasing amounts of information upon the evaluation of a stimulus person. If each added piece of information is positive then the summation interpretation predicts that the evaluation of the stimulus person should increase proportionately. A congruity or averaging point of view, however, predicts no change if the mean value of all of the information does not increase. In fact, if each added new piece of information is slightly less positive than the mean of the existing pieces of information then the congruity formula predicts decreased evaluation while the summation formula predicts increased evaluation. Subjects initially evaluated each of a series of positive adjectives and then evaluated a stimulus person (Mr. A) who was described with differing numbers of positive adjectives (one, two, four, or eight) for different subjects. An examination of the mean adjective evaluation based on the initial ratings indicated a nonsignificant tendency for the mean to decrease as the number of adjectives attributed to the stimulus person increased. Consistent with the summation point of view, however, evaluation of the stimulus person significantly increased with an increase in the number of attributed adjectives. No trend analyses were reported, but the function appears aproximately linear.

These results are intuitively compelling. It seems apparent that the more good things that are learned about an unfamiliar person the more positively he will be evaluated. There is a question, however, as to whether or not this process would keep on indefinitely. It seems very plausible that the more familiar a stimulus person becomes and the more certain the subject becomes in his evaluation of that stimulus person, the less likely it seems that additional positive information not differing from the existing overall evaluation would have much of an effect.

Anderson (1965a) has shown how an averaging formulation may account for the summation effect. As more and more positive adjectives are added to the description of the stimulus person that person is evaluated more and more highly. If the mean evaluations of the separate adjectives remain constant and the sum of the separate evaluations of the adjectives increases, then these results appear consistent with a summation formulation and inconsistent with an averaging formulation. Anderson has pointed out, however, that an averaging formulation can handle such results if it is assumed that the subjects initially begin with a neutral impression of the stimulus person. When this neutral impression is averaged with the separate evaluations of the adjectives, the mean evaluation increases with increasing numbers of highly polarized adjectives. With the aid of this notion plus some empirically derived weights for the separate adjectives, Anderson was able to predict the evaluations of the stimulus person more accurately than could a simple summation procedure.

Anderson's formulation predicts that with an increasing number of adjectives the evaluation of the stimulus person will increase more and more slowly. This is because each additional adjective will have a smaller and smaller effect on the mean as the number of adjectives increases. This fact should allow for a test of the relative predictive powers of Anderson's formulation and the summation formulation.

From the standpoint of congruity theory, however, Anderson's results are no more encouraging than are some of the previous results. Congruity theory is an averaging formulation but does not include any assumption regarding initial impressions that would account for the summation effect.

Comment. The research reviewed in this section is of two main types: studies in which the assertions are persuasive attempts and studies in which the assertions are perceptual groupings of stimuli, typically adjectives. The former group of studies is by and large more supportive of the congruity predictions than is the latter group. Except for problems involving the amount of change and the relevance of the source and concept, the attitude change studies give an encouraging degree of support to the congruity predictions. Congruity predictions with regard to the perceived evaluations of complex stimuli, however, are not nearly as accurate as some competing formulations, for example a simple summation procedure. It is of interest that no investigators have ever reported summation effects in an attitude change or persuasion situation. To the author's knowledge no one has ever reported that a favorable source's arguments in favor of a favorable concept has resulted in both the source and concept increasing in evaluation. This may reflect some rather basic differences between the persuasion and perceptual situations.

EVALUATION

Osgood and Tannenbaum's congruity theory is an impressive attempt to state exactly and mathematically some propositions that seem to have a fair amount of face validity. Many people, undoubtedly, would prefer a simple, verbally stated theory, arguing that any such mathematical theory is premature. It is evident, however, from an examination of the Osgood and Tannenbaum model that their mathematical statement has certain advantages. For one thing the mathematical statement allows for exact testing of the implications of the theory, and, for another, the mathematical statement makes obvious some of the inobvious implications of the theory.

One of the inobvious implications of the theory is that when an associative assertion links two objects of judgment of like sign or a dissociative assertion links two objects of judgment of unlike sign the more polarized object becomes less so. Osgood and Tannenbaum present some possibly artifactual data that are only mildly supportive of these predictions. A thorough testing of the theory will certainly need to involve further examination of these matters.

One thing that detracts from the elegance of the theory is that it is bolstered by two *ad hoc* corrections, one involving incredulity and the other, assertions. Neither of these corrections follows from the congruity principle and both are simply introduced, in an attempt to patch up and make more reasonable some of the congruity implications. The theory is also internally weak due to the fact that no definition of the crucial concept of assertion is given, and no satisfactory distinction between associative and dissociative assertions is made.

Kerrick's (1958) demonstration that congruity theory predicts significantly better for relevant than nonrelevant sources is evidence that Osgood and Tannenbaum need to further modify their theory. Despite the fact that Marilyn Monroe had considerable prestige her endorsement of some political candidate would have undoubtedly had little effect. Other variables not incorporated in the theory are those of intensity and repetition, which Osgood and Tannenbaum themselves mentioned. Osgood and Tannenbaum (1955) found that the obtained change was typically less than the predicted change and attributed this fact to "the limited effect of a single message" (p. 53).

Some of the most damaging evidence against congruity theory is that which indicates that summation effects occur in the perception of complex stimulus objects. Such summation effects will probably dictate an eventual revision of the theory.

Roger Brown (1962) has criticized congruity theory because it only allows for the resolution of incongruity or disequilibrium through the changed evaluations of the two associated objects of judgment. According to Brown, sometimes resolution may be achieved through a differentiation of one of the objects of judgment. For example, if a highly respected theatre critic writes a derogatory review after attending the opening performance of a highly respected play, resolution may be obtained by differentiating between the opening performance of the play and the subsequent performances of the play. Brown maintains that after such a process of differentiation it is not necessary to decrease the evaluation either of the play or of the theatre critic. This point is related to Asch's (1948, 1952) assertion that apparent prestige suggestion is a manifestation of a modified contextual meaning. Abelson (1959) discusses a number of responses to disequilibrium, not all of which involve attitude change. To the extent that equilibrium can be restored through change responses involving no attitude change, congruity theory obviously is inadequate. The theory nonetheless is a vast improvement over the old verbally stated doctrine of prestige suggestion.

7

Rokeach's Belief Congruence Theory

THEORY

Belief congruence theory was developed by Rokeach (Rokeach and Rothman, 1965) to get around some of the difficulties that he believed inherent in congruity theory. The theoretical statement is an extended elaboration of some earlier work by Rokeach (1960) and Rokeach, Smith, and Evans (1960).

Assertions

Rokeach and Rothman begin by assuming that any stimulus such as a verbal concept or event will tend to activate within the individual that portion of his belief system which is relevant to the stimulus. For example, the verbal concept "Communism" may activate relevant or associated beliefs dealing with such things as economics, politics, history, and war.

The more interesting situation, however, is one in which two stimuli are linked in some fashion. Following Osgood and Tannenbaum (1955), Rokeach and Rothman state that this linkage can be accomplished by either associative or dissociative assertions. (Osgood and Tannenbaum do not define associative and dissociative assertions but illustrate them with such examples as A likes B and A dislikes B, respectively.) Furthermore, these assertions can take any of four forms: linguistic qualification (beautiful woman), perceptual contiguity (picture of a celebrity smoking a particular brand of cigarettes), statement of classification (Jones is a psychologist), source-object assertions (Nasser opposes Israel).[1]

According to Rokeach and Rothman an assertion results in a unique cognitive configuration representing a *characterized subject* (*CS*). The characterized subject is a person, thing, or idea which is described in

[1] Presumably all four of these forms can be associative and only the last two dissociative, but Rokeach and Rothman do not discuss the matter.

some way. This CS has two components, a *subject* (S) capable of being characterized and a *characterization* (C) capable of being applied to subjects. For example, in the characterized subject "a white person who is a communist," "white person" represents the subject or S and "communist" represents the characterization or C.[2]

Relevance Comparison

According to Rokeach and Rothman when an individual encounters a CS the first thing he does is to ascertain whether or not the two components are relevant to each other. If he judges that they are not relevant, no new meaning derived from both components will emerge. One component will be ignored and the CS will have a meaning entirely attributable to the remaining component. If, however, the two components are judged relevant, then a second judgment dealing with importance will occur.

Relative Importance of C and S

Assuming at least some degree of relevance, the individual compares C and S for relative importance. This relative importance comparison allows for an overall evaluation of the entire CS. According to Rokeach and Rothman (1965) the evaluation of CS will be a simple average of the evaluations of C and S, each weighted by the judged relative importance of C and S within the context of CS. In symbols this is stated as follows:

$$d_{cs} = (w)d_c + (1 - w)d_s, \qquad (7\text{-}1)$$

where:

$d_{cs} =$ the degree of polarization of the characterized subject
$d_c =$ the degree of polarization of the characterization
$d_s =$ the degree of polarization of the subject
$(w) =$ the degree of importance of d_c relative to d_s
$(1 - w) =$ the degree of importance of d_s relative to d_c

This formula is analogous to Osgood and Tannenbaum's formula for predicting the equilibrium point for two associated objects of judgment.

---

[2] While in many instances, such as the above, it is perfectly clear what is subject and what is characterization, in other instances, such as "Nasser opposes Israel," it is not clear. Is Israel being characterized by Nasser's opposition or Nasser being characterized by his opposition to Israel? Again, Rokeach and Rothman offer no discussion.

In Osgood and Tannenbaum's formula, however, the associated objects of judgment, or components of the CS, are weighted according to their degree of polarization and not according to their judged relative importance.

Relative Importance of CS and C

In order to take into account possible overassimilation effects the theory is developed one step further. Assimilation results when the evaluation of CS more nearly conforms to the evaluation of one component than the other.[3] Overassimilation results when the evaluation of CS is even more polarized than the evaluation of either component. Rokeach and Rothman assert that when one of the components, for example C, reaches 100 percent in importance (and the other, of necessity, 0 percent in importance) then a third comparison process is activated. This is a comparison of the importance of one component with the importance of the characterized subject, CS. The necessity for this third comparison is illustrated with the hypothetical example of the individual who considers "irresponsible" as all-important in the context of "irresponsible father." On the basis of Formula 7–1 one would suppose that C would completely determine the evaluation of CS. Rokeach and Rothman argue, however, that this overlooks the possibility that the evaluation of CS may be even more extreme than the evaluation of C due to the interaction of C and S. "Irresponsible father" may be regarded as even more negative than "irresponsible" because of the feeling that fathers should not be irresponsible.

In the condition in which C reaches 100 percent in importance the combined effect of the comparison of C with S and CS with S is symbolically expressed as follows (Rokeach and Rothman, 1965, p. 130):

$$d_{cs} = d_c + (v)d_c, \qquad (7\text{--}2)$$

where d_{cs} refers to the degree of polarization of the characterized subject, d_c the degree of polarization of the characterization, and (v) the extent to which greater importance is attached to CS than to C. The latter value (v) is obtained from questionnaire responses in which subjects indicate the percent to which their feelings about some CS, like "irresponsible father," are more important than their feelings about the C, in this case "irresponsible."

One restriction for Formula 7–2 is that the value of d_{cs} cannot be allowed to exceed the most extreme score on the evaluation scale. There-

---

[3] A discussion of the relation between "assimilation" and "summation" will be delayed until the evaluation section.

fore if d_c equals the most extreme score, $d_c + (v)d_c$ is arbitrarily assigned the same score.

Principle of Belief Congruence

The principle of belief congruence is essentially a restatement of the above. When two stimuli are linked through an assertion they form a unique configuration activating two or possibly three comparison processes. The stimuli will first be compared for mutual relevance. If they are judged to be at least somewhat relevant they will then be compared for relative importance. Finally, in the special case in which one stimulus is 100 percent important and the other not at all important the total stimulus complex or CS will be compared with the more important stimulus. The quantitative results of the latter two comparisons are spelled out in terms of Formulas 7–1 and 7–2.

Comparison of Belief Congruence and Congruity Principles

Rokeach and Rothman further clarify the meaning of belief congruence through a comparison with Osgood and Tannenbaum's concept of congruity. First of all, Rokeach and Rothman point out that the congruity principle is an additive model in which the point of equilibrium is predicted on the basis of the evaluations of the two objects of judgment considered separately, while the belief congruence principle is a configurationist model in which the unique Gestalt formed by the two components cannot be predicted solely from information regarding their separate evaluations. Second, the congruity principle locates the incongruity between C and S (the two objects of judgment), while the belief congruence principle locates the incongruity between C and CS, or between S and CS, or both. This somewhat novel aspect of the belief congruence principle is expanded upon as follows:

The evaluative meaning of CS must somehow be made maximally congruent with one's belief system, which includes within it previously learned evaluative meanings of C and S. Since CS cannot be completely congruent with both C and S (assuming some discrepancy in the evaluative meaning of C and S), the question arises about the exact process whereby the evaluative meaning of CS will become maximally congruent with C and S. The principle of belief congruence attempts to describe how this outcome comes about. The more discrepant is the relative importance of C and S with respect to one another the greater the pressure to evaluate CS, positively or negatively, like C or like S, whichever is the most important, but not both. The more C equals S in importance, the more equalized the pressure from C and S. (Rokeach and Rothman, 1965, p. 132)

Third, Rokeach and Rothman point out that the congruity principle cannot account for overassimilation effects while the belief congruence principle can. Fourth, and finally, the congruity principle predictions are modified with an assertion constant guaranteeing relatively greater change in the object than in the source of an assertion, while the belief congruence predictions are not modified through any such *ad hoc* correction. Rokeach and Rothman argue that weighting C and S in terms of relative importance obviates the necessity for an assertion constant.

RESEARCH

Prejudice and Belief Similarity

Rokeach, Smith, and Evans (1960) have developed a theory of prejudice in terms of belief similarity. They argue that current conceptions of prejudice, simply in terms of intolerance for a homogeneous, undifferentiated, and stereotyped outgroup, are inadequate. Such conceptions ignore the fact that majority group members differentiate between minority group members who have beliefs similar to theirs and minority group members who have beliefs unlike theirs. The Ku Klux Klansman, for example, may regard the Negro who has beliefs agreeing with his as a "good nigger" and the Negro who has beliefs disagreeing with his as an "uppity nigger." Rokeach, Smith, and Evans (1960) state that ". . . *insofar as psychological processes* are involved, belief is more important than ethnic or racial membership as a determinant of social discrimination" (p. 135). In emphasizing psychological processes Rokeach, Smith, and Evans explicitly exclude institutionalized manifestations of prejudice. For example, "the southern white bigot would not want his daughter to marry the 'good' Negro any more than the 'bad' one" (p. 165).

This theoretical statement is a precursor to the full-blown version of belief congruence theory. In the language of belief congruence theory Rokeach, Smith, and Evans are talking about the belief similarity characterization of a subject belonging to a minority group. They specifically assert that the characterization in terms of belief similarity will have a greater effect upon the total evaluation than will the subject's membership in a minority group. In other words, the characterization will be weighted more heavily than the subject in the evaluation of the characterized subject. This sort of thing is, of course, allowed for in the belief congruence model.

In order to gain empirical support for their speculation Rokeach, Smith, and Evans carried out two separate studies. One of these studies is concerned with the Negro-white distinction and the other with the Jew-gentile distinction. In the first of the studies, students from Michigan State University and the University of Houston were given a questionnaire containing items requiring that the students indicate on a 9-point scale whether or not they could see themselves being friends with certain kinds of people. The people were always either Negroes or whites who either did or did not believe in such things as socialized medicine, God, Communism, segregation, etc. By systematically varying both belief and race it was possible to ascertain whether discrimination was made more frequently on the basis of race or of belief. For example, differential responses to the first two items below (Rokeach, Smith, and Evans, 1960, p. 136) indicate discrimination on the basis of race, while a differential response to the second two items indicates discrimination on the basis of belief:

   a. A white person who believes in God
   b. A Negro who believes in God

   a. A white person who believes in God
   b. A white person who is an atheist

The results indicated that the Northern and Southern students significantly discriminated both on the basis of race and belief, but that the racial discrimination was much less marked than the belief discrimination. A division of subjects into two subgroups on the basis of an anti-Negro attitude scale revealed no differences in the relative sizes of the race and belief effects.

In the second study the questionnaire was modified so as to be applicable to Jew-gentile discrimination and administered to a sample of Jewish children. In this study it was found that the subjects discriminated significantly on the basis of belief but not race. A division of subjects into subgroups on the basis of an anti-Semitism scale revealed essentially the same results for both subgroups.

Both of these studies were taken as supporting the hypothesis that belief discrimination is more marked than is race discrimination. In neither study, however, was this exact hypothesis tested for significance. Just because the probability value associated with the belief effect is smaller than the probability value associated with the race effect, it does not mean that the belief effect is significantly greater than the race effect. Although the obtained differences are sizeable, an appropriate test of significance would have been reassuring. Unfortunately, most other researchers have followed Rokeach's example of simply stating which effect is larger, race or belief.

Triandis (1961) has sharply criticized Rokeach's theory of prejudice. Triandis argues that belief similarity is a relevant variable for predicting friendship choice, Rokeach, Smith, and Evans' dependent variable, but not prejudice. Friendship or the lack of it relates to only small social distances, while prejudice relates to larger social distances such as the acceptance or rejection of someone as neighbor or schoolmate.

Rokeach's research technique used friendship as the variable under investigation, and so inevitably dealt only with a relationship involving small social distance. Prejudice and discrimination are much more relevant to acceptance or rejection of a relationship involving relatively large social distance, such as acceptance of a person as a neighbor or as a student in one's university. (1961, p. 184)

Triandis was sensitive to the Rokeach, Smith, and Evans study because of some data obtained from an earlier study by Triandis and Triandis (1960) which were interpreted as indicating that, although race, same-different social class, same-different religion, and nationality were all significant determiners of social distance, race was by far the most important determiner. In this study subjects, students at the University of Illinois, rated their social distance reactions to artificial stimulus persons who were described according to race (white-Negro), same-different social class, same-different religion, and nationality. In order to get information more directly relevant to the comparison of belief similarity and race, Triandis (1961) had subjects make social distance ratings of stimulus persons described according to race (white-Negro), same-different philosophy of life, occupation, and same-different religion. The subjects were instructed to think of "same philosophy" as the one philosophy of life with which they agreed out of a list of 13 such described philosophies. An analysis of variance of the social distance ratings indicated that all of the four aspects of the stimulus persons produced significant effects. Further, race proved to have a greater effect upon social distance than did philosophy.

Rokeach (1961) replied that: "Triandis' conclusions stem not so much from his use of a social distance scale, which he makes so much of, but from his use of the terms 'same philosophy-different philosophy,' which he makes so little of" (p. 187). Rokeach argues that describing someone as "Negro atheist" is a much more potent and concrete way of emphasizing belief dissimilarity than describing someone as "Negro different philosophy."

Byrne and Wong (1962) have reported a study that lends support to Rokeach's contentions. Students in an introductory psychology course were initially administered two attitude questionnaires, one of which was a measure of prejudice and the other a survey of attitudes toward a variety of topics such as undergraduate marriages, existence of God, political party, drinking, a Catholic president, premarital intercourse, musical comedies, and Westerns. The items in each of the questionnaires were responded to on agreement-disagreement scales. On the basis of the prejudice questionnaire the students were divided into two groups, high prejudiced and low prejudiced. A few weeks later the same subjects were asked to take part in an experiment on interpersonal prediction. Each subject was supplied with background information about and attitude survey responses from a supposedly real person. On the basis of this information the subjects made predictions about whether they would like or dislike the person and whether they would like or dislike working with him in an experiment. The background information was manipulated so that the stimulus person was either Negro or white, and the attitude survey responses were manipulated so that on all items the person either agreed or disagreed with the direction of response of each subject's own attitudes.

The results indicated that for both the dependent variables, general liking-disliking and preference for working with in an experiment, the F's for attitude similarity-dissimilarity but not for race or prejudice were significant. These findings were interpreted as indicating that within the limits of this experiment attitude similarity was of greater importance than either race or prejudice. (Relative to the size of the race and prejudice F's, all nonsignificant, the attitude similarity F's, 588.23 and 187.24, are quite large.)

For purposes of continuity with Triandis' research and theorizing, it is unfortunate that Byrne and Wong did not use a social distance scale for their dependent variable. However, their second dependent variable, preference for working with in an experiment, is at a relatively remote point on the social distance continuum. Thus their data do indicate that Triandis is incorrect in asserting that belief is more important than race in determining discrimination only at the proximal end of the social distance continuum.

Stein, Hardyck, and Smith (1965) obtained further support for the belief similarity hypothesis with the use of a social distance scale. A sample of 44 white ninth-grade students in a California school were presented with descriptions of four teenagers who were either white with like values, white with unlike values, Negro with like values, or Negro with unlike values. The similarity of value manipulation was accomplished by having the hypothetical teenager respond in a similar or different way than each subject had responded on the same questionnaire two months previously. The questionnaire was so constructed that it called for 5-point agreement-disagreement responses to such items as "Teenagers ought to . . . be good at dancing . . . live up to strict moral standards . . . be sincerely religious" etc. Along with the questionnaire responses of each hypothetical teenager the subjects were further provided with background information regarding such things as sex, grade in school, program being taken in school, average grades during the last year, and race. All of these things were kept constant except for sex, which was always the same as the subject's, and race, which was Negro for two of the hypothetical teenagers and white for two. Half of the subjects received the background information before the questionnaire responses and half after the questionnaire responses. Immediately following the description of each teenager the subjects responded both to a question regarding how friendly they would feel toward this person if they were to meet him or her for the first time, and to a teenage social distance scale. This scale contained such items as "I think I would be willing . . . to invite this person home to dinner . . . to have this person as one of my speaking acquaintances . . . to have this person date my sister (brother)" (p. 287).

The results for the friendliness dependent variable indicated that both belief and race had significant effects ($F = 37.72$ and 5.21, respectively), but that the belief effect is larger than the race effect.

Stein, Hardyck, and Smith also correlated the above friendliness scores with analogous friendliness scores obtained for "a Negro teenager" whose beliefs were not described. These additional data were obtained during the initial session when the subjects indicated their own beliefs. The correlation between "Negro-like" and "Negro teenager" is $+.15$ and the correlation between "Negro-unlike" and "Negro teenager" is $+.62$. Since the latter $+.62$ is significantly different from the nonsignificant $+.15$, Stein, Hardyck, and Smith concluded that their subjects responded to the undescribed Negro teenager as if he had dissimilar values. This, of course, provides even more support for Rokeach's hypothesis that prejudice is due to the ascription of dissimilar beliefs to minority group members.

The overall results for the social distance scale parallel those for the friendliness scale. Both race and belief had significant effects, but the belief effect is larger than the race effect ($F = 48.51$ and 7.20, respectively). An examination of each of the 11 separate items revealed that belief had a significant effect on all of them while race had a significant effect on only 3: "invite home to dinner," "live in same apartment house," and "date my sister (brother)." Stein, Hardyck, and Smith (1965) state that these latter three effects are possibly manifestations of institutionalized prejudice which lie outside the domain of the theory as Rokeach, Smith, and Evans have stated it. They suggest that the 3 items on which race had a significant effect seem to involve both "intimacy of contact and presence of others—in this case parents—who are the enforcers of social norms" (p. 288). It is true that the other items upon which race did not have a significant effect do seem to lack one or the other or both of these two components. For example, consider "go to the same school," "have as a member of a social group," and "close personal friend."

Stein (*1965*) replicated and extended the findings of Stein, Hardyck, and Smith. Friendliness and social distance reactions to four stimulus persons were indicated by 630 ninth-grade students from a Northeastern suburban city. As in the Stein, Hardyck, and Smith study belief similarity was manipulated through questionnaire responses that were either similar to or different from each subject's own previous responses to the same questionnaire; race was manipulated by providing the stimulus persons' responses to a question concerning race; and the sex of the subject and the four stimulus persons were always the same. Additional manipulations not included in the Stein, Hardyck, and Smith study were, among other things, the race of the subject (Negro or white), the age of the stimulus persons (teenage or adult), and the status of the stimulus persons (high or low).[4] For the adult stimulus persons, status was indicated through information regarding occupation (e.g., "doctor" versus "factory worker") and schooling (e.g., "some further education after college" versus "grade school"). For the teenage stimulus person, status was indicated through information regarding program in school ("college preparatory" versus "vocational") and last year's grade average ("about a 'B' average" versus "below a 'D' average").

Stein analyzed his data by doing three-factor analyses of variance involving race, belief, and status [5] separately for each of the eight subsamples generated from the combinations of sex of subject and stimulus person, race of subject, and age of stimulus person (e.g., Negro male subjects, adult stimulus persons, and white female subjects, teenage stimulus persons).

The results for the friendliness dependent variable indicated that belief had a significant effect in all eight subsamples (F's ranging from 21.96 to 80.31), race had a significant effect in none of the eight subsamples (F's from 0.01 to 3.54), and status had an effect in three of the eight subsamples (F's from 0.01 to 6.40). Stein also found that for the white sample the friendliness ratings of a lower status Negro with unlike values correlated significantly (+.53) with the previously obtained friendliness ratings of an otherwise undescribed Negro teenager. No other correlations with the undescribed Negro teenager are significant. For example, the correlation with the upper status Negro with unlike values is .00. These findings complement the similar findings of Stein, Hardyck, and Smith who did not manipulate status.

The results for the social distance dependent variable indicated that belief had a significant effect in all eight subsamples (F's ranging from 16.20 to 126.20), race had a significant effect in four of the subsamples

[4] There was also a manipulation of the stimulus persons' religion. For the full account see Stein (1965).

[5] All of these variables involved within-subject comparisons.

(F's from 0.18 to 26.42), and status had a significant effect in three of the subsamples (F's from 0.04 to 17.92).

Stein did not do any tests of significance with regard to the individual items on the social distance scales, but does report some data indicating a rough correspondence with the findings of Stein, Hardyck, and Smith. For example, the two largest race effects for the white males are "invite home to dinner" and "have close relative marry," and the two largest race effects for white females are "live in same apartment house" and "have close relative marry." In their mixed sex sample Stein, Hardyck, and Smith found that the same three areas were sensitive to the race manipulation.

Triandis and Davis (*1965*) report some evidence which they interpret as indicating that belief is important in determining large social distance behaviors and race is important in determining intimate or small social distance behaviors. Subjects were presented with eight stimulus persons generated from all possible combinations of the following characteristics: Negro-white, male-female, pro or con civil rights legislation. One of the eight stimulus persons, for example, was white, male, pro civil rights. Responses to each of these stimulus persons on a large number of items were grouped so as to form six dependent variables. One dependent variable was a semantic differential assessment of attitude and the other five were "behavioral differential scales" that Triandis (1964) had previously obtained from a factor analytic study. These scales, along with some illustrative items, are as follows: formal social acceptance versus formal social rejection ("I would admire the ideas of," "I would admire the character of"), marital acceptance versus marital rejection ("I would marry," "I would date"), friendship acceptance versus friendship rejection ("I would accept as an intimate friend," "I would eat with"), social distance ("I would exclude from the neighborhood," "I would prohibit admission to my club"), and subordination ("I would obey," "I would not treat as a subordinate").

According to Triandis and Davis the six dependent variables can be grouped into three clusters depending upon the amount of intimacy involved. Social distance and marital acceptance versus marital rejection involve the most intimate behaviors. Subordination and friendship acceptance versus friendship rejection are intermediate in intimacy. Attitude and formal social acceptance versus formal social rejection are least intimate or involve the most socially distant behaviors. The results of the study indicated that belief accounted for more of the variance in the most intimate cluster and race accounted for more of the variance in the least intimate cluster. For the intermediate cluster both belief and race were important determiners of the variance, but race was somewhat more important.

In addition to responding to the items constituting the six dependent variables the subjects also responded to a number of personality and attitude items. These items along with the items assessing the dependent variables were analyzed by a technique for factoring persons. Of the several factors extracted, two are directly relevant to the race-belief issue. One seemed to describe the "conventionally prejudiced." Subjects who scored high on this factor responded to the stimulus persons in terms of race. The other factor seemed to describe the "belief prejudiced." Subjects who scored high on this factor responded to the stimulus persons in terms of belief. The differences between these two types are most evident for the items of intermediate social distance.

As Triandis and Davis interpret the results of this study, the main conclusion appears in some respects opposite to the hypothesis originally stated by Triandis (1961). It now seems that race is relevant, not to large social distances, but to small social distances. The whole problem is complicated, however, by the fact that Triandis (1961) originally implied that friendship involves a smaller social distance than acceptance or rejection of someone as a neighbor, while Triandis and Davis seem to believe the opposite. They maintain that the friendship acceptance versus friendship rejection scale ("I would accept as an intimate friend," "I would eat with," "I would gossip with") involves more socially distant behaviors than the social distance scale ("I would exclude from the neighborhood," "I would prohibit admission to my club," "I would not accept as a close kin by marriage"). Perhaps part of the problem lies in the fact that the various items in these factors do not have uniform positions along the social distance dimension. For example, the two items, "I would exclude from the neighborhood" and "I would not accept as a close kin by marriage," are both on the social distance scale, and the two items, "I would accept as an intimate friend" and "I would eat with," are both on the friendship acceptance versus friendship rejection scale. In view of this ambiguity there is some reason to doubt the validity of Triandis and Davis' general conclusion regarding the differing effect of race and beliefs at various points along the social distance dimension.

Aside from this matter, there is a serious question regarding the extent to which Triandis and Davis adequately manipulated belief similarity. There was no attempt to assess the subjects' attitudes toward civil rights so that the stimulus persons could be systematically different from or similar to these beliefs, and only one belief or attitude was manipulated. It is, therefore, reasonable to suppose that the effect of belief similarity was not fully represented in this study. Byrne and McGraw (1964) present some evidence indicating that the number of belief items has an effect on the significance of belief similarity and its ability to overcome the effect of prejudice. In their study prejudice was a subject variable. If increasing the number of items facilitates the overcoming of a prejudice effect, it is probable that increasing the number of items would facilitate the overcoming of a race effect.

Rokeach and Mezei (1966) report three experiments which examined the effect of race and belief upon discrimination in actual social situations. Two of the experiments were done with college students in laboratory situations and one was done with unemployed adults in a field setting. The two college studies were essentially identical except for the fact that one utilized 20 subjects from an introductory sociology class and one used 48 subjects from an introductory psychology class. All of the subjects were white and male. At least 10 days before participating in the experiments the class instructors administered an anti-Negro scale to their students. On the basis of responses to this questionnaire the subjects were divided into two groups, high and low prejudiced. The experimental session involved a group discussion among four stooges and one naive subject. By prearrangement the naive subject was always elected chairman of the group. The experimenter provided the group with five discussion topics (invasion of Cuba, elimination of fraternities from campus, allowing girls to visit men's dormitories, Bible reading in the schools, the grading system) and the chairman picked one of them for discussion. Two of the stooges (one Negro and one white) agreed with the subject's point of view and two (one Negro and one white) disagreed with the subject's point of view. The agreeing and disagreeing roles were systematically rotated from subject to subject. At the conclusion of the experiment the experimenter informed the subjects that he wished to interview them individually and that there would be enough time for several of them to take a coffee break. He then asked the naive subject, as chairman, to select two of the participants to join him for coffee. In half of the cases the coffee was to be served next door in a private room and in half of the cases the coffee was to be purchased with research funds in a public grill.

The subjects in the field experiment were 26 Negro and 24 white male applicants for various positions (janitor, laundry worker, attendant, and recreation director) at two mental hospitals in Michigan. After filling out an application form the subjects were conducted to a room where four other "applicants" (actually stooges) were waiting to be interviewed. The experimenter distributed mimeographed sheets to everyone and suggested that, since the material described in these sheets was to be used in their training program, they might wish to look at them while waiting to be interviewed. The sheets listed five problems of working with mental patients (misses dinner, refuses to shave because of a delusion, takes off his clothes, asks to change his dining-room seat, and juvenile offenders) and suggested two alternative courses of action (one based on a rule and the other a more permissive alternative) for each problem. The experimenter then left the room and the stooges engaged in a "spontaneous" discussion of at least three of the five topics. Two of the stooges (one Negro and one white) agreed with the naive subject on each topic and two (one Negro and one white) disagreed with the subject on each topic. After 12 minutes the experimenter returned and asked the applicants to write down the names of the two people in the group with whom they would most prefer to work.

Rokeach and Mezei report their results in terms of the simple frequencies of each of the six possible choices (two of same race as subject, two of different race from subject, two who agreed with subject and two who disagreed with subject, one of same race who agreed and one of different race who disagreed, one of same race who disagreed and one of different race who agreed). Although, by and large, no tests of significance were reported, the results were interpreted as indicating that belief was a more important determiner of choice than was race. For all three experiments combined, 47 subjects chose the two stooges who agreed and four chose the two stooges who disagreed. On the other hand, 7 subjects chose the two stooges of the same race and 7 chose the two stooges of the different race. Belief then was a more important determiner of choice than was race. This general pattern of results is evident across all three experiments. In the two college experiments neither the prejudice of the subject nor the privacy of the place where the coffee was to be obtained made any appreciable difference in these effects. In the field experiment the same pattern of results was obtained from Negro and white subjects. The results for the choices based neither solely on race nor belief are somewhat more puzzling. For all three experiments combined, 22 subjects chose the stooge of the same race who agreed and the stooge of a different race who disagreed, and 31 subjects chose the stooge of the same race who disagreed and the stooge of a different race who agreed. These surprisingly high frequencies are largely due to the choices in the college experiments (18 and 23). Rokeach and Mezei state that it is not possible to know whether this difference between the college and field experiments is due to the nature of the subjects involved (students or workers), to the nature of the implied activity (coffee drinking or working with), or to the particular issues discussed (work related or nonwork related). They do, however, report some further data indicating that more than two thirds of the subjects who chose both agreeing and disagreeing stooges chose the agreeing stooge first. They interpret this finding as indicating that some subjects were motivated by "considerations of fair-mindedness" so that they tended to pick a second person who was opposite to the first in race or belief. They also report that when the subjects were questioned after the experiment many of the ones who had made inconsistent choices indicated that they had done so in order to "keep the discussion going." Apparently there are several plausible explanations for the occurrence of in-consistent choices.

Comment. All of the above studies which adequately manipulated belief similarity found that, in general, belief similarity produced a greater effect than did race. The consistency in the findings creates some confidence as to the reliability of the effect.

An interesting exception to the above general conclusion is the persistent finding that race is of considerable importance in determining responses to several types of behavioral items, such as ones dealing with interracial dating, marriage, and housing. These seem to be the areas in which institutionalized norms are operating. Rokeach, Smith, and Evans (1960) originally stated that their theorizing about the relatively greater effect of belief than race was limited to noninstitutionalized manifestations of prejudice. Existing data seem to indicate that this is an important and correct limitation.

Careful consideration of the above research indicates that it has failed to distinguish between two similar but yet different theoretical issues. One issue has to do with whether or not an individual's initial prejudicial reaction toward a particular minority group member could be altered if he learned that this person possessed beliefs that were similar to his. This is the problem that has been researched in the literature. The other issue has to do with whether or not the individual's prejudicial reaction toward a particular minority outgroup is due to the attribution of dissimilar beliefs to these people. This issue is at least part of Rokeach's theoretical concern, but it is not the issue that has been researched. In order to study this issue it would be necessary to manipulate the similarity-dissimilarity of just those beliefs with regard to which minority group members are perceived as being dissimilar. To the extent that the similarity-dissimilarity manipulation involved beliefs other than attributed dissimilar beliefs the results would be ambiguous insofar as this particular theoretical problem is concerned. Furthermore, the manipulation of similarity-dissimilarity ideally should reflect the amount of attributed dissimilarity.

An additional matter in need of clarification has to do with what the attribution of dissimilar beliefs implies with regard to the attribution of attitudes and traits. Rosenberg and Abelson (1960) maintain that beliefs tend to be consistent with attitudes. This means, for example, that the individual who believes that education contributes to the welfare of mankind will tend to have a positive attitude toward education. There is further, however, a close relation between traits, attitudes, and beliefs. For example, the person who is superstitious may have a negative attitude toward the number 13 and believe that in certain situations this particular number will hinder his welfare or "bring bad luck." Because of matters such as these it is not entirely clear what the attribution of dissimilar beliefs really implies. Perhaps it implies a lot more than has been recognized.

Rokeach and Rothman's Direct Test of Belief Congruence

At the present time the only directly relevant research on the adequacy of the belief congruence model is that reported by Rokeach and Rothman (1965) themselves. Rokeach and Rothman began their study with the idea of testing Osgood and Tannenbaum's (1955) congruity theory with component concepts which when examined separately would activate highly polarized evaluations. Initially, 42 subjects from an introductory psychology course evaluated 22 components and then 12 assertion-linked combinations of these components on semantic differential scales. For example, after having evaluated "my mother" and "insincere" along with 20 other components, they evaluated the combination, "my mother is insincere." Examples of other combinations are: "university professor favors extramarital sexual relations," "unfaithful romance," and "a prostitute who looks like Grace Kelly."

The results for the congruity predictions were not very encouraging. For 8 of the 12 combinations the congruity predictions differed significantly from the empirically obtained evaluations. Furthermore, for 9 of the 12 instances there is a marked tendency for the combination or CS to be evaluated like one of the components, the C, and not like the other, the S. For example, "my mother" was evaluated 6.51, "insincere" 1.86, and "my mother is insincere" 2.04. The 2.04 for the CS differs significantly from the 6.51 for the S, but not from the 1.86 for the C. This, of course, is evidence for assimilation. One of the 9 instances, in fact, showed a significant overassimilation effect; "white person who is a communist" was evaluated significantly more negatively than "communist." Rokeach and Rothman argue that these results are plainly contrary to the congruity or averaging predictions.

In order to test the adequacy of the belief congruence model it was necessary to obtain ratings of the relative importance of C and S in the context of CS. Since this had not been done on the original sample Rokeach and Rothman obtained the information from a later, hopefully comparable, sample. The rather complicated series of questions used to assess relative importance is presented in Rokeach and Rothman's Relative Importance Questionnaire. These questions ask first whether the respondent's feelings toward "irresponsible father" are completely determined by his feelings toward "irresponsible." If the answer is "no," he then is asked what percent of his feelings toward "irresponsible father" are determined by "irresponsible" and what percent by "father." If the

Rokeach and Rothman's Relative Importance Questionnaire

This is a scientific study in the meaning of words and combinations of words. There are no right or wrong answers. What we want is *your* personal opinion.

Consider, for example, the combination "IRRESPONSIBLE FATHER."

1. How do you feel about IRRESPONSIBLE FATHER? On the rating scale below indicate with a check mark how strongly you approve or disapprove of IRRESPONSIBLE FATHER.

    1   2   3   4   5   6   7

    Strongly   Strongly
    disapprove   approve

2. In rating IRRESPONSIBLE FATHER the way you did, how important, that is, how much weight did each word, IRRESPONSIBLE and FATHER, have in determining your rating of IRRESPONSIBLE FATHER? Did you feel about the combination IRRESPONSIBLE FATHER the same way you felt about the single word IRRESPONSIBLE or the same way you felt about FATHER? Estimate how much weight IRRESPONSIBLE and FATHER had in determining the way you actually rated the combination IRRESPONSIBLE FATHER.

    a. My feelings about IRRESPONSIBLE *completely* (100%) determined the way I rated IRRESPONSIBLE FATHER.

    Yes_____Now proceed to question *b*.

    No_____Now proceed to question *c*.

    b. In fact, my feelings about IRRESPONSIBLE FATHER are even more extreme than my feelings about other people who are IRRESPONSIBLE.
    _____No, my feelings about IRRESPONSIBLE FATHER and IRRESPONSIBLE are about of equal strength.
    _____Yes, my feelings about IRRESPONSIBLE FATHER are even stronger than my feelings about other people who are IRRESPONSIBLE.
    _____How much stronger? Slightly stronger (1% stronger)? Quite a bit stronger (50% stronger)? Much, much stronger (100% stronger)? My best guess is (fill in blank at left).
    Do not answer *c*. Go on to the next page.

    c. My feelings about IRRESPONSIBLE did not *completely* determine my rating of the combination IRRESPONSIBLE FATHER. I would guess that IRRESPONSIBLE influenced me about _____ percent in determining my rating of IRRESPONSIBLE FATHER and FATHER influenced me about _____ percent.

SOURCE: Rokeach and Rothman, 1965, p. 138.

answer to the initial question is "yes," the respondent is asked further if in fact his feelings toward "irresponsible father" are not even more extreme than his feelings toward "irresponsible," and if so by what per-cent. Rokeach and Rothman report that they had considerable difficulty in developing this relative importance assessment and that in their final sample of 71 subjects, 14 (19.1%) were eliminated because they did not follow or understand the instructions.

Rokeach and Rothman report that for 38 percent of all the asser-tions the subjects judged C to be 100 percent important in determining the meaning of CS, and, furthermore, that for 16 percent of the asser-tions the subjects judged CS to be more important than C. The informa-tion concerning the relative importance of C and S allowed Rokeach and Rothman to make belief congruence predictions. This was done simply by substituting mean relative importance ratings for each asser-tion along with the initial evaluations obtained for each subject into Formula 7–1 and in some cases also Formula 7–2. The results indicated that the predicted mean evaluation for the assertions differs significantly from the obtained mean evaluations in 3 of the 12 instances. This com-pares with the predicted means for congruity theory which differ from the obtained means in 8 of the 12 instances. Furthermore, Rokeach and Rothman report that the overall mean error in prediction is 1.07 for the congruity model and .34 for the belief congruence model. They, however, do not report any test of significance comparing these two figures.

What can be said in evaluating these data? The study seems to provide an encouraging degree of support for belief congruence theory. However, there are three things that should be pointed out. First, with-out an appropriate test of significance there is not any way of knowing whether the superior predictive power of the belief congruence model is generalizable. Just because the belief congruence model predicted better than the congruity model does not mean it predicted significantly better. Second, the belief congruence model itself made predictions for three assertions that significantly deviated from the empirically obtained results. While 9 out of 12 may be a fair batting average, it is still apparent that the theory can be improved upon. And third, almost 20 percent of the subjects were eliminated due to the complicated nature of the im-portance assessment. This is a very large percentage that may cast doubt on the generalizability of any findings.

EVALUATION

Rokeach and Rothman have made an interesting attempt to exactly and mathematically state a sophisticated type of consistency model. Rokeach and Rothman are properly impressed by Osgood and Tannenbaum's mathematical statement of congruity theory, but correctly perceive that congruity theory is somewhat inelegant in that it is forced to bring in *ad hoc* corrections for the direction of assertion, incredulity, and possibly the relevance-nonrelevance of the source and concept. They also perceive that a primary problem with congruity theory has to do with the adequacy of the basic equilibrium or averaging assumption. Quite reasonably, therefore, Rokeach and Rothman have attempted to develop a theory that does not have the same difficulties as does congruity theory.

One of the primary things with which Rokeach and Rothman are concerned is the possibility of assimilation or overassimilation effects. They do not exactly define these concepts, but judging from all of the examples presented, assimilation and overassimilation presumably refer to situations in which one component of the CS is initially evaluated positively and one initially evaluated negatively. In the example, "irresponsible father," "irresponsible" is initially evaluated negatively and "father" positively. This suggests that assimilation and overassimilation are quite different from what other investigators have referred to as summation. Kerrick (1959), for example, found that for half of the instances in which both of her components were initially evaluated on the *same* side of the scale the entire complex was evaluated even more extremely than either component. Perhaps, however, Rokeach and Rothman would be willing to say that overassimilation can result from components which are initially evaluated on the same side of the scale. The question would then become one of whether or not belief congruence theory, as it is formulated, can predict such summation or "overassimilation" effects. In order for the prediction to be successfully made subjects would have to be willing to state, first, that their feelings about one of the similarly evaluated components completely determined their evaluation of the entire CS, and, second, that their feelings about the entire CS are even stronger than their feelings about the component judged to be 100 percent in importance. Without empirical data it would be unwise to say that this will not occur, but certainly a thorough testing of belief congruence theory would involve the collection of such relevant data.

Even, however, in the case of components which are not similarly evaluated, a question can be raised about the meaningfulness of the comparison involving the relative importance of CS and the component judged to be 100 percent in importance. According to Rokeach and Rothman when one of the components is judged 100 percent in importance a second comparison process is activated, a comparison between CS and the component of 100 percent importance. This second comparison is supposedly to allow for the detection of interaction, or departure from simple summation, in the total effect of the two components. As the concept of interaction is commonly understood, however, it is impossible to achieve an interaction between two variables if the main effect of one of the variables contributes nothing to the total variance. In spite of this fact, Rokeach and Rothman only allow for interaction in the situation in which one variable is judged to be of zero percent importance (and the other of 100 percent importance). This is plainly nonsense in terms of the analysis of variance conception of interaction. Perhaps, however, Rokeach and Rothman have in mind some less well-defined "configurationist" conception of interaction. If so, it is certainly incumbent upon them to explain more carefully what they mean by interaction and, furthermore, how it operates. Rokeach and Rothman's major source of difficulty in constructing the importance questionnaire undoubtedly had to do with getting respondents to go along with the conception of interaction. As the questionnaire is constructed, if the respondent agrees that one component entirely determined his feelings about the CS, he is next asked if his feelings about the CS are not even stronger than his feelings about the component just judged to be 100 percent in importance. Many respondents may have thought that the investigators were trying to trick them into a contradiction.

In general, belief congruence theory does seem to have taken hold of some of the primary problems relating to an equilibrium point of view. It is quite plausible that in many situations there are interactions between CS components which produce assimilation or overassimilation effects. Unfortunately, however, there is very little empirical evidence directly relating to the theory, and the theory itself is not well formulated. The basic statement relating to the interaction between CS components needs to be reformulated or clarified. In view of these matters, any final statement as to the overall merit of the theory is very difficult and perhaps premature. The data with regard to belief similarity and prejudice are encouraging, but do not bear too directly on the belief congruence model itself. From the present vantage point the most promising aspect of Rokeach's work comes from the studies of prejudice.

8

Heider and Newcomb's

Balance Theories

THEORY

Heider (1946, 1958) and Newcomb (1953, 1959) have independently developed balance theories. Because of the high degree of similarity between these theories they will both be discussed in the same chapter. Heider and Newcomb's balance theories, like Osgood and Tannenbaum's congruity theory, are equilibrium theories.

Heider's Version

Relations. Heider (1946, 1958) theorizes about two types of relations between people or between people and events: sentiment relations and unit relations. A sentiment relation is an attitudinal relation that implies liking, admiring, approving, loving, and so forth. One person may approve of another person or of an event. Unit relations result in a perceived unity of the persons or persons and events. Examples of unit relations are similarity, proximity, causality, membership, and ownership. One person may be similar to another or may own a certain object.

Symbols. In Heider's system the person is symbolized by p, another person by o, an event, idea, or thing by x, a positive sentiment relation by L, a negative sentiment relation by nL, a positive unit relation by U, and a negative unit relation by nU. Thus pLo means that the person has a positive sentiment relation with another person, and $pnLx$ means that the person has a negative sentiment relation with an event, object, or idea.

Balance in General. By a balanced state Heider means a state in which everything fits together "harmoniously" without stress in the person's (p's) life space. Thus for Heider the concept of balance has Gestalt overtones and refers to intra-individual processes. A lack of balance results in stress and pressure toward change.

Balance as Homogeneity of the Sentiment Relation. Somewhat more specifically Heider discusses balance as involving a homogeneity of the sentiment relation. If all of the particular sentiments (admiration, liking, approval, etc.) agree in evaluation or have the same dynamic character then we have homogeneity of the sentiment relation. The relationship between p and o is balanced if pLo or $pnLo$ holds for all meanings of L. There is, therefore, a tendency to make all of the sentiment relations agree with each other, e.g., to love admired persons and admire loved persons.

According to Heider this tendency toward homogeneity of the sentiment relation results in the well-known halo phenomenon or judgment of another person as all good or all bad. There is thus an obvious similarity between this concept and Osgood and Tannenbaum's concept of a tendency toward maximal simplicity.

Balance as a Relationship Between or Among Parts. Heider also discusses balance as involving a particular type of relationship among or between persons, or among or between persons and events. In the dyadic situation involving p and x, balance exists if either both the sentiment relation and unit relation are positive or both the sentiment relation and unit relation are negative. (Symbolically, if either $pLx + pUx$ or $pnLo + pnUx$ obtains, the system is balanced.) For example, if p admires x and owns x then the system is balanced.

As in the dyad involving p and x, the dyad involving p and o is balanced if the sentiment relation and unit relation both have the same sign. In addition, however, the dyad is balanced if pLo and oLp both obtain. If p has a positive sentiment relation with o and o does not return the feeling, the dyad is not balanced. Examples of balanced dyadic relations between p and o are: p likes o and p is similar to o, p dislikes o and p is dissimilar to o, p likes o and p interacts with o, p dislikes o and p does not interact with o, p likes o and o likes p, p dislikes o and o dislikes p.

The theory implies then that persons who perceive each other as being similar should be attracted to each other; but what about the proverb which states that opposites attract? Heider (1958) maintains that such complementarity may facilitate the obtaining of a common purpose or goal and thus the individuals involved may in some sense or other be similar.

The apparent exception to the above relation between similarity and sentiment, namely that dissimilarity can lead to liking and association if two people fit together because they complement each other, may turn out to be a verification of the relation, at least in some instances. A good deal depends on the criteria for the designation of similar, dissimilar, and complementary entities. Two apparently dissimilar entities may in one sense be considered similar when they lead toward a common purpose. This is one kind of complementary relation and may be exemplified when "opposites attract," as male and female. In terms of this analysis, then, the fact, that dissimilarity can lead to liking, is not necessarily an exception to the balanced case under consideration, since the apparent dissimilarity may in effect become supplanted by a similarity, that of purpose for example. (1958, pp. 186–187)

The theory also implies that interaction and proximity result in the formation of positive sentiment relations. Once again, though, we are confronted by a contradictory proverb, "familiarity breeds contempt." Heider (1958) states that interaction will lead to the formation of a positive sentiment relation only if there is not too great a dissimilarity in attitudes. "With similar attitudes proximity will increase the degree of positive sentiment; with slight dissimilarity of attitudes a mutual assimilation might be produced, and with it an increase in friendliness; with strong dissimilarities the hostility will be increased" (p. 190).

In the case of the triadic relationship between p, o, and x, balance obtains if all three of the signs are positive or if two are negative and one positive. If p likes o and x, and perceives that o likes x, or if p likes o, dislikes x, and perceives that o dislikes x the system is balanced. A system in which two of the signs are positive and one negative is not balanced. If p likes o and x, and perceives that o dislikes x, or if p dislikes o, likes x, and perceives that o likes x the system is not balanced. Examples of balance and imbalance involving a unit relation as well as sentiment relations are the liking of the author of a liked book or the disliking of the author of a liked book.

What about the love triangle or situation in which p and his friend q both love the same girl, o. Here we have three positive relations, but the system is notoriously unbalanced. According to Heider (1946) "p does not want his girl friend o to fall in love with his boy friend q because oLq in this case implies $onLp$, which conflicts with pLo" (p. 110). In this case the triad of three positive relations is not balanced because of the potential imbalance of the dyad involving p and o.

According to Heider (1958) the case of three negative relations is "somewhat ambiguous" (p. 203). Heider does not say whether a system of three negative relations (p dislikes o and x and perceives that o dislikes x) is balanced or not. He does say that ". . . common negative attitudes toward x may readily bring about a feeling of similarity between p and o. The resulting unit (p similar to o) is in itself a positive relation, and as we have seen tends to induce a second positive relation (pLo)" (p. 206). The system of three negative relations will result in p perceiving his similarity to o in their mutual dislike of x. Similarity between p and o is a positive unit relation and induces a positive sentiment relation in order to balance the dyad. The result is a triadic system of one positive and two negative relations (p likes o and agrees with o in disliking x). Because of the fact that a system of three negative relations is unstable and tends toward a system of one positive and two negative relations there is some basis for considering the three-negative system imbalanced, but Heider does not commit himself.

Results of Imbalance. Imbalance results in tension which forces a change toward balance. This change can take any number of forms. Heider describes these changes with regard to a system of one positive sentiment relation, one positive unit relation, and one negative sentiment relation (p likes o who has done something, x, of which p does not approve). Balance can be restored by changing either of the sentiment relations so that, for example, p dislikes o or approves of x. Balance can likewise be obtained by changing the unit relation. For example, p may begin to think that o is not really responsible for x. Finally a kind of resolution but not balance can be obtained through differentiation. This differentiation can, for example, take the form of p recognizing that o has good and bad points. The bad points of which p disapproves are responsible for x of which p also disapproves, thus resulting in a balanced system of two negative relations and one positive relation. The good points of which p approves are not responsible for x, thus resulting in a balanced system of three positive relations. This sort of resolution obviously does not result in complete balance because of the fact that o consists of one positive and one negative part.

The Self-Sentiment. According to Heider the previous statements about balanced and unbalanced systems all assume that pLp or that p holds himself in high regard. It may be the case that $pnLp$ or that p does not hold himself in high regard, possibly because of guilt feelings, and may want to be punished. In such a situation if p's friend admires one of p's creations, x, the system is not balanced.

Mathematical Statement in Terms of Graph Theory. Cartwright and Harary (1956) have developed a statement of Heider's balance theory in terms of the mathematical theory of linear graphs. In this development individuals are represented by points, and relations between individuals by different types of connecting lines. With this type of mathematical tool Cartwright and Harary were able to extend balance theory to systems involving more than just two or three entities, to develop an index of the degree of balance, and to state theorems about when a system is or is not balanced. Expressed in algebraic terms Heider's system of two or three entities is balanced if the product of the signs is positive and not balanced if the product of the signs is negative. This means that systems of three positive relations, or one positive and two negative

relations are balanced; and that systems of one negative and two positive
relations, or three negative relations are not balanced.[1]

Newcomb's Version

Essential Constructs.   A key concept for Newcomb is that of *orientation*. Newcomb (1959) defines orientation as "that existing organization
of the psychological processes of an organism which affects its subsequent behavior with regard to a discriminable object or class of objects"
(p. 389). Orientations are divided into two basic types according to
whether they are directed at fellow communicators or at objects of
communication (person or nonperson). Orientations toward fellow communicators are called *attractions,* and orientations toward objects of
communication are called *attitudes.* Orientations can further be characterized according to their cathectic and cognitive aspects. The *cathectic*
aspect of an orientation is its location on an approach-avoidance or pro-
con continuum. The *cognitive* aspect of an orientation has "to do with
the ordering, or structuring, of attributes as cognized 'in' the object
of the orientation" (p. 391). The cognitive aspect of an orientation relates to the nonevaluative perception of an orientation object's attributes
and characteristics.

A *system of orientation* consists of the orientation of A (person)
toward B (fellow communicator) and X (object of communication),
and the judged orientation of B toward A and X. The totality of these
orientations is regarded as being a system because, under appropriate
circumstances, a change in one orientation will lead to a change in one
or more of the others. Two variables affecting the behavior of the system
are *importance* and *object relevance.* Importance refers to the amount
of cathectic orientation toward an object and is operationalized in terms
of the intensity of either a positive or a negative attitude. "*Object relevance* refers to the degree of joint dependence of two or more communicators upon a specific object of communication, as judged by one
of them" (pp. 392–393). Object relevance may be operationalized in
terms of statements concerning the closeness or frequency with which
the object is associated with the other person.

Finally, we have the two concepts of *strain* and *communication.*
A system of orientation may get out of balance or equilibrium and result in a strain toward symmetry or toward the regaining of balance.
One of the means by which the system moves from a state of greater
to lesser strain is through communication or the sending and receiving
of symbols.

[1] Feather (1964) has used Cartwright and Harary's graph theory statement of
balance theory to speculate about the balance theory implications for a communication structure relating the source, communication, issue, and receiver.

Conditions of Strain Induction. According to Newcomb, when given divergent orientations of A and B toward X, the greater the positive attraction of A for B the greater the strain. Furthermore, when given divergent orientations between A and B and positive attraction of A for B, strain increases with the importance and object relevance of X and the degree of commitment of A's and B's orientations toward X. Strain may also be produced by simple uncertainty as to discrepancy of orientation in conjunction with positive attraction between A and B.

In general, strain, according to Newcomb, varies in conjunction with five variables: (1) degree of orientation discrepancy, (2) sign and degree of attraction, (3) importance of X, (4) degree of commitment or importance of orientation, and (5) object relevance.

Communication as a Learned Response to Strain. Newcomb states that the instigation to communicate is an instrumental response which has been learned because of its value in reducing strain. For example, when there is some degree of positive attraction between A and B and a degree of discrepancy in cognitive orientation, communication may occur because A wants some information, wants to pass on some information, or wants to confirm a tentative observation. When there is discrepancy in cathectic orientation, again accompanied by positive attraction, A may attempt to persuade B on the point of disagreement or may expose himself to B's persuasive arguments. Also, uncertainty as to whether or not cathectic discrepancy exists may be an instigation to communication. Any of these communicative exchanges may serve to reduce strain and thus reward the instrumental behavior.

Newcomb states, however, that communication does not always lead to strain reduction and in some circumstances may serve to increase strain. Communication most readily produces strain reduction in the case of discrepancy in cognitive orientation (discrepancy with regard to unevaluated information). In the case of both cognitive and cathectic discrepancy an important variable determining whether or not communication will lead to strain reduction is the degree of respect and trust between A and B. An additional determining factor with regard to cathectic discrepancy only is the degree of commitment to existing attitudes. With a low level of respect and trust and a high degree of commitment, communication is not likely to reduce strain.

Autism as a Response to Strain. Strain may result in certain autistic responses that occur either alone or in conjunction with communication. These autistic responses include such things as rationalization, memory losses, and elaborations in fantasy. While communication may frequently result in an increase in strain, autistic responses almost always result in a decrease in strain. These responses are unaccompanied by communication when there are physical barriers preventing communication or when there is negative attraction between A and B.

Strain Reduction. As a result of communication and/or autism, strain may be reduced through changes in any of the following: (1) attraction, (2) object relevance, (3) perceived other's object relevance, (4) importance of X, (5) perceived other's importance of X, (6) cathexis or cognitive structure of own attitudes toward X (so that there is greater similarity with other's perceived attitudes), and (7) perceiv ed cathexis or cognitive structure of other's attitudes toward X (so that there is greater similarity with own attitudes).

Newcomb thus arrives at a complex system of interrelations among constructs. If attraction increases, for example, the resulting strain can be reduced by an increase in perceived similarity. Alternatively, the same increase in perceived similarity may be produced by an increase in object relevance. In every case the amount of change resulting from variance in one construct is modified by the existing states of the other constructs. The system finally evolved consists of five conditions of strain induction which may result in communication and/or autism that mediates any of seven intrasystem changes serving to reduce strain.

RESEARCH

There is a wide range of literature relevant to balance theory. However, most of this material, such as that dealing with person perception, interpersonal attraction, friendship, marital happiness, stability of the self-concept, etc., will not be discussed. This section will be limited to one topic, balance and imbalance in general.

Jordan (*1953*) presented subjects with 64 different hypothetical triadic situations involving either sentiment relations, unit relations, or both. The subjects were asked to rate the degree of pleasantness-unpleasantness of each situation. A sample hypothetical situation is as follows: "I dislike O; I like X; O has no sort of bond or relationship with X" (p. 277). The first two links of the triad always involved "I." The 64 triads were generated by combining the eight possible permutations of valences ($+++$, $+--$, $-+-$, $--+$, $++-$, $+-+$, $-++$, $---$) with the eight possible permutations of sentiment and unit relations (LLL, LLU, LUL, ULL, LUU, ULU, UUL, UUU). The first four valences, $+++$, $+--$, $-+-$, $--+$, are, of course, balanced, and the remaining four relations, $++-$, $+-+$, $-++$, $---$, imbalanced.

Jordan found that, in general, the balanced relations were judged more pleasant than the imbalanced ones. There were, however, complicating factors. The mean pleasantness-unpleasantness ratings of the four balanced situations were as follows: 26.2 ($+++$), 39.5 ($+--$), 55.3 ($-+-$), 62.4 ($--+$). For the four imbalanced situations the ratings were: 57.0 (++−), 58.2 (+−+), 54.8 (−++), 58.4 (−−−). (The lower the rating the greater the degree of pleasantness.) Negative valences in balanced situations seem to have been regarded as unpleasant, particularly if they involved the relationship between the first person, "I," and the other person "O," as in the −+− and −−+ triads.

Imbalance is theoretically stressful, and stress does imply or involve negative affect or unpleasantness. However, it is conceivable that if Jordan's subjects had been instructed to rate the degree of stress or instability generated by the triadic situations, data more consistent with the theory would have been obtained. This is particularly true if the subjects had been told that they were rating the kind of instability that is likely to produce a change in the relationship between two or more of the system objects.

Cartwright and Harary (1956) have pointed to an ambiguity in Heider's theory and thus in Jordan's data. They state that the opposite of liking is disliking, but that the opposite of a bond or relationship is not the absence of a bond or relationship. In the case of sentiments Heider talks about opposites and in the case of units, complements. Therefore, Cartwright and Harary argue that Jordan's triadic situations involving one or more negative unit relations are ambiguous as to their degree of balance or are "vacuously balanced." Furthermore, they point out that if the vacuously balanced situations are not averaged in with the balanced and imbalanced situations the difference between their mean unpleasantness ratings increases (balanced, 39; vacuously balanced, 51; not balanced, 66).

Morrissette (*1958*) used a somewhat different approach to obtain some of the same information in which Jordan (1953) was interested. Morrissette presented his subjects with a description of a social setting designed to produce positive unit relations between a group of three people including the subject. The social setting was simply one in which the subject had agreed to share an apartment with two other students, *a* and *b*, who had been living together for some time. This social setting was varied by manipulating the sentiment relation between the subject and *a* and between *a* and *b* so that they were either both positive, both negative, or one positive and one negative. The subjects were told that they had only briefly met one of their future roommates, *b*, and thus did not have an opportunity to form any sort of sentiment relation with him. They had, however, talked to the other future roommate, *a*, for some time and thus had ample opportunity to form a sentiment relation with him and to get an impression of *a*'s sentiment relation with *b*. All of the subjects (*Ss*) were presented with the same four sets of sentiment relations: *S* likes *a* and *a* likes *b*, *S* dislikes *a* and *a* likes *b*, *S* likes *a* and *a* dislikes *b*, *S* dislikes *a* and *a* dislikes *b*, and asked to predict how they would feel about *b*. After making each prediction the subjects marked rating scales indicating how comfortable they would feel in the situation, the probability that serious difficulty would arise among the roommates, and the amount of pressure toward changing the relationship.

The results are in agreement with balance theory predictions. In the situation with the two positive sentiment relations balance theory predicts that the third sentiment relation, the relation between S and b, will also be positive. A statistically significant percentage, 91 percent of 86 subjects, made this prediction. In the situation with two negative sentiment relations, balance theory again predicts that the third relation will be positive. This prediction was significantly upheld with 79 percent of the subjects designating the third relation as positive. It is evident, however, that even by making the third sentiment relation positive the total situation is not completely balanced. This is due to the fact that S will be rooming with a whom he dislikes, and a will be rooming with b whom he dislikes; i.e., the total situation contains two unbalanced dyads. In the two situations with one positive and one negative sentiment relation, balance theory predicts that the third sentiment relation is just as likely to be positive as negative. If the third relation is made negative then the triad of sentiment relations is balanced, but S is then rooming with one more person whom he dislikes and an unbalanced dyad is produced. The opposite occurs if the third sentiment relation is made positive. Morrissette found that in the situation in which there was a negative sentiment relation between S and a, 45 percent of the subjects predicted that the third sentiment relation would be positive and 55 percent negative, a nonsignificant difference. In the situation in which the sentiment relation between a and b was negative, the percentages (53 and 47, respectively) were also nonsignificant.

Using graph theory Morrissette was able to state two mathematical indices of the degree of balance resulting from each of the two possible solutions to each of the four social situations. Using both of these indices he found a perfect rank order correlation between the degree of imbalance and each of the three situational ratings made by the subjects. The greater the imbalance the greater the feeling of discomfort, probability of difficulty, and pressure to change.

Heider (1958) describes an unpublished study by Esch in which subjects were asked to predict the outcomes of certain social situations. The only one of these situations that Heider (1958) discusses is the following: "Bob thinks Jim very stupid and a first class bore. One day Bob reads some poetry he likes so well that he takes the trouble to track down the author in order to shake his hand. He finds that Jim wrote the poems" (p. 176). This unbalanced triad was resolved in the following ways: (1) 46 percent of the 101 subjects upgraded Bob's opinion of Jim; (2) 29 percent downgraded Bob's opinion of the poetry; (3) 5 percent questioned Jim's authorship of the poetry; (4) 2 percent differentiated the author so that the system consisted only of the positive part of Jim and the poetry, e.g., "Jim is smart in some lines but dumb in others"; (5) 19 percent of the subjects did not resolve the imbalance, but some (how many is not stated) were aware of the tension, e.g., "Bob is confused and does not know what to do. He finally briefly mentions his liking of the poems to Jim without much warmth."

Esch's data thus provide some, if not complete, support for balance theory. An obvious question about the data and the theory is how can one predict which of the various alternative methods of resolving tension will be selected. Heider does not discuss the matter at all.

Price, Harburg, and McLeod (1965) report a study of the extent to which hypothetical, balanced and imbalanced, interpersonal situations result in uneasy-pleasant feelings. College students were asked to select two people whom they liked best, two people whom they mildly liked, two people whom they slightly liked, and one person whom they strongly disliked. These people were to be college students of the same sex as the subjects. The subjects were then presented with a number of hypothetical interpersonal situations in which one of the two people who had previously been selected was represented as having a certain affective feeling toward the other. The interpersonal situations were so structured that the subjects' feelings for one of the persons (p to o) were either strong or slight liking and his feelings for the other person (p to q) were either strong, mild, or slight liking or strong disliking. The perceived feelings of one person for the other person (o to q) were described by the experimenter as being either strong, mild, or slight liking, or strong, mild, or slight disliking. Taking all possible combinations of these values for each of the three dyadic relationships gives 48 different interpersonal situations. Of these 48 situations 18 had three positive signs, 24 had two positive signs and one negative sign, and 6 had two negative signs and one positive sign. Due to lack of time in the experimental session, however, 4 of the 6 situations involving two negative signs and one positive sign were eliminated. In view of the further fact that none of the situations involved three negative signs, it is evident that the study was largely concerned with positive relations.

Each subject rated exactly half of the hypothetical situations on an uneasy-pleasant scale. The results by and large support the balance theory predictions. Only one of the balanced situations received a mean rating toward the uneasy end of the scale and only one of the imbalanced situations received a mean rating toward the pleasant end of the scale. The data were broken down to enable the testing of some of Newcomb's ideas regarding both the degree of affect between the subject and one of the other people, and the degree of agreement-disagreement (discrepancy of orientation) between the subject and one of the other persons with regard to their feelings about the third person. It was found that 70 percent of the comparisons significantly supported the predictions generated by the following two hypotheses: positive-negative affect varies with the degree of attraction between p and o (subject and one other person), holding constant discrepancy of orientation; positive-negative affect varies with the degree of orientation discrepancy, holding constant attraction between p and o.

Price, Harburg, and Newcomb (1966) report a study of hypothetical interpersonal situations in which all combinations of positive and negative signs were represented. Introductory psychology students were asked to select two best friends and two people whom they disliked. These people were to be students of the same sex as the subjects. The subjects were then presented with eight hypothetical situations in which one of the two people who had previously been selected was represented as having a certain affective feeling toward the other. These eight situations are presented in Table 8–1. The subjects responded to each of the eight situations by marking an uneasy-pleasant scale.

The data were analyzed by categorizing each subject's rating of each situation as either uneasy, neutral, or pleasant. The results are given in Table 8–1. Of the four balanced situations two (A and B) were regarded as significantly pleasant, and of the four imbalanced situations three (C, D, and E) were regarded as significantly uneasy. The remaining three situations (F, G, and H), all of which involve negative p to o relations, do not conform to expectations. The numbers of subjects rating situations G and H as uneasy or pleasant do not differ significantly, and significantly more subjects rated situation F as pleasant than uneasy (opposite of prediction).

Although Price, Harburg, and Newcomb do not draw this implication, these results possibly mean that balanced or imbalanced states are not most appropriately described along an uneasy-pleasant dimension. Imbalance is a hypothetical state that supposedly leads to some sort of balance restoring change. Balance, on the other hand, is a hypothetical state that does not lead to any change. This suggests that unstable-stable might be a more appropriate dimension for describing balance and imbalance than uneasy-pleasant. Uneasiness may be a reasonable approximation for instability but pleasantness is not a very good approximation for stability.[2]

Let's examine the three situations which did not conform to Price, Harburg, and Newcomb's expectations. In situation H the subjects dislike two people, one of whom likes the other. This balanced situation was

---

[2] In a study described in Chapter 9 Rosenberg (1965a) had subjects note the extent to which they were bothered by the "illogical" nature of certain hypothetical situations. Assuming that subjects do not take the word "illogical" literally, the logical-illogical dimension, like the stable-unstable dimension, is more theoretically appropriate than is the uneasy-pleasant dimension.

TABLE 8–1. *Percentage of Subjects Responding with Varying Signs of Affect to Eight Hypothetical Situations*

| | Sign of Affect | | |
Type of Situation	− (Uneasy)	N (Neutral)	+ (Pleasant)
A.[a] $p \xrightarrow{+} o$, $+\searrow \nearrow +$, q	6	7	87
B.[a] $p \xrightarrow{+} o$, $-\searrow \nearrow -$, q	5	6	89
C. $p \xrightarrow{+} o$, $+\searrow \nearrow -$, q	89	0	11
D. $p \xrightarrow{+} o$, $-\searrow \nearrow +$, q	84	8	8
E. $p \xrightarrow{-} o$, $+\searrow \nearrow +$, q	65	15	22
F. $p \xrightarrow{-} o$, $-\searrow \nearrow -$, q	17	38	45
G.[a] $p \xrightarrow{-} o$, $+\searrow \nearrow -$, q	43	22	35
H.[a] $p \xrightarrow{-} o$, $-\searrow \nearrow +$, q	28	39	33

[a] Balanced situations, all others being imbalanced.
SOURCE: Adapted from Price, Harburg, and Newcomb, 1966, p. 266.

not rated too pleasant possibly because it appears as if the subject's enemies are forming a coalition. At least to the present writer's phenomenology, however, the situation does seem to make sense and to imply a high degree of stability. This suggests that the situation would have been regarded as stable if the subjects had been asked to rate it in terms of the extent to which some sort of change in the signs would be expected. Consider situation *F*. In this imbalanced situation the subject dislikes two people, one of whom dislikes the other. Here we have a fair number of neutral and pleasant ratings, possibly because, unlike in situation *H*, the subject's enemies have not formed a coalition against him. The situation, however, does seem to be an unstable one in that some sort of movement toward coalition formation and a consequent change in one of the signs is likely. Finally, in situation *G* the subject's friend is disliked by someone whom the subject dislikes. The subjects may have felt uneasy about this situation because of the fact that their friends had to suffer the dislike of someone else. The situation nonetheless does seem to be a stable one. Suppose we learned that Castro disliked some democratic South American president of whom we approved. This situation is not as pleasant as it might be because the South American president would have to withstand the resultants of Castro's dislike. The situation is a stable one, however, in that we do not feel inclined to change any of the signs.

The above discussion does not imply that the pleasantness of any given social situation will not be an important causal consideration. It just means that a situation's balance or imbalance is only one of several important factors.

Burdick and Burnes (*1958*) tested the hypothesis that disagreement with a liked person produces tension or emotion. While the subjects were attached to GSR recording equipment, they first spent 5 minutes talking casually to the experimenter and then 30 minutes discussing two topics in succession, life after death and the draft. On one of these topics the experimenter agreed with the point of view taken by each subject and on one he disagreed. Both the order of the topics and the topic disagreed with were counterbalanced. Burdick and Burnes found that significantly greater GSR deflections were obtained under disagreement than agreement conditions. A postexperimental questionnaire revealed that 22 out of 24 subjects believed they would like the experimenter very much or fairly well if they had an opportunity to get to know him. An obvious next step would be to measure GSR while the sentiment relation is manipulated in either a positive or a negative direction.

Sampson and Insko (*1964*) tested the capability of Heider's balance theory for predicting autokinetic judgments. Two independent variables were manipulated in the experiment: sentiment relation between the subject and a stooge (liking-disliking) and discrepancy between the autokinetic judgments of the subject and stooge (large-small). The first period of the experiment was spent in an elaborate series of activities designed to give the stooge ample opportunity to get himself either liked or disliked. A postexperimental questionnaire revealed that the manipulation was successful. In the autokinetic situation, which was introduced during the second period as a new experiment, the stooge gave judgments that averaged either 11 inches or 1 inch more than those given by each subject in an initial series of five judgments.

According to balance theory the situation in which the subject likes and is dissimilar to the stooge, and the situation in which the subject dislikes and is similar to the stooge are both unbalanced. It is in these situations that change is expected. Furthermore, the change should be such as to increase the similarity between the subject and the liked stooge, and decrease the similarity between the subject and the disliked stooge. Both of these predictions were significantly upheld. Balance theory further implies that relative to the two balanced situations the two unbalanced situations should cause the subjects to feel more tense. Nervous-calm ratings of feelings while judging the light movement significantly upheld this prediction.

Comment. By and large the research reviewed in this section gives an encouraging degree of support to balance theory. The major problem raised by this literature concerns the most appropriate way of describing balanced and imbalanced states and whether or not the unpleasantness of some balanced states is very damaging to the theory.

EVALUATION

There are few theories within social psychology that appear to have such a wide range of applicability as does balance theory. Aspects of the topics of attitude change, person perception, interpersonal attraction, marital happiness, stability of the self-concept all appear to be related to balance formulations. Because of this fact balance theory is potentially a major theoretical orientation in social psychology, although it is not generally recognized as such.

Despite its wide range of applicability, however, balance theory has only begun to be experimentally investigated. For example, one problem that has not been investigated is whether or not balance really does imply complete stability. Suppose that p likes o, o likes x, and p likes x. Here we have a triadic system of three positive relations and the theory predicts no change. It is possible, however, that such a system will result in p increasing his evaluation of o and x; i.e., a summation effect may occur. Evidence with regard to the existence of summation effects in the context of congruity theory was reviewed in Chapter 6. Heider avoids the problem by not talking about degrees of either liking or disliking, but balance theory logically should be extended so as to cover small graduations in both sentiment and unit relations.

There may be difficulty, however, in conceptualizing the meaning of unit relation degrees. This illustrates the general vagueness of the whole unit concept. Two entities are connected by a unit relation if they are perceived as belonging together in some way or other. This sort of phenomenological conception may be acceptable as an initial starting point, but certainly not as a final theoretical definition.

It is this vagueness about the meaning of the term "unit" that leads to the confusion over the difference between the opposite and the complement of a relation, pointed out by Cartwright and Harary (1956). Heider (1958) admits that Cartwright and Harary are correct in their criticism and attempts to clarify matters by distinguishing between a negative and a neutral unit relation. He offers as examples of neutral and negative unit relations respectively the following two situations: "(1) p is unfamiliar with o who is seated next to him in the bus, and (2) p is unfamiliar with o whose ways and dress seem strangely different" (p. 202).

One of the most unsatisfactory aspects of balance theory is the fact that no statement is given as to which of many possible ways of reducing imbalance will be taken in any given situation.[2] The theory, as it has been developed, seems to have too many possible outcomes to the same circumstances. Newcomb lists seven possible resultants of imbalance.

Zajonc (1960) points out that it is not clear from balance theory what predictions are to be made when attractions among the entities of a triadic system are of differing origins and natures. To illustrate this point Zajonc reports a jocular inquiry of Festinger's as to whether, since he likes chickens and chickens like chicken feed, he ought also either to like chicken feed or to experience imbalance. Initially it might be thought that the primary difficulty with this example is the fact that o is a chicken and not another person. Even, however, if o were another person toward whom Festinger had cannibalistic intentions, this would still not mean that Festinger would either be attracted to the foods that o liked or suffer imbalance. The real problem, as Zajonc implies, is that liking to eat and evaluating positively for nongustatory reasons have to be distinguished. It is apparent that the owner of a chicken ranch, who might not even like to eat chicken, would suffer imbalance if he did not positively evaluate chicken feed.

Zajonc (1960) also raises the question about the imbalance of the love triangle, or competitive situation in which two young men who both love the same girl experience tension whether they are friends or enemies. Heider, however, has a reasonably satisfactory solution for this apparent theoretical difficulty. He points out that if the girl falls in love with one of the boys this implies that she does not love the other boy. The other boy is then involved in an imbalanced dyad in which he

[2] Steiner (1960) reports some evidence with regard to sex and personality differences in the utilization of different modes of imbalance resolution.

loves someone who does not love him. It is thus this possibility of an unbalanced dyad that produces tension between the suitors.

According to Osgood (1960) the major weakness of balance theory is the fact that it assigns both affective and connecting properties to the relations between cognitive entities. A positive sentiment relation, for example, implies that two entities are connected with an affective relationship. Congruity theory, on the other hand, assigns positive or negative values to two or more objects of judgment which then may or may not be connected with an assertion. Osgood (1960) argues that only if signs are applied to the associated objects of judgments does the cognitive interaction make sense. "When I see P *dancing with* O, and O is my girl or wife, the impact of this cognition obviously depends upon my attitude toward P (to say nothing of my attitude toward O), quite apart from the cognitive implication of *dancing with* (p. 348). But, of course, Heider would agree. Heider would handle the situation, not, however, by assigning values to wife and dancing partner, but by stating that the ego or husband has sentiment relations toward both. Whenever Osgood assigns a value to one of the associated objects of judgment Heider would simply say that the person or *p* has positive or negative sentiment relations toward both these objects. The theories thus use slightly different language to talk about the same thing.

Congruity and balance theory more clearly differ in the type of relationships that *p* perceives or infers as existing between the two objects of judgment or between *o* and *x*. According to congruity theory two objects of judgment are either associated by no assertion or by an associative or dissociative assertion; according to balance theory *o* and *x* are either associated by no relation or by positive or negative unit or sentiment relations. Associative assertions seem to involve either positive sentiment or unit relations or both, and dissociative assertions seem to involve either negative sentiment or unit relations or both. In our present state of knowledge there does not seem to be any way of deciding whether it is better to talk about assertions or about sentiment and unit relations, since both the concept of "assertion" and of "unit relation" are ill-defined.

9

Rosenberg and Abelson's
Affective-Cognitive Consistency Theory

THEORY

Affective-cognitive consistency theory has an initial and a later version. The initial version was developed by Rosenberg (1953, 1956, 1960a, 1960b, 1960c), and the later version was developed by Rosenberg in collaboration with Abelson (Abelson and Rosenberg, 1958; Rosenberg and Abelson, 1960). Each of these versions will be considered in turn.

Initial Version

Definition of Attitude. Rosenberg accepts as a starting point the common definition of attitude in terms of pro or con affect toward an object or class of objects. He maintains, however, that such affective sets are usually interconnected with cognitions or beliefs, so that it is preferable to conceive of attitudes as consisting of both affective and cognitive components. The cognitions of particular interest to Rosenberg are those relating attitude objects to other objects of affective significance in an instrumental way. For example, the physician's negative attitude toward socialized medicine involves negative affect for the object, socialized medicine, and also beliefs that it will lead to "debasement of medical standards" and the "loss of professional freedom." Thus attitudes consist of affect toward objects which are believed instrumentally related to other objects of affective significance.

Attitude Structure. In agreement with Peak (1955, 1958) Rosenberg maintains that attitudes possess psychological structures. To speak of psychological structure means that relations exist between psychological events so that change in one event will result in change in another. Thus

177

a change in the affective component of the attitude structure should result in a change in the cognitive components and vice versa. For example, if the doctor changed his attitude toward socialized medicine from negative to positive he would also be inclined to change his belief that socialized medicine leads to the debasement of medical standards, or if he changed his belief that socialized medicine leads to the debasement of medical standards he would also be inclined to change his attitude toward socialized medicine from negative to positive.

According to Rosenberg consistency in the attitude structure allows for prediction of the pro-con feelings toward an attitude object on the basis of the value placed upon various objects of affective significance and the perceived instrumental relations between these objects and the attitude object. This prediction is accomplished by computing an index that correlates with attitude. The index is obtained as follows. First, subjects rate the value placed upon various objects of affective significance. Second, subjects rate the extent to which each object of affective significance is perceived as being instrumentally relevant to the attitude object. Third, each subject's value rating for each object of affective significance is multiplied by his instrumentality rating for each of the same objects. Fourth and finally, the products of the value and instrumentality ratings are summed across objects to give an individual attitude index.

Attitudinal "Homeostasis." Change in the direction of maintaining consistency is the basis for Rosenberg's (1960a) " 'homeostatic' conception of attitude dynamics" (p. 22). This conception is stated in three propositions:

1. When the affective and cognitive components of an attitude are mutually consistent, the attitude is in a stable state.
2. When these components are mutually inconsistent, to a degree that exceeds the individual's "tolerance limit" for such inconsistency, the attitude is in an unstable state.
3. In such an unstable state the attitude will undergo reorganizing activity until one of three possible outcomes is achieved. These outcomes are: (a) rejection of the communications, or other forces, that engendered the original inconsistency between affect and cognition and thus rendered the attitude unstable, i.e. restoration of the original stable and consistent attitude; (b) "fragmentation" of the attitude through the isolation from each other of the mutually inconsistent affective and cognitive components; (c) accommodation to the original inconsistency-producing change so that a new attitude, consistent with that change, is now stabilized, i.e. attitude change. (1960c, p. 322)

Rosenberg asserts that the first of the three outcomes of attitude instability, rejection of influence attempt, will, in general, occur if the attacked affective-cognitive structure allows for the effective regulation of adaptive behavior. For example, a graduate student's positive attitude toward education and his belief that education is necessary for a higher standard of living allows for the effective regulation of his scholastic behavior and thus makes the rejection of any anti-education communication very likely. If, however, the influence attempt is too strong, either fragmentation of the attitude structure or attitude change will occur. Fragmentation results if attitude change is prevented by either objective reality or the needs of the individual. In order to rationalize his role behavior, our hypothetical graduate student, for example, may decide that some forms of education are good and some are bad.

Two Sequences of Attitude Change. According to Rosenberg all attitude change and acquisition can be understood as resulting from one or both of two distinct sequences. One sequence is cognitive change followed by affective change, the other is affective change followed by cognitive change. A change in feeling about an attitude object will result in a change in belief about this same attitude object and vice versa.

Later Version

Rosenberg (1960a) states that the two theoretical versions differ in that the later version deals with inconsistency reduction both more generally and more molecularly.

Cognitive Elements. Cognitive elements, for Rosenberg and Abelson, are the basic entities of human thought involving representation of concrete and abstract things. Three nonmutually exclusive classes of cognitive elements are distinguished: actors, means, and ends. Actors are cognitively represented persons, groups, or institutions; means are cognitively represented instrumental activities; and ends are cognitively represented goals. For example, if a student, in order to maintain the standards of the university, reports someone for cheating on an examination, we have the involvement of actor (the student), means (reporting the cheater), and end (the standards of the university).

Cognitive Relations. Abelson and Rosenberg theorize about four relations between cognitive elements (positive, negative, null, and ambivalent), which are symbolized by p, n, o, and a respectively. These relations are illustrated but not exactly defined. Positive cognitive relations are illustrated by the following: "likes," "uses," "possesses," "helps," "justifies," and "is consistent with." Negative cognitive relations are illustrated by: "dislikes," "opposes," "inhibits," "obviates," and "is incompatible with." Null cognitive relations are illustrated by: "is indifferent to," "is not responsible for," "does not affect," "does not interest," "cannot

ensue from," "is unconnected to." Ambivalent relations are combinations
of positive and negative relations.

Although Rosenberg and Abelson do not define what they mean by
cognitive relations, they do attempt to specify the basis on which certain
cognitive relations are eliminated from consideration. Relations such as
"has to do with," "is related to," "depends upon," and "is connected with,"
are eliminated because they are difficult to classify as to sign. Other relations such as "might have acted upon," "probably will help," and "ought
to seek" are eliminated from consideration because they involve time
sense, moral imperative, or conditionality and probability. Finally, any
cognitive relation is eliminated if it happens to connect cognitive elements (actors, means, and ends) at least one of which lacks affective
significance.

Cognitive Units. Cognitive units are pairs of cognitive elements
connected by a relation. If the elements are symbolized by A and B and
the relations by r, then ArB represents a cognitive unit. A simple sentence
in which two elements are affectively related in some manner thus constitutes a cognitive unit. Many more complex sentences may be reduced
to the simple ArB type by broadening the definition of element. Abelson
and Rosenberg (1958) illustrate this procedure with the following sentence: " 'Nasser (A) insists on (p) all Suez tools (B) belonging to (p)
Egypt (C)'" (p. 3). Symbolically this sentence is $Ap(BpC)$. By designating BpC as a new element D the sentence is reduced to the simple
form ApD. By such a procedure the number of sentences is reduced to
four: ApB, AnB, AoB, and AaB.

Rosenberg (1960a) maintains that what he has previously called
an attitude structure can be represented by a number of cognitive units
which are identical with regard to one of their cognitive elements, the
attitude object. The attitude structure consists of an attitude object of
affective significance which is instrumentally related to other objects of
affective importance. In terms of the later theoretical version each instrumental relation between the attitude object and another affective object
involves a cognitive unit. These rather abstract concepts are illustrated in
Figure 9–1. Here we see that a positive attitude object (education) has a
positive instrumental relation to two objects of positive affective significance (artistic appreciation and high standard of living) and a negative
instrumental relation to two objects of affective significance (ignorance
and poverty). In terms of the initial version of the theory this whole
complex is one attitude structure. In terms of the later version, however,
we have a number of cognitive units (such as education counteracts
poverty) which happen to have in common one component object (education).

The later version of the theory is both more molecular and more

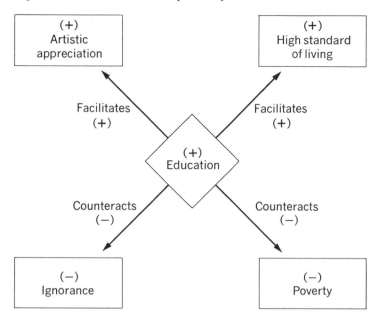

FIGURE 9-1. An attitude structure represented by a positive attitude object, education, that has a positive instrumental relation to two objects of positive affective significance and a negative instrumental relation to two objects of negative affective significance.

general than the early version. This is because the later version concentrates on the individual cognitive units within the attitude structure and makes use of cognitive relations other than instrumental ones.

The Conceptual Arena. The conceptual arena consists of all those related cognitive elements which are phenomenally relevant to a given issue or attitude object. Following Zajonc (1954), Abelson and Rosenberg (1958) describe a structured interview technique by means of which it is possible to map the conceptual arena in terms of the positive (p), negative (n), and null (o) relations existing among all possible parts of cognitive elements. This technique yields the structure of the conceptual arena which can be represented in matrix form. The rows and columns of the matrix represent each of the cognitive elements and the cells the relations between all possible pairs of elements.

Psycho-Logic. Whenever someone is motivated to think about the cognitive elements in his conceptual arena he is guided by "psychological" rules. These rules, which allow an individual to discover new symbolic sentences by combining two old sentences with a common element, are as follows (Abelson and Rosenberg, 1958, p. 4):

Rule 1. *ApB* and *BpC* implies *ApC*.

Rule 2. *ApB* and *BnC* implies *AnC*.

Rule 3. *AnB* and *BnC* implies *ApC*.

Rule 4. *AoB* and *BrC* implies nothing about the relation between *A* and *C*, irrespective of *r*.

Rule 5. If *ApC* and *AnC* are both implied, or if one is held initially and the other implied, then *AaC*. This is the definition of the ambivalent relation.

Rule 6. *AaC* and *CpD* implies *AaD*.

Rule 7. *AaC* and *CnD* implies *AaD*.

Rule 8. *AaC* and *CaD* implies *AaD*.

Except for the rules involving ambivalent or null relations the theoretical implications are identical with those of balance theory. In balance theory any triad involving an odd number of negative relations is not balanced; in the first three rules above, the implied relation is always one that would not create an odd number of negative relations. Abelson and Rosenberg (1958) point out that the above rules are psychological and not logical. For purposes of illustration they give the following example of rule 3:

India (*A*) opposes (*n*) U.S. Far Eastern policy (*B*). U.S. Far Eastern policy (*B*) is directed against (*n*) Communism (*C*).

Therefore, India (*A*) is in favor of (*p*) Communism (*C*).

Although such "deduction" is obviously illogical, Abelson and Rosenberg maintain that it occurs frequently.

Balance and Imbalance. Conceptual arenas or structure matrices may be either balanced or imbalanced. A balanced conceptual arena is one in which no amount of thinking or application of the psycho-logical rules leads to the discovery of ambivalent relationships; an imbalanced conceptual arena is one in which thinking does lead to the discovery of inconsistent or ambivalent relationships. Complete balance among a set of cognitive elements is, in commonsense terms, a black and white attitude.

Resolution of Imbalance. Inconsistency in the conceptual arena is only discovered through thought. Once inconsistency is discovered there will be some attempt to resolve the imbalance. Resolution can be accomplished in three ways: change in one or more of the relations, redefinition or differentiation of one or more of the elements, cessation in thinking about the inconsistency. Consider the Yale student who is in favor of having co-eds at Yale, wants good grades, but believes that having co-eds at Yale would interfere with getting good grades. The imbalance could be relieved by changing one of the three relations so that he is not in favor of having co-eds at Yale, or does not want good grades, or does not believe that having co-eds at Yale would interfere with getting good grades. The hypothetical Yale student could also resolve the imbalance by differentiating "getting good grades" into "getting C's" and "getting A's." If by getting good grades the student means getting C's there is no inconsistency. Finally, the student could resolve the inconsistency simply by not thinking about it.

In this illustration change in only one cognitive relation would resolve the imbalance. In many conceptual arenas, however, resolution of imbalance through change may require alteration of many cognitive relations. In this latter situation Abelson and Rosenberg (1958) maintain that, assuming all relations are equally resistant to change, the operation involving the fewest changes is the one that is most likely to occur. Abelson and Rosenberg provide a set of rules by which this balancing operation involving the fewest changes can be discovered from an examination of a matrix representation of a conceptual arena. These rules are obtained from a theorem resulting from a mathematical statement and development of the theory.

In a separate publication Abelson (1959) presents a somewhat different picture of imbalance resolution. He states that there are four modes of imbalance resolution: denial, bolstering, differentiation, and transcendence. Denial involves the alteration of one or more cognitive relations. This is illustrated by the previous example of the Yale student who might refuse to believe that having co-eds at Yale would interfere with getting good grades. Bolstering involves adducing additional consistent relations with one or the other of the inconsistent cognitive units. Bolstering does not resolve the inconsistency but simply "drowns it out." As Abelson points out this is the type of mechanism referred to by Festinger (1957) in his theory of cognitive dissonance. The smoker, for example, may attempt to reduce dissonance by telling himself that smoking is enjoyable, no more dangerous than driving, good for the nerves, etc. Differentiation is the previously discussed mechanism illustrated by the Yale student who redefines "getting good grades" so that it can mean either "getting C's" or "getting A's." Transcendence involves relating both the inconsistent cognitive units to a larger superordinate concept or element. For example, the inconsistency between science and religion may be transcended by reasoning that both science and religion are necessary in order to achieve a fuller life or deeper understanding of the universe.

Abelson further states that there is a hierarchy among the modes of belief resolution: denial, bolstering, denial (a second time), differentiation, and transcendence. This hierarchy is based on the relative ease with which balance may be restored using any one of the modes. If imbalance occurs through exposure to persuasive communications advocating cognitive units inconsistent with those already held, denial of the relevance or truth of the asserted relations is most likely to occur. If this fails, bolstering of the old relations will be attempted, and then, after opportunity for further thought, denial or change in one or more relations will occur. Abelson assumes that denial and bolstering are simpler, although not less effective, modes than differentiation and transcendence. Differentiation is more difficult than denial and bolstering because it requires intellectual skill and flexibility to split apart a cognitive element, particularly when it is of some affective significance. Transcendence is a last resort mode of resolution because of the great difficulty in creating a convincing superordinate structure.

RESEARCH

The research that is relevant to affective-cognitive theory will be discussed under two headings, attitude structure and structural change. The bulk of this reseach is more directly relevant to the initial than the later version of the theory.

Attitude Structure

Rosenberg (*1953, 1956*) attempted to demonstrate that attitudes toward free speech for Communists and toward segregated Negro housing could be predicted on two bases: personal values, and beliefs that the attitude objects are instrumentally related to personal values. Three to five weeks after subjects had indicated their attitudes toward free speech for Communists and segregated Negro housing, they were given a value importance test and a perceived instrumentality test. The value importance test required that the subjects rate a number of values, such as American prestige in other countries, equal rights for everyone, patriotism, and education, in terms of personal satisfaction. The perceived instrumentality test had two parts, one part for each attitude object. The test required that the subjects rate the above values in terms of whether a given attitude object (segregated Negro housing for example) contributed to or blocked their attainment. For every subject the value and instrumental scores for each value were multiplied and then summed so as to give a predicted attitude score. This was done separately for each of the two attitude objects. Rosenberg found that the predicted attitude scores were significantly related to the obtained attitude scores.

The results were taken as supporting the hypothesis that the affective significance of an attitude object is a function of whether or not it is perceived as facilitating or blocking the attainment of values and whether or not these values are of importance. Rosenberg discusses, but does not adequately explain away, the possibility that these results can be accounted for in terms of an attempt on the part of the subjects to appear consistent.

Woodruff and Di Vesta (1948) studied the relationship between attitude toward the abolishment of fraternities and sororities and importance values perceived as being relevant to this issue. Assessments were made of three things: attitudes toward the abolishment of fraternities and sororities; the perceived beneficial or detrimental economic, social, scholastic, and moral effect of fraternities and sororities; and the importance placed upon economic, social, scholastic, and moral values. For every subject scores were assigned to each value to reflect its general importance. These scores were in turn multiplied by +1 or 2 depending upon how beneficial fraternities and sororities were perceived as being in relation to any particular value, or they were multiplied by −1 or 2 depending upon how detrimental fraternities and sororities were perceived as being in relation to any particular value. The weighted value scores were then summed for each subject so as to give a predicted attitude score. The correlation between the predicted and obtained attitude scores was +.804 for a sample of 84 subjects.

Cartwright (1949) maintains that people who bought war bonds during World War II did it in part because of the existence of certain motivational structures. People tended to be persuaded by the war bond propaganda if the buying of war bonds was perceived as instrumental to the attainment of desired goals. When people were asked why they were buying bonds they gave responses consistent with this formulation. For example, they might say that they were buying bonds in order to win the war, to save for personal use in the future, or to help prevent inflation. Furthermore, it was found that at every income level and regardless of whether there had been personal solicitation, the more reasons that were given for buying bonds the greater the likelihood that bonds were actually purchased.

Cartwright also states that the data agree with the formulation that an alternative will not be chosen if it is seen as leading to an undesired goal or as not leading as directly to a desired goal as would different actions. Individuals who did not buy bonds gave some of the following reasons: the interest on bonds is lower than on other investments, bonds can not be redeemed, bonds prolong the war, bonds have too long a maturity period, and bonds will be of no value if we lose the war. If it can be assumed that bond purchasing activity is indicative of attitudes toward bonds, then Cartwright's data are obviously consistent with Rosenberg's concept of attitude structure.

Smith (1949) reports some interview data indicating that attitude toward Russia is related to the value placed upon liberty. A cross-sectional sample of 250 people from a suburb of Boston were questioned regarding their social relationships, values, and attitudes toward Russia. Early in the interview they were asked to name the things that they valued most or the things that were most important to them. Later in the interview the respondents were asked to select from a list the things that were most important in making them feel as they did toward Russia. The list included: the lack of free enterprise in Russia, the possibility of war with Russia, Russia's treatment of churches, Russia's concern for the welfare of her people, and the lack of freedom and democracy inside Russia. Smith found that significantly more of the respondents who had initially mentioned liberty as an important value indicated that the lack of freedom and democracy inside Russia was a determining aspect of their attitude toward Russia. However, the respondents who had initially mentioned economic security as a value did not indicate that Russia's concern for the welfare of her people was a determining aspect of their attitude. Smith maintains that two factors contribute to this latter finding. The first is the scarcity of information about the social welfare policies of Russia. The second is related to the fact that, as revealed by further interview data, the economic security respondents, relative to the liberty respondents, had narrow and circumscribed interests. Smith argues that economic security was not a value related to the world at large but simply an immediate, personal interest. Thus Smith concludes that a person will tend to orient an attitude in terms of one of his values to the extent that: (1) the value is of personal importance; (2) there is sufficient information available to relate the value to the attitude; and (3) the scope of the value is broad enough to extend to the attitude.

Fishbein (1963) presents some data indicating that attitudes toward Negroes can be predicted on the basis of beliefs or cognitions about the characteristics that Negroes possess and the value placed upon these characteristics. Three assessments were made. First, subjects indicated on evaluative semantic differential scales the value placed upon 10 characteristics, such as dark skin, athletic, tall, and lazy. Second, the subjects rated the extent to which they believed Negroes possessed each of these characteristics. Ratings were made on semantic differential scales containing such polar opposites as "probable-improbable" and "likely-unlikely." Third, the subjects indicated their attitudes toward Negroes on evaluative semantic differential scales. Fishbein obtained an estimated attitude score for each subject on the basis of the first two assessments. Each subject's estimated score was computed by summing the products of the belief and value scores for each of the 10 characteristics. In agreement with expectations the correlation between the estimated and obtained attitude scores was quite high, +.801. The correlations of obtained attitude with the value scores only and the belief scores only were +.468 and +.017, respectively. Both of these correlations are significantly lower than the correlation between estimated and obtained attitude. This was interpreted as demonstrating the necessity of considering both the value placed upon the characteristics and the beliefs about the relation between valued characteristics and the attitude object.

In this study the beliefs or cognitions were not concerned with instrumental relations between attitude object and values, as in Rosenberg's (1953, 1956) and Woodruff and Di Vesta's (1948) studies, but rather with the extent to which the attitude object possessed valued characteristics. The use of cognitive relations other than instrumental ones makes this study relevant to the later but not the initial version of affective-cognitive consistency theory.

Comment. The above studies of attitude structure all indicate that there is a good deal of consistency in the relationship between attitudes and values. While it is possible that some of the consistency found in these studies is due to rationalization, it seems unlikely that this is a sufficient explanation for all of the data.

Structural Change

Carlson (1956) presents evidence consistent with the hypothesis that attitude change results from a change in the perceived relevance of the attitude object for the attainment of certain values. The experimental manipulations involved an attempt to demonstrate that allowing Negroes to move into white neighborhoods would facilitate the attainment of four values: American prestige in other countries, protection of property values, equal opportunity for personal development, and being experienced, broad-minded, and worldly-wise. The change procedure involved two parts. The first part was a class assignment, presented in the guise of a "Test of Objectivity," to support the proposition that allowing Negroes to move into white neighborhoods would be a means of obtaining the above values. The second part of the change procedure was a discussion of the assignment by the class instructor in which the instrumentality proposition was further supported. An experimenter, not in any way connected with the change procedure, measured the subjects' attitudes, values, and perceived instrumentality relation between the attitude object and values both before and after the change manipulations. A control group was administered the same before and after measures without the intervening change procedure.

Carlson found that, as predicted, significantly more experimental than control subjects changed their instrumental ratings and attitudes in the anticipated direction. Further, the correlation between attitude change and the product of the value and instrumentality ratings summed over values for each subject was found to be a significant $+.27$.

Di Vesta and Merwin (1960) report evidence that attitudes toward teaching as a career can be made more favorable by changing the perceived instrumentality of teaching for the satisfaction of the achievement need. Two experimental groups were exposed to two different communications before and after receiving measures of attitude toward teaching as a career, the achievement need, and perceived instrumentality of teaching for the satisfaction of the achievement need. The communications were panel discussions recorded by the Department of Radio and Television of Syracuse University. Both of the panel discussions maintained that teaching is a desirable career but differed in the emphasis upon teaching as instrumental to the satisfaction of the achievement need. For example, one panel pointed out that teaching is a profession where one gets concrete evidence for one's accomplishments, and this provides opportunities for personal accomplishments and contributions to the community. The other panel pointed out the desirable lack of competitiveness with other teachers and the frequent vacations. A control group was exposed to a related non-need oriented communication before and after receiving the assessments.

Di Vesta and Merwin found that the achievement panel produced significant positive change in the perceived instrumentality of teaching for satisfaction of achievement need and in attitude toward teaching, while the nonachievement panel produced significant negative change in both of these dependent variables. There was no significant change in the control group. The correlation between attitude change and the products of the achievement scores by the instrumentality change scores was a significant but low +.26.

Rosenberg (1960a, 1960c) examined the reorganization in cognitive structure that follows attitude (affect) change produced through posthypnotic suggestion. Subjects were initially given a questionnaire designed to measure attitudes toward and interest in seven different social issues such as foreign aid, Negroes moving into white communities, federal medical insurance, and the city manager plan. Then each subject judged the importance of a series of values (equal rights, education, etc.) and the perceived instrumentality of one high interest and one low interest attitude object for the attainment of these values. This latter "Cognitive Structure Test," along with the attitude questionnaire, was administered before and shortly after the subjects were given posthypnotic suggestions to change their feelings toward the crucial high and low interest attitude objects. A control group, which was not capable of being deeply hypnotized, was administered the attitude questionnaire and the Cognitive Structure Test before and after being told to fall asleep.

Before-after change scores revealed that the experimental and control groups significantly differed in the predicted direction with regard to the manipulated high and low interest attitude objects but not with regard to the nonmanipulated attitude objects. Further, as predicted, there was significantly more change for the experimental than the control group in the cognitive structures associated with the high and low interest attitude objects. This structural change was due to significant changes in both the instrumentality and importance ratings. For example, if a subject changed his attitude toward federal medical insurance from negative to positive, this change may have been associated with increased perceived instrumentality of federal medical insurance to the attainment of equal rights and increased importance of the equal rights value.

Rosenberg reports that when the subjects were questioned prior to amnesia removal they insisted that their changed attitudes were genuine. Some of the subjects were not aware that they had changed and when presented with the evidence expressed great surprise. A typical response was that they must have misunderstood the instructions the first time they took the test. Other subjects who were aware of the change stated that they had initially misunderstood the instructions or the meaning of the test stimuli, or that their previous attitudes were simply incorrect. With the removal of the hypnotic amnesia Rosenberg indicates that all of the subjects were able to reestablish their original attitudes.

In a second experiment Rosenberg studied the effect of posthypnotic suggestion over a week rather than just over a few hours. Control subjects, untested for hypnotizability, and experimental subjects, capable of deep hypnosis, were given the Cognitive Structure Test and a questionnaire measure of three attitudes. The experimental subjects were given posthypnotic suggestions that upon awakening they would be against rather than in favor of foreign aid. The assessments were readministered to all subjects 2, 4, and 7 days after the experimental subjects were given the posthypnotic suggestions. The results indicated that at each of these testing periods the experimental group changed more than the control group both in the manipulated attitude toward foreign aid and in related cognitive structure. Further, the experimental group did not change more than the control group in the nonmanipulated attitudes or in related cognitive structures. After amnesia removal most subjects regained their former attitudes, although there was some tendency for a few subjects to retain the induced attitudes in a weakened form.

An interview held before amnesia removal revealed an interesting tendency for some subjects to justify their attitude change on the basis of having initially misunderstood the meaning of the test stimuli. Some of the subjects redefined the objects of judgment into good and bad components during the second testing. For example, one subject redefined foreign aid into financial aid which he considered bad and technological aid which he considered good. This is the sort of meaning change about which Asch (1948, 1952) made such a major theoretical point. Asch maintains that such a shift in meaning is responsible for the apparent, but not actual, change in judgment. However, as was previously pointed out, the results from the prestige suggestion literature are ambiguous as to the type of causal relation existing between judgment and meaning. Rosenberg's results, however, are not ambiguous in this respect. The hypnotically induced change in affect manifested in a changed judgment was rationalized through a change in meaning. In this situation it is evident that, contrary to Asch's theoretical statement, changed meaning was a resultant and not a cause of changed judgment or affect.

Rosenberg and Abelson (1960) report a study that is more directly relevant to the later than the initial version of the theory. The study is a test of the hypothesis that individuals follow the principle of least effort (make the fewest number of necessary changes) in resolving imbalance. Subjects were asked to play the role of a person who possessed an imbalanced cognitive structure and then were given a number of communications regarding various aspects of the cognitive dilemma. The communications were arranged so that the acceptance of one of them would restore balance through a single cognitive change. It was thus possible to see whether the subjects did in fact follow the principle of least effort in resolving imbalance. While this general description of the procedure is simple enough the details of the actual experiment are somewhat complicated.

The subjects were given the role of department store owner and provided with certain information about three separate concepts: the volume of sales; modern art; and Fenwick, the manager of the rug department. One third of the subjects were told to feel positively toward sales, modern art, and Fenwick; one third to feel positively toward sales, and Fenwick, and negatively toward modern art; one third to feel positively toward sales and negatively toward modern art and Fenwick. In addition, all of the subjects were given identical information with regard to the relations among the concepts: displays of modern art will reduce sales, Fenwick plans a display of modern art in the rug department, and Fenwick has in the past increased the volume of sales. The subjects were provided with various facts to support these ascribed relationships. The cognitive structures for the three groups are described in Figure 9–2. The locus of imbalance in each of the three structures differs. In the first structure imbalance results from the fact that positively evaluated modern art hurts positively evaluated sales. In the second structure imbalance results from the fact that positively evaluated Fenwick plans to mount a display of negatively evaluated modern art. And in the third structure imbalance results from the fact that negatively evaluated Fenwick has increased the volume of positively evaluated sales. Balance could be restored in each structure by altering a single cognitive relation.

Tests involving evaluation of the three concepts and the relations between them revealed that a number of subjects failed to accurately

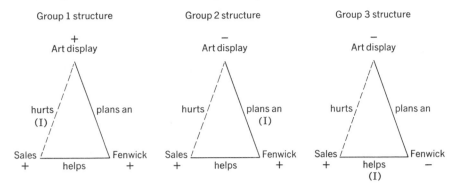

FIGURE 9-2. The three cognitive structures; I denotes the locus of imbalance; dashed lines indicate negative relations, solid lines positive relations. (After Rosenberg and Abelson, 1960, p. 128)

internalize the cognitive structures. These subjects were eliminated from the remainder of the experiment. Interestingly enough, approximately half of these subjects distorted the cognitive structures so as to achieve premature balance.

The remaining subjects for all groups were presented with three communications, all represented as coming from different store officers. These communications were: the Art-Sales communication which maintained that modern art displays increase sales, the Fenwick-Art communication which maintained that Fenwick does not intend to have a modern art display, and the Fenwick-Sales communication which maintained that Fenwick has failed to maintain sales. After reading each communication the subjects rated them on a number of 5-point alternative scales (pleased, persuaded, accurate). The primary prediction was that the subjects would evaluate most highly that communication allowing them to change the sign of the single imbalanced relation. Thus Group 1 should evaluate most highly the Art-Sales communication, Group 2 the Fenwick-Art communication, and Group 3 the Fenwick-Sales communication. A secondary prediction was that after the evaluation of the communication implying one change, the communication implying two rather than three changes would be evaluated more highly. Specifically, for Group 1 the Fenwick-Art communication would be evaluated more highly than the Fenwick-Sales communication, for Group 3 the Fenwick-Art more highly than the Art-Sales, and for Group 2 no differences between the evaluation of the Art-Sales and Fenwick-Sales communication because they both imply two changes.[1] An analysis of

---

[1] Although Rosenberg and Abelson do not mention the matter, this secondary prediction is based on the assumption that the positive evaluation of sales is unchangeable.

variance of the summed evaluative ratings for each communication revealed that both the primary and secondary predictions were significantly upheld and that there was no significant remaining residual.

Rosenberg and Abelson replicated the experiment using communications that were modified in an unspecified manner. Again the major and secondary predictions were significantly upheld; however, this time there was significant remaining residual. The major irregularity accounting for this significant residual was apparently the fact that Group 3 evaluated the communication asserting that Fenwick will be prevented from hanging the art display just as highly as the communication asserting that Fenwick has hurt sales. It was the latter Fenwick-Sales communication that theoretically should have been evaluated most highly.

In order to gain more information about this irregularity Rosenberg and Abelson did a third experiment in which the single imbalanced relation for each of the three groups was more strongly established. This was accomplished by supporting the imbalanced relation with more evidence. Again it was found that the F's for the major prediction, secondary prediction, and remaining residual were significant. The predictions, however, were less significantly upheld in this experiment than in the previous one. The major irregularity once more was in Group 3, where the Fenwick-Art communication was evaluated more highly than the Fenwick-Sales communication.

The subjects in the latter two experiments, after having evaluated the communications, rerated the three concepts and indicated their beliefs about the relations between them. It was thus possible to ascertain the extent to which the subjects actually achieved resolution of imbalance. The results were quite different for the three groups. In Group 1, 16 subjects achieved balance and 10 did not. The analogous numbers in Groups 2 and 3 were 6 and 18, and 4 and 18 respectively. Although no test of significance was reported, the numbers indicate more resolution of imbalance in Group 1 than in either Groups 2 or 3. Rosenberg and Abelson assert that the assumption that people are motivated to restore balance, while not disconfirmed, is part of a more complex picture.

This more complex picture, according to Rosenberg and Abelson, involves the tendency to maximize gain and minimize loss or more specifically in this case to maximize sales and minimize loss. For Group 1 the achievement of balance would mean that a liked Fenwick planned a liked art display that would facilitate sales. Thus the tendency to achieve balance and the tendency to maximize sales worked together. In the case of the other two groups, however, matters were more complicated. For Group 2 the achievement of balance would mean that a liked Fenwick did not plan a disliked art display which would hurt sales. Balance thus involved a maintenance of the status quo and no gain in sales. It is therefore understandable that the Group 2 subjects changed from negative to positive their attitude toward the Art-Sales relation. Thinking that a modern art display helps sales did not achieve balance, but it did satisfy the desire to increase sales. For Group 3 the achievement of balance would mean that a disliked Fenwick, who has hurt sales in the past, is planning a disliked art display which is going to further hurt sales. These subjects changed the Fenwick-Art relation so that Fenwick was not believed to be planning a modern art display. This change was coordinated with the unexpectedly high evaluation of the Fenwick-Art communication. By believing that Fenwick was not going to mount a modern art display the threat of further sales loss was averted, although balance was not achieved.

Rosenberg and Abelson speculate that the tendency to maximize gain and minimize loss may be a special case of the tendency to resolve imbalance. Thus the self $(+)$ associated with (p) a motive-frustrating state of affairs $(-)$ can be considered an imbalance situation, and the self $(+)$ associated with (p) a motive-satisfying state of affairs $(+)$, a balanced situation. In terms of the present problem the motive-satisfying state of affairs is, of course, an increased volume of sales. In the language of rules one and two, if the self likes increased sales (self p increased sales), and increased sales are facilitated by a certain situation (increased sales p situation), then the self will like this situation (self p situation); or if the self likes increased sales (self p increased sales), and increased sales are hindered by a certain situation (increased sales n situation), then the self will dislike this situation (self n situation). Rosenberg and Abelson state that such hedonic relations involving the self frequently form the basis for experiments on dissonance theory (Festinger, 1957).

It should be clear that just the simple involvement of the self as a cognitive element is not a sufficient explanation for the experimental results. When values were assigned to sales, Fenwick, and modern art, the self was implicitly involved in every case. If a subject were told to like Fenwick then the subject's self would be involved. The crucial matter is the involvement of the self in a motive-satisfying or -frustrating way. The subjects were told to play the role of a store manager and thus were motivated, not simply to maintain their positive attitude toward sales, but to actually increase sales.

Rosenberg (1965a) reports a study which explores the effect of two variables (hedonic-antihedonic and personal-general) upon feelings of being bothered by the "illogical nature" of certain hypothetical situations. Rosenberg argues that an inconsistent cognitive unit which forecasts gain is quite different from an inconsistent cognitive unit which forecasts loss. Cognitive units forecast gain when the last two signs are the same (both plus or both minus) and the relating cognition is either an instrumental relation or a sentiment relation. Consider the following two examples (1965a, p. 132):

My hated antagonist (−) supports (+) my favorite plan for reorganizing the department (+).
The charlatan Paracelsus (−) always loathed (−) those who victimized the poor (−).

In the first (−++ or −p+) example an inconsistent cognitive unit forecasts gain through a positive instrumental relation. In the second (−−− or −n−) example an inconsistent cognitive unit forecasts gain through a negative sentiment relation. The presence of hedonic meaning or forecasting of gain is dependent upon the last two signs being the same and the relating cognition being either an instrumental relation or a sentiment relation. In the case of cognitive relations having to do with common groupings (e.g., "belongs with" or "is a part of") hedonic implications are not always present.

The two remaining inconsistent cognitive units (++− and +−+) are antihedonic when they involve instrumental or sentiment relations. Rosenberg (1965a, p. 133) gives the following two examples:

The distinguished firm of Schlag and Sons (+) have put on the market (+) a completely worthless sphygmomanometer (−)

and

The church of my choice (+) is opposed to (−) the laudable goal of desegregation (+).

Rosenberg (1965a) specifically hypothesizes that *"reactive intolerance for inconsistency will be of lesser intensity if the attitudinal cognition in question conveys a hedonic assertion or promise of gain and of greater intensity if it conveys an antihedonic assertion or promise of loss"* (pp. 133–134).

A second consideration affecting "intolerance for inconsistency" is the extent to which the cognitive unit involves the individual's personal life situation as opposed to a more general impersonal situation. The distinction can be illustrated with the two previous examples of hedonic cognitive units. The first hedonic cognitive unit, which involves someone supporting "my favorite plan for reorganizing the department," is personal; and the second cognitive unit, which involves someone loathing "those who victimized the poor," is general. Rosenberg hypothesizes that intolerance for inconsistency is greater in the case of personal cognitive units than in the case of negative cognitive units.

In the experiment subjects rated the extent to which they were bothered by the "illogical nature" of each of 16 hypothetical situations. The hypothetical situations represented inconsistent cognitive units and were of four types: hedonic-personal, hedonic-general, antihedonic-personal, and antihedonic-general. In his instructions to the subjects Rosenberg put great emphasis upon making ratings in terms of the extent to which the situations were "illogical," "confusing," and "senseless."

An analysis of variance of the ratings indicated that both the hedonic-antihedonic and personal-general variables had highly significant effects in the predicted directions. There was also an interaction between these two variables indicating that the difference between hedonic and antihedonic was greater for personal than for general situations. Rosenberg (1965a) interprets the interaction as implying that "the hedonic or antihedonic import of a particular cognition is keyed to the person's perception of goal attainment or goal frustration for *himself*" (p. 141).

A possible criticism of the above findings relates to the fact that the subjects may have been responding to the situations in terms of hedonistic considerations and not in terms of consistency. In order to investigate this matter Rosenberg did an additional study in which the hypothetical situations differed in terms of consistency as well as in terms of the hedonic-antihedonic and personal-general dimensions. Consistent cognitive units were created by reversing the sign of the first cognitive element in each inconsistent cognitive unit. The results indicated that in every instance the subjects rated the inconsistent situation as more "illogical" than its similar consistent situation.

Rosenberg (1965a) interprets the results of the above study as implying additional generalizations concerning the attitude change process. The first of these generalizations is as follows: "*the production, through persuasive communication, of intra-attitudinal inconsistency will be easier in the case of originally negative attitudes than in the case of originally positive attitudes*" (p. 145). The basis for this generalization is simply that any inconsistent cognitive unit involving a negative first element (the negative attitude) will of necessity be hedonic ($-++$ or $---$) while any inconsistent cognitive unit involving a positive first element (the positive attitude) will of necessity be antihedonic ($+-+$ or $++-$). The second generalization is that "*when equal degrees of internal inconsistency have been generated the originally positive attitude is more likely to undergo reorganization toward the negative than will the originally negative one change toward becoming positive*" (p. 146). Due to the fact that inconsistent cognitive units involving negative attitudes are hedonic they may be easy to get established or accepted, but once they have been established they are less likely to stimulate reorganizing change than are the antihedonic cognitive units containing positive attitudes.

Comment. The research reviewed in the first part of this section is consistent with the assertion that there are two sequences of attitude change, cognitive change followed by affective change and affective change followed by cognitive change. The studies of Carlson (1956), and Di Vesta and Merwin (1960) indicate that cognitive change produces affective change, and two of Rosenberg's experiments (1960a, 1960c) indicate that affective change produces cognitive change. Rosenberg's procedure of manipulating affect directly through hypnosis is an interesting one. It is somewhat difficult to evaluate, however, due to our lack of knowledge about what hypnosis actually involves.

The two studies by Rosenberg and Abelson (1960) and Rosenberg (1965a) have suggested some interesting possibilities as to how a hedonistic tendency operates along with the tendency toward consistency. Rosenberg and Abelson found that their subjects did not always act so as to achieve consistency if a loss in sales or no gain in sales would be the result. Rosenberg and Abelson perceived, however, that a consistency orientation could account for the data through the postulation of a cognitive unit involving the self (+) in association with (p or +) a motive-satisfying (+) or motive-frustrating (−) state of affairs. If the self is associated with a motive-satisfying state of affairs the cognitive unit is both hedonic and consistent; if the self is associated with a motive-frustrating state of affairs the cognitive unit is both antihedonic and inconsistent. In cognitive units in which the first element is positive the hedonic tendency and the tendency toward consistency exactly parallel each other, i.e., the two consistent cognitive units (+++ and +−−) are hedonic and the two inconsistent cognitive units (+−+ and ++−) are antihedonic. In cognitive units in which the first element is negative the hedonic tendency and the tendency toward consistency operate against each other, i.e., the two consistent cognitive units (−−+ and −+−) are antihedonic and the two inconsistent cognitive units (−++ and −−−) are hedonic. Since the self is typically positive, cognitive units involving the self as the first element are characterized by the parallel action of the hedonic tendency and the tendency toward consistency. Conceivably Rosenberg (1965a) could have invoked these facts to account for his subjects' perception of inconsistent antihedonic situations as more "illogical" than inconsistent hedonic situations. If the antihedonic situations were indeed motive-frustrating and the hedonic situations were indeed motive satisfying, then this is a reasonable interpretation of the results. Some reservation, however, may be voiced about the extent to which Rosenberg's general situations were really motive-satisfying or frustrating. It is interesting, though, that the hedonic-antihedonic difference was significantly greater in the personal than in the general situations. This is exactly what would be expected if the presence of motive satisfaction or frustration were an important consideration.

EVALUATION

Rosenberg and Abelson's affective-cognitive consistency theory, particularly in its later version, is one of the most sophisticated and compelling statements of the consistency point of view. The formal statement of the "psycho-logical" rules, the notion of the conceptual arena, and the theorizing about imbalance resolution all seem to be definite improvements. One of the main shortcomings of Heider's balance theory, for example, is the lack of any statement concerning which of several modes of imbalance resolution will be utilized in any particular situation. In both the initial and the later version of affective-cognitive consistency theory, however, there is some attempt to handle this problem. To a great extent, of course, Rosenberg and Abelson have profited and built upon Heider's pioneer efforts. Some of the defects of Heider's theory, however, still remain in Rosenberg and Abelson's theory. For example, neither theory has been elaborated so as to account for varying strengths of relations.

For both congruity theory and balance theory there is some ambiguity about the meaning of the relating concepts. Neither the concepts of "assertion" (associative or dissociative) nor of "unit relation" are adequately defined. Rosenberg and Abelson also do not exactly define what they mean by "cognitive relation," but they do make some attempt to state the categories of relations that are not encompassed by the theory. Assuming that there are proper grounds for eliminating various categories of relations, this gain in explicitness is an improvement.

One interesting point about Rosenberg's (1953, 1956) procedure of predicting attitude on the basis of the sum of the products of value and instrumentality ratings is the close parallel with Fishbein's summation formula (Triandis and Fishbein, 1963). Obviously there is not necessary antagonism between a summation approach and a consistency approach. Apparently, however, whether consistency theories should be formulated in terms of averaging (as in congruity theory) or in terms of summation (as in the early version of affective-cognitive consistency theory) is an open question.

The research relevant to Rosenberg and Abelson's theory is highly consistent and supportive. Although many aspects of the theory are still untested, the existing evidence is strong enough to produce considerable faith in the general adequacy of the formulation.

10

Festinger's Dissonance Theory

THEORY

The theory of cognitive dissonance developed by Leon Festinger (1957) is still another statement of the consistency point of view. Dissonance theory, as will become evident, however, is uniquely different from the previously discussed consistency theories.

General Statement

Cognitive Elements. The basic units of dissonance theory are cognitive elements. According to Festinger cognitive elements are "knowledges" about various objects, facts, circumstances, behaviors, etc. As Festinger uses the term "knowledges" it includes beliefs, opinions, and attitudes. It is thus a rather global concept.

When is a "knowledge" a cognitive element instead of a cluster of cognitive elements? Festinger states that he does not know, but that as a matter of practical concern it does not matter. Measurement of the "element" is possible in any case.

Relations between Cognitive Elements. Two cognitive elements may have irrelevant or relevant relations between them. If the cognitive elements are completely unrelated to each other then the relationship between them is one of irrelevance. For most people the knowledge that it rained 2 weeks ago would be irrelevant to the knowledge that the mail on a certain day came 1 hour late. If some person possessed information relating these two events then the relationship between them would, of course, be one of relevance for that person.

Relevant relations are of two types, dissonant and consonant. According to Festinger (1957), *"two elements are in a dissonant relation if, considering these two alone, the obverse of one element would follow from the other"* (p. 13). For example, if someone who was in debt bought a car there would be a dissonant relation between the two cognitive elements; not buying a car follows from being in debt. Festinger further states that different meanings can be given to the phrase "follow from" in the above definition of dissonance. Dissonance may arise because the obverse of one cognitive element follows from another in a strictly logical fashion. Dissonance may also arise because the obverse of one's present behavior follows from cultural mores, or because the obverse of one's present experience follows from expectations based on past experience, and so on. The term "follow from" is obviously used very loosely.

Consonant relations imply that one cognitive element does follow from another. Consonant and dissonant relations are thus in some sense or other the opposite of each other.

Magnitude of Dissonance. The magnitude of the dissonance between cognitive elements is dependent upon both the importance of the elements and the proportion of relevant elements that are dissonant. The greater the importance of the cognitive elements that are in a dissonant relationship the greater the magnitude of the dissonance. For example, giving a dime to a beggar who is not in need would create only mild dissonance because little importance is attached to the cognitive elements. On the other hand, not adequately studying for an important examination would create much more dissonance. The magnitude of the dissonance also increases with an increase in the proportion of cognitive elements that are in a dissonant relationship. For example, the more reasons known to a smoker to stop smoking, the greater the dissonance created by continued smoking.

Dissonance Reduction. Cognitive inconsistency gives rise to pressure to reduce the dissonance. This pressure is a function of the magnitude of the dissonance. Dissonance reduction can be achieved in any of three ways: changing a behavioral cognitive element, changing an environmental cognitive element, adding new cognitive elements. The changing of a behavioral cognitive element is illustrated by the smoker who stops smoking when he learns that smoking is detrimental to health. Changing an environmental cognitive element is illustrated by the person who cuts a hole in his living-room floor to make more reasonable the fact that he always jumps over that spot, or who distorts the perceived political orientation of a candidate in order to justify the fact that he has voted for him. Adding new cognitive elements is illustrated by the smoker who reads material critical of the research linking smoking to lung cancer or material on the high death rate resulting from automobile accidents.

Limit in the Magnitude of Dissonance. Festinger (1957) states that: *"The maximum dissonance that can possibly exist between any two elements is equal to the total resistance to change of the less resistant element"* (p. 28). The reason for this is simply that when the less resistant element changes, the magnitude of dissonance is thereby reduced.

Specific Implications

Festinger amplifies his general statement of dissonance theory by discussing its implications for a number of specific situations or events.

Decisions. When a person is faced with making a choice between a number of alternatives he is in a conflict situation. After a decision is made the conflict is resolved, but dissonance is created. If a person decides to buy car A rather than car B the cognitive elements concerning the desirable characteristics of car B are dissonant with the cognitive element that car A has been chosen. In the present context Festinger definitely distinguishes between conflict and dissonance.

The person is in a conflict situation before making the decision. After having made the decision he is no longer in conflict; he has made his choice; he has, so to speak, resolved the conflict; he is no longer being pushed in two or more directions simultaneously. He is now committed to the chosen course of action. It is only here that dissonance exists, and the pressure to reduce this dissonance is *not* pushing the person in two directions simultaneously. (1957, p. 39)

Dissonance thus seems to involve postdecisional conflict.

According to Festinger the magnitude of dissonance is dependent upon three things: the importance of the decision, the relative attractiveness of the unchosen compared to the chosen alternative, and the degree of cognitive overlap, or similarity, among the dissonant cognitive elements. Other things being equal, the greater the importance of a decision the greater the degree of dissonance. For example, a choice between two makes of automobiles will create more dissonance than a choice between two brands of soap. It is also the case that the greater the attractiveness of the unchosen alternative the greater the degree of dissonance. A choice between two equally attractive automobiles will create more dissonance than a choice between one attractive and one unattractive automobile. Finally, the greater the degree of cognitive overlap (or similarity) between two alternatives the less the dissonance resulting from the choice of one of them. Cognitive overlap is high if many of the cognitive elements belonging to one alternative are shared by the other alternative. Festinger states that a choice between two books would probably arouse less dissonance than a choice between a book and a theater ticket.

Dissonance resulting from decisions or "free choices" [1] can be reduced in any of four ways: revoking the decision, increasing the attractiveness of the chosen alternative, decreasing the attractiveness of the unchosen alternative, or establishing cognitive overlap or similarity between the alternatives. Dissonance reduction through the revoking of a decision may occur if the person encounters information indicating that his previous decision was inappropriate or incorrect. This revoking of the previous decision, however, throws the person back into the conflict situation and thus may not be very satisfying. A more usual manner of reducing postdecisional dissonance is through either decreasing the attractiveness of the unchosen alternative or increasing the attractiveness of the chosen alternative. The success of this procedure depends both upon the mental capacity of the person and upon the availability of various types of support or information. Dissonance reduction through the establishment of cognitive overlap is illustrated by the boy who, having chosen to go to a movie rather than the circus, decides that both the movies and the circus are forms of entertainment.

Forced Compliance. By forced compliance Festinger means compliance to public pressure without or prior to an accompanying change in private opinion. Such forced compliance may result from either the threat of punishment for noncompliance or the offer of reward for compliance. Once forced compliance has occurred, however, there is dissonance between opinion and behavior. The cognitive elements corresponding to the opinion and the behavior are in a dissonant relationship.

The magnitude of the dissonance resulting from forced compliance is a function of the amount of reward or punishment that is offered to induce the behavior and the importance of the opinion or behavior involved. Assuming that compliance occurs, the greater the reward or punishment used to induce the behavior the less is the dissonance. If an adult accepted a million dollars to state publicly that he liked comic books, he would suffer very little dissonance. On the other hand, if the reward were only 10 cents the dissonance would be considerably greater. Similarly, assuming that compliance has occurred, the greater the importance of the behavior or opinion the greater the dissonance. Accepting a bribe to claim that one liked comic books would create less dissonance than accepting a bribe to be disloyal to one's country.

What happens, however, if the individual decides not to be forced into compliance? This decision also results in dissonance that is dependent upon the amount of reward or punishment and the importance of the opinion or behavior. In this situation, however, the greater the reward or punishment and the less the importance of the opinion or

[1] The term "free choice" was coined by Brehm and Cohen (1962).

behavior the greater the dissonance. If an individual decides not to accept a large bribe there may be considerable dissonance. The decision not to accept a small bribe would create far less dissonance. Similarly the less the importance of the behavior the individual decides not to engage in, the greater the dissonance. The decision not to accept a bribe to claim one likes comic books would create more dissonance than the decision not to accept a bribe to betray one's country.

The dissonance that results from forced compliance can be reduced in three ways: reducing the importance of the opinion or behavior involved, changing the private opinion so as to agree with the public behavior, or magnification of the reward or punishment used to induce the behavior. If a person can convince himself that his act of betrayal to his country is of little importance or that he really is not being disloyal to his country then he can reduce the dissonance resulting from such an act. Also, if he can convince himself that the rewards or punishments used to force his behavior were so great that he had no choice but to betray his country, then the dissonance can be reduced.

Festinger does not make explicit the essential difference between the forced compliance situation and the decision or "free choice" situation. It is evident that decisions are involved in both situations. Dissonance results both from the decision between a number of alternatives and from the decision either to be or not to be forced into compliant behavior. The first situation involves a decision in what Lewin (1935) calls an approach-approach conflict, i.e., a conflict between a number of desirable alternatives. The individual, for example, may be confronted with deciding which of several articles to purchase. The second situation involves either Lewin's avoidance-avoidance or approach-avoidance conflict. In the avoidance-avoidance conflict the individual is forced to choose between a number of undesirable alternatives, e.g., a choice between betraying one's country and being shot. In the approach-avoidance conflict the individual is confronted with the choice between engaging in or not engaging in behavior that has both desirable and undesirable consequences, e.g., a choice between accepting and not accepting a million dollars to betray one's country. The essential difference between the "free choice" and forced compliance situations is thus in the nature of the conflict that leads to the decision.

Involuntary Exposure to Information. According to Festinger if information is fairly widespread it may be difficult to avoid encountering it either through the mass media or through interaction with other people. For whatever reason, however, involuntary exposure to new information is potentially dissonance arousing. If the new information implies the obverse of cognitions already held, then dissonance will result. In this situation, unlike in the "free choice" and forced compliance situations, Festinger makes no mention of choice or decision as being of crucial importance in the production of dissonance.

The dissonance resulting from involuntary exposure to new information may be reduced through defensive misperception of the information, avoidance of or escape from the information, or opinion change. Such defensive actions help to eliminate the newly introduced dissonance and also to prevent further introduction of dissonance.

Voluntary Exposure to Information. Voluntary exposure to information may result from the desire to obtain information that is relevant for future action. For example, a person trying to decide between two makes of automobiles may seek out information about the advantages and disadvantages of each. Voluntary exposure to information may also, however, result from the pressure to reduce dissonance. If a person has purchased an automobile he may seek dissonance reducing information about the advantages of the chosen automobile and the disadvantages of the rejected automobile.

If the level of dissonance, however, is too high then the person may seek information to further increase the dissonance to a point where the decision will be revoked. If he can increase the dissonance to a point greater than the resistance to change of one or more cognitive elements, then the level of dissonance may eventually return to a low level. In order to obtain an eventual decrease in dissonance a temporary increase in dissonance is sought out.

Social Support. According to Festinger agreement with other people reduces dissonance and disagreement with other people increases dissonance. The magnitude of dissonance resulting from disagreement is a function of a number of variables: the testability of the point of disagreement through empirical observation, the number of agreeing and disagreeing people, the importance of the issue in dispute, the attractiveness of the disagreeing person, the credibility of the disagreeing person, and the extent of the disagreement. Social disagreement will produce little dissonance if the point of disagreement is readily testable in terms of physical reality. Further, the greater the number of people who agree, the less the dissonance produced by someone else who disagrees. The production of a large amount of dissonance through disagreement is, of course, dependent upon the issue being an important one. Finally, the magnitude of dissonance also increases with the attractiveness and credibility of the source as well as with the extent of disagreement.

Festinger lists three ways in which dissonance resulting from disagreement may be reduced: change in opinion so as to agree with the disagreeing person, persuasion of the disagreeing person to change his opinion, and an increase in the perceived noncomparability of the disagreeing person. The first two points are obvious; the third is illustrated by the person who reduces dissonance by perceiving the disagreeing person as stupid, unfriendly, and bigoted. It is evident that the dissonance theory treatment of social support is, in some respects, similar to that of balance theory and assimilation-contrast theory.

Brehm and Cohen's Extensions of Dissonance Theory

Brehm and Cohen (1962) have speculated both about the role of commitment and volition in the production of dissonance and about the relation of dissonance and conflict.

Role of Commitment. According to Brehm and Cohen most of the empirical investigations of dissonance theory have dealt with the special case of commitment. They consider a person to be committed if he has made a choice between two or more alternatives or between doing or not doing a certain thing. The role of commitment in dissonance theory is to aid first in the specification of psychological implication and second in the specification of the ways in which a person may attempt to reduce dissonance. Assuming that a person is motivated to benefit himself and to avoid harm, if he has made a choice between a number of alternatives the specification of what is consonant or dissonant with this commitment is fairly straightforward. For example, if someone decides to take up cigar rather than cigarette smoking, the knowledge that cigar smokers are less likely than cigarette smokers to get lung cancer is consonant with the decision, but the knowledge that cigars smell worse than cigarettes is dissonant with the decision. However, before there is a commitment to either cigars or cigarettes the above knowledges have no power to arouse dissonance.

How does commitment aid in the specification of the ways in which dissonance may be reduced? If a person experiences dissonance he will change the least resistant dissonant elements. Therefore dissonance aroused through commitment is most likely to be reduced through the changing of elements other than those related to the commitment. Recourse to the revoking of a decision, choice, or commitment will be a last resort.

Brehm and Cohen further state that commitment allows for the deduction of inobvious implications that are directly contrary to the commonsense implications of other theories. Reinforcement theory, congruity theory, balance theory, and affective-cognitive consistency theory all imply that liked communicators will have more influence than disliked communicators. According to dissonance theory, however, if a person chooses to listen to a communicator, the greater the dislike for the communicator the greater the influence. This is due to the fact that the dissonance between the commitment and the negative characteristics of the communicator increases with increased disliking for the communicator. Since the individual is committed to listening to the communicator, dissonance cannot readily be reduced by rejecting the communicator or his views, but can most easily occur through opinion change. Hence, the greater the dislike for the communicator to which one is committed to listening, the greater the influence.

In both the forced compliance and "free choice" situations the individual may acquire a commitment and thus create dissonance. Festinger, however, maintains that dissonance may also be created when there is involuntary exposure to information. Brehm and Cohen, in disagreement with Festinger, state that it is equivocal whether or not dissonance is created by such exposure; due to theoretical ambiguities it is not clear whether or not exposure creates dissonance. Furthermore, the predictions made from dissonance theory about such exposure situations are similar to the ones made by other theories. Thus they prefer to concentrate on the special case of commitment.

Role of Volition. Brehm and Cohen maintain that volition also provides a source of psychological implication. Volition implies control of and responsibility for one's behavior. Like commitment, volition is necessarily involved with choice or selection. Brehm and Cohen state that other things being equal the greater the volition the greater the dissonance—the greater the control of and felt responsibility for a choice the greater the resultant dissonance.

According to Festinger the amount of potential postdecisional dissonance increases as the choice alternatives become more nearly equal in attractiveness. Brehm and Cohen, however, maintain that such an increased equalization in the attractiveness of the alternatives may or may not be positively correlated with an increase in volition. Thus if the amount of volition does not increase the dissonance resulting from the decision will not increase either.

Brehm and Cohen argue that the concept of volition helps to clarify some of the theoretical ambiguity concerning dissonance in the involuntary exposure situation. If the individual is involuntarily exposed to unpleasant information the production of dissonance depends upon whether or not there is any personal responsibility for the unpleasant consequences. If past volition could have easily prevented the unpleasant consequences then dissonance would be created. Brehm and Cohen discuss the example of a farmer who at the beginning of the season decides to plant tobacco rather than corn and then later hears that tobacco causes a deadly disease. Since the inconsistency created by growing a crop that produces a deadly disease could have been prevented by growing corn, the farmer experiences dissonance. On the other hand, if land taxes were raised no dissonance would be created due to the planting of tobacco. This would particularly hold true if the farm had been inherited; if, on the other hand, the farm had been recently purchased, dissonance would be created by the increase in taxes. Volition is thus considered to be of crucial importance in the production of dissonance through involuntary exposure.

Brehm and Cohen state that not all of the possible variables producing dissonance are known. They do theorize, though, that commitment and volition are necessary conditions for the creation of dissonance. Furthermore, commitment and volition in conjunction with importance and discrepancy of cognitions constitute sufficient conditions for the production of dissonance.

Dissonance and Conflict. Dissonance, as Brehm and Cohen conceive it, occurs only after a choice of some kind. This makes it appear as if dissonance is relevant to the postdecisional conflict situation but is not relevant to the predecisional conflict situation. However, Brehm and Cohen point out that before the conflict is resolved in terms of a final decision, there will be many temporary, vacillating decisions or choices. As long as decisions, temporary or otherwise, are being made before the conflict is finally resolved, dissonance theory is theoretically relevant to the whole process.

RESEARCH

There is a rather large body of research relevant to dissonance theory and no attempt will be made to cover all of it. We will concentrate on research in which attitude or belief change is the main dependent variable.

Revaluation of the Alternatives Following the Resolution of Approach-Approach Conflicts

In his chapter on decisions Festinger (1957) maintains that the choice of one of several positive alternatives results in dissonance. Dissonance thus results from decisions in approach-approach conflicts or in "free choice" situations. Theoretically one of the main ways in which such dissonance can be reduced is through increasing the desirability of the chosen alternative and decreasing the desirability of the rejected alternative. The present section will review the literature pertinent to this theoretical expectation.

Brehm (1956) tested three dissonance theory predictions with regard to choice in approach-approach situations: dissonance resulting from a choice should be reduced by increasing the desirability of the chosen alternative and decreasing the desirability of the rejected alternative; the more equal the desirability of the alternatives the greater the dissonance and consequent attempts to reduce dissonance resulting from the choice; exposure to relevant information after the choice should facilitate dissonance reduction. In the experiment female subjects were asked to rate the desirability of a number of items such as a portable radio, automatic coffee maker, stop watch, fluorescent desk lamp, etc. The subjects were told that the manufacturers of these items were interested in ascertaining consumers' reactions and that in payment for their time they could have one of the items. Due to the short supply of items, however, they would have to choose between two. In the high dissonance condition the subjects were allowed to choose between an item previously rated highly desirable and another item rated ½ to 1½ points lower on an 8-point scale. In the low dissonance condition the subjects were allowed to choose between a desirable item and another item rated about 3 points lower. After making the choice and being given the item the subjects were asked to read research reports dealing with four of the items. For approximately half of the subjects in both the high and low dissonance conditions two of the four research reports dealt with the choice items, and for the remaining subjects the research reports did not deal with the choice items. The research reports were simple discussions of the good and bad points about the items and thus constituted a manipulation of relevant information. Finally, the subjects were asked to rate all of the items a second time. The subjects were told that the manufacturers wanted to see how the evaluation of items change after the customers had looked them over and left the store. Of the 165 subjects in the four choice conditions 48, or approximately 29 percent, were eliminated because they chose the item initially rated as less desirable.

The results were only partially confirmatory. Brehm's first prediction concerning the increased desirability of the chosen alternative and decreased desirability of the rejected alternative was reasonably well supported. The difference between the increased desirability of the chosen alternative and the decreased desirability of the rejected alternative is significant in the high dissonance-information, high dissonance-no information, and low dissonance-no information conditions. The effect is not significant in the low dissonance-information condition. Brehm's second prediction concerning the greater dissonance and attempts to reduce it with alternatives more similar in desirability was partially confirmed. Although the effect is in the predicted direction, it is significant only in the information condition. Finally, Brehm's third prediction concerning the facilitation of dissonance reduction by the exposure to relevant postchoice information was not at all supported.

All of the above significance information was based on separate t tests; no attempt was made to do an overall analysis of variance, possibly because of the unequal cell frequencies. In a footnote Brehm (1956) states that the changes in the desirability ratings of the eliminated subjects "were, if anything, in the direction of reducing dissonance" (p. 385). This is comforting to know.

Deutsch, Krauss, and Rosenau (*1962*) tested the hypothesis that the magnitude of dissonance resulting from a decision will increase as the individual's self-involvement increases. In a supposed study of consumer preferences, subjects tasted and then rated six different spreads for bread (jam, jelly, peanut butter, etc.). The ratings were done on two scales: an overall comparison of each spread with all others, and a flavor scale. Self-involvement was manipulated by telling half of the subjects that ability to judge the quality of foods was associated with a number of characteristics such as leadership, aptitude, executive potential, and artistic judgment and by telling the other half nothing. The spreads were rated a second time after the subjects had chosen one of two spreads in payment for participating in the experiment. The two spreads offered to the subjects were ones that on the overall comparison scale had been rated at or near the center. Deutsch, Krauss, and Rosenau did two-factor analyses of variance on the change scores for each of the two rating scales. One factor concerned the difference among treatment conditions (high and low self-involvement) and the other the difference between the chosen spread, rejected spread, and a matched noncritical spread. The matched noncritical spreads were ones which received approximately equal ratings with the chosen and rejected spreads but were not involved in the choice situation. For the overall comparison scale only the factor for the three alternatives is significant. Over both the high and low self-involvement conditions the chosen alternative increased in evaluation, the rejected alternative hardly changed at all, and the matched noncritical "alternative" increased by an intermediate amount. The difference between the chosen and rejected alternative is bigger in the high than in the low self-involvement conditions, but the crucial interaction between conditions and alternatives is not significant. For the flavor scale, as for the overall comparison scale, the factor for the three alternatives is significant. Collapsing the high and low self-involvement conditions, the chosen alternatives increased in evaluation, the rejected alternative decreased in evaluation, and the noncritical "alternative" changed by an intermediate amount. This general pattern of differences, however, is not evident in the low self-involvement condition where there were small, inconsistent changes. Once again, however, the predicted interaction between alternatives and involvement is not significant. A chi square test, though, did reveal that more subjects in the high as compared with the low self-involvement conditions changed the flavor ratings so as to increase the difference between the chosen as compared to the rejected alternative. The similar effect for the overall comparison is not significant.

This experiment is notable in that apparently no subjects were eliminated from the sample. The main dissonance theory prediction concerned with an increase in the evaluation of the chosen and a decrease in the evaluation of the rejected alternative was fairly well supported. Deutsch, Krauss, and Rosenau's prediction, however, that this effect would only be evident under high self-involvement was rather inconsistently supported. There is probably good reason for supposing that their manipulation of self-involvement was less than adequate. They apparently made no attempt to assess the success of the manipulation.

Brehm and Cohen (*1959b*) tested the predictions that dissonance reducing revaluation of the chosen and unchosen alternatives in an approach-approach conflict will increase with an increase in the number and qualitative dissimilarity of the alternatives. Using a sample of children, they obtained results which they interpreted as confirming the predictions. For various reasons, however, their original sample of 203 children was reduced by 130 (65 percent). In a footnote Brehm and Cohen state that the entire sample yielded support for the similar-dissimilar manipulation but failed to show any effect for the number of alternatives. As Chapanis and Chapanis (1964) point out, though, this could mean a significant effect or a nonsignificant trend in the predicted direction. Brehm and Cohen eliminated some subjects because they failed to choose the alternative initially marked as most liked. These subjects were considered to have given unreliable or invalid ratings. Chapanis and Chapanis (1964) maintain that selection of subjects on this basis may automatically produce the mean differences that Brehm and Cohen predicted. A simplified statement of their argument is as follows: By discarding those subjects who chose the alternative not initially most liked, that part of the distribution of subjects who decreased their liking of the initially preferred alternative and/or increased their liking of the initially least preferred alternative was eliminated. This leaves the subjects who, on the average, increased their liking for the initially most preferred alternative and/or decreased their liking for the initially least preferred alternative. Thus the remaining subjects will of necessity show increased liking for the chosen alternative and decreased liking for the rejected alternative.

Chapanis and Chapanis, however, are apparently unaware of the fact that Brehm and Cohen (1962) detailed exactly the same argument about the effects of subject loss. Brehm and Cohen were less impressed by the argument because they doubted the validity of the assumption that choice reversal is always due to a genuine change in the evaluation of the alternatives. It may be that a choice reversal is not due either to an increased evaluation of the initially less preferred alternative or to a decreased evaluation of the initially more preferred alternative, but simply to an invalid initial rating. They do state, though, that continued research which is ambiguous because of subject loss would be inexcusable. It simply is not known what causes choice reversals, and all experiments which eliminated subjects on this basis should be regarded with suspicion.

In the previously discussed study by Brehm (1956), 29 percent of the subjects were eliminated because of choice reversal. However, Brehm (1956) does state in a footnote that the ratings of the eliminated subjects "were, if anything, in the direction of reducing dissonance" (p. 385). He further implies that an analysis of the entire sample supported the predictions.

Brock (1963) tested the dissonance formulation that a choice between two similar objects produces less dissonance than a choice between two dissimilar objects. He also investigated the effect of irrelevant tension or drive on such decisionally produced dissonance. An original sample of 141 children indicated how much they liked three kinds of small toys (ring toss, spinning top, Yo-Yo) and three kinds of crackers in plastic bags (Saltine, graham, cheese). After making the ratings the children were told that they could win two movie tickets if they guessed correctly which 3 of a list of 12 toys were in a box shown them by the experimenter. Then the experimenter left the room for 5 minutes, giving the children ample opportunity to cheat by looking into the box. After the experimenter returned to the room the children guessed which toys were in the box and chose between either two similar objects (two bags of crackers or two toys) or two dissimilar objects (a bag of crackers and a toy). One of the objects had previously been given a moderate to high liking rating and the other a rating that was no more than 1½ scale units lower on an 8-point scale. Twenty-four subjects who did not have two initial ratings meeting this criterion were eliminated. After the choice was made the objects were rated a second time. Nine subjects who chose the object initially rated as less desirable were eliminated from the analysis.

If the subjects picked the correct three objects in the box, they were considered to have cheated. Ratings by the experimenter and another observer indicated that the peekers significantly more often than the nonpeekers manifested fidgeting, refusal to look at the experimenter, hurry to leave, spontaneous denial of having cheated, etc. Thus the classification of subjects as peekers or nonpeekers was taken as a classification of subjects who were under either high or low irrelevant tension. Taking the difference in increased liking for the chosen alternative and decreased liking for the unchosen alternative as the dependent variable, a three-factor analysis of variance was performed. The three independent factors in this analysis were: peeking versus no-peeking, dissimilar versus similar alternatives, and age group (3–4, 5–6, 7–9, 10–12). The only significant effects were peeking versus no-peeking, dissimilar versus similar alternatives, and the interaction between these two variables. As dissonance theory predicts, more increased liking of the chosen alternative and decreased liking of the rejected alternative (dissonance reduction) occurred with dissimilar than with similar choices. Also, as the conception of irrelevant drive or tension would lead one to expect, more dissonance reduction occurred among peekers than nonpeekers. The interaction means that the difference between dissimilar and similar choices was greater among the peekers than among the nonpeekers. Inspection of the tabled results indicates that in all 16 of the cells there was both an increase in liking for the chosen alternative and a decrease in liking for the rejected alternative. Brock further reports that the inclusion or exclusion of the 9 subjects who picked the alternative initially considered less desirable makes no difference in the overall results. Except, then, for the limitation of generality due to the elimination of the 24 subjects who did not make two appropriate initial ratings, the experiment appears to provide good support for the dissonance theory interpretation of choice in an approach-approach conflict.

Davidson and Kiesler (1964) obtained evidence indicating that more revaluation of the alternatives occurs after than before the resolution of an approach-approach conflict. In a decision making experiment female subjects were asked to play the role of a person who had the responsibility of hiring a vice-president for a firm which they owned. After ranking eight qualities, such as leadership and experience, in terms of their importance for people filling this job, the subjects were given sequential information about two candidates, Mr. Brown and Mr. Jones. This sequential information consisted of a series of cards given to the subjects one at a time. Each card described Mr. Jones as excelling on one of the previously ranked qualities on which Mr. Brown was average and Mr. Brown excelling on one of the previously ranked qualities on which Mr. Jones was average. The subjects were told that they would be given a total of 10 cards of increasing importance and that it would be impossible to reach a valid decision until they had read all of the cards. Actually they were given only 4 cards, each card relating to two of the previously ranked eight qualities. After receiving the fourth card half of the subjects were asked to indicate which candidate they would hire at this point and, after a 2-minute wait, to rerank the eight qualities (postdecision measurement condition). The other half of the subjects reranked the eight qualities before making their decision (predecision measurement condition). It is possible from these data to see whether the four qualities belonging to the chosen candidate increased in ranking more than the four qualities of the rejected candidate. Davidson and Kiesler found that significantly greater increased ranking of the qualities belonging to the chosen candidate than of the qualities belonging to the rejected candidate occurred in the postdecision measurement condition than in the predecision measurement condition. Making the decision apparently created dissonance that resulted in the spreading apart of the qualities. This finding was replicated in both a condition in which there were 5-second intervals between cards and a condition in which there were 2½-minute intervals between cards. Davidson and Kiesler point out, however, that this does not rule out the possibility that some revaluation of the alternatives did occur because of predecision processes. In the predecision measurement conditions some increased ranking of the qualities belonging to the subsequently chosen candidate did occur, but this effect was significantly greater than zero only when coupled with the longer time interval between cards. The data strongly support the assertion that more dissonance reducing revaluation occurred after than before the decision.

Out of the original 85 subjects, 1 was eliminated because she failed to understand the instructions. No subjects were eliminated because they chose the candidate possessing the qualities initially ranked as less desirable. Apparently such choice reversals did occur, but Davidson and Kiesler do not directly discuss the matter.

Jecker (1964) obtained more evidence indicating that postdecisional rather than predecisional processes are important in producing the revaluation of alternatives. Female high school students rated 15 popular records on a 7-point scale and then chose which of 2 of the records they would like in payment for their help in this "market research." The two records were ones that had been given moderate ratings not more than 2 scale units apart. Half of the subjects were told that the chances were 1 out of 20 that they would get both records (high conflict), and half were told that the chances were 19 out of 20 that they would get both records (low conflict). Whether they actually got one or both of the records was "randomly" determined by drawing a number out of a box. Actually half of the subjects in both the high and low conflict conditions got both records (no dissonance) and half only got the chosen record (dissonance). At the conclusion the subjects rated the records for a second time. An analysis of variance of the before-after change scores indicated that more revaluation of the records occurred in the dissonance than the no-dissonance condition, but that neither conflict nor the conflict × dissonance interaction had an effect. Furthermore, the revaluation was significantly different from zero in both the high conflict dissonance condition and in the low conflict dissonance condition, but in neither of the no-dissonance conditions. The data for the increased evaluation of the chosen record and the decreased evaluation of the rejected record were not reported separately. A check on the adequacy of the conflict manipulation indicated that significantly more time was spent considering the decision in the high than the low conflict conditions.

Of the 88 subjects tested 4 (5 percent) were eliminated because they did not make appropriate initial ratings one scale unit apart in the moderate range of the scale, and 4 were eliminated because they chose the record initially rated as less desirable. Assuming that the small percentage of eliminated subjects did not bias the results, the experiment certainly points to the greater importance of postdecisional processes (dissonance) over predecisional processes (conflict) in producing the revaluation of alternatives. It is interesting to note that the manipulation of dissonance involved involuntary exposure to information about whether one or both of the two records would be obtained. Apparently the involuntary exposure to information regarding the effects of a past decision can, at least in some circumstances, create dissonance.

In a second experiment Jecker investigated the effect of withholding information about whether one or both of the records would be obtained until after the second rating. The subjects were assured of getting one record but not told about the other until after the second rating. In both a high and a low conflict condition, dissonance reducing revaluation did not occur. In fact, the alternatives were rated closer together the second time than the first. In a third condition in which the subjects were not told about any possibility of obtaining both records, significant dissonance reducing revaluation did occur. (Jecker does not report whether any subjects were eliminated, and he does not give the data for revaluation of the chosen and rejected alternatives separately.) The results of the study appear to indicate that conflict alone is not sufficient to produce revaluation of the alternatives. The results also seem to indicate, as Festinger (1964b) points out, that making a decision to resolve the conflict is not sufficient to start the dissonance reducing process. As long as the subjects thought that there was some chance that they would obtain both records (either 1 in 20, or 19 in 20), revaluation of the alternatives did not occur. When there was no chance of obtaining both records dissonance reduction did occur.

In the light of these results Festinger (1964b) states that he is inclined to accept Brehm and Cohen's (1962) emphasis on commitment. Simply making a decision is not sufficient; the person has to be committed to his decision and its possible consequences. In Jecker's experiment the subjects who chose one record but still thought there was a possibility of obtaining the other, presumably were not committed to the consequences of their decision.

Festinger further states, however, that Brehm and Cohen are somewhat vague about the meaning of commitment. According to Festinger (1964b), "It seems that a decision carries commitment with it if the decision unequivocally affects subsequent behavior" (p. 156). For example, someone might express a preference for one of several paintings without necessarily being committed. A decision has been made that carries no commitment. If, however, the artist offers to give this individual the painting that he likes best, then the decision does carry commitment because consequences for subsequent behavior are implied.

Allen (*1964*) investigated the effect of the possibility or impossibility of obtaining the unchosen alternative and the certainty or uncertainty of obtaining the chosen alternative. Using a procedure similar to Jecker's, Allen had female high school students rate 15 popular records on a 7-point scale and then choose which 2 of the records they would like in payment for their help. Before making the second rating the subjects were given information designed to create four different conditions. In one condition the subjects were told that they would definitely receive only the chosen record (impossibility of obtaining the unchosen alternative and certainty of obtaining the chosen alternative). In a second condition the subjects were told that they had equal chances of obtaining the chosen record or neither record (impossibility of obtaining the unchosen alternative and uncertainty of obtaining the chosen alternative). The subjects drew numbers supposedly to determine whether they were to obtain the chosen record or neither record. In a third condition the subjects were told that they would either obtain the chosen record or both records (possibility of obtaining the unchosen record and certainty of obtaining the chosen record). And in a fourth condition the subjects were told that they had equal chances of obtaining neither record, the chosen record, or both records (possibility of obtaining the unchosen alternative and uncertainty of obtaining the chosen alternative).

Of the 121 subjects tested 24 chose the record initially rated as less desirable. The data for the 97 subjects who chose the record initially rated as more desirable indicate a different pattern of results for the increased desirability of the chosen record and the decreased desirability of the rejected record. In all four conditions there were moderate but apparently nonsignificant increases in the desirability of the chosen record. In the two conditions in which it was impossible to obtain the rejected record there was a significant decrease in the desirability of the rejected record, and in the two conditions in which it was possible to obtain the rejected record there was no change in the desirability of the rejected record. The certainty or uncertainty of obtaining the chosen record had no significant effect. Due to the small number of "choice reversal" subjects the certainty variable was collapsed and the differences between the possible and impossible conditions examined. Although the differences were not significant, the pattern of results is similar to that obtained from the other 97 subjects. The largest difference is the greater reduction in the desirability of the rejected record when it was impossible rather than possible to obtain it.

Allen's results appear roughly consistent with Jecker's (1964) finding that when there is some possibility of obtaining the rejected alternative, revaluation of the alternatives does not occur. Allen's data, however, appear to indicate that it is the rejected alternative that is not revaluated. (No significance test was reported comparing the differing effects of the possibility of obtaining the rejected record upon revaluation of the chosen and rejected records.) It makes some sense that the cause of dissonance reduction would not be served by devaluing an object that may be eventually possessed. Jecker, unfortunately, does not present separately his data for the revaluation of the chosen and rejected alternatives.

Festinger and Walster (1964) attempted to support the hypothesis that immediately after a decision in a conflict situation there is a period of increased salience of dissonance or regret due to having made a decision. Theoretically in some situations such regret may produce a reversal of the previous choice. Festinger and Walster tested this prediction with a very simple procedure. Female subjects rated a series of hair styles, ranked the same hair styles, chose which of two hair styles they would like to have for themselves, and finally rated the hair styles a second time. The subjects were given coupons to be presented at a local beauty salon. Half of the subjects were told that they could have a choice between two hair styles after the ranking (no prior decision), and half before (prior decision). Festinger and Walster thus assumed that the ranking was a preliminary choice and that any regret produced by this choice would be manifested in a large number of choice reversals when the final decision was made. They, in fact, found that significantly more selections of the hair style initially rated as less desirable occurred in the prior decision condition (62 percent) than occurred in the no-prior decision condition (28 percent). Festinger and Walster further report that for both conditions slightly more than half of the choice reversals were evident during the ranking, but argue that this does not modify the interpretation of the results. They state that many of the subjects went over their initial rankings and changed the rank position of some of the hair styles. Conceivably then, regret produced some choice reversal during the period of ranking. An examination of the dissonance reduction scores (difference between the increased evaluation of the chosen alternative and decreased evaluation of the rejected alternative) revealed significant effects in both of the experimental conditions for both the choice reversal and consistent choice subjects. Furthermore, the amount of dissonance reduction was greater, although not significantly so, in the prior decision condition than in the no-prior decision condition. Festinger and Walster interpreted this nonsignificant effect as indicating that the process of dissonance reduction takes some time to overcome postdecision regret.

Festinger (1964b) points out that the Festinger and Walster (1964) experiment involved a number of questionable assumptions. First of all it assumed that the ranking procedure involved a decision that would initiate the same regret as the final irrevocable decision. But more important it assumed that the experimentally produced regret would be manifested in choice reversal. Festinger states that a direct approach to the measurement of regret would be more convincing.

Walster (*1964*) attempted to obtain more direct evidence for the existence of regret. She reasoned that regret, if it is a genuine phenomenon, should result in the chosen alternative becoming less attractive and the rejected alternative becoming more attractive. The period in which this type of revaluation occurs should be a very brief one right after the decision has been made. Previous studies, however, had measured evaluation of the alternatives several minutes after the decision and had not found evidence of regret. Walster reasoned that regret is more likely to occur if subjects choose between alternatives that have negative as well as positive attributes. She thus designed an experiment involving a double approach-avoidance conflict.

Army draftees from the reception center at Fort Ord rated a series of occupational specialties, chose which of two they wanted to be assigned to for the next 2 years, and then rated the occupational specialties a second time. The alternatives were initially described to the subjects so that they each had desirable and undesirable characteristics. The time between the decision and the second rating was systematically varied for different groups of subjects so as to be either 0, 4 minutes, 15 minutes, or 90 minutes. During these time intervals the subjects were isolated from each other in small cubicles.

Of the 244 subjects in the experiment, 51 (21 percent) chose the alternative initially rated as less desirable. The 193 subjects who made consistent choices showed significant variation in alternative revaluation over the four time interval conditions. The mean dissonance reduction score for the immediate condition is .71; for the 4-minute condition, −1.34; for the 15-minute condition, 2.14; and for the 90-minute condition, .31. (A positive number indicates a revaluation of the alternatives so as to reduce dissonance and a negative number, the opposite.) The only score that differs significantly from zero is the 2.14 in the 15-minute condition. However, the negative score in the 4-minute condition is significantly less than both the positive score in the immediate condition and the positive score in the 15-minute condition. This dissonance increasing score was taken as a manifestation of regret.

The 51 subjects who chose the alternative initially rated as less desirable did not show significant variation in revaluation over the four time interval conditions. The mean score for the immediate condition is 6.73; for the 4-minute condition, 5.11; for the 15-minute condition, 7.12; and for the 90-minute condition, 5.43. The rank order of these conditions, as Walster points out, is exactly the same as that for the subjects making consistent choices. The least spreading apart of the alternatives in a dissonance reducing fashion occurred in the 4-minute condition. However, it is quite obvious that the magnitude of the scores is much larger for the choice reversal subjects. Furthermore, it should be pointed out that the average score for all subjects in the 4-minute condition is .03, practically zero. It is true that this is not dissonance reduction, but, on the other hand, in an absolute sense neither is it revaluation in the direction of regret. The data from the entire sample seem to indicate that regret operates so as to prevent dissonance reducing revaluation from occurring, and not so as to finally decrease the evaluation of the chosen alternative and increase the evaluation of the rejected alternative. However, it is unclear at this point whether a more valid conclusion can be reached by examining the data from all of the subjects or just the data from the nonreversal or consistent choice subjects. It should be pointed out, though, that the mean score for the consistent choice subjects in the 4-minute condition is *not* significantly less than zero.

The most puzzling aspect of the results is the low score in the 90-minute condition. Why should the amount of dissonance reducing revaluation decrease with the increase in time from 15 minutes to 90 minutes? According to Walster (1964): "It is possible that after some dissonance had been reduced, the continued focusing on the remaining dissonance without further successful dissonance reduction could produce the effect obtained in the 90-minute condition" (p. 126). But why could further dissonance reduction not occur? Walster argues that in most situations dissonance is ultimately reduced through social support or the obtaining of bolstering information. In the present experiment this was impossible since the subjects were isolated from each other. Thus since the subjects were unable to reduce all of their dissonance, the continued focusing on the remaining dissonance produced a decrease in the dissonance reducing revaluation of the alternatives. While this explanation is very speculative, it does sound reasonably plausible and should be explored with further research.

Comment. Evaluation of this literature on the revaluation of the alternatives following the resolution of an approach-approach conflict is difficult due to the repeated elimination of subjects, particularly those subjects who chose the alternative initially rated as less desirable. With regard to the overall prediction that revaluation of the alternatives does occur, however, we can have some confidence. Deutsch, Krauss, and

Rosenau (1962) and Davidson and Kiesler (1964) did not eliminate any subjects and did find significant dissonance reducing revaluation. Further, Festinger and Walster (1964) found significant revaluation effects separately for the choice reversal and consistent choice subjects. Jecker (1964) found significant revaluation when only 5 percent of his sample was eliminated because of choice reversal. Other studies either report nonsignificant tabular data in the predicted direction for the few choice reversal subjects (Allen, 1964; Walster, 1964) or state in footnotes that the eliminated subjects show the same trends or would not change the conclusions if included in the reported results (Brehm, 1956; Brock, 1963). The one exception to this is the study by Brehm and Cohen (1959b) in which it is stated in a footnote that for the entire sample one manipulation (similarity of the alternatives) had an effect upon revaluation and one did not (number of alternatives). In any event, it is probably safe to maintain that dissonance reducing revaluation of the alternatives following a decision in an approach-approach conflict does occur.

Also the evidence with regard to the greater importance of post-decisional over predecisional processes in producing alternative revaluation (Allen, 1964; Davidson and Kiesler, 1964; Jecker, 1964) is fairly compelling, although not completely free from ambiguity. The evidence with regard to regret is less compelling, but certainly provides a very provocative lead for further study. Beyond this, the evidence with regard to the effect upon revaluation of such variables as equality of alternative desirability, exposure to information after the choice, ego-involvement with the choice, and number of alternatives is either weak or inconsistent.

In 1962 Brehm and Cohen stated that continued research with ambiguity due to loss of choice reversal subjects would be inexcusable. Since that time, however, such ambiguous research has continued to be reported. It is quite possible, though, that two simple changes in methodological procedure would eliminate the problem. Suppose that the subjects initially rated the desirability of only two rather than of 10 to 15 alternatives. When people rate a large number of alternatives they cannot easily compare every alternative with every other one, so it is quite possible that when later asked to choose between any two of the alternatives they will pick the one initially rated as less desirable. If the subjects rate only 2 alternatives the situation is simpler and confusion less likely. If we have only 2 alternatives, however, we have the problem of the subjects' being able to remember their first rating at the time of the second rating. This is one of the justifications for having the subjects rate a large number of alternatives. This problem can be easily handled by switching to an after-only design in which the pretest is eliminated. The pretest possibly creates more problems than it eliminates anyway

(Campbell, 1957). In an after-only design one group of subjects would rate the alternatives and then make a choice, and another group would make a choice and then rate the alternatives. The latter group should have a higher desirability score for the chosen alternative and a lower desirability score for the rejected alternative than the former group. The main problem with this design is one of selecting alternatives that have small variability in desirability. Small variability theoretically should guarantee that any subject's choice would be dissonance arousing. Note, however, that it is not necessary for each subject to choose the same alternative. The comparison between groups could be done separately for the subjects choosing each alternative.

Counterattitudinal Role-Playing

According to dissonance theory if an individual argues for a point of view inconsistent with his beliefs or plays a role inconsistent with his beliefs, dissonance is created. The individual can theoretically reduce the dissonance by changing his beliefs so as to be more consistent with his behavior. Thus dissonance theory predicts that counterattitudinal role-playing will result in consistency-producing attitude change. Counterattitudinal role-playing is in Festinger's terminology one type of forced compliance.

The research to be discussed in this section deals with the simple effect of counterattitudinal role-playing upon attitude change. We will not include studies which examine the general effect of role-playing upon beliefs and attitudes (e.g., Jansen and Stolurow, 1962). We are interested specifically in counterattitudinal role-playing, because it is when behavior is inconsistent with cognitions that dissonance theoretically arises. Also, other research dealing with the use of reward, punishment, justification, and so forth to induce the forced compliant behavior will be discussed in later sections.

Janis and King (*1954*) report an early investigation of attitude change produced by counterattitudinal advocacy. They expected that arguing against one's own point of view would produce change consistent with the arguments. Preliminary interviews with collegiate debaters had produced support for this expectation. Four weeks before the experimental sessions an opinion questionnaire was administered to male college students in a large class. The questionnaire contained three key opinion items: number of movie theaters that would be in existence 3 years hence, total supply of meat available to the United States in 1953, and number of years it would take to find a cure for the common cold. In the experimental session, groups of three subjects were told that they were taking part in a research project designed to develop a new aptitude test for assessing oral speaking ability. The subjects were asked to give an informal talk based on the material in a prepared outline. Each subject was given a different outline relating to one of the three above opinion items. The outlines presented arguments advocating a decrease in the opinion estimates below that given by any of the students on the before test. While each of the three subjects gave his talk the other two subjects listened. After the third talk the subjects filled out a questionnaire containing items assessing the performance of the other subjects and opinion regarding the three key issues.

The results indicated that the active participants (speakers) changed significantly more than the passive participants (nonspeakers) on the movie theater and meat supply issues and nonsignificantly more on the common cold issue. All of the changes were consistent with the arguments. An examination of data obtained from observing and interviewing the subjects indicated that the subjects who gave talks on the cold cure issue engaged in less improvisation and were less satisfied with their performance than the subjects who gave talks on the two other issues. This difference was possibly produced by the fact that the material in the outline dealing with the common cold was considerably more technical than the material in the outlines dealing with movie theaters and the supply of meat. Janis and King assert that either improvisation or satisfaction could have been the key factor producing the difference between the cold cure issue and the other two issues.

Janis and King regard their results as being consistent with a role-playing interpretation of attitude change. When people play certain roles they take on the attitude consistent with those roles. As Festinger (1957) has pointed out, though, it is also apparent that Janis and King's results are consistent with dissonance theory. Dissonance is theoretically created by engaging in attitude discrepancy behavior such as arguing against one's own point of view. It is furthermore reasonable in the context of dissonance theory to assume that the more thoroughly the counter-attitudinal arguments are developed the greater the amount of dissonance and consequent attitude change.

King and Janis (1956) report a study designed to give evidence on the separate effects of improvisation and satisfaction in the production of attitude change. There were three conditions in the experiment: improvisation, oral reading, and silent reading. In the improvisation condition the subjects read and then gave their own improvised version of a communication containing arguments to the effect that over 90 percent of the college students would be drafted 1 year after graduation and the length of military service for these students would be at least 3 years. The improvised speeches were taped. In the oral reading condition the subjects read the communications into the tape recorder, and in the silent reading condition the subjects simply read the communications to themselves. Before-after change scores revealed a significant difference between the improvisation condition and the oral and silent reading conditions but no significant difference between the latter two conditions. In all conditions there was a tendency to change in the direction of the influence, but this change was significantly greater with improvisation. Additional questionnaire data revealed that the subjects in the oral reading condition felt more satisfied with their performance than the subjects in the improvisation condition. The subjects in the improvisation condition, however, were the ones who changed the most. The data are thus consistent with the hypothesis that improvisation and not satisfaction is the crucial variable producing opinion change in this forced compliance situation.

Harvey and Beverly (1961) present further evidence indicating that counterattitudinal advocacy changes attitudes. Subjects from a small college opposed to the sale and drinking of alcoholic beverages were exposed to a pro-alcohol communication and asked to write down what they considered to be the main arguments contained in the communication. Half of the subjects were then further asked to write a pro-alcohol communication of their own that could be used in a collegiate debate. Before-after change scores indicated that these role-playing subjects became significantly more pro-alcohol than the other subjects who did not write pro-alcohol communications. Once again it is apparent that counterattitudinal advocacy changes attitudes in a consistency producing direction.

Culbertson (1957) demonstrated that role-playing in a psychodrama can change attitudes toward Negroes. Preselected subjects who were not extremely pro-Negro directly participated in or simply observed a psychodrama session. The problem for the psychodrama was structured as follows: Due to the construction of a defense plant in a certain neighborhood it was expected that there would be a considerable influx of Negroes. The government was interested in developing an education program that would facilitate integration and prevent racial disturbance. What, however, would be the theme of this education program? This was the problem with which the psychodrama dealt. Each of the three participants in any given session was given 3 minutes to prepare the advocacy and defense of one particular pro-integration theme. The psychodrama sessions were observed by three nonparticipating subjects.

Before-after change scores revealed a significantly greater change in attitude for the participating than for the observing subjects. Participating in the psychodrama resulted in the creation of more favorable attitudes toward Negroes.

Stanley and Klausmeier (1957) failed to obtain a significant effect as a result of counterattitudinal advocacy. In the context of a classroom demonstration groups of eight graduate students in education argued the pros and cons of world government. Half of the people in each group argued for world government and half against. Of the people who argued for world government half were actually pro and half con. Similarly, of the people who argued against world government half were pro and half con. The other students in the class observed the group discussion.

Before-after change scores revealed that the role-playing manipulation had no significant effect. The subjects who argued against their own point of view, argued for their own point of view, or simply observed did not differ significantly from each other. Stanley and Klausmeier also report some data indicating that the individuals who argued for their own point of view were perceived by the observers as being more convincing than the individuals who argued against their own point of view. This suggests that the counterattitudinal role-players contributed very little to the discussion. This may account for the fact that the counterattitudinal role-players failed to show the predicted greatest amount of attitude change. An unconvincing or minimal counterattitudinal performance may produce very little dissonance and consequent attitude change.

Janis and Mann (1965) found that role-playing a lung cancer patient produced both attitude change and a reduction in smoking. Female moderate and heavy smokers played the role of a patient who after waiting in a doctor's waiting room is told by the doctor that she has a severe case of lung cancer and must go to the hospital for an immediate but probably unsuccessful operation. The details of the procedure were elaborately and convincingly worked out. A control group listened to a tape recording of one of the more dramatic sessions but did not actually engage in role-playing.

Before-after change scores indicated that the role-playing group relative to the control group showed significantly more belief that smoking causes lung cancer, fear of personal harm from smoking, willingness to attempt modification of smoking, and intention to stop smoking. In addition, the role-playing group reported significantly more fear about their health, worry about lung cancer, and 2 weeks later a greater reduction in the number of cigarettes smoked per day.

Janis and Mann's experiment is a dramatic illustration of the potent effect that counterattitudinal role-playing can have. Not only was there a change in attitude toward smoking, but there was also a change in actual smoking behavior. This experiment is one of the few demonstrations that experimentally produced attitude change can lead to actual behavior change outside the laboratory.

Comment. The above evidence seems to indicate that counterattitudinal role-playing is an exceedingly powerful attitude change technique. Of the six reviewed studies five support this conclusion (Culbertson, 1957; Harvey and Beverly, 1961; Janis and King, 1954; Janis and Mann, 1965; King and Janis, 1956) and one does not (Stanley and Klausmeier, 1957). Relative to the inconsistency in many research areas the research on counterattitudinal role-playing is fairly consistent.

It would undoubtedly be unwise, however, to suppose that all types of role-playing will necessarily be more influential than simple exposure to information. McGuire (1966) and McGuire and Papageorgis (1961) have argued that if the individual is too unmotivated to become actively involved in the role-playing or is too unpracticed to perform adequately in the assigned role, then the passive exposure to information may have a superior effect. In an experiment discussed in more detail in Chapter 12, McGuire and Papageorgis found that writing an essay defending a cultural truism (e.g., "Mental illness is not contagious") had less of an effect than the passive reading of defensive material. This differential effect was evident with regard to both direct strengthening of the belief and resistance to subsequent attacking arguments. According to McGuire individuals are unmotivated to defend cultural truisms because they regard them as unassailable, and they are unpracticed in defending cultural truisms because they have never had to defend them in the past. McGuire's results, of course, are limited to role-playing consistent or consonant with existing opinions.

Reward and Forced Compliance

If an individual engages in behavior inconsistent with his own beliefs, he exhibits forced compliance. Such forced compliance is illustrated by the person who publicly argues for a point of view that he privately does not accept. There are many reasons why someone might engage in such dissonance producing behavior. In this section we will examine the research which has used reward in an attempt to induce forced compliance. This research then is concerned with dissonance reduction following the resolution of one particular type of approach-avoidance conflict. The individual has the choice of either engaging in the inconsistent behavior and receiving the reward or not engaging in the inconsistent behavior and not receiving the reward. Dissonance, of course, results no matter which choice is made. If the inconsistent behavior is engaged in, the greater the reward the less the dissonance. If the inconsistent behavior is not engaged in, the greater the reward the more the dissonance.

Kelman (1953), working before the formulation of dissonance theory, obtained the first evidence concerning the effect of reward on forced compliance. After taking a questionnaire measure of the relative merits of jungle (Tarzan) versus fantastic hero (Superman) comic books, seventh-grade school children were offered various rewards for writing essays that argued for the greater value of one type of comic book. The majority of the subjects preferred fantastic hero to jungle comic books. The subjects were given different instructions according to whether they were in a control group, high restriction group, or low restriction group. The control group was told that anyone who wrote a pro-fantastic hero essay would get a copy of *Huckleberry Finn*. The low restriction group was also told that anyone who wrote a pro-fantastic hero essay would get a copy of *Huckleberry Finn*, but that the *five* who wrote the best pro-jungle essays would get free passes to a movie of *Huckleberry Finn*. The high restriction group was told that anyone who wrote a pro-fantastic hero essay would get a copy of *Huckleberry Finn*, but that *all* who wrote pro-jungle essays would get free passes to a movie of *Huckleberry Finn*. Thus the subjects in all groups were promised a free book for writing pro-fantastic hero essays. The two restriction groups differed in that in one all subjects would get a free movie pass for writing pro-jungle essays, and in one only five subjects would be so rewarded. In his discussion of this experiment Festinger (1957) implies or points out that the control group, thus, has moderate incentive toward fantastic hero stories, the low restriction group has low incentive toward jungle stories, and the high restriction group has high incentive toward jungle stories.

Kelman found that in the control group 42 percent of the subjects wrote pro-jungle essays, in the low restriction group 68 percent wrote pro-jungle essays, and in the high restriction group 80 percent wrote pro-jungle essays. These percentages differ significantly in the anticipated direction. The mean before-after change scores broken down according to the three experimental conditions and the type of essay written are presented in Table 10–1. An analysis of variance of these data

TABLE 10–1.   Mean Before-After Change in
Kelman's Six Subgroups [a]

| Experimental Treatment | | Type of Essay | |
Degree of Incentive	Direction of Incentive	Jungle Hero	Fantastic Hero
Moderate	Fantastic Hero	+2.62	−4.57
Low	Jungle	+5.49	+1.89
High	Jungle	+3.81	−5.00

[a] A positive sign indicates change in the direction of greater preference for jungle stories.
SOURCE: Adapted from Festinger, 1957, p. 117.

indicates that the variation between experimental treatments and type of essay written are both significant and the interaction is not. Over all experimental conditions, writing a pro-jungle essay resulted in greater pro-jungle change than writing a fantastic hero essay. This is in accord with the theoretical prediction that the dissonance created by arguing for jungle comics when fantastic hero comics are preferred can be reduced by increased valuation of jungle comics. The overall difference between experimental groups means that the low restriction group changed the most and the control group the least. Festinger (1957) discusses the results by considering first those who wrote jungle essays and then those who wrote fantastic hero essays. He assumes that the subjects who wrote jungle essays in the control condition are subjects who did not comply in order to get the free book. This should have produced moderate dissonance which could have been reduced by a moderate increase in the evaluation of jungle comics. On the other hand, some of the subjects in the low restriction group must have conformed for a small reward (the possibility of getting a free book), and thus have suffered appreciable dissonance. The subjects in the high restriction group should have experienced less dissonance since they conformed for a larger reward (the certainty of getting a free movie pass versus a free book). This speculation leads to the conclusion that the low restriction group should show the greatest increase in valuation of jungle comics, but does not specify what differences should exist between the control and high restriction groups. As can be seen from Table 10–1 the low restriction group does manifest the most change, while there is little difference between the remaining two groups. Festinger presents a similar argument for the subjects who wrote fantastic hero essays. In the control group some of the subjects who wrote fantastic hero essays undoubtedly complied in order to get the free book. Since this is not a large reward they should have been subjected to considerable dissonance. This dissonance, of course, could be reduced through increased valuation of fantastic hero comics. The subjects in the low restriction group did not comply under the influence of the small reward (possibility of getting one of five movie passes versus a free book) and therefore should have been subjected to minimal dissonance, resulting in small change. The subjects in the high restriction group who wrote fantastic hero essays did not comply under the influence of considerable reward (certainty of a movie pass versus a free book). Their resulting dissonance could have been reduced by increased valuation of fantastic hero comics. This speculation leads to the prediction that the low restriction group should show the least negative change in evaluation of jungle comics but does not specify the nature of the difference between the high restriction and the control groups. As can be seen from Table 10–1 the low restriction manifests the only positive change.

The dissonance theory prediction is that for both types of essays the low restriction condition should show more positive change (in-

creased valuation of jungle comics) than either of the other two conditions. Unfortunately, Kelman did not exactly test this prediction. He
did an overall F test comparing the total variance in all three groups. On
the basis of this test we can say for certain that the two extreme groups,
high restriction and control, do differ significantly. However, we have no
test of significance for the comparison between the high restriction and
low restriction groups. All that can be done is to note that the difference
is in the predicted direction.

Mills (1958) tested the hypothesis that cheating for a small reward
results in a greater decreased evaluation of honesty than cheating for a
large reward, and that not cheating for a large reward results in a
greater increased evaluation of honesty than not cheating for a small
reward. Measures of attitudes toward cheating were taken before and
after sixth-grade students were tested on one of two tasks (number
circling or dot counting). For the number circling task, motivation to
cheat was manipulated by offering the two best students either 5 dollars
or 50 cents. For the dot counting task, motivation to cheat was manipulated by offering everyone who improved either 5 dollars or the honor
of having their names announced. Since accurate scores were virtually
impossible, it was possible to tell who had cheated by examining the
subjects' self-graded papers.

Mills reports that some subjects were eliminated because they were
initially so opposed to cheating that there was little or no room on the
scale for an indication of increased honesty. In addition, other subjects
who improved in their performance on the dot counting task were eliminated. Mills plausibly argues that subjects who through honest improvement expected to win the reward would not be subjected to dissonance
because they did not cheat. This matter, however, raises a question concerning the accuracy of discrimination between honest improvers and
cheaters. Mills does report that for the number circling contest there
were some doubtful cases.

Since the patterns of results for the two tasks are very similar the
data were combined for purposes of analysis. Mills found that across
all conditions the cheaters decreased their evaluation of honesty, and
the honest subjects increased theirs. The other effects, however, are by
and large nonsignificant. With regard to the honest subjects, there was
a nonsignificantly greater increase in evaluation of honesty in the high
motivation (high reward for cheating) condition than in the low motivation (low reward for cheating) condition. In the high motivation condition this increased evaluation is significantly different from similar change
in a control group. With regard to the cheaters, evaluation of honesty
was nonsignificantly decreased in the low motivation condition compared with the high motivation condition. Thus we have nonsignificant

results in the predicted direction for both cheaters (conformers) and honest subjects (nonconformers).

Festinger and Carlsmith (1959) report some findings indicating that forced compliance produced by a small reward results in more dissonance reducing attitude change than forced compliance produced by a large reward. Individual male subjects initially spent 1 hour working at tasks designed to be boring (spool packing and peg turning). At the end of the hour the subjects were told that the experiment was over, but that the experimenter would like to hire some help to introduce the next subject to the experiment. It was explained that the assistant who normally did this had failed to show up. The assistant's job was to act like a subject who had just finished the experiment and to tell the waiting subject that the experiment was enjoyable and fun. As an incentive some of the subjects were offered 1 dollar (low reward) and some, 20 dollars (high reward). The payment was for acting as assistant at that time and also for being on call in case of future emergencies. After the subjects talked to the individual waiting for the experiment (a female stooge), they were taken down the hall and introduced to an interviewer in another office. All of the students in the class from which the subjects were drawn had been told earlier that a sample of them would be interviewed concerning their reactions to the research being carried out in the psychology department. During the course of the interview the subjects were asked to indicate how enjoyable they considered the experimental tasks and whether or not they were suspicious about the experiment.

Of the 51 subjects in the two reward groups, 11 were eliminated. Five subjects were suspicious about the procedure; 2 subjects told the female stooge that the experiment was really boring; 3 subjects refused to be hired (conform); and 1 insisted on waiting to explain things to the female stooge. The results for the remaining subjects indicate that the task enjoyment score for the low reward subjects (+1.35) is significantly greater than the task enjoyment score for the high reward subjects (−.05). Further, the task enjoyment score for a control group which did not tell the waiting stooge that the task was fun (−.45) differs significantly from the task enjoyment score for the low reward subjects but not for the high reward subjects.

These results then seemingly indicate that for subjects who conform, low reward produces more dissonance than high reward. This experiment, unlike the previously discussed ones, does not present any evidence concerning the effect of reward magnitude upon subjects who do not conform. In the experiment only three subjects refused to conform—not enough to justify a separate analysis.

Chapanis and Chapanis (1964) have criticized this experiment because the high reward subjects were given an implausibly large incentive, 20 dollars, for a few minutes' work. They argue that such a large reward should have aroused suspicions about what was going on and that this may account for the fact that their evaluations of the enjoyableness of the tasks were evasive or neutral. The low reward subjects, on the other hand, were given a plausible reward, 1 dollar. Chapanis and Chapanis further argue that the results fit the pattern of previous research on credulity and refer to the Fisher and Lubin (1958) study on communicator discrepancy. As Silverman (1964) points out, however, the Fisher and Lubin study does not appear very relevant. But, in any event, Chapanis and Chapanis may have a good point concerning the reason why the high reward subjects rated the tasks as neutral in enjoyability. Perhaps the higher rating of the low reward group was due to a simple effect of a plausible, reasonable reward. Brehm (1965), on the other hand, argues that while 20 dollars may be given in such a way as to create suspicion or puzzlement, Festinger and Carlsmith were not this inept. The money was a payment both for present services and for being on call in case of future emergency. In return for being on call 20 dollars is not an unreasonable sum.

Cohen (1962c) carried out a forced compliance experiment in which rewards were varied over four intervals. He was interested in testing the nondissonance explanation that the inverse relationship between magnitude of rewards and attitude change would disappear if rewards were small enough so as not to arouse suspicion and resistance. Yale students were contacted in their dormitory rooms and asked to write essays in support of the actions of the New Haven police in handling a recent student riot. At that time the dominant attitude toward the police was negative. The subjects were told that the experimenter, a student, was collecting various arguments on the issue as part of a research paper being done for The Institute of Human Relations. As an incentive for writing the essay the subjects were offered either 10 dollars, 5 dollars, 1 dollar, or 50 cents. After writing the essay the subjects marked a 7-point rating scale indicating how justified they thought the actions of the New Haven police were. According to an after-only design this was the only measure taken. A control group marked the rating scale without writing the essay.

Apparently no subjects refused to comply with the request to write the essay, although Cohen does not directly discuss the matter. The empirical data are very clear-cut; the less the reward the more positive the attitude toward the actions of the police. In the control condition the mean attitude score is 2.70; in the 10-dollar condition, 2.32; in the 5-dollar condition, 3.08; in the 1-dollar condition, 3.47; and in the 50-cent condition, 4.54. (The higher the mean the more positive the attitudes toward the New Haven police.) In the experimental conditions the over-all linear trend as well as numerous differences between conditions are significant. Of particular significance for Cohen's argument is the fact that the difference between the 1-dollar and 50-cent conditions is significant. Both the 1-dollar and 50-cent conditions differ significantly from the control condition.

Cohen's experimental test is based on the assumption that suspicion may occur in the high reward conditions (5- or 10-dollar conditions), but not in the low reward conditions (1-dollar or 50-cent conditions). It may be the case, however, that suspicion varies uniformly with reward. If this is so, then the crucial theoretical question concerns whether or not the difference in suspicion between the 1-dollar and 50-cent conditions is large enough so as to have produced the significant attitudinal differences.

Leventhal (1964) tested a "two-process" model that involves a combination of Rosenberg's (1956) instrumentality notions and dissonance theory. An assumption of Rosenberg and Abelson's affective-cognitive consistency theory is that the liking for an instrumental task varies directly with the magnitude of the reward. Dissonance theory, on the other hand, makes the opposite assumption if the magnitude of the reward is considered inadequate. According to dissonance theory, so long as an individual considers the reward for engaging in some activity inadequate, the less the reward the greater the dissonance-produced liking for the task. Leventhal combined the instrumentality and dissonance theory assumptions into a two-process model that predicts a V-shaped relation between reward magnitude and liking for the instrumental task. If the reward is considered inadequate the greater the reward the less the liking for the task, but if the reward is considered adequate the greater the reward the greater the liking for the task.

After a short preliminary session of copying random digits under time pressure, students from an introductory psychology course were asked to decide whether or not they would agree to come back a week later for a 3-hour session of the same thing. As incentives the subjects were offered either 2, 4, or 8 credit points toward their course grade. A control group had indicated that they considered 3.54 credit points fair compensation for being in the experiment. After making their decisions the subjects marked two rating scales indicating their enjoyment of the task and feelings about taking part in the experiment. Three subjects were eliminated; one because he did not know what the credit points were and two (both in the 2-credit condition) because they refused to participate in the later session. The results indicated that the 8-credit condition differed from both of the other two conditions in showing greater liking for the task and the experiment. On both rating scales the

2- and 4-credit point conditions were practically identical. Leventhal had expected that there would be less liking for the task and experiment in the 4-credit condition than in either of the other two conditions.

These results support the instrumentality part of the theory but not the dissonance part. Leventhal states that his results suggest an important restriction in the generality of the dissonance theory. This restriction is that inadequate reward will lower rather than raise liking for the instrumental task when the importance and/or amount of dissonant information is low. Leventhal thus implies that his experimental manipulation probably induced very little dissonance in his subjects. In this he may be correct. Deciding to accept an insufficient reward for a boring task may not create nearly as much dissonance as accepting money to argue for a point of view contrary to one's own.

Rosenberg (1965*b*) attempted to directly test the hypothesis that the inverse relation between reward magnitude and attitude or opinion change is due to suspicion created by being offered a sizeable reward for performing a simple task. According to Rosenberg the typical subject experiences "evaluation apprehension" in an experiment and acts in a manner that he thinks will result in his being evaluated favorably. Thus a large reward for engaging in attitude discrepant behavior may be regarded as a bribe to change one's attitude. Rosenberg argues that the subject who has formulated such a hypothesis will not give evidence of attitude change for to do so would convey something unattractive about himself thereby leading to a negative evaluation.

Rosenberg's test of his evaluation apprehension hypothesis was modeled after the Cohen (1962c) experiment in which reward magnitude was varied over several levels. The crucial difference between the two experiments is the fact that in Rosenberg's experiment, after the subjects wrote the attitude discrepant essays, attitude assessment was done by a different experimenter at a different location in a supposedly unrelated study. When the subjects individually arrived at Rosenberg's office he told them that he was very busy and asked them to wait for about 20 minutes. After they agreed he "remembered" that a graduate student in education had called the previous day requesting volunteers for some attitude research. Rosenberg explained that inasmuch as this graduate student had some funds to pay for their help they might like to go over to the education department and participate in the attitude research while waiting for the present experiment. (Out of 65 subjects, 3 refused to participate in the other study.) When the subjects arrived in the education department an experimenter offered them rewards of either 50 cents, 1 dollar, or 5 dollars for writing essays arguing that their football team should not participate in the Rose Bowl despite the fact that they were the Big Ten champions. After writing their essays and receiving payment for their labors the subjects returned to Rosenberg's office where they filled out an attitude questionnaire containing a crucial item on participation in the Rose Bowl. A control group simply filled out the questionnaire without writing the essay.

On the basis of a postexperiment interview 2 subjects were eliminated because they saw through the deceptions. Analysis of the data for the reduced sample indicated that, contrary to the dissonance prediction, the greater the reward the greater the attitude change. The mean scores in the control, 50-cent, 1-dollar, and 5-dollar conditions are 1.45, 2.24, 2.32, and 3.24 respectively. In addition to an overall significant F, the control condition is significantly less than all of the other conditions, and the 5-dollar condition is significantly greater than the 50-cent condition.

Rosenberg argues that his results do not call the general status of dissonance theory into question. He does think, however, that dissonance theory has been overextended.

In the author's view the kind of counterattitudinal performance that best fits the dissonance paradigm is a simple overt act that directly violates one's private attitude (for example, eating or agreeing to eat a disliked food; expressing approval of a disliked proposal or candidate; merely *committing* oneself to develop counterattitudinal arguments; etc.). But when a person actually *does* elaborate a set of arguments opposite to his own attitude the dissonance he experiences is probably of much wider scope than dissonance analysis would have it; it encompasses considerably more than merely realizing that he has argued against his own position. (1965b, p. 39)

Rosenberg thus believes that certain types of counterattitudinal behavior, such as eating a disliked vegetable or committing oneself to develop counterattitudinal arguments, fit the dissonance model fairly well, but when the person actually develops counterattitudinal arguments other complicating factors become involved. In the latter case the person is confronted not just by the fact that he has argued against his own point of view but also by inconsistency between the plausibility of the new arguments and the affect originally associated with the attitude object. Rosenberg describes this inconsistency as follows:

Thus the subject who opposes the Rose Bowl ban and then argues in favor of it may come up with some good arguments (for example, "If we ban going to the Rose Bowl we will improve our reputation as a serious University . . . we will draw better students," etc.). In so doing he may become convinced of the validity of those arguments. This will produce intraattitudinal inconsistency; that is, the newly established beliefs relating the Rose Bowl ban to positive ends and values will be inconsistent with the original negative affect toward the ban. (1965b, p. 39)

This is the sort of inconsistency that affective-cognitive consistency theory takes as being the basic cause of attitude change.

How can affective-cognitive consistency theory account for the results of the present experiment? According to Rosenberg the reward may act so as to increase the quality of the counterattitudinal arguments that are developed, or reward may act as a reinforcer to facilitate the acceptance of the counterattitudinal arguments once they have been developed. In either case the result would be an increase in the degree of cognitive inconsistency. In order to obtain some information regarding these mediational processes, Rosenberg had two judges rate the persuasiveness of the subjects' essays. It was thus possible to make a comparison of the subjects who wrote essays below the median persuasiveness with the subjects who wrote essays above the median persuasiveness. With the 50-cent and 1-dollar conditions combined, the analysis revealed a significant tendency for the subjects who wrote the most persuasive essays to have the most positive attitudes toward the Rose Bowl ban. A similar analysis in the 5-dollar condition revealed nothing of significance. In addition, Rosenberg found that the subjects in the 5-dollar condition, in general, wrote more persuasive essays than the subjects in the low reward conditions. He thus concluded that one of the factors mediating the obtained results is the effect of reward on the development of persuasive arguments.

An additional analysis, however, revealed that this is not the whole story. When those subjects in the low reward conditions who wrote unpersuasive essays were eliminated, the various reward groups were approximately equated in terms of essay persuasiveness. Even with this reduced sample Rosenberg still found that the high reward group had significantly more positive attitudes. Thus there is evidence that the reward acted as a reinforcer for the acceptance and possibly the learning of the counterattitudinal arguments.

In an attempt to defend dissonance theory Brehm (1965) has pointed out that Rosenberg did not demonstrate that his manipulations could have produced Cohen's (1962c) dissonance reduction results. Brehm specifically argues that Rosenberg's experiment may not have shown dissonance reduction results because of the failure of the reward manipulation to produce an effect on perceived choice. Rosenberg reports evidence indicating that the subjects in all conditions felt relatively free to refuse to write the essays. Cohen, on the other hand, found an inverse relation between amount of reward and perceived choice. If you take the position, as Brehm and Cohen (1962) have, that variation in choice is the crucial variable producing dissonance, then Rosenberg's negative findings are more understandable.

In discussing Rosenberg's results Brehm reveals an interesting bias with regard to the people whom he thinks are most capable of disproving dissonance theory.

Perhaps in practice the person best equipped to disprove a dissonance hypothesis is one who has been successful in supporting it. When such a person designs a test, he is more likely to do so in a sensitive and adequate way and is thus in a position to produce and to recognize disconfirming evidence when it appears. (1965, p. 64)

Janis and Gilmore (*1965*) also failed to support the dissonance predictions concerning the effect of reward upon counterattitudinal advocacy. Their experiment involved three independent variables: amount of monetary reward, favorable versus unfavorable sponsorship, and commitment to compliant behavior versus actual compliance. Male university students were individually contacted in their dormitories and asked to participate in a study. (Before being told anything about the purpose of the study approximately 10 percent refused to participate.) Half of the subjects were told that the experimenter was collecting information on students' attitudes toward science and mathematics courses for a national research organization on behalf of the leading universities in the country (favorable sponsorship). The other half of the subjects were told that the experimenter was collecting information to be used in an advertising campaign by a publisher of science and mathematics textbooks (unfavorable sponsorship). All of the subjects were then asked to write an essay in favor of a required year of mathematics and physics for college students. Half of the subjects were offered 20 dollars for writing the essay and half 1 dollar. As soon as each subject agreed to write the essay he was paid in advance. The final manipulation had to do with whether or not the subjects actually wrote the essays. Half of the subjects were given a questionnaire assessment of attitude immediately after receiving payment and half after they had spent 10 minutes writing the essay.

Theoretically more dissonance should be aroused by the small reward than the large reward and by the unfavorable sponsor than by the favorable sponsor. Commitment to writing the essay, however, should arouse approximately as much dissonance as actually writing the essay. Thus dissonance theory simply predicts most attitude change with small reward and unfavorable sponsorship. Janis and Gilmore interpret reinforcement theory, on the other hand, so that attitude change is predicted only when the essay is written under favorable sponsorship. The favorable sponsor is regarded as providing incentives for a "biased scanning" of the evidence. If the essay is actually written there is, of course, most opportunity for the biased scanning to occur. Thus the combination of the favorable sponsor with the actual writing of the essay, according to Janis and Gilmore's interpretation of reinforcement theory, should produce the most attitude change. In view of Rosenberg's (1965b) results regarding the suspicion aroused by large monetary rewards and the fact that their subjects reported being "puzzled" by the 20 dollars, Janis and Gilmore did not interpret reinforcement theory as making any prediction regarding the monetary manipulation.

The results of the experiment generally support the reinforcement theory predictions. Owing to the fact that most attitude change occurred for the subjects who actually wrote the essays under favorable sponsorship, the crucial favorable versus unfavorable sponsorship and commitment versus actual writing variables interacted significantly. There was no significant effect for the monetary variable. These results then are inconsistent with dissonance theory and consistent with Janis and Gilmore's interpretation of reinforcement theory. A puzzling aspect of Janis and Gilmore's results, however, relates to the failure of the monetary variable to produce any effect whatsoever. If the suspicion interpretation of Festinger and Carlsmith's (1959) results is correct, why was there no inverse relation between reward and attitude change in the present experiment?

One final result was a nonsignificant tendency for the subjects who did not write the essays to change more with unfavorable than favorable sponsorship. This finding weakly supports Rosenberg's (1965b) contention that the dissonance formulation is applicable to the situation where there is commitment but not actual counterattitudinal advocacy.

Elms and Janis (1965) report a study similar to that of Janis and Gilmore (1965). As in the Janis and Gilmore study three independent variables were manipulated: amount of monetary reward, favorable versus unfavorable sponsorship, and commitment to compliant behavior versus actual compliance. Elms and Janis, however, attempted to make the large monetary reward plausible enough to generate positive feelings of satisfaction and to make the difference between the favorable and unfavorable sponsors rather extreme. The monetary rewards were 50 cents and 10 dollars and the sponsors were the Soviet Union and the United States governments. According to Elms and Janis, if a large monetary reward generates positive feelings it should produce more attitude change than a small monetary reward. They expected, however, that the large reward would generate positive feelings only when coming from the favorable sponsor. They thus predicted the most positive attitude change for the condition in which the large reward was paired with the favorable sponsor. As in the Janis and Gilmore study, however, this interaction was expected only if the compliant behavior actually occurred or, more specifically, if the essay was actually written. The reward was conceived of as providing an incentive for the "biased scanning" of the evidence.

The subjects were students in a New England teachers' college who volunteered for the experiment following class announcements promising payment for their services. All of the subjects were given an initial questionnaire measurement of attitude toward sending Americans to the Soviet Union to obtain 4 years of college education. It was then explained that negotiations were currently under way between the U.S. State Department and the Soviet Union regarding such an exchange program. The Soviet Union was reported to be strongly in favor of the program, but the State Department was withholding judgment until some assessment of student attitudes could be made. In the unfavorable sponsorship condition the experimenter presented himself as a representative of a private research firm which had been hired by the Soviet Embassy (with the permission of the State Department) to collect information favorable to the exchange program. This information was to be put in pamphlets that would be circulated on U.S. college campuses. In order to provide this information the subjects were asked to write essays favorable to the exchange program. In the favorable sponsorship program the experimenter presented himself as a representative of a firm which had a contract with the State Department to assess student attitudes toward the exchange program. Attitudes were to be assessed after a sample of U.S. students was given the opportunity to read a pamphlet presenting arguments on both sides of the issue. In order to help in the preparation of this pamphlet the subjects were asked to write essays in favor of the exchange program. It was explained that enough essays unfavorable to the program had already been obtained. As incentives for writing the essays some of the subjects in both the favorable and unfavorable sponsor conditions were paid 50 cents and some 10 dollars. All payments were made as soon as the subjects agreed to write the essays. (One subject in the low reward, unfavorable sponsor condition refused.) The final manipulation concerned whether or not the essay was actually written. Some of the subjects wrote the essays and then filled out the attitude questionnaire a second time, and some filled out the attitude questionnaire a second time without writing the essays.

The before-after attitude change scores are presented in Table 10–2. Elms and Janis refer to the group which actually wrote the essays as the experimental group and the group which did not write the essays as the control group. From the data for the experimental group it can be seen that, in agreement with the prediction, the greatest amount of positive change occurred in the large payment, favorable sponsorship condition. This change is significantly different from all of the other changes in the experimental group. This pattern of results, however, is not replicated in the control group. An analysis of variance of the data resulted in a significant triple order interaction, which Elms and Janis interpreted as supporting their theoretical hypotheses. In disagreement with Rosenberg's expectations, the control (non-essay writing) subjects did not change more with unfavorable than favorable sponsorship.

There is one puzzling thing about this experiment which Elms and

TABLE 10-2. Mean Net Attitude-Change Scores [a]

Sponsorship of role-playing task		Control Groups: No overt role-playing			Experimental Groups: Overt role-playing		
		Small payment, $0.50	Large payment, $10.00	Total	Small payment, $0.50	Large payment, $10.00	Total
Favorable: U.S. Gov't.	N	5	5	10	18	16	34
	M	+0.2	+0.8	+0.5	+0.9	+2.4	+1.7
Unfavorable: Soviet Union	N	5	5	10	17	19	36
	M	−2.0	+1.6	−0.2	+0.6	−0.1	+0.3

[a] Positive scores indicate change in counter-norm direction.
SOURCE: Elms and Janis, 1965, p. 57.

Janis do not directly discuss. Theoretically the 10 dollars did not arouse any suspicion in the favorable sponsorship condition. The question then is why not? Ten dollars is a fairly sizeable sum for a few minutes' work writing an essay. A number of things may have contributed to the lack of suspicion. For one thing the subjects were recruited with the understanding that they would be paid for their services. Thus an offer of money, even an exceedingly large one, may not have appeared suspicious. Second, since the subjects were students on a small college campus they may not have been inclined to mistrust the cover story given them by the experimenter. Students on large campuses where a lot of research is done become rather "experiment-wise" after a while. Third, the money was supposedly coming from a plausible source, either the U.S. or Soviet government. Governments are known to spend large sums of money for various unusual activities.

Brehm (1965) has offered a dissonance interpretation of the Elms and Janis (1965) results. He points out that dissonance can theoretically be reduced in a number of ways other than through attitude change in the counternorm direction. Elms and Janis' subjects, for example, could have magnified the pressure to comply or bolstered their existing attitudes. Brehm argues that positive attitude change was rather unlikely in the unfavorable sponsor condition, since the unfavorable sponsor had such obviously propagandist and dishonest motives. In view of this fact dissonance could have been reduced through the bolstering of the existing attitudes, particularly in the condition in which the essays were not actually written. As can be seen from Table 10–2, in the unfavorable-control condition the small reward resulted in sizeable negative change (−2.0) and the large reward in sizeable positive change (+1.6). Brehm points out that Elms and Janis have no explanation for this finding. What about the unfavorable-experimental condition? Brehm argues that actually writing the essay would commit the subjects and make dissonance reduction through bolstering more unlikely. As can be seen from Table 10–2 there is small positive change with the small reward (+.06) and slight negative change (−0.1) with the large reward. While this effect is undoubtedly not significant, Brehm believes that it probably does differ significantly from the opposite effect in the unfavorable-control condition.

What about Elms and Janis' results in the favorable sponsor conditions? Brehm is not explicit about the matter, but seems to imply that the forces to comply may have been so great as to create little dissonance. In any event, he does state that if compliance creates no dissonance, then any finding that a large reward creates more positive attitude change than a small reward is not contrary to dissonance theory. There is, of course, really no way of knowing whether any dissonance was aroused by compliance in the favorable sponsor condition. In general, Brehm's arguments, while in some respects plausible, seem highly speculative. As he admits (personal communication) he could not have predicted all of the obtained results before actually seeing the data.

  Carlsmith, Collins, and Helmreich (1966) found that anonymous, written counterattitudinal advocacy produced a positive relation between attitude change and reward, while public, oral counterattitudinal advocacy produced a negative relationship. Carlsmith, Collins, and Helmreich argue that if an individual is asked to anonymously write arguments that are opposed to his opinions this will not necessarily create dissonance. The subject may look upon the task as an opportunity to prove that he is an open-minded intellectual. The experimenter, after all, knows that the subject is not expressing his true opinion. Thus anonymous essay writing should produce little dissonance between existing cognitions and the *cognition that a counterattitudinal essay has been written*. On the other hand, the counterattitudinal essay may arouse dissonance of another sort, dissonance between the arguments contained in the essay and the opinions held by the subject. This kind of dissonance, however, is similar to that discussed by "incentive theory" and is not the kind of dissonance studied by Festinger and Carlsmith (1959). When the subject publicly deceives someone else through counterattitudinal advocacy, there is dissonance between the existing cognitions and the cognition that counterattitudinal advocacy has been engaged in. Thus the dissonance prediction regarding the negative relation between reward and counterattitudinal advocacy holds only in the situation in which the counterattitudinal advocacy is publicly deceptive with regard to the subject's true opinions. In the situation in which the counterattitudinal advocacy is not publicly deceptive, dissonance theory, according to Carlsmith, Collins, and Helmreich, predicts no relation between reward and attitude change.

  The experiment was modeled after Festinger and Carlsmith's (1959). After spending an hour performing a boring task (crossing out certain numbers in tables of random numbers) male high school students were offered either 5 dollars, 1 dollar and 50 cents, or 50 cents to advocate that the experimental task was interesting and fun. In a role-playing condition the subjects were asked to orally explain how interesting and fun the experiment was to a waiting subject. In an essay-writing condition the subjects were asked to write anonymous essays to the effect that the task was interesting and fun. The experimenter explained that he was going to take several such essays and combine them into one essay which would eventually be shown to subjects before they undertook the experimental task. No one but the experimenter would see the original essays or know who wrote them. The subjects in both conditions were told that the experiment was concerned with the effect upon performance of being told that a task is interesting and fun and that they themselves had been tested in a control condition. An after-only assessment of the extent to which the experiment was regarded as interesting and fun was taken by a different experimenter in a different room.

For both the ratings of "interesting" and "fun" the attitude change manifested a significant positive linear trend with reward in the essay-writing condition and a significant negative trend with reward in the role-playing condition. These results thus replicate Festinger and Carlsmith's (1959) in the comparable oral or role-playing condition.

Two things are apparent about this experiment. First, dissonance theory, as it is currently interpreted, cannot account for the positive relationship between reward and attitude change which was obtained in the essay-writing condition. Second, unless it is assumed that more suspicion was aroused in the role-playing condition than in the essay-writing condition, Rosenberg's notion of evaluation apprehension cannot account for the negative relation between reward and attitude change which was obtained in the role-playing condition.

In commenting upon this experiment Rosenberg (1966) argues that his hypothesis concerning the situations in which dissonance theory does and does not apply can account for the results. Rosenberg (1965b) had previously hypothesized that dissonance theory applies most directly to those situations in which the subject states a counterattitudinal position but does not elaborate it with a series of persuasive arguments. Rosenberg (1966) argues that the essay-writers came closer than did the role-players to engaging in the kind of complex counterattitudinal advocacy that involves the elaboration of counterattitudinal arguments. He notes that Carlsmith, Collins, and Helmreich report that writing the essays took a maximum of 16 minutes while oral role-playing took a maximum of 2 minutes. He also points out that a film reenactment of the Festinger and Carlsmith (1959) experiment indicates that the subjects in this experiment, like the role-playing subjects in the Carlsmith, Collins, and Helmreich experiment, did not engage in elaborate counterattitudinal advocacy.

Rosenberg further elaborates his hypothesis by bringing in some ideas that are similar to those contained in the theoretical orientation presented by Carlsmith, Collins, and Helmreich. Rosenberg states that the dissonance effect in a counterattitudinal situation in which there is not too great an elaboration of counterattitudinal arguments will be most evident if the subject adopts a duplicity set or consciously attempts to mislead the individuals he is addressing. On the other hand, if the subjects elaborate a sizeable number of counterattitudinal arguments under a self-examination set rather than a duplicity set, the dissonance interpretation will be particularly inappropriate. In this latter situation reward will positively affect the quality of the arguments and hence the amount of attitude change.

One difficulty with Rosenberg's reconciliation is the fact that Cohen (1962c) obtained a negative relationship between influence and reward in an experiment that involved written counterattitudinal advocacy. Rosenberg (1966) argues that either evaluation apprehension or unreported subject loss may account for Cohen's result. Unlike several of the experiments in this tradition Cohen used the same person to conduct both the initial part of the experiment and the final assessment of opinion. This makes the operation of evaluation apprehension more likely. Furthermore, Rosenberg suggests that the subjects who refused to participate in the experiment may have differed from condition to condition. In the low reward condition the subjects who refused to participate would have most likely held opinions contrary to the direction of advocacy, while this type of self-selection would not be expected in the high reward condition. Such biased subject loss could account for opinions being more in accord with the arguments in the low reward conditions. This is sheer speculation, however, since Cohen does not discuss whether there was any subject loss, let alone whether it differed from condition to condition. An additional matter that Rosenberg does not mention has to do with the possibility that Cohen's subjects adopted a duplicity set rather than a self-examination set. Since the essays apparently were not anonymous it is at least possible that a feeling of duplicity or guilt may have facilitated the dissonance effect and the negative relationship between influence and reward.

Collins and Helmreich (1965) failed to find an effect of reward on attitude change in a context in which counterattitudinal essays were written under either "process instructions" or "consequence instructions." Collins and Helmreich argue that dissonance theory puts major emphasis on the consequences of a response rather than on the actual response itself. Thus, according to dissonance theory, a set of instructions designed to emphasize the consequences of counterattitudinal advocacy through an emphasis on the advocacy's possible persuasive impact should maximize dissonance. Other theoretical approaches from the reinforcement or role-playing tradition emphasize the importance of the actual response rather than the consequences of the response. Thus, according to reinforcement theory, a set of instructions designed to emphasize the process of counterattitudinal advocacy through an emphasis on the soundness of the advocacy's arguments should maximize self-persuasion.

Nursing school students tasted and evaluated on rating scales 16 supposedly different solutions. Actually all of the solutions were unsweetened quinine, a very unpleasant tasting substance. During a break which occurred after rating the first 8 solutions, the subjects were offered either 50 cents or 2 dollars to write a counterattitudinal essay pointing out the pleasant aspects of the previously rated solutions. Half of the subjects wrote the essays under process instructions and half under consequence instructions. The subjects given the process instructions were told to *"Think carefully about the samples, and try to find aspects of them which are pleasant, exotic, and not bitter-tasting"* (p. 11), and that they need not sign their names since no one but the experimenter would read their essays. The subjects given the consequence instructions were told to write essays *"that would persuade someone that the samples are pleasant, exotic, and not bitter-tasting"* (p. 12), and that their signed essays would be used in an experiment next semester. After finishing the essays the subjects rated the remaining 8 solutions.

Before-after change scores indicated that reward had no effect in either the process or consequence conditions but that there was significantly more overall change in the process condition than in the consequence condition. Ratings of the essays indicated that, despite the fact that more attitude change occurred in the process condition, the essays were more positive or pro in the consequence condition. The correlation between attitude change and extent of essay positiveness was found to be +.85 in the process condition and −.50 in the consequence condition. These significant correlations seemingly indicate that different mechanisms mediated attitude change in the two instructional conditions. Collins and Helmreich state that the results lend support to the theories which place major emphasis upon the processes involved in counterattitudinal advocacy.

Rosenberg (1966) argues that Collins and Helmreich's process instructions created a self-examination set and the consequence instructions a duplicity set. Thus the greater superiority of process over consequence instructions in producing attitude change is consistent with his hypothesis that attitude change in the counterattitudinal situation is mediated through responsiveness to the merits of the counterattitudinal arguments. Rosenberg may be correct in this assertion. The puzzling thing about Collins and Helmreich's results, however, has to do with the failure of the reward manipulation to produce a significant effect in either instructional condition. Supposedly the self-examination set produces or at least facilitates a positive relation between reward and attitude change, and the duplicity set produces or facilitates a negative relation between reward and attitude change. Such relationships, however, did not occur. Collins and Helmreich's results thus constitute negative evidence with regard to Rosenberg's hypothesis concerning the interaction between reward and type of set (self-examination or duplicity).

Nuttin (1966) studied the effect of reward by using a procedure similar to Festinger and Carlsmith's (1959) except for the addition of a consonance control condition. After participating in a boring experiment, subjects (students at the University of Louvain, Belgium) were offered either 0, 20, or 500 Belgian francs for acting as a stooge and interacting with the next subject who was waiting in an adjacent room. It was explained that the money was also a payment for being on call in case of future emergencies. The subjects were asked to explain to the waiting subject (who was actually a stooge) that the experiment was either enjoyable and interesting (dissonance condition) or boring and uninteresting (consonance condition). After completion of the interaction the subjects were introduced to a supposedly unrelated interviewer who assessed their reactions to the experiment in terms of three main dimensions: enjoyable-disagreeable, interesting-boring, and varied-monotonous.

The results in the dissonance condition indicated that reward had no significant effect on any of the three dependent variables. The results in the consonance conditions indicated that reward had a significant effect on the interesting-boring ratings and similar, but nonsignificant, effects on the other two ratings. In the consonance conditions the general pattern of results on all three dependent variables was for the 20-franc reward to produce the most favorable reaction, the 500-franc reward the least favorable reaction, and the no-reward condition an intermediate reaction. No overall test of significance for all three dependent variables is reported.

Nuttin interprets his results as indicating that the subjects in the 500-franc consonance condition were so embarrassed by the large reward that they attempted to justify it by accentuating the unfavorable aspects of the experimental tasks. Responses from the postexperimental interview, in fact, indicated that the subjects in this condition, more than the subjects in any other condition, considered the reward unnecessarily large. Subjects in the 20-franc consonance condition did not consider the smaller reward unnecessarily large and thus responded with a "pure reward effect." Nuttin thus offers a partial dissonance interpretation of his results which he considers consistent with the broader framework of Festinger's theory, even though different from Festinger and Carlsmith's (1959) interpretation of their results.

Jones and Cooper (1966) report evidence indicating that money offered after agreement to engage in counterattitudinal advocacy produces a positive relationship between reward magnitude and attitude change (reinforcement results), and that money offered before agreement to engage in counterattitudinal advocacy produces a negative relation between reward magnitude and attitude change (dissonance results). Freedman (1963) found that the temporal placement of justification for engaging in an unpleasant task determines whether reinforcement or dissonance results are obtained. On the basis of these findings with regard to justification, Jones and Cooper hypothesized that the same thing might be true of reward.

Subjects, students at Duke University, were paid either 50 cents or 2 dollars and 50 cents for writing counterattitudinal essays justifying a state law forbidding Communists and Fifth Amendment pleaders from speaking at state supported institutions. Through casual conversation it was initially determined that all but one of the original sample of subjects were in fact opposed to the law. (This one subject was eliminated from the final sample.) Half of the subjects were offered the money as an incentive for writing the essays and half were given the money after they had agreed to write the essays but before they actually began writing. At the conclusion of the experiment the subjects marked a scale indicating their attitudes toward the Speaker Ban Law.

The results indicated that in the condition in which the money was offered as an incentive for writing the essays there was a negative relation between the reward magnitude and attitude and that in the condition in which the money was offered after the commitment to write the essays there was a positive relationship between reward magnitude and attitude. The crucial interaction between reward magnitude and time of commitment is significant. Control subjects who did not write counter-attitudinal essays were about as opposed to the Speaker Ban Law as were the subjects offered 2 dollars and 50 cents as an incentive for writing the essays or the subjects offered 50 cents after committing themselves to writing the essays.

Jones and Cooper interpret their results as supporting their initial hypothesis as to the crucial importance of the timing of reward in producing either dissonance or reinforcement results. They also point out that Rosenberg's (1965b) procedure of having one experimenter obtain a commitment from the subjects to participate in the experiment before learning of the required essay writing from a second experimenter may possibly account for the obtained results. The money was offered by the second experimenter after the commitment was obtained by the first experimenter.

Jones and Cooper's provocative findings are the best news that the supporters of dissonance theory have heard in some time. There is a question, however, as to how well the temporal placement of reward hypothesis can systematize the existing literature. Several previous investigators (e.g., Carlsmith, Collins, and Helmreich, 1966) have obtained reinforcement results with rewards that were offered prior to commitment. At the very least it appears as if the temporal placement of reward hypothesis needs to be supplemented with additional considerations.

Comment. According to dissonance theory the greater the reward the less the attitude change produced by compliance and the more the attitude change produced by noncompliance. Almost all of the research has concentrated on testing the prediction for compliant subjects. The results of this research, however, are highly inconsistent. In the counter-attitudinal situations some studies have found a positive relationship between reward and attitude change (Carlsmith, Collins, and Helmreich, 1966; Elms and Janis, 1965; Jones and Cooper, 1966; Leventhal, 1964; Rosenberg, 1965b), some studies have found a negative relationship (Carlsmith, Collins, and Helmreich 1966; Cohen, 1962c; Jones and Cooper, 1966; Festinger and Carlsmith, 1959; Kelman, 1953), and some studies have found no relationship (Collins and Helmreich, 1965; Janis and Gilmore, 1965; Mills, 1958; Nuttin, 1966). Attempts to understand this literature in terms of such notions as suspicion, evaluation apprehension, self-examination versus duplicity sets, extent to which counterattitudinal arguments are elaborated, and temporal placement of reward have not been completely successful, but may eventually prove helpful. At present no existing hypothesis appears to completely systematize all of the existing literature. The one evident thing is that dissonance theory is in trouble and, at the very least, is in need of revision.

Punishment and Forced Compliance

There are two basic types of studies dealing with the effect of punishment on forced compliance. One type is concerned with punishment used to encourage a disliked activity, and the other type is concerned with punishment used to discourage a liked activity. The first type, of course, involves an avoidance-avoidance conflict and the second an approach-avoidance conflict.

Raven and Fishbein (*1961*) tested the dissonance prediction that failure to report the reception of ESP images when encouraged with electric shock to do so, produces a reduction of belief in ESP. On the assumption that lying is a disliked activity the experiment involves an avoidance-avoidance conflict. Raven and Fishbein initially measured subjects' beliefs in and attitudes toward ESP on semantic differential scales. The subjects were then put in a situation in which on each of 12 trials they pressed buttons indicating whether they did or did not receive ESP images of the word "contemporary" from a "sender" in an adjacent room. Half of the subjects were given an electric shock on each of the trials in which they failed to report receiving an ESP image and half were not. The shock levels were individually adjusted for each subject so as to be the maximum reported as endurable. After the last trial the semantic differential scales were marked for a second time. Out of the original sample of 82 subjects 30 were eliminated, 17 because their initial belief scores were so extreme as to preclude change in one direction or the other, 1 because he preferred not to be shocked, and 12 because they reported receiving ESP images on some of the trials. Raven and Fishbein did not report whether these subjects consistently conformed over the last trials in the series. For any subjects who could be unambiguously classified as compliant, dissonance theory, of course, has definite predictions. For the noncompliant subjects or subjects who reported receiving no ESP images on any of the 12 trials, Raven and Fishbein found no overall change in *belief* in ESP. According to dissonance theory noncompliance in the shock condition (failure to report ESP images) should have resulted in a greater reduction in belief in ESP than noncompliance in the no-shock condition. However, a breakdown of the data according to sex revealed a tendency for females but not males to show the predicted effect. A comparison of the shock females with the other three groups (no-shock females, shock males, no-shock males) revealed significantly greater belief reduction on the part of the shock females. This *post hoc* comparison was justified by the fact that the latency of response in pushing the buzzer on each trial was markedly and significantly longer only for the females in the shock condition. Presumably, then, it was only in the females that the shock produced a real conflict and difficult decision. Raven and Fishbein state that perhaps the males perceived the shock as a test of their masculinity and gained some intrinsic reward from responding rapidly. This argument thus leads to the conclusion that it is only the females in the shock condition who were punished in a theoretically relevant manner.

Raven and Fishbein point out that there is an alternative interpretation of their results in terms of a shock-produced generalized negative attitude toward the experiment and ESP. Such a negative *attitude* could produce a reduction of *belief* in ESP. However, the before-after change scores in *attitude* toward ESP revealed no significant effect for either males or females in either of the experimental conditions. This interpretation was therefore regarded as unsupported by the data.

While Raven and Fishbein do succeed in making their results consistent with dissonance theory, the fact that this was done on a *post hoc* basis makes the support for the theory not terribly convincing. The prediction needs to be tested in another situation with a different procedure.

Brehm (1962) attempted to test the dissonance prediction that the less the threatened punishment for noncompliance the greater the attitude change following compliance. Since the threatened punishment was used to encourage a disliked activity, this experiment also involves an avoidance-avoidance conflict. The experimenter, a fraternity member, asked 20 of his fraternity's pledges to spend three hours copying random numbers. He explained that as part of a research project for a psychology course he was required to collect such normative data. The pledges were threatened with either high coercion or low coercion if they failed to comply. The high coercion threat was a tribunal and possible rejection by the fraternity, and the low coercion threat was a paddling. After signing a schedule sheet the subjects were given an anonymous questionnaire that they themselves were to send to the Interfraternity Council. The experimenter explained that I.F.C. had prepared the questionnaire to determine the advisability of using pledges in psychological research.

The questionnaire responses indicated that the high coercion condition was indeed regarded as more threatening, but, unexpectedly, the low coercion threat was regarded as significantly less likely to be carried out. This means, of course, that the greater amount of dissonance existing in the low coercion condition may have been due both to the minimal severity of the threat and to the belief that it was less likely to be carried out. With regard to the main dependent variable it was found that there was less reported dissatisfaction with the experiment in the low coercion than in the high coercion condition. This was taken to mean that the greater dissonance in the low coercion condition was reduced through a decrease in dissatisfaction with the experiment. An alternative interpretation, though, is that the severe threat in the high coercion condition produced a greater dissatisfaction with the experiment than the minimal threat in the low coercion condition.

Aronson and Carlsmith (*1963*) tested the dissonance prediction that the less the threatened punishment for manipulating a desirable object the more the dissonance reducing derogation of this object by compliant subjects. Here we have an approach-avoidance rather than an avoidance-avoidance conflict. The experimenter first individually tested the preferences of preschool children for five attractive toys by means of a paired-comparison procedure. He then told each child that while left alone he or she could play with all of the toys except one. The forbidden toy was the toy ranked second by each subject. The experimenter informed half of the subjects that he would be annoyed if they played with the forbidden toy (mild threat) and half of the subjects that he would be angry and take away all of the toys if they played with the forbidden toy (severe threat). All subjects were run in both the severe and mild threat conditions, but there was a 45-day interval between the sessions as well as counterbalancing of the order. During the 10-minute interval in which the experimenter was out of the room the subjects were observed through a one-way mirror. When the experimenter returned he had the subjects evaluate the toys for a second time.

Of the 28 children in the original sample 6 did not complete the experiment. Two moved from town; 3 were unable to make consistent paired-comparison rankings; and 1 did not wish to continue. No children played with the forbidden toy while the experimenter was out of the room. The results indicated that the expected decrease in attractiveness of the forbidden toy in the mild threat condition was significantly different from the unexpected increase in attractiveness of the forbidden toy in the severe threat condition. In order to check into the possibility that this increase in attractiveness of the forbidden toy was due to satiation with the other toys, some of the same subjects were run in a control condition in which the experimenter took the second-ranked toy with him when he left the room and in no way threatened the subjects. This procedure produced a marked increase in liking for the second-ranked toy just as occurred in the severe threat condition, although no test of significance was reported. By and large, these results provide fairly convincing support for the dissonance prediction.

Freedman (*1965*) found that the less the threatened punishment for manipulating a desirable object the greater the tendency of compliant subjects to avoid the object after removal of the threat. The experimental procedure was very similar to Aronson and Carlsmith's (1963). Individually tested second-, third-, and fourth-grade boys initially rated five toys and then were told with either a high or low threat that they were not to play with the most expensive one, a battery controlled robot. After leaving the room for 5 minutes the experimenter returned and had the boys rate the toys for a second time. A concealed electric timer recorded whether or not the robot's switch had been turned on during the experimenter's absence. Approximately 40 days later a different experimenter again left the boys alone with the toys.

Two experimental subjects (one in each of the threat conditions) violated the norm against playing with the robot in the first session and were not included in the analysis. For the remaining subjects the results indicated as predicted that playing with the robot during the second session occurred for significantly more of the subjects in the high threat condition than in the low threat condition. The number of subjects playing with the robot in the high threat condition did not differ significantly from the number of subjects who played with the robot in two control conditions. The two control conditions differed from the two experimental conditions solely in that the experimenter did not leave the room during the first session. Before-after changes in the desirability ratings of the toys during the first session indicated that the robot decreased more and the other toys increased more in the mild threat experimental group than in any of the other groups. This predicted difference, however, is not significant. Freedman speculates that his failure to replicate Aronson and Carlsmith's (1963) findings in this respect may be due to the fact that the obviously attractive robot was more difficult to disparage than the forbidden toys used by Aronson and Carlsmith. Freedman further speculates that dissonance in the low threat condition may have been reduced, not by disparagement of the forbidden toy, but by acceptance of the idea that it was wrong to play with the forbidden toy.

Aronson and Mills (1959) tested the hypothesis that the liking of a group by its members varies directly with the severity of initiation. The more unpleasant (punishing) the initiation procedure the more the resulting dissonance in noncompliant individuals (individuals who are not deterred by the punishment) is reduced through increased liking for the group. The subjects were college women who had volunteered for participation in a series of group discussions on the psychology of sex. When the subjects individually showed up for the group discussion the experimenter told them that in order to prevent embarrassment the participants in the discussion would communicate via headphones and microphones and would not actually see each other. There were three conditions in the experiment: severe initiation, mild initiation, and control. In the two initiation conditions the subjects were required to take an "embarrassment test" before participating in the discussion. One subject who declined was excluded. (At this point in the procedure the experiment involved an approach-avoidance conflict.) In the severe condition the embarrassment test was to read 12 obscene words and 2 vivid descriptions of sexual activity from contemporary novels in the presence of the male experimenter. In the mild condition the embarrassment test was to read 5 sexual but nonobscene words in the presence of the experimenter. In the control condition there was no embarrassment test at all. After these manipulations the subjects were told that, since the group discussion was already underway and since they had not done the required preparation, it would be better if they just listened and did not say anything. The group discussion to which the subjects listened was concerned with the secondary sexual behavior of animals. This discussion, which (unknown to the subjects) was taped, had been purposely made dull and boring. At the conclusion of the recording the subjects filled out a questionnaire giving their evaluation of the discussion. One subject, who upon questioning revealed definite suspicions about the experiment, was excluded from the sample.

The results indicated that the discussion was evaluated more highly in the severe initiation condition than in either the mild initiation condition or the control condition, and nonsignificantly more highly in the mild initiation condition than in the control condition. These results, then, support the dissonance prediction. Chapanis and Chapanis (1964) argue that the results are explicable in terms of a successful feeling of accomplishment in overcoming a painful obstacle. The subjects in the severe initiation condition overcame more of an obstacle and thus evaluated the discussion more highly. Silverman (1964) argues that this explanation would most directly account for the evaluation of the initiation procedure rather than the discussion that followed. It seems, however, that a successful feeling of accomplishment would most directly affect the evaluation of one's performance. If this is the case, then the crucial theoretical question concerns whether or not the subjects' evaluation of their initiation performance generalized to the evaluation of the discussion. Unfortunately, we do not have the answer. This generalization assumption does, however, make the Chapanis and Chapanis explanation appear somewhat strained.

Schopler and Bateson (1962) tested an explanation of Aronson and Mills' (1959) results derived from Thibaut and Kelley's (1959) "exchange" theory of interpersonal behavior. From the standpoint of exchange theory Aronson and Mills' subjects in the severe initiation condition were forced to endure an unpleasant experience or a poor "outcome" by virtue of their low power position. Such a state of affairs theoretically leads the low power person to engage in behaviors that will increase his power and thus eventually the value of his outcomes. One of the most potent of such behaviors is simple conformity to the opinions of the high power person. This strategy gives the low power person the option of withdrawing his support for the high power person's opinions if the high power person engages in behavior that is unrewarding for the low power person. The implication of this line of reasoning is that Aronson and Mills' subjects in the severe initiation condition conformed to the experimenter's opinion regarding the value of the group discussion simply in order to increase their power and thus prevent the recurrence of future unpleasant experiences.

Schopler and Bateson's experiment involved four conditions: severe initiation, mild initiation, disparage, and increased power. The severe initiation and mild initiation conditions were the same or similar to the analogous conditions in Aronson and Mills' experiment. The disparage condition differed from the severe initiation condition solely in that after completion of the initiation procedure the experimenter told the subject that the group discussion was actually dull and unexciting. The increased power condition differed from the severe initiation condition solely in that the subjects were given the opportunity to evaluate the competence of the experimenter supposedly as part of a routine procedure being used in all psychology experiments. Schopler and Bateson interpreted exchange theory as implying that subjects in the two latter conditions, unlike subjects in the severe initiation condition, would not highly evaluate the group discussion. Conformity to the experimenter's opinion in the disparage condition would certainly not produce a high evaluation of the group discussion, and the subjects' opportunity to evaluate the experimenter in the increased power condition should obviate the necessity for conformity to the experimenter's evaluation of the group discussion. Besides the addition of these two groups the experiment differed from Aronson and Mills' mainly in that the subjects did not come to the experiment with the purpose or expectation of joining a group discussion on the psychology of sex.

The results indicated that the subjects in the severe initiation evaluated the group discussion more highly than the subjects in the mild initiation condition. This finding replicates Aronson and Mills' main results. In addition, it was found that the subjects in the disparage condition evaluated the discussion less highly than the subjects in the severe initiation condition and that the subjects in the increased power condition evaluated the discussion nonsignificantly differently from the subjects in the severe initiation condition. The significant difference between the disparage and severe initiation conditions supports the exchange theory interpretation, but the nonsignificant difference between the severe initiation condition and the increased power condition does not. However, in view of the fact that a postexperimental questionnaire revealed that the subjects in the increased power condition did not regard themselves as having more influence over the experimenter than did the subjects in the other conditions, the latter test was not regarded as crucial for the exchange theory interpretation. In general, the experiments pose an interesting alternative explanation for the Aronson and Mills results.

Gerard and Mathewson (*1966*) report an experiment which attempted to rule out a number of alternative explanations for the Aronson and Mills results. Gerard and Mathewson list a sizeable number of interesting explanations. First, there is the family of interpretations that relate to the fact that the content of the initiation and the discussion both had to do with sex. Possibly the severe initiation sexually aroused the girls so that they were more anxious to get into the group in order to discuss sex. Or possibly the subjects in the severe initiation condition were intrigued by the obscene material and believed that sometime in the future such matters would be discussed. Second, there is the "relief" hypothesis that the severe initiation condition built up anxiety which was subsequently reduced by the banal discussion. Third, there is Schopler and Bateson's (1962) dependency or exchange theory interpretation. Fourth, there is Chapanis and Chapanis' (1964) "afterglow" hypothesis that the subjects evaluated the discussion highly because of a feeling of accomplishment at having overcome the severe initiation test. Finally, there is the contrast hypothesis that the group discussion seemed pleasant by contrast to the unpleasant severe initiation.

The experiment involved severely or mildly shocking subjects prior to exposing them to an uninteresting discussion on cheating in college. Half of the subjects came to the experiment with the idea of volunteering for a discussion club concerned with campus morality and half came with the idea of participating in an ordinary psychology experiment. These conditions further differed in that the subjects who came to join the club were led to believe that the shocks were part of an initiation procedure while the other subjects were led to believe that the shocks were simply given in order to determine their reactions.[3] One final variation was concerned with whether or not the "initiated" subjects, or subjects who believed that they were being screened for entrance into the club, were told that they had passed the initiation.

The results indicated that the initiated subjects evaluated the discussion more highly in the severe initiation condition than in the mild initiation condition and that severity of shock had no effect on the noninitiated subjects. The relevant initiation by shock interaction is sig-

[3] None of Schopler and Bateson's subjects came to the experiment with the expectation of joining a club, but all of them believed that they were initiated for the club.

nificant. Furthermore, the difference between severe and mild shock conditions was not affected by whether or not the initiated subjects were told that they had passed the initiation. Gerard and Mathewson interpret these results as simultaneously supporting the dissonance interpretation and eliminating the alternative explanations. The fact that the content of the initiation procedure was unrelated to the content of the group discussion eliminates those explanations that focus on the fact that the Aronson and Mills initiation procedure and group discussion both related to sex. The fact that the difference between severe and mild shock did not produce differential evaluations of the group discussion in the non-initiation conditions eliminates the relief and contrast hypotheses. Finally, the fact that whether or not the initiated subjects were told that they had passed the initiation had no effect on the difference between discussion evaluations in the severe and mild conditions eliminates Chapanis and Chapanis' afterglow hypothesis and Schopler and Bateson's dependency interpretation.

This is an interesting experiment and most of Gerard and Mathewson's arguments are cogent ones. Some reservation, however, can be voiced as to whether or not the results really eliminate the dependency interpretation. It is true that by telling the subjects that they had passed the initiation they were given somewhat more favorable outcomes and hence perhaps less motivation for conformity to the experimenter's presumably favorable opinion of the group discussion. There is no way of knowing, however, whether the increased favorable outcomes would have been sufficient to obviate the necessity for conformity. From the standpoint of exchange theory the test was not a crucial one. Gerard and Mathewson offer no explanation for Schopler and Bateson's finding that subjects in the severe initiation condition did not favorably evaluate the discussion when they were led to believe that the experimenter considered the discussion uninteresting.

Comment. It is difficult to give an overall evaluation of the research relating to the effect of punishment, threatened or actual, on dissonance reduction in a forced compliance situation. There are two experiments which used avoidance-avoidance conflicts: Raven and Fishbein (1961) and Brehm (1962). The Raven and Fishbein experiment, which was concerned with noncompliant subjects, is consistent with dissonance theory only through a *post hoc* analysis and interpretation of the data. And the Brehm experiment, which was concerned with compliant subjects, can be interpreted as readily in terms of avoidance motivation as in terms of dissonance reduction. The research that has involved approach-avoidance conflicts provides somewhat more convincing support for the theory. Studies of compliant subjects (Aronson and Carlsmith, 1963; Freedman, 1965) in general agree with the dissonance expectations, although there is some ambiguity over the role of decreased evaluation of the forbidden object as a mode of dissonance reduction. Studies of noncompliant subjects (Aronson and Mills, 1959; Gerard and Mathewson, 1966; Schopler and Bateson, 1962) support the dissonance expectations, although exchange theory provides an equally cogent explanation of the findings in terms of dependency.

Matters are made more ambiguous by the fact that the above research on punishment has focused on the four possible types of relevant situations. These four situations are noncompliant subjects in avoidance-avoidance conflicts, compliant subjects in avoidance-avoidance conflicts, noncompliant subjects in approach-avoidance conflicts, and compliant subjects in approach-avoidance conflicts. In view of this diversity one cannot assume that the experiments provide much mutual support. Thus, at the present time it would seem premature to draw any overall conclusions concerning the effect of punishment in a forced compliance situation.

Justification and Forced Compliance

According to dissonance theory, the greater the justification for engaging in an unpleasant activity or an activity that is inconsistent with one's cognitions, the less the dissonance. This justification typically takes the form of rational reasons why it would be helpful to the experimenter if the subjects complied. Some of the research on justification has explicitly given the subjects a choice as to whether or not to comply, and some has not. In either case, however, a conflict is undoubtedly created if the compliant behavior is unpleasant enough.

Cohen, Brehm, and Fleming (1958) were the first to report an investigation concerned with the effect of justification on dissonance reduction. In a classroom setting Yale undergraduates were asked to write essays contrary to their opinions as to whether or not Yale should be made coeducational. Before and after writing the essays anonymous questionnaires on the subject were filled out. In a high justification condition the subjects were given a variety of reasons as to why they should write the essays: their cooperation would help the experimenter with a research paper, other students had been willing to cooperate, considering the other side of any issue facilitated comprehension, etc. In a low justification condition no justification whatsoever was given for writing the opinion discrepant essays. Furthermore, the subjects were told that they did not have to comply if they did not want to. All subjects in both conditions did in fact comply.

Theoretically compliance in a low justification condition should produce more dissonance than compliance in a high justification condition. As a result the subjects in the low justification condition should show the most change in opinion so as to agree with their essays. This in fact happened, but to a very minor and nonsignificant degree. The hypothesis was tested a second time after eliminating 51 percent of the subjects whose before scores were extreme in either direction. This was justified on the basis that extreme scores were inversely related to opinion change, and more extreme scores were in the low than high justification group. With this selected sample, however, the results still are not significant ($p < .07$, one-tailed), even though Cohen, Brehm, and Fleming seemingly imply that they are.

Rabbie, Brehm, and Cohen (*1959*) investigated the effect upon attitude change both of justification and of engaging or not engaging in the compliant behavior once the commitment has been made. Yale freshmen were individually contacted and asked to write essays advocating the elimination of athletic competition between schools. They were all told that their essays would help the administration in considering such a course of action. Some of the subjects were then given further high justification for writing the essays and some further low justification. An additional variation was in whether attitudes were measured immediately after having agreed to write the essay or after having actually written the essay. According to an after-only design this measure was the only one taken.

Of the 60 students contacted, 46 percent refused to write essays in favor of the elimination of interschool athletics. Rabbie, Brehm, and Cohen report that these subjects were approximately equally distributed among the four conditions. For the remaining subjects there is a significant difference between high and low justification only in the condition in which attitude was measured before rather than after writing the essay. In this condition attitudes toward interschool athletics were, as predicted, more positive for low than for high justification. No overall significance test of high versus low justification is reported.

Brehm and Cohen (1962, pp. 122–123) state that subjects are likely to refuse to participate in forced compliance studies if the required compliant behavior is too dissonant with their cognitions. Therefore more subjects with cognitions contrary to the compliance may be lost from high dissonance than from low dissonance conditions. This means that the subjects remaining in the high and low dissonance conditions will of necessity have differing cognitions simply because of differential subject loss. Brehm and Cohen do, however, state that this problem can be handled with a before measure. Unfortunately, Rabbie, Brehm, and Cohen (1959) did not have a before measure. Thus it may be the case that the subjects who remained in the low justification condition were more in favor of eliminating interschool athletics than the subjects who remained in the high justification condition. Rabbie, Brehm, and Cohen do state that the numbers of subjects who refused to write the essays were approximately equally distributed among the four conditions, and that therefore no serious bias resulted from subject loss. If subject loss is due to too much dissonance then more subjects should have been lost from the high than the low dissonance conditions. The fact that such was not the case is at least some evidence that the results are not artifactual.

The one thing that can be said with certainty about these results is that the elimination of such a large percentage of the sample through self-selection poses severe and to a great extent unspecifiable restrictions on the generality of the findings.

Brock and Blackwood (1962) present the first really convincing evidence concerning the effect of justification upon attitude change. College students were individually asked to write essays advocating higher tuition. There was no explicit choice manipulation; i.e., the subjects were not given a choice as to whether they could or could not write the essays. Low justification was given to 32 subjects for writing the essays and 30 subjects received high justification. After having written the predetermined essay title the subjects were interrupted and given a questionnaire. According to an after-only design this was the only measure taken. The subjects did not actually write the essays. The results unambiguously and significantly indicated that, as predicted, attitudes were more favorable toward the tuition increase in the low justification condition than in the high justification condition.

Cohen (1962b) reports a study on the effect of repeated dissonances. Three weeks after the administration of an initial attitude questionnaire Yale students were asked to write essays on each of five topics: (1) compulsory chapel, (2) compulsory coats and ties at all times and places, (3) compulsory Latin and Greek, (4) compulsory attendance at all classes, (5) elimination of intercollegiate athletics. Yale students were opposed to all of these potential changes. In a preconsonance condition the subjects were asked to write opposing essays on the first four topics, and in a predissonance condition subjects were asked to write supporting essays on the first four topics. All subjects were asked to write opposing essays on the last topic. The last or fifth essay was written under either a high or a low justification set. There was no explicit choice manipulation for any of the subjects on any of the essays. After finishing the last essay the subjects filled out the attitude questionnaire a second time.

Apparently no subjects refused to participate in the experiment or to write the requested type of essay. An analysis of variance indicated that, although the main effect of justification is not significant, the interaction between justification and the predissonance-preconsonance manipulation is. In the predissonance condition high justification resulted in small positive (dissonance-reducing) change and low justification in minimal negative change, while in the preconsonance condition high justification resulted in small positive change and low justification in sizeable positive change. The results in the preconsonance condition, of course, parallel those predicted and sometimes obtained by other investigators. (No t test comparing high and low justification in the preconsonance condition is reported.)

In addition to assessing attitude the final questionnaire also contained a measure of perceived obligation for writing the final essay. Cohen found that overall high justification resulted in significantly greater perceived obligation than did low justification. However, within the low justification condition, predissonance resulted in significantly greater perceived obligation for writing the final essay than did preconsonance. Cohen suggests that possibly the predissonance, low-justification subjects used perceived obligation rather than attitude change as a mode of dissonance reduction. The fact that these subjects had previously written four attitude discrepant essays may have made this mode of dissonance reduction more salient.

Brehm (1960) attempted to study justification in conjunction with commitment. Eighth-grade students were induced by a reward (movie tickets or records) to eat a disliked vegetable. Liking for the vegetables was measured by a questionnaire administered sometime prior to the experimental session. After the subjects had eaten they read a research report describing the vegetable's vitamin and mineral content and filled out the questionnaire for the second time. Two variables were manipulated in the experiment: high versus low eating (commitment) and support versus no support (justification). In the low eating condition the subjects simply ate a small portion of the disliked vegetable. In the high eating condition the subjects ate a small portion and in addition were told they would have to return three or four times during the week to eat more of the vegetable. Brehm conceived of the high eating condition as being high commitment and the low eating condition as being low commitment. The support or justification manipulation was accomplished by having the research report describe the disliked vegetable as either extremely high or extremely low in vitamin and mineral content.

Brehm reports that the overall rate of refusal to eat was 5 percent and did not differ among the four conditions. The results indicated that in the high commitment condition no support resulted in nonsignificantly more change than support ($p = .09$), and in the low commitment condition support resulted in nonsignificantly more change than no support ($p = .06$). If one will settle for one-tailed probability values the two opposite effects may be considered significant. In any event, the interaction between eating and support (commitment and justification) is significant. Brehm interpreted these results as indicating that only substantial commitment will produce the predicted effect for support or justification. When subjects are highly committed then the dissonance produced by low support or low justification for having eaten a disliked vegetable is reduced by increased liking for the vegetable.

Freedman (*1963*) reports a number of experiments on justification, one of which is directly relevant to the Brehm (1960) study. Freedman argues that Brehm's results can be interpreted in terms of the time at which the justification was given. In the low eating condition the justification was given after eating a small portion of the vegetable. In the high eating condition the justification was given after eating a small portion of the vegetable but before the times at which the subjects believed they would have to return and eat more. Freedman notes that if justification is a reinforcer it should be most effective when given after rather than before the dissonance-producing behavior, and Brehm in fact found that high justification was more effective than low justification in the low eating condition in which the justification occurred last. In the high eating condition, on the other hand, the earlier occurrence of the justification produced the expected dissonance reducing effect, i.e., low justification was found more effective than high justification. Freedman thus argues that not commitment but the time of justification is the crucial factor accounting for Brehm's results.

In order to test this hypothesis Freedman designed an experiment in which high or low justification was given either before or after engaging in dissonance-producing behavior. Undergraduates in an English class were asked to spend some time writing "random" numbers. It was explained to all of the subjects that the experiment was a study of people's implicit assumptions about the number system revealed through the deviations from randomness in the numbers they wrote. In the high justification conditions the subjects were told that the data from their class would be extremely useful since they would allow the experimenter to complete the study. In the low justification condition the subjects were told that the data from their class would be of no use since all of the necessary data had been collected the previous week. Their class was being used simply because they had previously been scheduled. This justification manipulation was given either before or after actually writing the numbers.

Analysis of a task-enjoyment rating revealed a significant interaction between time of justification and type of justification. As predicted when the justification was given before writing the numbers, low justification resulted in significantly more task enjoyment than high justification, and when the justification was given after writing the numbers, high justification resulted in significantly more enjoyment than low justification. These results support Freedman's contention that justification given before a decision or action produces dissonance reduction effects and justification given after a decision or action produces reinforcement effects. This may be a very important theoretical contribution.

In further research Freedman investigated the effectiveness of various high and low justification instructions in producing dissonance-reducing evaluation of a boring and tedious task. In the first such experiment the task was one of writing plus and minus symbols left to right in the squares on a piece of paper. In the last two experiments the task was one of writing the numbers 0 through 9 in the squares. In all experiments the subjects were stopped after working for 12 minutes in order to indicate their enjoyment of the task. It was implied, however, that they would have to work much longer.

High justification instructions in the first experiment described the task as a study of ESP in which the subjects would attempt to match the symbols with the ones existing on a master sheet. In addition the subjects were told that the information would be used for discussion in a class in statistics. The low justification instructions mentioned only the latter reason for performing the task. The justifications were given before performing the task and there was no choice manipulation. The results indicated, as predicted, that task enjoyment was significantly higher with low than with high justification.

High justification instructions in the second experiment described the task as a study of the relation between the ability to write random numbers and personality, as measured by a previously taken MMPI. In addition, the subjects were told that the numbers collected would be used for class discussion in a statistics course. The low justification instructions mentioned only the second reason. Again the results indicated, as predicted, that there was significantly more enjoyment of the task with low than with high justification.

In the third experiment Freedman investigated the effect of high and low justification instructions that differed only in usefulness. All subjects were told that the nonrandom numbers written by people were needed for discussion in their class in statistics. In the high justification condition the subjects were further told the numbers produced by people are always better for demonstration than those from tables, and also their numbers would be used to demonstrate how numbers actually deviate from randomness. In the low justification condition the subjects were told that the numbers they wrote would not be much of an improvement over other tabled numbers and therefore not very useful. The results, once again, indicated that enjoyment of the task was significantly higher in the low justification condition than in the high justification condition.

The four experiments on justification reported by Freedman provide very convincing support for dissonance theory. In none of these experiments were any subjects eliminated. This, of course, is a resultant of the fact that the subjects were not given an explicit choice as to whether or not to perform the tasks.

With regard to the lack of a choice manipulation in any of the experiments Freedman points out that his results do not agree with Brehm and Cohen's (1962) theorizing that some volition is a necessary condition for the arousal of dissonance. Freedman admits that people may feel some degree of responsibility for their actions unless this responsibility is explicitly excluded, but nonetheless argues that his results convince him that dissonance can be aroused in the absence of choice. Freedman suggests that perhaps Brehm and Cohen stated their case too strongly. Choice may be one of the most important determiners of the amount of dissonance produced without being a necessary condition for dissonance arousal.

Comment. Due to subject elimination and nonsignificant results in the predicted direction, much of the research on the effect of justification is rather inconclusive. However, the research of Brock and Blackwood (1962) and of Freedman (1963) appears to have greatly straightened things out. The one study by Brock and Blackwood and the four studies by Freedman obtained significant results in the predicted direction, did not eliminate subjects, utilized appropriate tests of significance, and did not involve design flaws. Furthermore, Freedman's demonstration of the differing effects of justification before and after an action may possibly point the way to a major rapprochement of reinforcement theory and dissonance theory.

Choice and Forced Compliance

Festinger's (1957) original statement of dissonance theory does not make explicitly clear the role of choice in the production of dissonance. From Festinger's discussion of decisional and forced compliance situations, however, it is apparent that choice is sometimes bound up with the production of dissonance. Further, it seems reasonable in the context of the theory to suppose that the greater the degree of choice the greater the amount of resultant dissonance. A high degree of choice should produce a high degree of felt responsibility for the consequences of the decision, and this felt responsibility should produce dissonance if these consequences are undesirable in any respect. The question still remains, though, whether choice is a necessary condition for the production of dissonance. Festinger (1957) discusses the production of dissonance resulting from involuntary exposure to information. In this situation the individual does not choose to be exposed to information contrary to his beliefs but nonetheless suffers from dissonance following exposure. The question then becomes one of whether some prior choice is a necessary condition for the production of dissonance. Suppose our hypothetical individual chooses to go to a political rally not knowing who is going to speak. There, however, he is exposed to a speech that is unexpectedly contrary to his political beliefs. Is the prior choice a necessary condition for the production of dissonance? Brehm and Cohen (1962) would say yes, but Festinger (1957) does not comment about the matter.

The following section deals with the literature concerning the role of choice in the production of dissonance.

Brehm (1959) reports an experiment concerned with whether involuntary exposure to information can create dissonance. Eighth-grade boys were offered an incentive (two movie tickets or two phonograph records) if they would eat a small portion of a supposedly randomly selected vegetable. Actually the boys were asked to eat a vegetable which they had 3 weeks earlier indicated that they disliked. The experimenter represented himself as being from a fictitious consumers' organization. After eating, the boys indicated the extent to which they liked or disliked the vegetable. There were two conditions in the experiment: high consequences and low consequences. In the high consequences condition the boys were casually told while eating the vegetable that a letter would be sent to their parents telling them what vegetable their son had eaten. According to Brehm this implied that the boys would have to eat more of the vegetable at home. In the low consequences condition the boys were not told anything while eating the vegetable. The boys thus had a choice as to whether or not to eat the vegetable but no choice as to whether or not the information concerning the vegetable they had eaten would be sent to their parents.

The results indicated that attitudes toward the disliked vegetables became significantly more positive in the high consequences condition than in the low consequences condition. Being told that their parents would be informed about which vegetable had been eaten resulted in more positive change than not being told that their parents would be so informed. A further breakdown of the data indicated that this significant difference between the consequences conditions was due to the subjects who had previously indicated a large discrepancy between the frequency with which the crucial vegetable was served at home and the frequency with which they ate it. It is reasonable to suppose that it is for these subjects that the high consequences manipulation created the most dissonance.

Brehm interprets these results as indicating that a *fait accompli*, or event outside of immediate control, can create dissonance. However, as Brehm points out, there was a prior choice manipulation that conceivably may have been of crucial importance. The question then is whether dissonance would have occurred if the subjects had not been given an explicit choice about whether or not to eat the disliked vegetable. Since no subjects chose not to eat the disliked vegetable it is apparent that this choice was not a difficult one to make. Beyond this, however, the experiment provides no additional information.

Brehm and Cohen (*1959a*) report an investigation in which there was an attempt to study the effect of choice upon dissonance reduction. Subjects were told that the experiment involved 3 hours of copying random numbers. Choice was manipulated by not giving some of the subjects the opportunity to be excused and by telling the rest of the subjects that they could be excused from the experiment by making an appointment with the "Psychology Department's Director of Undergraduate Studies" concerning their excuse. An additionally manipulated variable was relative deprivation (high or low). In the high relative deprivation condition the subjects were told that most persons would receive 10 dollars for participating in the experiment but that in order to study the effect of reward upon copying numbers it had been randomly determined that they would receive nothing. In the low relative deprivation condition the subjects were told that most persons would receive 1 dollar for participating in the experiment but that in order to study the effect of reward upon copying numbers it had been randomly determined that they would receive nothing. Thus the subjects in both the high and low relative deprivation conditions actually received nothing, but differed in how much they thought the other subjects would receive. This manipulation of relative deprivation occurred after the choice manipulation. Brehm and Cohen thus were interested in the effect of prior choice upon the dissonance created by degree of relative deprivation. The subjects did not actually have to copy the random numbers.

A questionnaire that immediately followed the above instructions indicated that the manipulation of relative deprivation was successful but the manipulation of choice was not. Brehm and Cohen therefore relied upon a measure of perceived choice to divide their subjects into high and low groups. The experiment was carried out in five separate regularly scheduled classes. Each of the classes was divided at the median so as to obtain approximately equal numbers of high and low choice subjects within each class. Since high relative deprivation theoretically creates more dissonance than low relative deprivation the subjects in the former condition should have the most positive attitudes toward the experiment. The creation of the positive attitude theoretically serves as a mode of dissonance reduction or justification for the anticipated number copying. Brehm and Cohen found that for the high choice subjects high relative deprivation resulted in more positive attitudes than low relative deprivation in four of the five classes. For the low choice subjects, on the other hand, low relative deprivation resulted in more positive attitudes than high relative deprivation in all five classes. Tests of the crucial choice × deprivation interaction in each of the five classes indicated that it was clearly nonsignificant in two classes, borderline significant in two classes (.07 and .06), and significant in one class. As Chapanis and Chapanis (1964) point out, without one overall test of significance it is exceedingly difficult to interpret these results as being contrary to or in agreement with expectations.

Cohen, Terry, and Jones (1959) attempted to test the hypothesis that only with choice does increasing communicator discrepancy result in increasing dissonance and consequent attitude change. Yale freshmen were individually contacted in their dormitories and asked to indicate on a rating scale their attitudes toward men marrying by the age of 23. After marking the rating scale the subjects were given a written communication advocating a conclusion contrary to their own (pro or con). Some of the subjects were explicitly given a choice as to whether or not to read the communication and some were not given a choice. After reading the communication the subjects marked the rating scale for a second time. In addition to the choice variable there was a second variable, degree of discrepancy. Subjects were classified as being in a high or a low discrepancy condition on the basis of the distance between their positions on the first rating scale and the position taken by the communication. Discrepancy thus was not manipulated experimentally.

Three subjects in the high choice condition refused to read the communication and consequently were eliminated. The results, in general, support the initial prediction. With high choice the mean attitude change increased from low (.63) to high discrepancy (1.17). With low choice, however, mean attitude change decreased from low (.76) to high discrepancy (.32). The crucial interaction between choice and discrepancy is significant by *t* test. These results are in accord with Cohen, Terry, and Jones' expectations except for the fact that with low discrepancy, high choice resulted in slightly less change (.63) than low choice (.76).

There are two obvious things to be said about this experiment. First, as Cohen, Terry, and Jones themselves point out, the "manipulation" of discrepancy was not adequate. Individuals at different locations on a pro-con attitude dimension differ in many ways other than in attitude. Second, studies of the discrepancy variable have found that frequently increasing discrepancy results in increasing change. In view of the fact that this research did not explicitly manipulate choice it is evident that Cohen, Terry, and Jones' initial hypothesis is incorrect. It is simply not true that only under high choice conditions does increasing discrepancy result in increasing change.

In spite of all this, however, it appears that choice had some kind of effect in *this* experiment. One possibly important reservation has to do with the fact that the three eliminated subjects all came from the high-choice-high-discrepancy cell. Since the cell originally contained only 18 subjects, the elimination of three subjects reduces the number of observations by 17 percent. The problem would not be too bad except for the fact that it is the high change score in this cell (1.17) that is mainly responsible for the significant interaction. The results from this experiment thus do not constitute very solid evidence concerning the role of choice and communication discrepancy in the production of dissonance.

Davis and Jones (1960) investigated the effect of choice on dissonance reducing revaluation of a stimulus person. Male subjects were individually exposed to a taped interview and a personality assessment of another "subject" supposedly in an adjacent room. Under the pretext of investigating how people react to extreme evaluations of themselves the subject was then asked to read a rather unfavorable evaluation of the other "subject" into a microphone connecting the two rooms. Half of the subjects were given an explicit choice as to whether to read an unfavorable or a favorable evaluation but were urged to read the unfavorable evaluation. The other subjects were given no choice. In addition to the manipulation of choice there was also a manipulation of anticipated interaction. Half of the subjects were told that they would have an opportunity to explain everything to the subjects after the experiment was over, and half were told that there would be no opportunity to do this. The dependent variable was the change in evaluation of the stimulus person or dummy subject from before to after reading the negative evaluation. The investigators expected that the greatest amount of dissonance would be created in the choice-no-anticipated-interaction, condition and, consequently, that this condition would produce the greatest amount of negative revaluation of the stimulus person. Davis and Jones reasoned that dissonance would be greatest when there is choice and also no opportunity to "explain all" to the stimulus person after having insulted him.

Of the 52 subjects tested 12 (23 percent) were eliminated because they either suspected that the stimulus person was not genuine, or refused to read the negative evaluation, or later indicated that the choice and anticipated interaction manipulations were not successful with them. The results indicated that, as predicted, there was significantly more negative change in the evaluation of the stimulus person in the choice-no-anticipated-interaction condition than in any of the other three conditions. The other three conditions all manifested approximately equal amounts of negative change. These results are consistent with the hypothesis that choice, at least under some conditions, can serve to create dissonance. The one reservation concerning this study has to do with sampling bias resulting from nonrandom elimination of 23 percent of the sample.

Brock (1962) reports a study of the effect of choice on both attitude change and cognitive restructuring. Brock points out that dissonance theoretically may be reduced through either revaluation or modification of the relevant cognitive structures. For example, dissonance resulting from the knowledge that one more belligerent nation has nuclear weapons could be reduced either by positive revaluation of war (attitude change) or by convincing oneself that it will be a long time before the belligerent nation can develop long-range delivery systems (cognitive restructuring). One hundred eighty-three non-Catholic Yale freshmen were individually approached in their dormitories and given a test of their attitude toward becoming Catholic and a test of the related cognitive structure. The latter test involved a number of steps. First, the subjects completed as many sentences beginning with "For me, becoming a Catholic would mean" as they could. Each sentence was written on a separate slip of paper. Second, the subjects grouped the sentences into as many categories or piles as they wished. And third, the subjects indicated as many bonds or relations between all of the sentences as they could. The latter task was accomplished by indicating all of the sentences that would have to be modified or changed if any given sentence was modified or changed. A week later all of the subjects were contacted by telephone and asked to come to a room near their dormitory for a "follow-up" of the original survey. (Of the 183 subjects initially contacted, 38 refused.) In the experimental room the subjects were asked to write essays on the theme "Why I Would Like to Become a Catholic." Some of the subjects were explicitly given a choice as to whether they would have to write the essays and some were not. (Seven subjects in the choice condition refused to participate.) After writing the essays the subjects were asked either to rank the individual sentences in their essays in terms of their originality and persuasiveness (high confrontation) or to indicate the number of syllables in each word in the essays (low confrontation). The high and low confrontation conditions were intended to differ only in the extent to which attention was focused on the meaning of the essays. In addition to the manipulations of choice and confrontation there was also a manipulation of the order of measurement for the two dependent variables, evaluation (attitude) and cognitive restructuring. Some of the subjects received the measures in a structure-evaluation order and some in an evaluation-structure order.

In the absence of explicit theory concerning the effect of dissonance upon cognitive restructuring, Brock only made predictions concerning the effect of dissonance on revaluation (attitude change). First, Brock predicted that there would be more attitude change with high than with low choice. And second, he predicted that with high choice there would be more attitude change under high than low confrontation, but with low choice there would be more attitude change under low than high confrontation. Brock reasoned that if a person has made a choice and thus feels personally responsible for what he has done, confrontation with the meaning of his action should increase dissonance and consequent attitude change. However, if a person has not made a choice and does not feel responsible, confrontation should bring about resistance to attitude change. Both of these predictions were confirmed. There was more attitude change with high than with low choice, and there was a significant choice × confrontation interaction. Brock also found that choice interacted significantly with order of measurement. This interaction indicates that more attitude change occurred when evaluation was measured before rather than after structure. Brock points out that this effect is reasonable if it is assumed that restructuring reduces dissonance and that subjects avail themselves of the most opportune mode of dissonance reduction. When the structure measure was taken first, the subjects utilized the restructuring mode of dissonance reduction so that the necessity for dissonance reduction through attitude change was somewhat reduced.

Brock's data with regard to the restructuring dependent variable are more ambiguous. There were no significant changes in the number of implications seen (sentences written) or in the grouping of the implications. There was, however, a significant choice × confrontation interaction in the change in number of perceived bonds or relations. Overall there was a tendency for the number of bonds or relations to decrease, possibly due to fatigue. The significant interaction indicates that this decrease in the number of bonds was less in the high-choice-confrontation and low-choice-confrontation conditions than in the two conditions in which choice and confrontation were not uniformly high or low. This is interesting because of the fact that dissonance theoretically was greatest in the high-choice-confrontation and low-choice-confrontation conditions. Thus Brock reasoned that dissonance was reduced by a *relative* increase in the number of bonds or relations between the implications of becoming a Catholic. It is not clear, however, why an overall relative increase in the number of bonds is any more dissonance reducing than some other kind of change. Some additional light could be shed on the matter if we knew what kind of bonds were involved. Certainly a positive bond such as "would facilitate" is quite different from a negative bond such as "would hinder" (Abelson and Rosenberg, 1958).

Brock and Buss (1962) report a study concerned with the effect of choice on the evaluation of pain. The subjects were 43 students from introductory psychology classes who had indicated on a previously administered questionnaire that they were either "opposed" or "very opposed" to the use of electric shock on humans in scientific research. Such responses were given by 34 percent of the students in these classes. The subjects were asked to act as experimenters in an experiment in which another subject, actually a stooge, was shocked every time he made an incorrect response in a concept formation task. The subjects were given an opportunity to feel and rate the painfulness of the shocks at the beginning of the experiment. Half of the subjects were given an explicit choice as to whether or not to act as experimenters and deliver the shocks and half were not. (Three subjects in the choice condition refused.) During the experiment the subjects could hear but not see the stooge. Although the stooge gasped after the supposedly more intense shocks, he was actually not shocked at all. At the conclusion of the concept formation task the subjects again felt and rated the painfulness of the shocks. Before-after change in these ratings indicated a highly significant difference between the high and low choice conditions. Consistent with expectations, subjects in the high choice condition decreased their painfulness ratings and the subjects in the low choice condition increased their painfulness ratings.

For a subsample of his subjects Brock also took after measures of attitude toward the use of shock in psychological research. Before-after change scores in this dependent variable, however, revealed no significant effect. Brock speculates that this lack of significance may be due to the fact that the prior occurring painfulness rating provided ample opportunity for dissonance reduction.

In general, Brock's results provide fairly convincing support for the hypothesis that choice produces dissonance. Approximately 7 percent of the subjects were eliminated because they refused to shock the stooge. However, the F for the difference between high and low choice is so large, 33.2, that there undoubtedly is no reason for concern.

Cohen and Latané (1962) report a study of the effect of choice upon forced compliance. Yale students who had previously indicated that they were opposed to a compulsory religion course were individually contacted in their dormitories and asked to make oral statements concerning a compulsory religion course. These statements were taped, supposedly so that they could be played for an alumni board. Twenty-six of the subjects were given no explicit choice as to whether they made favorable or unfavorable statements, and 25 were given an explicit choice. All of the subjects were told that enough unfavorable statements had already been obtained, and that what was really needed were some favorable statements. (All of the subjects in both the high and low choice conditions complied with the request.) After making their statements the subjects indicated their attitudes toward a compulsory religion course and rated the quality of their speeches.

Cohen and Latané found that overall there was nonsignificantly more before-after change in the high choice than the low choice condition. In an effort to salvage something they split their subjects according to whether they were above or below the median in amount of attitude change. A chi square test of a fourfold table relating high and low change to high and low choice proved to be significant. This significant effect is because of the fact that most of the low choice subjects were below the

median in amount of change and most of the high choice subjects were
above the median in amount of change. This then provides some weak
support for the hypothesis that choice is an important dissonance-producing variable.

An additional finding has to do with an interaction between choice
and the rated quality of the statements. In the low choice condition
there was more change with high than with low quality, and in the high
choice condition there was more change with low than with high quality.
It is understandable why making a high quality statement or speech
would create more dissonance than a low quality statement or speech, as
apparently happened in the low choice condition. As Brehm and Cohen
(1962) point out, however, the opposite finding in the high choice condition is not readily interpretable.

Cohen and Brehm (1962) attempted to test the hypothesis that
choice is the crucial dissonance-producing variable in forced compliance situations. Brehm and Cohen (1962) argue that small reward produces more dissonance than large reward because there is more choice
or volition with small reward. When the reward is very large the person
may have little choice as to whether or not he engages in the attitude
discrepant behavior. Similarly, low coercion (threatened punishment)
produces more dissonance than high coercion because there is more
choice or volition with low coercion. Festinger (1957) theorizes about
these forced compliance situations in terms of the ratio of dissonant to
consonant cognitions. All of the cognitions consistent with a given decision are considered consonant, and all of the cognitions inconsistent with
the decision are considered dissonant. Thus, since engaging in attitude
discrepant behavior for a small reward is more dissonant than engaging
in attitude discrepant behavior for a large reward, the ratio of dissonant
to consonant cognitions differs in the high and low reward situations.
Relative to the number of consonant cognitions there are more dissonant
cognitions in the low reward situation. The same reasoning applies to
the action of coercion upon attitude discrepant behavior. Thus it typically
is the case that Festinger's (1957) notion of the ratio of dissonant to
consonant cognitions and Brehm and Cohen's (1962) notion of choice
or volition lead to identical predictions. According to Festinger the
greater the number of dissonant cognitions relative to the number of consonant cognitions the greater the dissonance, and according to Brehm and
Cohen the greater the amount of choice the greater the dissonance.

Cohen and Brehm (1962) designed an experiment which theoretically allowed choice to vary inversely and not directly with the
ratio of dissonant to consonant cognitions. This inverse relationship, unlike the typical direct relationship, allows for differential predictions. The
experiment involved an attempt to create more choice and thus more
dissonance with high coercion than with low coercion by making the

coercion illegitimate or contrary to ethical standards. When the coercion is legitimate, theoretically there is less choice and less dissonance with high than with low coercion.

Fraternity pledges who had been told by their pledgemaster to report for a 15- to 20-minute experiment were informed by the experimenter (a professor) that they were expected to spend 3 to 4 hours copying random numbers. The experiment involved three conditions: high coercion, low coercion, and control. In the high coercion condition the subjects were threatened with an extension of their pledge period or rejection by the fraternity if they did not agree to copy the numbers; in the low coercion condition they were threatened with some hours of extra duty as a pledge; and in the control condition they were simply told that their cooperation was needed. Cohen and Brehm intended for the subjects to regard the coercion as illegitimate. The experimenter was a professor who had no connection with the fraternity. Furthermore, it is highly unusual for a professor to have any influence on a fraternity's business, whether with regard to the treatment of pledges or anything else. After the coercion manipulation the subjects indicated the hours in which they would like to participate in the experiment. Immediately following this they were given a questionnaire which ascertained their evaluation of the number copying task and perceived choice about whether or not to participate.

Of the 31 subjects tested, 1 subject refused to participate. The data for the remaining subjects are, in general, in line with Cohen and Brehm's expectations. There was higher evaluation of the task in the high coercion condition than in either the low coercion or control conditions. There was nonsignificantly higher evaluation of the task in the low coercion than in the control condition. With regard to perceived choice the only significant difference is between the high coercion and control conditions. There was greater perceived choice in the high coercion condition than in the control condition and nonsignificantly greater perceived choice in the low coercion condition than in the control condition.

This experiment definitely provides support for Cohen and Brehm's assertion that choice and not the ratio of dissonant to consonant elements is the crucial dissonance-producing factor in forced compliance situations. Cohen and Brehm, though, do point out one possible ambiguity in the interpretation of the results. It is not known whether the pledges considered the severe punishment as likely to be carried out as the mild punishment. No direct assessment of this matter was incorporated into the procedure. Since it was found that the high coercion subjects were significantly more annoyed than the low coercion subjects, Cohen and Brehm argue that the high coercion subjects did take the threatened punishment seriously.

Even more convincing support for the choice interpretation of forced compliance could be provided by an experiment in which the legitimacy of the coercion and the degree of coercion were both varied. What Cohen and Brehm specifically predict is an interaction between legitimacy (choice) and coercion such that with legitimate coercion, evaluation varies inversely with amount of coercion and with illegitimate coercion, evaluation varies directly with amount of coercion.

Watts (1965) failed to find that choice had the predicted effects on dissonance reduction following an unconfirmed expectancy. In a purported study of individual differences in taste resulting from electrical stimulation of the tongue, subjects were given either a pleasant or an unpleasant "anaesthetic" to alleviate the pain. The supposed anaesthetic was iron and quinine in the unpleasant condition and mint-flavored colored water in the pleasant condition. Half of the subjects were given a choice as to whether to take the anaesthetic and half were not. (Of the 41 subjects in the choice condition all but one chose to take the anaesthetic.) Before taking or choosing to take the anaesthetic the subjects were told whether it was pleasant or unpleasant and the subjects given the unpleasant solution were further told that the anaesthetic would not completely eliminate the pain. After taking the anaesthetic the experiment was terminated supposedly due to the fact that the physician who was going to administer the shocks had been called out on an emergency. The subjects were thus asked to fill out a questionnaire similar to one they had completed at the beginning of the session in order to provide some control data.

According to Watts the failure of the physician to appear should have created the most dissonance in the high choice, unpleasant condition. Before-after changes in numerous measures, however, revealed no tendency for greater dissonance reduction to occur in this condition than in the remaining three conditions. There was in fact a general tendency for choice to affect the dependent variables in the direction opposite to that predicted. Subjects in the high choice condition (pleasant or unpleasant) thought the experiment was significantly less valuable, were significantly less willing to recruit other subjects for the experiment, and perceived the anaesthetic as nonsignificantly more unpleasant than subjects in the no choice condition.

In view of the fact that assessments of the two independent variables (pleasantness of the anaesthetic and choice) revealed that the manipulations were both successful, Watts' experiment possibly constitutes damaging negative evidence. It is possible, however, that the primary problem relates to the expected unpleasantness of the electric shocks. Even though the subjects did choose to take a distasteful anaesthetic in preparation for the shocks, the knowledge that the shocks were not to be administered may have resulted in considerable relief. Such relief may conceivably have overcome any dissonance resulting from disconfirmation of the expectancy that shocks were to be administered.

Comment. It is extremely difficult to make an overall evaluation of this material on the effect of choice in a forced compliance situation. One difficulty has to do with nonrandom subject loss. If subjects are given a choice as to whether or not to engage in attitude discrepant behavior some of them will invariably refuse and thereby leave the researcher with a biased sample. On the other hand, if the researcher does not give his subjects an explicit choice he is not able to study the effect of choice. The problem is thus an inherently slippery one.

The single most convincing evidence concerning the effect of choice upon dissonance production is the research of Brock and Buss (1962). In this experiment only 7 percent of the subjects were nonrandomly eliminated, and the F for the choice manipulation is extremely large. If one is willing not to be concerned with nonrandom subject loss and, in some cases, qualifying interactions, three additional experiments also indicate that choice in a forced compliance situation increases dissonance (Brock, 1962; Cohen, Terry, and Jones, 1959; Davis and Jones, 1960). Although not involving an explicit manipulation of choice, the experiment of Cohen and Brehm (1962) on illegitimate coercion should probably be added to this list. One big difficulty, however, is the fact that Watts (1965) failed to confirm the choice prediction in an experiment in which only one subject was eliminated.

Even if it were granted that choice increases the level of dissonance, there is still a question as to whether or not an explicit choice to engage in attitude discrepant behavior is a *necessary* condition for the production of dissonance. The evidence from Brehm's (1959) experiment seems to indicate that a *fait accompli* can create dissonance. This evidence is consistent with the results of Freedman (1963) which indicate that even without an explicit choice manipulation, inadequate justification for forced compliance behavior produces dissonance. There, however, is still the problem as to whether some prior choice is a necessary condition for dissonance arousal. For example, consider the college sophomore who in the context of an experiment writes an essay contrary to his religious beliefs. He may not have had an explicit choice about whether or not to write the essay, but he supposedly had made some prior decisions which resulted in his being in the experiment. Examples of these prior decisions or choices might be: the decision to be in this experiment rather than another experiment, the decision to take an introductory psychology course rather than an introductory sociology course, and the decision to go to college rather than to get a job. The theoretical problem is one of specifying the critical prior choice or choices. This may prove exceedingly difficult. Certainly from our present vantage point

Brehm and Cohen's (1962) assertion that some prior volition is a necessary condition for dissonance arousal is an unproven one.

Predecision Familiarity and Postdecision Time

Davidson (1964) conducted the one study which is concerned with the effect upon dissonance reduction of predecision familiarity and postdecision time. According to Davidson, dissonance reduction is work and possibly takes time. He was interested in finding out whether predecision activity would facilitate dissonance reduction and also whether time after the decision would allow more dissonance reduction to occur. The experiment was modeled after an earlier study by Davis and Jones (1960). High school students were individually exposed to a taped interview and personality assessment of another "subject" supposedly in an adjacent room. Under the pretense of investigating how people react to extreme evaluations of themselves the subjects were asked to read a rather unfavorable evaluation of the other "subject" into a microphone connecting the two rooms. All of the subjects were given an explicit choice as to whether to read an unfavorable or a favorable evaluation but urged to read the unfavorable evaluation. After having read the unfavorable evaluation the subjects indicated the extent to which they liked the stimulus person. Dissonance reduction should produce decreased liking for the stimulus person.

Two independent variables were manipulated in the experiment: degree of predecision familiarity (high or low) and measurement delay (0 or 8 minutes). In the high-predecision-familiarity condition the subjects, after hearing the taped interview and personality assessment, filled out a questionnaire that called for ratings of the stimulus person in terms of various traits such as introversion and dominance. In the low-predecision-familiarity condition the subjects filled out the same questionnaire with regard to themselves. Measurement delay was accomplished by having the subjects indicate their attraction for the stimulus person either immediately after or 8 minutes after reading the negative evaluation. The 8-minute delay period was spent writing about the stimulus person's supposed characteristics.

Of the 82 subjects tested in the experiment 6 were eliminated, 2 because they guessed that there was no other subject and 4 because they expressed spontaneous dislike for the stimulus person. The data for the remaining subjects quite unambiguously indicated more liking for the stimulus person (less dissonance reduction) in the low-predecision-familiarity and no-delay-measurement condition than in any of the other three conditions. The other three conditions, in which there was oppor-

tunity before and/or after the forced compliance decision to think about
the stimulus person, did not differ significantly from each other. Dissonance reduction is apparently facilitated by consideration of the relevant facts either before or after the decision is made. This experiment
points to the possibly crucial importance of predecision familiarity and
postdecision time upon dissonance reduction.

Effort

Effort that is needlessly expended or that is expended on unpleasant
activities theoretically results in dissonance. A number of experiments
have studied the dissonance arousal of effort in various contexts.

Aronson (1961) argues that if a person exerts considerable effort
in attempting to reach a goal and fails, dissonance is created. If repeated
attempts are made to reach the goal the dissonance cannot be readily
reduced through convincing oneself that the goal never was desired.
The most convenient mode of dissonance reduction is through increased
valuation of the task or stimuli associated with the task. Thus Aronson
predicts that continual and unsuccessful exertion of effort to reach a goal
will result in increased valuation of the stimuli associated with the effort.

Subjects fished for cans, two thirds of which were empty and one
third of which contained two, three, or four dimes. The cans containing
money were of one color and the cans not containing money were of
another color, but the subjects could not tell what they had snared until
the cans were pulled out from under a cardboard covering. The subjects in the low effort condition had the relatively easy task of pulling
the cans out with a horseshoe magnet. This took an average of 14 seconds. The subjects in the high effort condition had the more difficult
task of pulling the cans out by catching a hook in the metal ring attached
to each can. This took an average of 52 seconds. All of the subjects
worked until they had snared 16 unrewarding containers. This means that
each subject obtained approximately 8 rewarding containers. The relative attractiveness of the two container colors was rated before and after
carrying out the task.

Aronson expected that there would be more dissonance in the low
effort condition than in the high effort condition, and that this dissonance
would be reduced through increased valuation of the unrewarding color.
When the subjects exerted considerable effort fishing for a can that
turned out to contain no money the resulting dissonance should theoretically be reduced through increased valuation of the stimuli associated with the task—perhaps the color of the can. Aronson further
expected, however, that the dissonance reduction effect would be counter-

acted by a secondary reinforcement effect. According to the secondary reinforcement concept, stimuli that have been associated with reinforcers take on reinforcing properties of their own. Aronson actually found that the rewarding color was considered significantly more attractive in the low effort than in the high effort condition. In the high effort condition the colors were, in fact, considered approximately equal in attractiveness. Aronson interpreted these results as supporting his hypothesis. In the low effort condition secondary reinforcement resulted in increased valuation of the rewarding color but in the high effort condition dissonance reduction overcame and neutralized the secondary reinforcement effect. As Aronson points out, it would have been more elegant if the unrewarding color actually had been considered more attractive in the high effort condition. However, he points out that the obtained results are nonetheless consistent with his hypothesis.

Chapanis and Chapanis (1964) have criticized the Aronson experiment because of the fact that the high and low effort conditions differed in reinforcement rate. The subjects in the high effort condition received reinforcement at a much slower rate than the subjects in the low effort condition. Thus if secondary reinforcement is a function of reinforcement rate, the significantly greater attractiveness of the rewarding color in the low effort (high reinforcement rate) condition could be explained without any reference to dissonance reduction. Silverman (1964), though, points out that the high and low effort conditions were equated in terms of the total amount of reinforcement, and furthermore, that studies of partial reinforcement (Ferster and Skinner, 1957) suggest that low rate of reinforcement produces more secondary reinforcement than high rate of reinforcement. The Ferster and Skinner studies, however, were concerned not with the strength of secondary reinforcement but with the nature and rate of responding during acquisition and extinction. This evidence then is indirectly, but certainly not directly, relevant to the question of the effect of reinforcement rate upon the creation of secondary reinforcement effects.

Yaryan and Festinger (1961) obtained evidence consistent with the hypothesis that the greater the amount of effort expended in preparing for a possible future event the greater the belief that the event will in fact occur. Theoretically dissonance is created when a great deal of effort is exerted preparing for an event that may not occur. The dissonance, however, can be reduced by increasing the belief that the event will occur and the effort is justified. Subjects were told that half of them would be required to take a new kind of aptitude test and half of them would not. There were two conditions in the experiment, high effort and low effort. In the high effort condition the subjects were required to memorize the abstract definitions of 25 symbols in preparation for the aptitude test. In the low effort condition the subjects simply read over the list of definitions in preparation for the test. After either memorizing or reading over the definitions all of the subjects indicated the perceived likelihood that they would have to take the aptitude test. As predicted, the subjects in the high effort condition considered it significantly more likely that they would have to take the test than the subjects in the low effort condition.

Johnson and Steiner (1965) present some evidence which they interpret as indicating that Yaryan and Festinger's (1961) results were due to the experimenter's behavior rather than to the subjects' own efforts. Johnson and Steiner note that in Yaryan and Festinger's study the experimenter spent more time with the subjects in the high effort condition than in the low effort condition. Since the subjects were told that the experimenter knew whether or not they would take the test, it seems reasonable that the experimenter's behavior would have been used as a cue to affect the probability ratings.

Johnson and Steiner repeated Yaryan and Festinger's experiment with the addition of two variables. As in Yaryan and Festinger's experiment, subjects expended high or low efforts in the preparation for a test which never occurred. The two additional variables concerned whether the experimenter himself expended high or low effort in preparing the subjects for the test and whether the subjects were told that the experimenter knew or did not know if they would take the test. Johnson and Steiner expected that the subjects would rate the test as probable in the conditions in which the experimenter expended considerable effort and was believed to know whether or not they would take the test. The results indicated no significant differences among any of the experimental conditions. However, an examination of the subjects' ratings of the experimenter's concern with their preparedness and how prepared they themselves felt did reveal some positive results. Within the condition in which the subjects believed that the experimenter knew whether or not they were to take the test, it was found that the greater the perceived experimenter's concern with preparedness and the greater the subjects' feelings of being prepared the higher were the probability ratings. These variables were not significantly related within the condition in which the subjects believed that the experimenter did not know whether or not they would take the test. (No test of significance comparing the size of the relationships across these conditions is reported.) Johnson and Steiner interpret these results as supporting their interpretation that subjective probability ratings are a function of the experimenter's behavior rather than the subjects' effort. Why is it, though, that the differences between condition means do not support this conclusion? The answer to this question is not apparent. But in any event, the simple fact that Johnson and Steiner failed to replicate Yaryan and Festinger's results does constitute negative evidence with regard to the dissonance prediction.

Cohen (1959) attempted to test some implications of dissonance theory relating to effort and communicator-communicatee discrepancy. According to Cohen dissonance theory implies that when considerable effort is exerted in understanding a communication, dissonance is produced by the knowledge that work is put into understanding something with which one does not agree, so that the greater the discrepancy the more the attitude or opinion change. On the other hand, when little effort is put into understanding a communication, little or no dissonance is aroused, so that the greater the discrepancy the less the amount of change. While it is clear that Cohen is correct in asserting that increased effort should result in increased dissonance and thus an even greater amount of change with increasing discrepancies, it is not clear why an absence of effort should result in a complete reversal of the relationship. According to Festinger (1957) and Zimbardo (1960) the greater the degree of discrepancy the greater the amount of dissonance and consequent attitude or opinion change. There is no implication that this relation holds only when considerable effort or work is exerted in understanding the communication.

In Cohen's experiment subjects were given a before questionnaire which contained an item concerning the advisability of foster homes for juvenile delinquents as a means of curbing delinquency. Three weeks later the experimenter contacted those subjects who had indicated that they were opposed to the foster home idea and asked them if they would agree to read a communication contrary to their point of view. All subjects received this choice manipulation prior to the effort manipulation. Half of the subjects were told that they would have to put out a great deal of mental effort to comprehend the arguments and the point of view advocated. The other half of the subjects were told that the communication would be easy to comprehend and understand. Discrepancy was not manipulated experimentally, but was defined in terms of the distance between initial opinion and the communication as being either large or small. Discrepancy was thus confounded with initial position.

The results indicated that under low effort significantly more change was produced by the small than the large discrepancy, and that under high effort significantly more change was produced by the large discrepancy. A number of things can be said about this experiment. First, the manipulation of the effort variable, as Cohen himself points out, may have been somewhat less than adequate. Second, although the results specifically support Cohen's predictions, the results in the low effort conditions do not seem to be in accord with what would be expected on the basis of dissonance theory as stated by Festinger (1957) and Zimbardo (1960). Third and most important, the confounding of discrepancy and initial position makes an unambiguous interpretation of the results impossible.[4]

Lerner (*1965*) found that high school students who exerted effort reading a civil defense pamphlet regarded nuclear war as more probable than control subjects who did not read the pamphlet. Since the civil defense pamphlet, "Ten for Survival," did not mention or discuss the probability of nuclear war, Lerner interpreted the results as being due to a reduction in dissonance produced by the effort exerted in reading the pamphlet. It is entirely possible, however, that the belief effect was due to the pamphlet's implicit suggestion that nuclear war is probable.

Zimbardo (*1965*) tested the hypothesis that counterattitudinal advocacy carried out under high effort conditions will produce more attitude change than counterattitudinal advocacy carried out under low effort conditions. In the guise of an aptitude test subjects were asked to either read or improvise a counterattitudinal speech arguing for the admission of Red China to the United Nations. Improvisation was accomplished with the aid of a prepared outline supplied by the experimenter. Half of the subjects delivered their speeches with a delayed auditory feedback of 0.25 seconds (high effort) and half with a delayed auditory feedback of 0.01 seconds (low effort). Before-after change scores indicated that more attitude change occurred in the high effort condition than in the low effort condition, but that the reading versus improvisation manipulation had no significant effect. The failure to obtain more attitude change with than without improvisation disagrees with King and Janis's (1956) results, but the success in finding more attitude change with high than with low effort supports the main dissonance prediction. Zimbardo argues that the results cannot be accounted for by Chapanis and Chapanis' (1964) "sweet smell of effortful success" notion due to the fact that satisfaction ratings bore no relation to the attitude change scores.

Comment. In general, the results reviewed in this section do not provide very convincing evidence for the various dissonance hypotheses concerning effort. The prevalence of alternative explanations, the failure to replicate previous findings, and inadequacies in experimental design all serve to create considerable scepticism. The single most convincing evidence comes from Zimbardo's (1965) study of effort exerted in counterattitudinal advocacy. At the present time any overall generalizations about this literature would be premature.

---

[4] A thorough discussion of the methodological problem created by confounding discrepancy and initial position is contained in Chapter 3.

Disliked Experimenters and Low Credibility Communicators

Several studies have been concerned with the effect of compliance to the demands of a disliked experimenter or low credibility communicator upon attitude change. Theoretically more dissonance is created by compliance to a disliked or low credibility person than by compliance to a liked or high credibility person. Since the dissonance can be reduced through increased evaluation of some aspect of the compliant behavior or situation, more attitude change supposedly results from compliance to a disliked or low credibility person than from compliance to a liked or high credibility person.

Smith (1961) investigated the effect of liking-disliking for an experimenter who induces attitude discrepant behavior. Group-tested army reservists were told that they were to be subjects in an experiment to determine the reaction of men asked to eat unusual food in an emergency. All of the men were offered 50 cents if they would eat one grasshopper. In a positive communicator condition the experimenter was "friendly, warm, and permissive"; in a negative communicator condition the experimenter was "formal, cool, and official." A check on the success of this manipulation revealed that the positive communicator was in fact better liked. The number of subjects actually eating the grasshoppers (conforming) was 19 out of 20 in the positive communicator condition and 10 out of 20 in the negative communicator condition. The conforming subjects gave the grasshoppers a higher hedonic rating in the negative communicator condition than in the positive communicator condition. For the entire sample, including conformers and nonconformers, there was no significant difference between the positive communicator and negative communicator conditions.

Zimbardo, Weisenberg, Firestone, and Levy (1965) replicated and extended Smith's (1961) findings. Subjects were induced to eat fried grasshoppers by an experimenter who adopted either a friendly, positive role or an unfriendly, negative role. (An after assessment validated the manipulation.) Half of the subjects were army reservists and half were college students. All of the college students were tested individually, but only half of the reservists were tested individually. The college students were told that the experiment was concerned with the relation of physiological and intellectual reactions to food deprivation and eating behavior; the reservists were told that the experiment was concerned with providing the Quartermaster Corps with information on food preference. All subjects were urged to eat the grasshoppers, but it was made plain that the decision was entirely voluntary. Approximately 50 percent of the subjects in all conditions ate the grasshoppers.

Before-after change scores indicate that the pattern of results for college students and individually tested reservists is approximately the same. Eating resulted in significantly more positive attitudes toward grasshoppers than did noneating. Noneating in fact resulted in more unfavorable attitudes, a boomerang effect. With regard to the difference between experimenter conditions, as predicted, almost all of the positive change produced by eating occurred when the experimenter was disliked. The noneaters manifested approximately equal amounts of negative change in the two experimenter conditions.

The results for the army reservists who were tested in groups are ambivalent. Some groups showed the predicted effects and some did not; overall the experimenter manipulation had no significant effect. The groups in which the eaters showed the most marked positive change were the ones in which the majority did not eat. These findings support Zimbardo, Weisenberg, Firestone, and Levy's initial supposition that Smith's (1961) group procedure is not the ideal one for testing the dissonance prediction regarding disliked or unattractive experimenters.

While these results agree with the predictions that Zimbardo, Weisenberg, Firestone, and Levy stated, a question can be raised concerning whether or not dissonance theory also predicts that the noneaters in the positive experimenter condition should have shown more negative change than the noneaters in the negative experimenter condition. This prediction rests on two assumptions: first, that refusal to eat would create more dissonance in the positive experimenter condition than in the negative experimenter condition, and second, that the dissonance would be reduced through decreased evaluation of grasshoppers. The data, in fact, indicate that the individually tested subjects in both experimenter conditions showed approximately equal amounts of negative change.

Powell (*1965*) presents evidence that low credibility sources are more influential than high credibility sources in producing attitude change in compliant subjects. In a regular classroom setting college students were exposed to a persuasive communication advancing the American Red Cross blood program and urging them to donate blood. The person delivering the communication was introduced either as a "Public Relations Counsel, American National Red Cross" (high credibility source) or as a "Volunteer Worker, Ingham County Red Cross Chapter" (low credibility source). (An after-assessment indicated that the credibility conditions differed as expected.) In addition to the manipulation of credibility there was also a manipulation of compliance. Subjects in a voluntary compliance condition were urged to make an appointment for contributing blood. (Of the 31 subjects exposed to the high credibility source 3 refused to make appointments, and of the 38 subjects exposed to the low credibility source 7 refused to make appointments.) Subjects in an involuntary condition were told that they had no choice but to permit the taking of blood and that the blood would be taken within

the next few minutes. And the subjects in a noncompliance condition
were told that they should contribute blood if the opportunity ever
presented itself.

A before-after assessment of attitude toward the American Red
Cross blood program revealed results that are largely in accord with
theoretical expectations. In the voluntary compliance condition significantly more attitude change occurred in response to the low credibility source than in response to the high credibility source. A similar
difference occurred in the involuntary condition, although the effect is
far from significant. In the noncompliance condition, on the other hand,
more attitude change occurred in response to the high credibility source
than in response to the low credibility source. The interaction between
source credibility and type of compliance is significant.

Comment. The several experiments reviewed in this section appear
to support reasonably well the dissonance prediction concerning the
effect of disliked experimenters and low credibility communicators upon
attitude change. The major reservation is the familiar one concerning
the nonrandom loss of subjects who refused to comply. Research on this
problem requires that subjects be allowed to choose whether or not
they will comply. If the experimental situation is rigged so that the
compliance choice is in fact a real one, then nonrandom subject loss will
inevitably occur. There does not seem to be any easy solution to this
problem.

Social Support

Most of the research previously discussed in this chapter is concerned with the production of dissonance in a situation in which a choice
or decision is made. According to Festinger (1957), however, dissonance
may also arise through a lack of social support or through exposure to
information that does not agree with an already held cognition or belief.
This dissonance can be reduced through any of a number of modes
(Aronson, Turner, and Carlsmith, 1963; Festinger and Aronson, 1960):
conforming to the communicator, disparaging the communicator, attempting to persuade the communicator that he is wrong, or seeking
social support for the already held cognitions. The literature that is specifically concerned with communicator-communicatee discrepancy is reviewed in Chapter 3. This section contains a few additional studies that
are concerned with various other aspects of exposure.

Freedman and Steinbruner (1964) found that high perceived choice
produces resistance to persuasion by a subsequent communication. Subjects were told that they were going to be asked to rate a number of
candidates in terms of their acceptability for graduate school. Actually

only one candidate was rated. The rating was based on grade-point average, aptitude scores, letters of recommendation, etc. For half of the subjects the information portrayed the candidate favorably and for the other half, unfavorably. Before making the ratings the subjects were told either that they were entirely free to rate the candidate in any way they wished (high choice) or that the information was so one-sided that there was not much choice as to how this candidate should be rated (low choice). After making their ratings the subjects were exposed to subsequent information that contradicted the previous impression. This information was an interview with the candidate conducted by a member of the Stanford Psychology Department. The interview implied either that the candidate was extremely creative and a good prospect despite his poor grades or that he was rather uncreative and a poor prospect despite his good grades. After reading this material the subjects made a second rating. The results indicated that for both the favorable and unfavorable candidates the subjects in the high choice condition showed significantly less before-after opinion change. High choice resulted in greater resistance to the countercommunications.

Why should high choice have resulted in greater resistance to influence? Freedman and Steinbruner convincingly argue that with high choice the individual feels more personally responsible for his action, and this personal responsibility prevents admission of error or opinion change.

Festinger, Riecken, and Schachter (1956) report a field study of prophecy failure and proselytizing. According to Festinger, Riecken, and Schachter if an individual is confronted with evidence that unquestionably refutes a prophecy concerning future events, he may believe even more fervently that he was correct and attempt to so convince others. The cause of dissonance reduction is served through the proselytizing of other people and the obtaining of social support. Festinger, Riecken, and Schachter state five conditions that must be satisfied before prophecy failure can be expected to lead to proselytizing. First, a belief must be held with deep conviction and must be related to behavior. Second, the person holding the belief must have publicly committed himself in a manner that is difficult to undo. Third, the belief must be sufficiently specific so that events can unquestionably refute it. Fourth, events must in fact undeniably disconfirm the belief. Fifth, the individual must have social support from other like-minded people.

These theoretical expectations were tested by joining and observing close at hand a group of people who believed that on a specific date the world was going to be destroyed by earthquake and flood. The leader of the group, a Mrs. Keech, had received messages in automatic writing from creatures in outer space who had warned her of the coming disaster. These creatures were going to land in a flying saucer and save the faithful followers a few hours before the flood. Many of the members of the group had given up their jobs and most all of them had made public declarations of their convictions. There was a marked tendency to shun publicity and newspaper reporters were avoided. When the appointed hour passed and no space ship arrived to pick up the faithful, there was at first disappointment and disillusionment. Finally, however, Mrs. Keech received a message via automatic writing indicating that their little group had generated so much goodness and light that the world was going to be spared. The message was received with enthusiasm by the group. A few minutes later Mrs. Keech received a second message instructing the group to publicize the explanation. She called the newspaper for the first time, and in the ensuing days she and her followers made many efforts to publicize and proselytize.

A few of Mrs. Keech's followers were students who had gone home for the Christmas holidays. They thus waited for the flying saucer surrounded by nonbelievers and without social support from like-minded individuals. These students reacted to the disconfirmation by either completely giving up or seriously doubting their beliefs. There was no attempt at proselytizing. Festinger, Riecken, and Schachter argue that the differing effects of disconfirmation for these isolated individuals as opposed to the main group point to the crucial importance of social support.

Hardyck and Braden (1962) failed to replicate the previous results concerning prophecy failure and proselytizing. They studied a group of 29 families from a Pentecostal church that had spent 42 days and nights in large underground fallout shelters. The families had gone into the shelters because one of the leaders of the group had prophesied that a nuclear disaster was imminent. When the 135 people left their cramped, uncomfortable quarters their rationalization was that they had misinterpreted God's message and, furthermore, that God had been testing their faith. They, however, made no noticeable attempt at proselytizing.

Hardyck and Braden argue that their group and the circumstances surrounding it meet all five of Festinger, Riecken, and Schachter's necessary conditions for prophecy failure to result in proselytizing. Why then did proselytizing not occur? Hardyck and Braden offer two possible explanations. First of all, they point out that the group may have been large enough to supply an adequate amount of internal social support. If the internally obtained social support was sufficient to reduce the dissonance below a certain level then the necessity for proselytizing may have been obviated. The group studied by Festinger, Riecken, and Schachter (1956) was much smaller. Second, Hardyck and Braden point out that their group was not ridiculed by nonmembers, while Festinger, Riecken, and Schachter's group was. It seems reasonable that ridicule would produce an impetus toward proselytizing. In any event it is apparent that Festinger, Riecken, and Schachter's original theoretical statement is in need of some revision or elaboration.

Marlowe, Frager, and Nuttall (1965) present evidence indicating that subjects who suffered large monetary loss because of their favorable attitudes toward Negroes were more willing to commit themselves to action congruent with their attitudes than were subjects who suffered small monetary loss. College students who were being paid 1 dollar and 50 cents for participating in the experiment initially filled out a questionnaire assessing their attitudes toward Negroes. As the experimenter scored the questionnaire he told the subjects that if they had the "right" attitudes he would pay them additional money to fill out a second questionnaire. Half of the subjects were told that this additional money was 20 dollars and half that it was 1 dollar and 50 cents. All of the subjects were told that they did not have the right (unfavorable) attitudes. The subjects then marked a rating scale indicating the perceived importance of their ethnic attitudes and were asked to go upstairs and see one of the professors who "wants to talk to all students who are in the building." Upon arriving at the appointed office the professor asked them if they would be willing to devote at least 3 hours to guiding a group of visiting Negro students around the campus.

Marlowe, Frager, and Nuttall had expected that the subjects in the 20-dollar condition would consider their attitudes toward Negroes more important and would be more likely to volunteer to guide a group of Negroes around campus than would the subjects in the 1-dollar-and-50-cent condition. The expectations regarding importance were not borne out but the expectation regarding volunteering was. In the 20-dollar condition 77 percent of the subjects volunteered, and in the 1-dollar-and-50-cent condition 42 percent volunteered, a significant difference. A control experiment in which the subjects were denied the opportunity to earn the additional money (supposedly on a random basis) did not result in any significant difference between the 20-dollar and the 1-dollar-and-50-cent conditions.

According to Marlowe, Frager, and Nuttall, volunteering allowed the subjects to demonstrate how personally important their beliefs were, thereby minimizing the dissonance resulting from having lost the money. The failure of the perceived importance ratings to differ significantly between conditions was interpreted as being due to a ceiling effect. Most of the subjects considered their attitudes fairly important.

EVALUATION

Judging by the amount of literature, dissonance theory appears to be the single most popular theory in the field of attitude change. In any event there can be no doubt that dissonance theory has some devoted advocates who are active researchers. Much of the appeal of dissonance theory undoubtedly relates to its ability to generate nonobvious predictions that frequently can be empirically supported. It is these nonobvious predictions that set dissonance theory off most sharply from all other theories of attitude change.

How is it that dissonance theory makes nonobvious predictions and other consistency theories, such as congruity theory, balance theory, and cognitive-affective consistency theory, do not? Dissonance theory's nonobvious predictions arise from the treatment of choices or decisions in various conflict situations. Once a decision has been made, certain nonobvious implications follow; for example, the less the incentive or reward inducing some distasteful activity the greater the increased liking for the activity. Since congruity theory, balance theory, and cognitive-affective consistency theory do not deal with decisions in conflict situations they do not make analogous predictions. Further, as Brehm and Cohen (1962) point out, it is this difference between dissonance theory and the other consistency theories which allows for a possible test of relative predictive powers. According to dissonance theory if a person chooses to listen to a disliked communicator, the greater the disliking the greater the influence. The other consistency theories, of course, imply that the greater the disliking for a communicator the less the influence. Suppose, however, that our hypothetical individual did not choose to listen to the disliked communicator. In this situation the dissonance theory prediction is similar to or the same as that of congruity theory. This points up the fact that in an involuntary exposure situation, dissonance theory is basically very similar to the other consistency theories. The differences here have to do mostly with matters of language and conceptualization of the modes of inconsistency reduction. It is in these areas, of course, that all of the consistency theories differ from each other.

What can be said by way of evaluation of dissonance theory? From an internal point of view the most glaring weakness of the theory has to do with the vague way in which dissonance is defined. According to Festinger (1957) *"two elements are in a dissonant relation if, considering these two alone, the obverse of one element would follow from the other"* (p. 13). This definition makes everything sound very neat and tidy. Festinger goes on, however, to confuse matters by enumerating various meanings of "follow from." Dissonance may arise because the obverse of one cognitive element follows from another in a strictly logical fashion, because the obverse of one's present behavior follows from cultural mores, or because the obverse of one's present experience follows from expectations based on past experience, etc. The net result of all this is that we are left, not with a precise definition of dissonance, but with an intuitive feeling. Two cognitive elements are in a dissonant relationship if they are somehow or other "unreasonably" related.

There is a similar, although possibly less important, lack of precision in the conceptualization of cognitive elements. When do we have a single cognitive element rather than a cluster of cognitive elements? Festinger candidly admits that he does not know. We are therefore left with a peculiar situation in which an entire theory is erected on the foundation of two poorly conceptualized constructs, dissonance and cognitive elements. In defense of the theory, however, it should be pointed out that this foundational imprecision does not seem to have hampered subsequent theoretical and empirical work.

It is apparent that there are many topics or areas within the theory that are in need of further theoretical and empirical development. These include specification of such things as the situations in which the varying modes of dissonance reduction will be utilized,[5] the role of commitment and volition, the relation of pre- and postdecisional processes,[6] and the course of dissonance reduction over time. Festinger enumerates various modes of dissonance reduction but does not give a systematic account of the situations in which each mode will be utilized; and despite Brehm and Cohen's (1962) insistence that commitment be considered a necessary condition for the arousal of dissonance and Festinger's (1964b) admission that they may be right, the evidence is not at all unambiguous. Further, the relation of pre- and postdecisional processes, as Davidson (1964) has demonstrated, is something that should not be neglected. It seems very reasonable that the processes occurring before the decision should have an effect upon the dissonance reduction occurring after the decision. Finally, Walster's (1964) research has drawn attention to the important matter of the course of dissonance reduction over time. Are there changes in the amount of dissonance reduction at varying times since the decision, and, if so, how can these changes be explained?

What can be said to evaluate dissonance theory in the light of the existing empirical evidence? This is not an easy question to answer. The empirical evidence is frequently made rather ambiguous due to the non-random elimination of subjects for various theory based reasons. From the present vantage point, however, it appears as if the research in some areas is at least fairly supportive. These areas include: revaluation of the alternatives following the resolution of approach-approach conflicts, the simple effect of counterattitudinal advocacy, and the effect of justification upon forced compliance. Other areas in which the research is somewhat less supportive include: the effect of punishment upon forced compliance, the effect of choice upon forced compliance, and the effect of effort upon forced compliance. At the present time overall conclusions

---

[5] Steiner and Johnson (1964) and Steiner and Rogers (1963) report some data bearing on this problem.

[6] Janis (1959) has developed conflict theory so as to have theoretical implications regarding predecisional and postdecisional conflicts.

about the implications of this research would be premature. There are two areas, however, in which the research definitely implies that some revision of dissonance theory is necessary; these are selective exposure and reward in forced compliance situations.[7] In an excellent review of the selective exposure literature Freedman and Sears (1965) find little support for the dissonance predictions. According to Freedman and Sears (1965): "The evidence does not support the hypothesis that the greater the magnitude of cognitive dissonance the greater will be the relative preference for exposure to supportive as opposed to nonsupportive information" (p. 94). The research dealing with the effect of reward in forced compliance situations also indicates that dissonance theory, at least in its present form, is either oversimplified or incorrect. If the theory is to be salvaged some revisions are definitely in order.

[7] Due to the fact that the dependent variable in selective exposure studies is not an attitudinal one, no attempt has been made to discuss this literature.

II

Sarnoff's Psychoanalytic Theory

THEORY

Sarnoff (1960a, 1962) has developed a theory which attempts to spell out the implications of Freudian psychology for attitudes and attitude change. Sarnoff appropriately calls this theory psychoanalytic theory.

Motives and Conflicts

According to Sarnoff (1960a): "*A motive is an internally operative, tension-producing stimulus which provokes the individual to act in such a way as to reduce the tension generated by it and which is capable of being consciously experienced*" (p. 252). Furthermore, "*Whenever two or more motives are activated at the same time, their coalescence produces a state of conflict*" (p. 253).

When the simultaneously aroused motives differ in intensity the conflict may be readily reduced in favor of the stronger motive. Simultaneously aroused motives, however, are frequently of equal intensity. Under these circumstances the manner of conflict resolution is dependent upon whether the motives are associated with intolerable fear and thus consciously unacceptable or not associated with intolerable fear and thus consciously acceptable. If the motives are consciously acceptable, the individual may suppress his perception of one of the motives or simply inhibit one of the motives while remaining conscious of its presence. On the other hand, if one of the motives is consciously unacceptable it may be deferred by a defense mechanism.

Ego Defense

According to Freud and Sarnoff the child, in the course of development, learns a configuration of perceptual and motor skills which helps to reduce motivational tension within the limitations of environmental constraints. This configuration, which is called the ego, allows the child to seek out and obtain tension reducing objects, such as food, or to avoid threatening objects, such as an irate parent. Because of the child's relative helplessness, however, he is frequently unable to respond to threatening objects in an adaptative, tension reducing manner. In such circumstances the ego may lose its perceptual function and/or the individual may lose consciousness and faint. To avoid such a "catastrophic state of helplessness" the individual covertly responds to the intolerable fear in such a way as to preserve the ego's perceptual function. These covert responses, which are called ego defenses or defense mechanisms, eliminate from consciousness the fear motive and any other motive which is responsible for the arousal of fear.

Ego defenses can take any number of forms such as repression, projection, denial, or identification with the aggressor. Repression involves a forgetting of the anxiety-provoking motives and circumstances, projection involves the attribution of consciously unacceptable motives to others, denial means the failure to perceive threatening circumstances, and identification with the aggressor means the adopting of the attitudes and behavior of a threatening and fearful person. All of these defenses of the ego unconsciously operate in different ways so as to eliminate the perception of consciously unacceptable motives.

Although the ego defenses may be effective in eliminating the perception of unacceptable motives, this does not guarantee that the tension produced by these motives is reduced. In order for tension reduction to occur the individual must make some overt response. These overt responses are called symptoms. According to Sarnoff (1960a) a symptom is *"an overt, tension-reducing response whose relationship to an unconscious motive is not perceived by the individual"* (p. 260). For example, suppose a mother harbors unconscious hatred for her child. This motive cannot be openly expressed or admitted because it would arouse too much guilt. Ego defenses thus prevent the perception of the unacceptable motive. However, tension produced by this motive can nonetheless be reduced if the mother smothers the child with overprotection. In this case being overprotective is a symptom that allows for tension reduction of an unacceptable hate motive.

Attitudes

In agreement with many psychologists Sarnoff (1960a) defines attitude as *"a disposition to react favorably or unfavorably to a class of objects"* (p. 261). These dispositions to react favorably or unfavorably, according to Sarnoff, are developed in the process of making tension reducing responses to various classes of objects. More specifically *"an individual's attitude toward a class of objects is determined by the particular role these objects have come to play in facilitating responses which reduce the tension of particular motives and which resolve particular conflicts among motives"* (p. 261). The motives that are involved may be either consciously acceptable or unacceptable.

Attitudes as a Function of Consciously Acceptable Motives

In the process of reducing tension arising from consciously acceptable motives, the individual develops favorable attitudes toward the objects facilitating tension reduction and unfavorable attitudes toward the objects interfering with tension reduction. He is, furthermore, aware of the functional relationship between his motives and the related attitudes. For example, someone with a strong achievement motive develops favorable attitudes toward facilitating work conditions and unfavorable attitudes toward interfering work conditions. He is, in addition, aware of the reasons why he holds the attitudes that he does.

Attitudes as a Function of Consciously Unacceptable Motives

Attitudes also develop as a function of consciously unacceptable motives. In this regard attitudes are determined by the extent to which they facilitate both ego defensive reactions which prevent perception of the unacceptable motives and symptomatic reactions which facilitate tension reduction of the unacceptable motives.

Attitudes facilitate ego defensive reactions by contributing to the perceptual obliteration of threatening stimuli that are either external or internal. Such defense mechanisms as denial and identification with the aggressor prevent perception of threatening *external* stimuli. By identifying with or adopting the behavior and *attitudes* of an aggressor the individual becomes less capable of perceiving the aggressor as separate from or different from himself. Thus adopting appropriate attitudes facilitates perceptual obliteration of a threatening external stimulus. Denial occurs when the individual refuses to admit the existence of danger. In this case we have a failure to believe in the existence of danger and the consequent lack of a strong negative attitude toward the danger. Again there is perceptual obliteration of a threatening external stimulus.

Defense mechanisms such as projection and reaction formation prevent perception of threatening *internal* stimuli. Projection occurs when the individual attributes his own inferiority or guilt feelings to other people so that he thinks it is not he but the other people who are inferior or bad. In this case adopting a negative attitude toward other people facilitates the perceptual obliteration of threatening inferiority and guilt feelings. Reaction formation occurs when the individual covers up his unacceptable feelings toward other people by acting in an opposite manner toward them. Someone, for example, may feel negatively toward other people and yet act very positively toward them. Here, once again, the adoption of a particular attitude produces perceptual obliteration of a threatening internal stimulus.

According to Sarnoff attitudes may also facilitate the occurrence of symptomatic reactions which reduce the tension arising from consciously unacceptable motives. For example, by adopting extremely moralistic attitudes toward sex some individuals are able to rationalize their presence on censorship boards and consequent exposure to large amounts of pornographic literature. Exposure to the pornographic literature reduces tension arising from unacceptable sexual urges, but the moralistic attitude toward sex helps in rationalizing and maintaining the behavior.[1]

Psychoanalytic Theory and Dissonance Theory

Sarnoff (1966) has further pointed out some interesting relationships between psychoanalytic theory and dissonance theory. He first notes that the two theories are similar in that they both refer to a basic dissonant or homeostatically imbalanced state that is a source of inner tension and motivation. According to dissonance theory dissonance results when the individual decides to do something with unpleasant consequences. According to psychoanalytic theory homeostatic imbalance is produced by competing motives. Dissonance theory maintains that the individual may react to the inner tensions with one or more modes of dissonance reduction, and psychoanalytic theory maintains that the individual may react with one or more defensive reactions. The particular defensive reactions that are invoked depend upon the nature of the specific motives involved and the habitual way in which the individual reduces tensions from these motives.

Sarnoff illustrates the above discussion by showing how psychoanalytic theory can account for the results obtained by Festinger and Carlsmith (1959). Festinger and Carlsmith found that subjects who were paid 1 dollar for informing a waiting subject that a very dull experiment is actually interesting and fun reacted by rating the experiment as more enjoyable than subjects who were paid 20 dollars for engaging in the same behavior. According to Festinger and Carlsmith the dissonance produced by engaging in deceitful behavior for a minimal incentive was reduced through increased evaluation of the experimental task. Sarnoff,

---

[1] In the above discussion the reader may have noticed the omission of any reference to displacement and the related scapegoat theory of prejudice. Sarnoff (1960a) does not mention these matters in his main theoretical treatment of attitudes, although he does do so in the context of his general theory of prejudice (1962).

however, interprets the experiment as having aroused two conflicting motives, a need for approval and a need to reduce shame. The 1-dollar subjects engaged in the deceitful behavior in order to satisfy their need for approval from the high status experimenter. Enactment of the behavior, though, produced shame for having succumbed to this need for approval. They thus reacted defensively in order to push the shame out of consciousness. Specifically the subjects rationalized their behavior by evaluating the experiment favorably, thus allowing for resolution of the motivational conflict.

Sarnoff further maintains that psychoanalytic theory contributes to an understanding of dissonance-related phenomena and that dissonance theory contributes to an understanding of psychoanalytically-related phenomena. Psychoanalytic theory contributes to an understanding of dissonance-related phenomena, for example, by providing concepts such as compartmentalization which explain why some individuals do not become disquieted by behaviors that should be dissonance producing. Dissonance theory contributes to an understanding of psychoanalytically-related phenomena through the use of concepts such as choice, commitment, and volition. Psychoanalytic theory conceives of man as involuntarily driven by unconscious urges. A more realistic picture is obtained, however, if the theory is complemented by concepts which in addition refer to conscious voluntary behavior.

RESEARCH

The few experimental studies that are directly relevant to Sarnoff's psychoanalytic interpretation of attitudes will be presented under two headings: psychoanalytic interpretation versus rational argument, and miscellaneous studies of defensive reactions. Other studies relating to social affiliation (Sarnoff and Zimbardo, 1961) and personality correlates of anti-Semitism among Jews (Sarnoff, 1951) will not be discussed.

Psychoanalytic Interpretation versus Rational Argument

Katz, Sarnoff, and McClintock (1956) present some evidence indicating that a communication which interprets prejudice in psychoanalytic terms is more persuasive than a communication which presents rational arguments against prejudice. Katz, Sarnoff, and McClintock reasoned that in a Northern college population where there is adequate opportunity to gain information regarding Negroes, prejudicial attitudes are more likely to be a resultant of defensive reactions than misinformation. They further reasoned that the interpretative approach should be most effective on subjects who are intermediate in defensiveness and the informational approach most effective on subjects who are low in defensiveness. Presumably, nothing less than prolonged individual therapy would change attitudes in highly defensive people; rationally presented information will only be effective in combatting attitudes based on nondefensive processes.

There were three conditions in the experiment: interpretation, information, and control. In the interpretation condition the subjects read a communication which described and illustrated the dynamics of scapegoating and projection in the development of prejudicial attitudes. In the information condition the subjects read a communication which provided information regarding Negroes and was intended to make a prejudicial attitude appear unreasonable. In the control condition the subjects were not given any communication whatsoever. A Likert-type scale of attitudes toward Negroes was administered 1 week before, immediately after, and 6 weeks after the communication manipulation. In terms of change from before to immediately after, the interpretation condition produced an effect that was significantly greater than that which occurred in the control condition and nonsignificantly greater than that which occurred in the information condition. The intermediate effect produced by the information condition did not differ significantly from the effects in either the interpretation or control conditions. In terms of change from before to 6 weeks after, the interpretation condition produced an effect that was significantly greater than that found in either the information or control conditions. This latter finding was taken as supporting the main initial hypothesis with regard to the superiority of interpretative over informational communications.

In order to examine the relative effectiveness of the two communications upon subjects differing in defensiveness, a TAT was given during the first session. This test consisted of a card depicting a number of girls, one of whom was definitely Negro, one of whom was definitely white, but the majority of whom were ambiguous with regard to racial indentity. The stories written in response to the picture were coded for projection, denial, and extrapunitiveness and then combined into one ego-defensive score. Attribution of hostile feelings to the Negro girl, for example, was taken as an indication of projection, and failure to identify the Negro girl as Negro was taken as an indication of denial. Katz, Sarnoff, and McClintock had originally predicted that the interpretative approach would be most effective for the subjects who were intermediate in defensiveness. The results, however, indicated that the interpretative communication was most effective for the subjects who were either intermediate or low in defensiveness. While the intermediate and low groups combined differed significantly from the high group, the intermediate and high groups did not differ significantly from each other. Katz, Sarnoff, and McClintock interpreted this finding as meaning either that their measure of defensiveness was not very sensitive or that there are very few people so low in defensiveness that they cannot be affected by exposure to interpretative materials. The prediction that the informational approach would be most effective for the subjects low in defensiveness was not supported. The three subgroups of subjects in the information condition, in fact, did not significantly differ in any way. This was interpreted as being due to the low defensive subjects possessing enough defenses so as not to be overly persuaded by information and the high defensive subjects being persuaded by the conformity aspects of the experimental situation.

The very audacity of this experiment makes it both intriguing and suspect. The idea that someone would attempt to successfully carry out psychoanalytic interpretation in a single written communication seems absurd. However, the qualification that this interpretative approach will only be effective with subjects intermediate in defensiveness, along with the subsequent finding that the approach is effective with subjects who are both intermediate and low in defensiveness, does lend an added degree of plausibility. What about the overall finding that the interpretative approach was more effective than the informational? This finding may indeed indicate that interpretation is a more effective means of reducing prejudice than is rational argument, but it also may mean that an interpretative approach is simply a very powerful way of producing conformity. After all, most people do not want to manifest characteristics that are diagnostic of neuroticism. One may also wonder just how rational and informative the information communication actually was. Perhaps a better constructed information communication would have produced different results.

Katz, McClintock, and Sarnoff (1957) report a follow-up investigation which attempted to get at differences in defensiveness among subjects who were exposed to an interpretative communication. The subjects were female education students from an urban university. As in the Katz, Sarnoff, and McClintock study, the experiment was conducted in three sessions. During the first session the subjects completed various measures of defensiveness and a premeasure of prejudice toward Negroes. One week later during the second session the subjects read the interpretative communication and completed the measure of prejudice the second time. Five weeks later during the third session the subjects completed the measure of prejudice for a third time. Four measures of defensiveness were taken: a two card TAT, a sentence completion test, the ego defense scale of the MMPI, and that part of the F scale which theoretically assesses authoritarianism resulting from defensiveness rather than from conformity. The TAT card used by Katz, Sarnoff, and McClintock (1956) was supplemented by an additional, highly similar card.

Since there was no control group it is impossible to assess the communication's effectiveness. However, between sessions one and two, and between sessions one and three the percentages of subjects showing positive change were 65 and 67, respectively. Change, however, did not prove to be related to defensiveness as assessed through either the TAT or the sentence completion test. When defensiveness was assessed with either the MMPI scale or the F scale, though, the subjects who were medium in defensiveness changed significantly more from the first to the third session than the subjects who were high in defensiveness and nonsignificantly more than the subjects who were low in defensiveness. The F scale and MMPI ego defensiveness scale turned out to be significantly related to each other but unrelated to either the TAT or sentence completion test.

Comment. Since the TAT measure of defensiveness differentiated amount of change in the first study but not in the second, there is considerable room for scepticism about what is actually occurring when a subject is persuaded by an interpretative communication. Does an interpretative communication actually relax defenses or does it simply persuade through other means? This is the crucial question which certainly has not been satisfactorily answered.

Miscellaneous Studies

Two other studies bear directly on Sarnoff's theory, one relating to castration anxiety and one relating to reaction formation.

Sarnoff and Corwin (1959) tested the hypothesis that individuals with a high degree of castration anxiety have a greater fear of death after exposure to sexually arousing stimuli than individuals with a low degree of castration anxiety. During the Oedipal period the little boy theoretically represses sexual cravings for his mother in order to control the castration anxiety arising from his father's real or imagined threats. After puberty sexual arousal by women other than his mother may bring back the castration anxiety if the original castration threat was too severe. The unconscious castration anxiety, furthermore, may manifest itself either in fear of moderate bodily harm or in fear of extreme bodily harm, death. Thus Sarnoff and Corwin argue that the exposure of individuals with high castration anxiety to sexually arousing stimuli will produce fear of death.

The experimental design involved two independent variables, high or low sexual arousal and high or low castration anxiety. Sexual arousal was manipulated by exposing male subjects to pictures of nude females or to pictures of fully clothed fashion models. Subjects were classified as being high or low in castration anxiety on the basis of responses to one of the cards from the Blacky Test. The card depicts one dog looking at another blindfolded dog who is about to have his tail cut by a descending knife. Subjects were instructed to rank three summary statements for this picture: a low castration anxiety statement which indicated that the amputation had little emotional significance for the onlooking dog, a medium castration anxiety statement which indicated that the amputation was frightening for the onlooking dog, and a high castration anxiety statement which indicated that the amputation was deeply upsetting and anxiety provoking for the onlooking dog. All of the subjects who considered the low anxiety statement least appropriate and the high anxiety statement most appropriate were classified as high in castration anxiety. The dependent variable for the study was the before-after change in response to a 22-item fear of death scale.

The results fully support Sarnoff and Corwin's expectations. In the high sexual arousal condition the high castration anxiety subjects manifested significantly greater increased fear of death than did the low castration anxiety subjects, and in the low sexual arousal condition the high and low castration anxiety subjects did not differ significantly. Furthermore, in agreement with the above *t*-test results, the interaction between sexual arousal and castration anxiety is significant. This latter finding means that the difference between high and low castration anxiety subjects in the high sexual arousal condition is significantly greater than the comparable difference in the low sexual arousal condition.

Sarnoff (1960b) tested the hypothesis that individuals who are high in reaction formation against affection become more cynical after arousal of their affectionate feelings than persons who are low in reaction formation against affection. Reaction formation occurs when the individual acts in a manner opposed to his unconscious impulses in order both to expend energy in the control of these impulses and to misperceive the true nature of these impulses. Sarnoff reasons that some individuals who have affectionate impulses may seek to control these impulses by adopting a hostile or cynical attitude toward other people and the world.

The experimental design involved two independent variables, high or low affectionate feelings toward others and high or low reaction formation against affection. Affection was manipulated by exposing subjects either to a live dramatic presentation of an excerpt from William Saroyan's play *Hello Out There,* or to a tape recording of the same excerpt. Subjects were classified as high or low in reaction formation against affection on the basis of their rankings of summary statements relating to four TAT pictures. A 7-item cynicism scale was administered 2 weeks before and immediately after the experimental manipulations.

The results indicated that, contrary to Sarnoff's expectations, all four groups manifested a decrease in cynicism. The pattern of shifts, however, was consistent with the initial hypothesis. In the high-affection-arousal condition the high reaction formation subjects showed significantly less decrease in cynicism than the low reaction formation subjects, and there was no significant difference between the high and low reaction formation subjects in the low-affection-arousal condition. Furthermore, after utilizing a special statistical technique to take into account the differing regressions of the before scores on the after scores in the various conditions, Sarnoff found a significant interaction between arousal and reaction formation. This interaction indicates that the difference between the high and low reaction formation subjects in the high arousal condition is significantly greater than the corresponding difference in the low arousal condition. Despite the fact that Sarnoff's high reaction formation did not show an actual increase in cynicism the results still lend support to his theoretical speculations.

EVALUATION

For the majority of social psychologists who approach attitude change with an experimental orientation Sarnoff's work on psychoanalytic theory is undoubtedly "way out." There are two reasons for this. First, the theory sounds utterly bizarre and far too speculative. Second, both the theory and the research are couched in terms of individual differences. With regard to the first point it should be realized, however, that sober evaluation does not eliminate a theory simply because it sounds bizarre, and that as long as any theory, no matter how speculative, does lead to empirical research it should not be ruled out of court on any *a priori* basis. The second point is a far more serious one. It is possible to argue quite forcefully that unless psychology takes into account the numerous individual differences, it is burying its head in the sand. Sarnoff (1965) maintains that "progress in psychology will best be facilitated by experimental designs that permit the simultaneous study of: the separate effects of organismic and situational variables on behavior, and the behavioral effects of the interaction of those variables" (p. 284). On the other hand, it is also equally obvious that the experimental grouping of people who differ in one known characteristic may also involve the grouping of people who differ in many other unspecified characteristics and thus make the causal interpretation of any obtained results highly questionable. This is one of the primary problems facing contemporary psychology. Perhaps part of the solution lies in utilizing only psychometric instruments which correlate with some instruments and do not correlate with other instruments in a manner required by Campbell and Fiske's (1959) multi-trait-multimethod matrix.

Sarnoff's translation of Freudian theory into a theory of attitude change is a forthright and interesting attempt to make a unique contribution. Unfortunately the theory is so incompletely tested that at the present time any overall evaluation would be premature. It is interesting to note, however, that Sarnoff (1966) himself considers psychoanalytic theory inadequate insofar as it focuses totally on unconscious impulses to the complete exclusion of conscious volitional choices.

Festinger and Bramel (1962), like Sarnoff (1966), have discussed the relationship between psychoanalytic theory and dissonance theory. Festinger and Bramel, however, are somewhat more explicit in specifying the difference between dissonance arousing and defense arousing situations. They maintain that psychoanalytic theory is mostly concerned with situations in which a person's perception of himself is discrepant from what he thinks he should be (his superego). For example, if the person perceives that he has homosexual tendencies and at the same time considers homosexuality immoral or bad, then he may react defensively in order to avoid anxiety and guilt. Dissonance theory, on the other hand, is concerned with situations in which a person's immediate perception of himself is discrepant from his previously acquired self-conception. Thus a person with a favorable self-conception will experience more dissonance upon perceiving that he has homosexual tendencies than a person who has an unfavorable self-conception. Dissonance is aroused not by a discrepancy between a self-perception and one's superego but by a discrepancy between a self-perception and one's self-conception. Festinger and Bramel report an investigation in which subjects with favorable self-conceptions who learned that they had homosexual tendencies reacted by attributing homosexual tendencies to other people (projecting) to a greater extent than similarly treated subjects with unfavorable self-conceptions. Projecting or attributing homosexual tendencies to other people, particularly if they are respected, theoretically allows for dissonance reduction through favorable revaluation of homosexuality. This investigation helps greatly in clarifying what is possibly the most important difference between dissonance theory and psychoanalytic theory. If a person who believed himself to be homosexual were confronted with information that he were not homosexual, dissonance would be created. According to psychoanalytic theory, however, tension and consequent defensive reactions would occur only if the individual conceived of homosexuality as good or desirable. Psychoanalytic theory, like affective-cognitive consistency theory, puts relatively more emphasis upon values and relatively less emphasis upon cognitions or beliefs.

McGuire's Inoculation Theory

THEORY

McGuire's (1962a, 1964) inoculation theory is concerned with how to make attitudes resistant to change. Although, as McGuire (1964) points out, other theories of attitude change do have implications concerning ways of inducing resistance to persuasion, inoculation theory is the only major formulation that focuses primarily upon this problem.

A Biological Analogy

Inoculation theory is based on an analogy with the means of creating biological resistance to disease. What is the best procedure for creating resistance to disease? There are two possible ways: first, supportive therapy (going on a special diet, vitamins, and exercise regime), and second, being inoculated. If someone has been living in a germ free environment inoculation is definitely the best procedure. When inoculated, a person is given a weakened or killed form of the disease-producing bacteria and is thereby stimulated to develop defenses capable of handling stronger bacteria.

What is the best procedure for making someone resistant to counterattitudinal propaganda? Following the biological analogy there are two possible ways. One way is to make the attitude healthier by providing supportive information and arguments. The other way is to inoculate the attitudes by presenting the individual with weakened counterattitudinal propaganda. If the individual has been living in an environment where his attitudes have not been threatened, the inoculation procedure will be the superior one.

Selective Exposure and Cultural Truisms

To what extent do attitudes exist in a germ free environment or in an environment in which they are not attacked? According to the selective exposure postulate nearly all attitudes should be relatively free of attack. Individuals should defensively avoid encountering information contrary to their attitudes. However, in view of the contradictory evidence relating to selective exposure (Freedman and Sears, 1965; Steiner, 1962), McGuire is and was not convinced that attitudes are to any great extent sheltered and protected. Therefore, in the development and test of inoculation theory, he turned to the study of cultural truisms or widely shared beliefs that most individuals have never heard attacked. After much pretesting he discovered that the area of health abounds in almost unanimously accepted propositions. By far the majority of his student samples checked 15 on a 15-point scale to indicate agreement with such propositions: "It's a good idea to brush your teeth after every meal if at all possible"; "The effects of penicillin have been, almost without exception, of great benefit to mankind"; "Everyone should get a yearly chest X-ray to detect any signs of TB at an early stage"; "Mental illness is not contagious" (McGuire, 1964, p. 201).

Utilizing these health truisms it is possible to test the analogical implication that beliefs existing in an attack free environment can be made most resistant to subsequent counterpropaganda through inoculation. Inoculation consists of the presentation of weakened or refuted counterarguments.

Motivation and Practice

Theoretically a truism that has previously existed in a nonthreatening environment should be quite vulnerable to attacking counterpropaganda. According to McGuire there are two main reasons for this vulnerability: lack of practice in defending the truism and lack of motivation to defend the truism. The individual is unpracticed because he has never had to defend the truism, and he is unmotivated to start practicing because he regards the truism as unassailable.

Why should the presentation of refuted counterarguments produce resistance to subsequent stronger counterarguments? McGuire's answer is in terms of motivation and practice. The inoculation poses a threat that motivates the individual to develop bolstering arguments for his somewhat weakened belief. This, of course, leads to practice in the development of bolstering arguments. Thus the motivation to develop bolstering arguments plus the practice acquired in such development produces resistance to subsequent counterarguments.

Three Defensive Variables

McGuire distinguishes and has experimentally investigated three defensive variables: the amount of threat contained in the truism defenses, the amount of active participation in the defenses required of the subjects, and the amount of time between the defense and the attack of the truism. For his manipulation of the amount of threat McGuire uses two basic types of defenses, supportive and refutational. The supportive defenses are nonthreatening arguments favorable toward the truism, and the threatening defenses are arguments unfavorable toward the truism followed by refutations of these arguments. By analogy the supportive defenses correspond to supportive therapy and the refutational defenses to inoculations. There are two subtypes of refutational defenses, refutational-same defenses and refutational-different defenses. Refutational-same defenses present and refute the same arguments that are in a subsequent attack, and refutational-different defenses present and refute different arguments from those that are in a subsequent attack.

The second defensive variable is the amount of active participation in the defenses required of the subjects. In a passive condition the subjects simply read a defensive essay that has already been prepared for them. In an active condition, on the other hand, the subjects, with some small help, write the defensive essays themselves. This manipulation is relevant to the matter of motivation and practice.

The third defensive variable, interval between attack and defense, is of obvious importance since building up immunity may require some time and any immunity that is built up may decay over time. The investigated time intervals vary between several minutes and 1 week.

The above theoretical framework in conjunction with the defensive variables has allowed McGuire to make a sizeable number of deductions. For example, it can be predicted that a refutational defense will be more effective in inducing resistance to subsequent attacking arguments than will a supportive defense. However, many of the deductions are somewhat complex, and, following McGuire's example, discussions of these matters will be delayed until the presentation of the related research evidence.

RESEARCH

Supportive and Refutational Defenses

According to inoculation theory a refutational defense should provide greater resistance to subsequent attacking arguments than a supportive defense. By analogy this is because the refutational argument immunizes subjects against the subsequent attacks. McGuire and his associates have, in some cases, used passive defensives in which the supportive and refutational materials are already prepared for the subjects, and, in some cases, active defenses in which the subjects themselves prepare the supportive and refutational materials, either with or without the aid of outlines. Discussion of the theoretical developments and empirical findings relevant to the active-passive manipulation will be presented mostly in a subsequent section. The present section will be concerned with this issue only insofar as it is relevant to the general question of the relative effectiveness of supportive and refutational defenses in offering resistance to subsequent attacking arguments.

McGuire and Papageorgis (1961) demonstrated that refutation-same defenses produce greater resistance to subsequent attacking arguments than do supportive defenses. The experiment was conducted in two 1-hour sessions that were 48 hours apart. During the first session the subjects were exposed to supportive and refutational defenses and during the second to attacking arguments. In the first session each subject wrote an essay defending one truism and read a 1000-word essay defending another. To support the cover story that the experiment was concerned with the relationship between reading and writing skills the subjects answered a series of questions relating to the essay they had read. Besides the reading-writing manipulation which involved a within-subject comparison, there were two manipulations involving between-subject comparisons. The first manipulation had to do with whether the subjects wrote their essays with or without the benefit of an outline and read the prepared essays with or without underlining the key sentences. The second manipulation had to do with whether the defenses were both supportive or both refutational. In the reading condition the supportive and refutational defenses were five paragraph essays. For the supportive defense each paragraph after the initial one consisted of the elaboration of separate arguments favorable to the truism, and for the refutational defense each paragraph after the initial one consisted of the presentation and refutation of arguments unfavorable to the truism. In the writing-from-outline condition the subjects were given either four one-sentence synopses, each consisting of a different supportive argument, or four two-sentence synopses, each consisting of a different attacking argument and its refutation. In the writing-without-outline condition the subjects were simply instructed either to write an essay giving arguments in support of the truism or to write an essay refuting possible counter-arguments against the truism. At the conclusion of the first session the subjects filled out a questionnaire measuring their belief in four truisms, including the two that were defended. The subjects were told that the measure was to ascertain whether or not belief had any effect upon their performance in the "verbal skills test."

In the second session the subjects read and underlined the key sentences contained in attacks against three truisms, including the two that had been previously defended. The attacks were five paragraph essays, each paragraph after the initial one elaborating separate argu-

ments against a given truism. In the case of the two attacks against the
previously defended truisms the arguments were the same as those which
had previously been refuted. After reading the attacks the subjects filled
out a comprehension test and the same belief questionnaire that they
had taken in the previous session. Each subject thus provided information with regard to four truisms, two which were defended and attacked,
one which was attacked only, and one which was neither attacked nor
defended. The four truisms were systematically rotated among the four
different conditions for different subjects.

The results generally confirm McGuire's expectations. In the condition in which the truisms were neither attacked nor defended the mean
belief was 12.62 on a 15-point scale. This mean is significantly greater
than the similar mean belief in the attack-only condition, 6.64. In the
absence of defenses the attacks were, thus, very successful. The results
with regard to the defensive conditions are presented in Table 12–1.
Overall mean belief in the refutational defense conditions (10.33) is

TABLE 12–1. Mean Belief After Attacks [a] Preceded by
Refutational-Same or Supportive Defenses

| | Reading | | Writing | |
	Passive	Underline	Outline	No Outline
Refutational Defense then Attack	11.51	11.13	9.19	9.46
Supportive Defense then Attack	7.47	7.63	7.94	6.53

[a] Neither-attack-nor-defense = 12.62; attack-only = 6.64.
SOURCE: Adapted from McGuire and Papageorgis, 1961, p. 331.

significantly higher than the mean belief in both the attack-only condition (6.64) and the supportive defense conditions (7.39). The mean
belief level in the supportive defense conditions, in fact, does not even
differ significantly from the mean belief level in the attack-only condition. The refutational defenses were obviously much superior to the
supportive defenses in conferring resistance to the attacks. The effect is
statistically significant in each of the four defense conditions: passive
reading, reading and underlining, writing-with-outline, writing-without-
outline.

What about the immediate effect of the defenses which were presented before the attacks in the second session? The mean belief score
for the supportive defenses was 14.34, and the mean belief score for the
refutational defenses was 13.91. Paradoxically, the supportive defenses

appear to have immediately strengthened belief more than the refutational defenses, although the effect is not significant ($p < .10$, two-tailed). McGuire refers to this as the "paper tiger" phenomenon.

The experiment fairly convincingly demonstrates that refutational-same defenses are superior to supportive defenses in conferring resistance to subsequent attacks. What would happen, however, if the attacks did not contain the same arguments that were previously refuted in the refutational defenses? This is the question answered by the next experiment.

Papageorgis and McGuire (*1961*) found that refutational-different defenses are as effective as refutational-same defenses in inducing resistance to persuasion. According to inoculation theory refutational defenses are effective because their threatening nature motivates the individual to acquire belief bolstering material. This stimulated belief bolstering should assure resistance to attacking arguments other than those specifically refuted in the refutational defense. On the other hand, if the conferred resistance is specifically due to the refutations contained in the defense, then an attack utilizing nonrefuted arguments should be very damaging.

This experiment differs from the previously discussed McGuire and Papageorgis (1961) experiment in a number of ways. First, only passive reading and not active writing conditions were used. Second, the main comparison was between refutational-same and refutational-different defenses with no involvement of supportive defenses. Third, the defenses and attacks were shortened from five to three paragraphs and from four to two counterarguments. Fourth, the interval between the immunizing and attacking sessions was lengthened from 2 days to 1 week. And fifth, a somewhat different design was used in which each subject provided information on only two truisms. This design involved two nondefensive conditions: attack-only and neither-attack-nor-defense; and three defensive conditions: refutational-same, refutational-different, defense-without-attack. Each subject served in one nondefensive condition and in one defensive condition. The two truisms were counterbalanced between the nondefensive and defensive conditions.

The results agree with Papageorgis and McGuire's expectations. With defense-and-no-attack and with neither-attack-nor-defense the mean second session beliefs were 14.15 and 13.23 respectively. These means are both significantly greater than the mean belief for the attack-only condition, 5.73. In the refutational-same and refutational-different conditions the mean belief levels were 9.25 and 8.70 respectively. These means do not significantly differ from each other but are both significantly greater than the mean for the attack-only condition. These results, then, indicate that refutational-same and refutational-different defenses are approximately equal in inducing resistance to persuasion.

In an attempt to gain some information on the underlying process producing these resistance effects Papageorgis and McGuire included two additional measures at the end of the second session. One was the number of supportive arguments that the subjects could write down in a short period of time, and the other was a semantic differential, credibility rating of the attacking argument. The latter measure revealed that the counterarguments were seen as significantly less credible when preceded by either a refutational-same or a refutational-different defense than when preceded by no defense. The former measure revealed that the subjects who received the refutational defense were able to think up only slightly more supportive defense than the subjects who received no defenses ($p < .20$). This measure is crucial for the theory since the resistance supposedly results from the accumulation of belief-bolstering material. Papageorgis and McGuire, however, argue that the lack of significance may be due to having provided insufficient time for writing out the defensive arguments. Their subjects, in fact, complained about the lack of time.

One further matter has to do with the responses obtained from a question concerning what the experiment was about besides verbal and reading skills. A question of this type was apparently not included in the previously discussed McGuire and Papageorgis (1961) study but was included in the present experiment. Of the 73 subjects in the defensive conditions, 16 (22 percent) gave responses indicating they had perceived that the experiment was concerned with persuasion. Papageorgis and McGuire argue that much of this awareness may have been created by the rating of the credibility of the counterarguments and by the listing of supportive arguments. All of this activity occurred after the belief ratings were made and therefore possibly did not contaminate these ratings. In any event, since the belief ratings of the aware and nonaware subjects did not differ appreciably Papageorgis and McGuire did not eliminate any subjects.

McGuire and Papageorgis (1962) report an investigation on the effect of attack-forewarning in inducing resistance to persuasion. They theorized that an attack-forewarning would produce greater attention to the defenses and thus greater resistance to the subsequent attack. They further theorized that the forewarning would enhance the immunizing efficacy of the supportive defenses more than the refutational. This interaction prediction is based on the assumption that the refutational defenses already contain threatening information while the supportive defenses do not. The forewarning makes up a greater deficit in the case of the supportive than the refutational defenses.

Half of the subjects served in a no-forewarning group and half in a forewarning group. The subjects in the no-forewarning group were told that the experiment was a test of verbal skills; the subjects in the forewarning group were told that the experiment was concerned with study-ing susceptibility to persuasion and that after reading some defenses of their beliefs they would be exposed to strong attacks against these be-liefs. Each subject served in four conditions, three defensive and one control. The defensive conditions involved supportive, refutational-same, and refutational-different defenses. All of the defenses were followed by attacks during the same experimental session. For half of the subjects the control condition was neither-defense-nor-attack and for half it was attack-only. Different truisms were systematically rotated among the various conditions.

The results of the experiment are presented in Table 12–2. The

TABLE 12–2. Mean Belief after the Various
Experimental Treatments

Experimental Treatment	Foreknowledge of Attack		
	No	Yes	Combined
Neither-attack-nor-defense condition	13.20	12.52	12.86
Defense-then-attack conditions:			
Supportive defense	10.11	12.09	11.10
Refutational-same defense	11.68	11.79	11.73
Refutational-different defense	10.98	11.12	11.05
Refutational defenses combined	11.93	11.46	11.39
All defenses combined	10.93	11.67	11.30
Attack-only condition	10.23	9.95	10.09

SOURCE: Adapted from McGuire and Papageorgis, 1962, p. 31.

mean belief in the attack-only condition (10.09), is significantly less than the mean belief in the neither-attack-nor-defense condition (12.86). Combining the scores with and without forewarning, the mean beliefs in the supportive, refutational-same and refutational-different conditions (11.10, 11.73, 11.05) are all significantly greater than the mean belief in the attack-only condition. Of these three means the 11.73 for the refutational-same condition is significantly greater than the other two. Why are not both of the refutational means greater than the supportive mean? McGuire (1962a) argues that the explanation lies in the lack of time between defense and attack. Supportive defenses theoretically dis-sipate over time and refutational defenses increase in strength over time.[1] It is the case, however, that in the condition without forewarning the mean belief following the supportive defenses (10.11) is somewhat less than the means for the refutational-same and refutational-different defenses (11.68 and 10.98). No test of significance comparing these means is reported.

[1] This prediction and related evidence is described in detail in a later section.

What about the effect of the forewarning manipulation? As predicted, for all defenses combined the mean belief with forewarning (11.67) is significantly greater than the mean belief without forewarning (10.93). As McGuire and Papageorgis point out, however, this evidence by itself does not prove that the forewarning increased the effectiveness of the defenses; the forewarning could have decreased the effectiveness of the attacks. Apparently this did not happen, though, because in the attack-only condition the mean in the forewarning group (9.95) is slightly less than the mean in the no-forewarning group (10.23). There is thus no reason for supposing that with forewarning the attacks were any weaker.

The last prediction has to do with an interaction between forewarning and type of defense. As expected, the supportive defense gained significantly more from the presence of forewarning than did the refutational defenses.

Tannenbaum (*in press*) briefly reports a study concerned with the effect of attack forewarning or alerting. There were five different levels of alert varying from very general to very specific. In the most general level the subjects were informed that various health practices, including toothbrushing (the single issue that was later attacked), "were worthy of periodic evaluation and discussion," and in the most specific level the four main arguments contained in the attack were presented without refutation. The intermediate levels varied in the explicitness with which the details of the four arguments were presented. All five levels of alert were followed by an attack. The results indicated that none of the five alerting conditions produced a final belief level significantly different from that of an attack-only control. Furthermore, these results agree with McGuire and Papageorgis' (1962) finding that alerting or forewarning did not significantly affect belief in the attack-only control groups.

These results make it apparent that forewarning all by itself is not a sufficient condition for the conferral of resistance to persuasion. But as Tannenbaum points out, inoculation theory does not maintain that forewarning alone is sufficient. The individual must also have the "wherewithal" to produce defenses. Supposedly this wherewithal is provided by the information contained in the refutations.[2] Although Tannenbaum does not discuss the matter, it is also possible that the added elements beyond the forewarning would be obtained if the individual were given sufficient time to accumulate belief bolstering information.

Anderson and McGuire (*1965*) report an investigation dealing with the effect of predefense reassurance (bogus information given before

---

[2] Tannenbaum mentions that he failed to find a supportive defense plus a forewarning more effective than a refutational defense. If McGuire and Papageorgis (1962) had obtained such results, the predicted interaction between forewarning and type of defense would have been weaker, although possibly still significant.

the defenses concerning peer belief in the truisms). They interpret inoculation theory as implying that predefense reassurance reduces the immunizing effectiveness of the various defenses, and furthermore that the weakening is greater for the supportive than the refutational defenses. The predefense reassurance theoretically produces overconfidence so that the defensive material is not adequately assimilated, but this overconfidence is to some extent overcome by the threatening component of the refutational defenses. The net result is a greater weakening of the supportive than the refutational defenses.

After initially indicating their beliefs in 12 medical truisms on 15-point scales the subjects were given bogus information regarding the group average for those truisms that the experimenter supposedly had had time to compute. Purportedly to reduce the possibility of later clerical errors on the part of IBM key punch operators the subjects were asked to record these averages in their booklets. Subjects in the reassurance group were told that the mean belief in four key truisms was quite high (about 14.5 on a 15-point scale). Subjects in the no-reassurance group were not given any information regarding these key truisms. All subjects served in three experimental conditions (supportive, refutational-same, and refutational-different) and one of two control conditions (attack-only or neither-attack-nor-defense). The attacks and defenses all occurred in the same session.

The results of the experiment are reported in Table 12–3.

TABLE 12–3. Mean Belief With and Without Reassuring Feedback of Peer Group Adherence Before the Defenses

| | Defense and Attack Conditions | | | | |
Feedback Condition	Neither-Attack-nor-Defense	Refutational-Same Defense	Refutational-Different Defense	Supportive Defense	Attack-only
Reassurance	12.40	11.52	10.80	9.58	10.20
No reassurance	12.68	12.12	11.41	11.06	10.74
Combined	12.54	11.82	11.10	10.32	10.47

SOURCE: Adapted from Anderson and McGuire, 1965, p. 54, with permission of the American Sociological Association.

The mean belief in the attack-only condition (10.47) is significantly less than the mean belief in the neither-attack-nor-defense condition (12.54). The mean belief for the supportive defenses (10.32) is significantly less than the mean belief for both the refutational-same defense

(11.82) and the refutational-different (11.10). For these data the supportive defense is therefore less effective even when the attacks follow
immediately after the defenses. McGuire and Papageorgis (1962) did
not find such a significant difference for an analogous situation in which
the attacks followed immediately after the defenses.

What about the effects of the reassurance manipulation? All three
defenses were more effective in the no-reassurance group than in the
reassurance group, but the effect was significant at only the .06 level.[3]
Furthermore, there was a nonsignificant tendency for reassurance to
reduce the effectiveness of the supportive defenses more than the refutational defenses. The data, then, are suggestive but not supportive.

McGuire (1964, pp. 213–215) reports an investigation in which he
sought to determine whether the immunizing efficacy of refutational defenses derives from the threatening component (attacking arguments
mentioned in the first paragraph) or the reassuring component (refutations of the attacking arguments in the subsequent paragraphs). According to inoculation theory the threatening component is the theoretically
important one because it motivates the individual to bolster his defenses.
Two independent variables were manipulated in the experiment, threat
(high or low) and reassurance (high or low). In the high threat condition four attacking arguments were mentioned in the first paragraph, and
in the low threat condition two attacking arguments were mentioned in
the first paragraph. In the high reassurance condition two of the attacking arguments were refuted in the subsequent paragraphs, and in the
low reassurance condition none of the attacking arguments was refuted.
All of the defenses were of the passive reading type and attacks followed the defenses by 2 days.

The results indicated that both the threat variable and the reassurance variable had significant effects. As predicted, in the high threat
condition there was more resistance to the attacks (11.02) than in the
low threat condition (10.14). There was also, however, more resistance
in the high reassurance condition (10.75) than in the low reassurance
condition (10.23). In discussing this latter effect McGuire (1964) states:
"The theory did not rule out the possibility that other components of
the refutational defense also would contribute to resistance to persuasion, any more than Boyle's law implies the invalidity of Charles's law"
(p. 215). He thus does not regard the significant reassurance effect as
being contrary to inoculation theory. In this he is undoubtedly correct.
However, it is apparent that inoculation theory insofar as it refers only
to the threatening component is not the whole story.

Comment. The research in this section is by and large very supportive of inoculation theory. Although the data are not entirely clear

[3] In discussing this effect McGuire (1962a, 1964) asserts that it is significant
at the .01 level.

as to whether or not refutational defenses are superior to supportive defenses when the attacks follow immediately after the defenses (Anderson and McGuire, 1965; McGuire and Papageorgis, 1962), it is clear that with a delay between the defenses and the attacks both refutational-same and refutational-different defenses are superior to supportive defenses (Papageorgis and McGuire, 1961).[4] It is perhaps not too surprising that refutational-same defenses are more effective than supportive defenses, but that refutational-different defenses are also superior to supportive defenses is a very provocative finding. Even more provocative is the fact that, as required by inoculation theory, the threatening component of the refutational defense is instrumental in producing the immunizing effect (McGuire, 1964, pp. 213–215). This latter study, however, also found that the reassuring component of the refutational defenses had a significant effect, even though this is not required by inoculation theory.

From the standpoint of inoculation theory the most unsatisfactory evidence comes from Anderson and McGuire's (1965) study of reassuring social support for truism beliefs. The predicted greater reduction of the immunizing effectiveness of supportive defenses following reassuring social support was not found. Perhaps the prediction needs to be rethought or perhaps the study needs to be redesigned.

Active and Passive Defenses

In an active defense condition the subject is assigned the task of writing a defense (supportive or refutational) either from an outline or without any guidance at all. In a passive defensive condition the subject simply reads a defense that is already prepared for him. In theorizing about the differences between these two types of defenses McGuire makes use of the concepts of practice and motivation. Theoretically people are unpracticed at defending truisms because they have never been called on to do so, and they are unmotivated to defend truisms because they believe the truisms unassailable. It thus might be thought that active defenses are superior to passive, first, because they provide the individual with practice and, second, because they motivate the individual by getting him actively involved in the defense. McGuire, however, takes a different approach. He argues that because of the individual's lack of practice he performs so poorly in the active condition as to actually obtain little or no practice. The net result is that the individual becomes motivated to defend his beliefs by the inadequacy of his own performance. Thus active defenses gain their strength simply

---

[4] Tannenbaum (in press) reports some evidence indicating that without a delay between attacks and defenses a refutational-different defense confers resistance when it precedes the attack but not when it follows the attack.

from their motivating effects. What about passive defenses? The practice deficit does not prevent the individual who is exposed to the passive defense from becoming involved in the relevant material (at least in the case of supportive and refutational-same defenses). Further, refutational defenses contain a threatening component that motivates the individual to defend his beliefs. In general, then, passive defenses gain their strength from, first, immersing the individual in the relevant material and, second, with refutational defenses at least, motivating the individual to bolster his defenses. Active defenses, on the other hand, gain strength only from their motivating effects. McGuire therefore hypothesizes that passive defenses are superior to active defenses in conferring resistance to persuasion.

Within the framework of this main order effect, McGuire formulates two interaction hypotheses. First, the superiority of passive over active defenses will be greater with refutational-same defenses than with supportive defenses, and, second, the superiority of passive over active defenses will be greater with supportive defenses than with refutational-different defenses. The first interaction hypothesis is based on two arguments. One argument is related to the fact that the active supportive, the active refutational, and the passive refutational defenses are benefited by their threatening or motivating power while the passive supportive defenses have no threatening or motivating power. The net result is that the superiority of the passive defenses over the active defenses is greater in the case of refutational-same than supportive defenses. The other argument supporting the first interaction has to do with the inadequate performance of individuals in the active conditions due to lack of practice in defending their beliefs. McGuire maintains that this lack of practice is less pronounced with regard to supportive defenses than with regard to refutational defenses. People have had some practice in developing or repeating arguments why they should brush their teeth after every meal even if they have not had practice in refuting arguments against brushing their teeth after every meal. Thus the active supportive defenses are not quite as bad off as the active refutational-same defenses. The net result, once again, is to make the superiority of the passive over the active defenses greater in the case of refutational-same defenses than in the case of supportive defenses.

It might be thought that the above arguments would also apply to the interaction involving refutational-different defenses. McGuire, however, maintains that there is an overriding consideration which implies that the superiority of passive over active defenses is greater with supportive defenses than with refutational-different defenses. This consideration has to do with the fact that the greater confrontation with refutational-different defensive arguments in the passive rather than the active condition is of little defensive use, since the refutations are of counterarguments not contained in the subsequent attacks. In the supportive passive defense, however, the material is relevant to warding off the subsequent attack. McGuire states the argument as follows:

The reason for the reversal of the interaction prediction when we turn from the refutational-same to refutational-different defense involves the second, detrimental mechanism produced by the active participation requirement, namely, the fact that the person participates so poorly that he is exposed to very little defensive material in the active participation as compared to the passive reception condition. As pointed out above, he participates poorly in the supportive defense but even more poorly in the refutational defense and hence, under the active participation condition, gets exposed to very little material as compared with the passive reception condition, where he reads a carefully prepared defensive essay. But in the case of the refutational-different defense this greater exposure in the passive condition is of very little use since he is receiving refutations of counterarguments different from those with which he will actually be attacked later. Hence, with the refutational-different defense it makes little difference whether he is in the active or passive condition as far as the beneficial mechanism is concerned. In either case, he receives very little material that is useful in enabling him to handle the specific counterarguments with which he will actually be attacked: in the active condition, because he is unable to formulate refutational material; in the passive, because the carefully formulated material which he does receive refutes the "wrong" counterarguments. In the supportive defense, on the other hand, the carefully formulated essay presented in the passive condition does give supportive arguments for the right truism, which arguments are much less adequately formulated by the believer himself in the active defense condition. Hence, the beneficial mechanism involved in the passive reception condition will be much more operative with the supportive than the refutational material, making for the predicted interaction effect. (1962a, p. 4/–10)

McGuire and Papageorgis (*1961*) report evidence supporting the hypothesized greater superiority of passive over active defenses in the case of refutational-same defenses than in the case of supportive defenses. The experimental procedure for this study has been described in detail in a previous section. The procedure involved two sessions 48 hours apart. In the first session the subjects received a passive (reading) defense on one truism and an active (writing) defense on another. In the second session each subject read two attacks against the previously defended truisms, an attack against a previously undefended truism (attack-only control), and no attack against a fourth truism (neither-attack-nor-defense control). The attacks utilized the same arguments that were refuted in the refutational defenses.

The results are presented in Table 12–1. The main order effect of the superiority of passive over active defenses is significant and the greater superiority of passive over active defenses in the case of refutational-same defenses than in the case of supportive defenses is of borderline significance ($p < .08$).[5] The results, then, tend to be supportive of McGuire and Papageorgis' expectations.

McGuire (*1962a*) reports evidence relating to both the hypothesized main effect and the two interactions. The experiment was carried out in a single session, and each subject served in four different conditions. The conditions were: a passive (reading and underlining) defense followed by an attack, an active (writing from outline) defense followed by an attack, an attack without a prior defense, and neither a defense nor an attack. Four different truisms were systematically rotated among the four conditions. For different subjects the defenses were either both supportive, both refutational-same or both refutational-different.

The results agree with all three hypotheses. First, the main order passive-active effect was significant. The passive defenses conferred more resistance than the active ones. As expected, though, this main order effect was qualified by the two hypothesized interactions. The superiority of the passive over the active defenses was greater for the refutational-same defenses than for the supportive defenses and for supportive defenses than for the refutational-different defenses.

Comment. The research discussed in this section is remarkably supportive of the hypotheses. One cannot help but be impressed with McGuire's ability to intuit and empirically support nonobvious predictions.

One, however, can raise a question concerning the extent to which the hypotheses concerning active and passive defenses follow from the biological analogy of inoculation theory. There is no such thing as an active or passive immunization. Since active defenses are assumed to be more threatening than passive ones, McGuire studied the differential effects of active and passive defenses in order to gain information concerning the efficacy of threat. This, however, led to the introduction of assumptions that are not obviously related to the biological analogy. One such assumption has to do with the beneficial effect of being involved in the relevant material. McGuire uses this notion to help explain why passive supportive and refutational-same defenses are superior to active supportive and refutational-same defenses and to help explain why the superiority of passive refutational-different defenses over active refutational-different defenses is less than the superiority of passive supportive defenses over active supportive defenses. It is unclear in what way this assumption is related to the biological analogy. In addition to the assumption that being exposed to the relevant material is beneficial, McGuire also implicitly makes assumptions regarding the relative amount of effect produced by the practice deficit, the motivation to bolster defenses, and being exposed to relevant material. It is therefore legitimate

[5] McGuire (1962a, 1964) states that this effect is significant at the .05 level.

to ask to what extent McGuire is testing one coherent theory as opposed to a miscellaneous collection of explicit and implicit assumptions.

Sequential and Combinational Effects

McGuire has developed inoculation theory so that it has implications concerning various sequences and combinations of defenses. This development has focused both on sequences and combinations of supportive and refutational defenses and on sequences and combinations of active and passive defenses. Each of these matters will be considered in turn.

McGuire has two hypotheses concerning combinations of supportive and refutational passive defenses. The first hypothesis is that supportive and refutational defenses combined are significantly more effective than either alone. This hypothesis is based on the following considerations. The refutational defenses (particularly the refutational-different defense) do not provide the individual with any useful belief bolstering material. The defenses motivate the individual to acquire such belief bolstering material, but due to lack of practice this material is not easily come by. Theoretically, if sufficient time is allowed, the individual will accumulate such material from his environment; however, in a short time interval this is not possible. Therefore if the experimenter provides the individual with supportive material along with the refutational defense, it is understandable why the double defense is immediately superior to the refutational-only defense. The double defense supplies both the motivation to acquire the belief bolstering or supportive material and the supportive defense. The supportive defense by itself, of course, is not very effective because the individual is not motivated to pay attention to or absorb the material. The refutational defense thus has something that the supportive defense lacks and the supportive defense something that the refutational defense lacks. The combination of defenses therefore should be more effective than either defense alone.

McGuire's second combinational hypothesis is that the superiority of the double defense over the refutational-only defense is greater for refutational-different defenses than for refutational-same defenses. This hypothesized interaction is based on the fact that the refutational-same defenses contain some relevant belief bolstering material while the refutational-different defenses do not. Therefore, the supportive defense has less to add to the refutational-same defense than to the refutational-different defense.

Four sequence hypotheses regarding passive defenses were formulated. The first is that within the double defense combination the supportive-then-refutational sequence is less effective than the refutational-then-supportive sequence. This is because the latter sequence first provides the motivation to assimilate the belief bolstering material and then the material to be assimilated. The other three sequence hypotheses all were concerned with the effectiveness of an immunization sequence, defense-then-attack, versus a restoration sequence, attack-then-defense. One hypothesis is a main effect prediction that the restoration sequence will be more effective than the immunization sequence. This prediction is based on the fact that a person is more motivated to assimilate the belief bolstering material if it follows rather than precedes the attack. Another sequence hypothesis is that the superiority of restoration over immunization is less with refutational than with supportive defenses. This is because an immunization sequence involving refutational defenses supplies an individual with the motivation to assimilate the defensive material even before the attack while this is not the case with an immunization sequence involving supportive defenses. Finally, there is a predicted sequence interaction within the double defense condition. This prediction is that the superiority of restoration over immunization will be less with the refutational-then-supportive sequence than with the supportive-then-refutational sequence. This, once again, is because the refutational-then-supportive sequence supplies a motivating threat even when it occurs before the attack.

The above hypotheses relate entirely to passive defenses. With regard to both active and passive defenses McGuire has one combinational and one sequential hypothesis. The combinational hypothesis is that double (active plus passive) refutational-same defenses will produce more resistance than either a single active or passive defense but that the single active or passive defense will be at least as effective as the double (active plus passive) refutational-different defense. In the language of analysis of variance this is a predicted interaction between the single versus double refutation variable and the refutational-same versus refutational-different variable. The hypothesis is based on two main assumptions. The first assumption is that the single defense provides more or as much motivation-inducing threat as the double defense and the double defense provides more reassuring, belief bolstering material than the single defense. The second assumption is that the reassuring, belief bolstering material will be most useful in combating the same counterarguments and that the motivation inducing threat will be most useful in combating different counterarguments. These assumptions allow for the deduction that the double refutational-same defense will produce more resistance than the single defense but that the single defense will be at least as effective as the double refutational-different defense.

McGuire's sequential hypothesis has to do with the double defense (active and passive) condition. He hypothesizes that the passive-active sequence of refutational-same defenses is superior while the active-passive sequence of refutational-different defenses is superior. McGuire believes that the passive defenses are particularly strong in supplying useful defensive material or reassurance and the active defenses particularly strong in supplying motivation. When the defenses occur in a passive-active sequence, however, the individual is able to practice with the previously encountered reassuring material and consequently gain the most total reassurance. Thus the passive-active sequence should be the most effective in combating attacks utilizing the same counterarguments. The active part of the active-passive sequence is largely wasted as far as supplying further reassurance is concerned. With regard to combating attacks utilizing different counterarguments, however, the active-passive sequence is considered superior. The reason for this is simply that the active-passive sequence theoretically does the best job of demonstrating that previously formidable sounding arguments can be refuted. Supposedly it is this factor rather than the presence of reassurance that is important in combating attacks utilizing different counterarguments. McGuire states the argument as follows:

The active-then-passive sequence provides the subject with a threat-then-reassurance experience with regard to his belief which should be particularly useful in immunizing him against later attack by strong forms of different counterarguments. The previously threatened and reassured believer can say to himself regarding the new counterarguments: "Those earlier ones also looked pretty formidable when first I heard of them, but turned out to be easily punctured in that later essay; these too are probably full of holes that one could pick out if he had time to really study them." (1962a, p. 5/−4)

McGuire (1961b) supported his combinational but not his sequential hypotheses relating to passive defenses. The experiment was conducted in one 2-hour session. Besides the usual attack-only and neither-defense-nor-attack control conditions, there was an immunization condition in which the defenses preceded the attacks and a restoration condition in which the defenses followed the attacks. There were seven types of defenses, including three single defenses and four double defenses. The single defenses were supportive, refutational-same, and refutation-different, and the double defenses were supportive-then-refutational-same, supportive-then-refutational-different, refutational-same-then-supportive, and refutational-different-then-supportive. Each subject served in four different conditions, every condition involving a different truism. The four truisms were systematically rotated among conditions.[6]

The results in the control conditions indicated that the manipulations were successful. The mean belief in the attack-only condition

---

[6] The various control and experimentation conditions were combined in a complex fashion. Suffice it to say that any one variable involved a pure between or a pure within error term.

(9.94) is significantly less than the mean belief in the neither-attack-nor-defense condition (12.44). Furthermore, the mean for all of the defense and attack conditions (11.32) is significantly lower than the mean for the neither-attack-nor-defense condition and significantly higher than the mean for the attack-only condition. The results with regard to the predicted sequence effects are not at all confirmatory. Both the immunization and restoration sequences produced significant reduction in the effects of the attacks but differ only minimally from each other in all seven of the defensive conditions. Furthermore, within the double defense condition there is no significant difference between the supportive-then-refutational sequence and the refutational-then-supportive sequence.

The results with regard to the predicted combinational effects are more encouraging. As hypothesized, the supportive and refutational defenses combined are significantly more effective than either alone. And, furthermore, the superiority of the double defense over the refutational-only defense is greater for refutational-different defenses than for refutational-same defenses.

While the confirmation of the combinational predictions is gratifying, McGuire is somewhat embarrassed by the failure of the sequential predictions. This is the first experiment that has failed to support the bulk of McGuire's predictions.

McGuire (1961a) presents evidence supporting his hypothesis concerning combinations of active and passive refutational defenses but not his hypothesis concerning sequences of active and passive refutational defenses. The experiment was conducted in two sessions 48 hours apart. All of the attacks occurred in the second session. Four types of defenses were employed: active, passive, active-passive, and passive-active. Each of these defenses could be followed by no-attack, attack with the same counterarguments, or attack with different counterarguments, thus giving 12 defensive conditions. In addition, there were two control conditions: attack-only and neither-attack-nor-defense. Each subject served in four of the 14 conditions, a different truism being used in each of his conditions. The truisms were systematically rotated among the four conditions for different groups of subjects.[7]

This experiment was concerned entirely with refutational defenses; there were no supportive defenses. In the active defensive condition the subjects were presented with two counterarguments and asked to refute each of them; in the passive condition the subjects were presented with already prepared refutations of the same two counterarguments and asked to select and underline the crucial sentence in each paragraph. In the double, or active plus passive, defense conditions the same two counterarguments were used in both the active and passive parts.

[7] McGuire does not state which of the manipulations involved between-subject comparisons and which within-subject comparisons.

As usual the mean in the attack-only condition is significantly lower than the mean in the neither-attack-nor-defense condition, and the mean for all of the defensive conditions is intermediate to and differs significantly from these two control means. Within the single defense condition it was found that passive refutational-same defenses were superior to active refutational-same defenses but that passive refutational-different defenses were inferior to active refutational-different defenses. This is a replication of a previous finding which McGuire earlier predicted.

The results with regard to the combinational prediction support McGuire's expectations. The double (active plus passive) defense was superior to the single (active or passive) defense only when the refuted counterarguments were the same ones that were contained in the attacks. In the refutational-different conditions single and double defenses were practically identical in their effectiveness. The sequential prediction, however, was not supported. The passive-active and active-passive sequences were practically identical for both refutational-same and refutational-different defenses.

Tannenbaum, Macaulay, and Norris (1966) and *Tannenbaum and Norris (1965)*, in research described in more detail in a later section, report that immunization sequences of passive defenses were more effective in conferring resistance to attacks than were restoration sequences. Furthermore, Tannenbaum (in press) briefly reports that in a number of additional studies the results have consistently favored immunization over restoration, although not always significantly. These results are exactly opposite to McGuire's theoretical expectations.

Comment. The research described in this section has consistently supported the combinational but not the sequential predictions. In discussing the failure of his sequential predictions in the 1961b study, McGuire (1962a) argues that the theory is probably correct, the deductions of the sequential hypotheses valid, but the manipulation of sequence inadequate. Allowing a longer time interval between the defensive messages would possibly allow for the first one to become more obviously "set." However, in view of the fact that Tannenbaum, Macaulay, and Norris (1966) had a 1-week interval between the defensive messages this hypothesis does not appear too plausible. It thus seems likely that some revision either of the sequential deductions or more basically of inoculation theory itself will be necessary.

Temporal Effects

McGuire (1962a, 1964) has elaborated inoculation theory so that it has implications concerning the persistence of induced resistance to persuasion over time. This elaboration begins by focusing upon the two postulated mechanisms by which defenses induce resistance: the threatening component which supplies the needed motivation to obtain or assimilate belief bolstering material and the belief bolstering material contained in the defense itself. McGuire assumes that the threatening mechanism manifests a nonmonotonic (rising and then falling) trend over time. For some time after receiving the threat the individual continues to accumulate belief bolstering information, thus producing increasing resistance to persuasion. After a while, however, as the induced motivation begins to fall off, the individual ceases to accumulate belief bolstering material. McGuire points out that this rising and then falling curve is similar to that for the typical biological inoculation. The second mechanism, the actual communication of the belief bolstering material, is assumed to drop off over time like the ordinary forgetting curve.

McGuire next argues that different defenses involve the two above mechanisms to different extents and thus theoretically manifest different persistence effects. All types of active defenses, whether supportive refutational-same or refutational-different, depend primarily upon the threatening component and therefore manifest nonmonotonic persistence effects over time. This means that the resistance conferred by active defenses first increases and then decreases. The situation with regard to passive defenses is somewhat more complicated. Passive supportive defenses confer resistance solely on the basis of the second mechanism, the direct communication of belief bolstering material, and therefore show monotonic persistence effects; i.e., the persistence of resistance effects drops regularly over time. Passive refutational-different defenses, on the other hand, depend mainly on the threatening mechanism and therefore manifest the same nonmonotonic persistence effects as do the active defenses. Passive refutational-same defenses depend upon both mechanisms and thus show a persistence effect that is a composite of the nonmonotonic and monotonic trends. Initially the persistence effect is relatively steady as the nonmonotonic trend increases and the monotonic trend decreases. After a while, however, the persistence effect drops off markedly as the nonmonotonic trend turns downward with the monotonic trend.

McGuire has no suggestions with regard to the theoretically important temporal intervals. In designing his tests of the above formulation he relied upon information gained from the previously discussed research in which the time intervals between defenses and attacks were varied from experiment to experiment.

McGuire (*1962b*) tested his hypotheses with regard to the persistence of resistance conferred by passive defenses. The experiment was conducted in two sessions that were either 2 or 7 days apart. The design included four blocks of subjects. Subjects in the first block received four refutational defenses, two in the first session 2 days before the attacks and two in the second session immediately before the attacks. In each session one defense was refutational-same and one refutational-different. Subjects in the second block received the same treatment as those in the first block except that the time between sessions was 7 days instead of 2 days. Subjects in the third block received two supportive defenses, one in the first session 2 days before the attack and one in the second session immediately before the attack. These subjects also provided attack-only and neither-attack-nor-defense controls on two other truisms. Finally, the fourth block of subjects was treated identically with the third except for the fact that the time interval between sessions was 7 days instead of 2 days. Four truisms were systematically rotated among the subjects within each of the four blocks.

The results of the experiment are presented in Table 12–4.

TABLE 12–4. *Persistence of the Resistance to Persuasion Conferred by Three Types of Prior Belief Defense* [a]

| | Type of Defense Preceding Attack | | |
Interval Between Defense and Attack	Supportive Defense	Refutational- Same Defense	Refutational- Different Defense
Immediate	9.71	11.36	10.41
Two days	8.51	11.08	11.45
Seven days	8.82	9.49	9.68

[a] Neither-defense-nor-attack = 11.74; attack-only = 8.49.
SOURCE: Adapted from McGuire, 1962b, p. 245.

The mean belief in the attack-only condition (8.49) is significantly less than the mean belief in the neither-attack-nor-defense condition (11.74). The mean belief for the three defensive conditions (10.17) is significantly greater than the mean for the attack-only condition and significantly greater than the mean for the neither-attack-nor-defense condition.

As predicted, the mean belief for the supportive defenses dropped off significantly over time. The mean beliefs in the 2- and 7-day interval conditions (8.51 and 8.82, respectively) are very near the mean for the attack-only control condition (8.49). In the refutational-same condition, on the other hand, the drop-off was much slower, although still significant. The interaction between time (immediate versus 2 days) and defense (supportive versus refutational-same) is significant. The predicted nonmonotonic trend for the refutational-different defense was also obtained. The rise in mean belief from immediate to 2 days is significant as well as the interaction between time (immediate versus 2 days) and defense (refutational-same versus refutational-different). The results, in general, give striking confirmation to all of McGuire's expectations regarding the persistence of passively conferred defenses.

McGuire (1962a) reports that in this experiment 5 of the 160 subjects stated in a postquestionnaire that the experiment had to do with influence; However, since these subjects did not appear any different from the nonsuspicious ones they were kept in the analysis.

McGuire (1962a, 1964) describes a study which compared the relative persistence of actively and passively conferred defenses. The experiment was conducted in two sessions 1 week apart. In the first session all subjects received an active (essaywriting) defense of one truism and a passive (reading) defense of another. In the second session the subject received active and passive defenses of two additional truisms followed by attacks against all four of the previously defended truisms. For one-third of the subjects the defenses were all supportive, for one-third they were all refutational-same, and for one-third they were all refutational-different. There were no attack-only or neither-attack-nor-defense control conditions. The time between defenses and attacks was either immediate or 1 week.

TABLE 12–5.   Persistence of the Resistance to Persuasion Conferred
by Active and Passive Defenses

Type of Defensive Material	Active Defense		Passive Defense		All Four Combined
	Imme-diate Attack	Attack One Week Later	Imme-diate Attack	Attack One Week Later	
Supportive	8.30	9.89	9.72	9.47	9.34
Refutational-same	9.61	10.13	12.12	10.42	10.57
Refutational-different	9.77	9.98	9.61	9.99	9.84
All three combined	9.22	10.00	10.48	9.96	9.91

SOURCE: Adapted from McGuire, 1964, p. 226.

The results of the experiment are presented in Table 12–5. As predicted, all three of the active defenses increased in resistance conferral over time. The effect for all of the active defenses combined is significant. All three of the passive defenses combined show a drop-off over time that is significant by one-tailed test. However, as expected, it is the supportive and refutational-same defenses which are mainly responsible for this overall decline. The passive refutational-different defense in fact shows a slight increase over time (in the previous experiment this effect was found to peak at 2 days). The interaction produced by the overall decrease in the passive defenses and the overall increase in the active defenses is highly significant. In general, the results are in accord with McGuire's expectations.

Comment.   This research on persistence of conferred resistance provides convincing support for McGuire's formulation of inoculation theory.

The fact that the active defenses and the passive refutational-different defenses actually increased in effectiveness over time is particularly interesting. Perhaps there really is something to this concept of threat induced motivation to build up defenses. The evidence presented in this section is at least highly suggestive that such a process is genuine.

Defensive Mechanisms

Inoculation theory is most directly concerned with the production of immunity to attacking arguments through the creation of threat-produced defenses. The individual theoretically reacts to the threatening inoculations through increased motivation to gain practice in defending beliefs previously thought unassailable. Eventually this process results in the accumulation of a store of belief bolstering arguments.

Beyond these defense alerting and defense producing mechanisms, however, it is entirely possible that other mechanisms result in the creation of defenses. This section will be devoted to a discussion of research which has illuminated various defensive mechanisms other than the threat reaction mechanism emphasized by inoculation theory.

Tannenbaum, Macaulay, and Norris (1966) have used congruity theory concepts to generate four defensive mechanisms. According to congruity theory, if a favorable source makes a negative assertion about a favorable concept then incongruity results. As Tannenbaum, Macaulay, and Norris interpret the theory, any of four defensive mechanisms may be used to reduce the incongruity or make the concept more invulnerable to change. The mechanisms are denial, source attack, refutation, and concept boost. Denial consists of severing the cognitive link between the source and concept. By denying that the source has made a negative assertion regarding the favorable concept, incongruity is reduced. Source attack consists of decreased evaluation of the source. If the source which made the negative assertion is no longer regarded favorably, incongruity is reduced. Refutation consists of invalidating the assertion. The weaker the assertion or argument attacking the favorable concept the less the incongruity.[8] Finally, concept boost consists of strengthening the attitude toward the concept. If attitude toward the favorable source is strengthened, then the incongruity is less likely to be reduced through decreased evaluation of the concept. According to congruity theory more intense or highly polarized attitudes are less likely to change.

Tannenbaum, Macaulay, and Norris (1966) designed an experiment which tested the efficacy of the four mechanisms or strategies in con-

[8] In the original formulation of congruity theory Osgood and Tannenbaum (1955) recognized such a factor by utilizing an "assertion constant" and by stating that an adequate theory should include an intensity of assertion parameter.

ferring resistance to attacking arguments. The attacking arguments dealt, for different subjects, with attitudes toward one of three public health issues (toothbrushing, regular medical checkups, and X-ray tuberculosis examinations) and were attributed to the United States Public Health Service (USPHS). Each of the defensive mechanisms was represented by a different defensive treatment. The denial treatment took the form of a press release in which the USPHS denied any connection with recent statements which had been "erroneously" attributed to it. The source attack treatment took the form of an Associated Press news story regarding a report by an investigating committee of medical practitioners. The report described USPHS as "incompetently staffed, riddled with political appointees, and generally not serving the public interest." The refutational treatment took the form of a report by either the American Medical Association or the American Dental Association, depending upon the issue involved. The report, which contained the materials from McGuire's refutational defense, offered a point by point rebuttal of the attacking arguments. Finally, the concept boost treatment took the form of a report by either the American Medical Association or the American Dental Association and contained the materials from McGuire's supportive defense. Some subjects received the messages in an immunization order (defense then attack) and some in a restoration order (attack then defense), but the interval between messages was 1 week for all experimental subjects. There were also attack-only and neither-attack-nor-defense control groups.

An analysis of covariance was used to adjust posttest scores on the basis of pretest scores. The adjusted means in each of the conditions are presented in Table 12–6.

TABLE 12–6. Adjusted Mean Beliefs for Different
Experimental and Control Conditions

Sequence	Denial	Source Attack	Refuta- tion	Concept Boost
Control	11.77	11.86	11.70	11.22
Immunization	9.06	10.62	12.46	10.85
Restoration	9.96	8.54	10.45	
Attack-only	8.56	8.30	8.82	8.39

SOURCE: Tannenbaum, Macaulay, and Norris, 1966, p. 235.

In the denial condition neither the immunization nor restoration sequences differ significantly from the attack-only control, but in the source attack condition the immunization, but not the restoration, sequence produced significant resistance to the attacks. The refutational condition produced significant resistance in both sequences and the concept boost condition produced significant resistance in the only sequence tested, immunization. In all treatment conditions which contained the two sequences, immunization was found to be somewhat more effective in conferring resistance than was restoration. This significant effect, however, is totally due to the results in the source attack and refutational conditions.

In general, the results seem to indicate that the refutational and concept boost mechanisms are more effective than are the denial and source attack mechanisms. Tannenbaum, Macaulay, and Norris point out, however, that the messages used to evoke these various mechanisms differ in numerous ways (length, format, source, etc.) so that any conclusions based on the differences between treatment conditions would of necessity be tentative. It is nonetheless of interest that the concept boost (supportive) and particularly the refutational treatments produced the greatest amounts of resistance. These are the two treatments which McGuire repeatedly used in his research. McGuire, however, interprets the refutational treatment as evoking threat-produced mechanisms. Tannenbaum, Macaulay, and Norris, on the other hand, interpret the refutational treatment as directly weakening the assertion or attacking arguments. It is, of course, not impossible that the refutation treatment evokes both types of defensive mechanisms.

Tannenbaum and Norris (1965) report a study which investigated the congruity theory implication that refutation and source attack are independent mechanisms of resistance conferral. If refutation and source attack are independent mechanisms then the resistance conferred by both mechanisms together should be equal to that conferred by both mechanisms separately. In addition to the usual attack-only and neither-attack-nor-defense controls, the experiment involved four single defense conditions and four double defense conditions. The single defense conditions were source attack in the restoration sequence (AS), source attack in the immunization sequence (SA), refutation in the restoration sequence (AR), and refutation in the immunization sequence (RA). The four double defense conditions were either massed (ASR, SRA) or distributed (RAS, SAR). All of the messages dealt with one issue, annual chest X rays for the detection of TB. The attack was attributed to a member of the Columbia University medical faculty, "Dr. William J. McGuire," and cited four arguments against the obtaining of annual chest X rays. The source attack was a news story reporting that the Columbia University medical faculty had recommended that Dr. McGuire be fired because of his "unethical and unprofessional behavior" in making various statements regarding public health practices. The refutational message countered each of the four arguments raised in the attack. Following exposure to all messages within a single session, belief was measured on a 15-point agree-disagree scale.

The results are presented in Table 12–7. All four of the single defenses produced effects intermediate to those in the attack-only control (4.70) and neither-attack-nor-defense control (13.75). An analysis of variance for the four single defense conditions revealed that the refutational defenses were superior to the source attack defenses. Both defenses

TABLE 12–7. Mean Beliefs for the Single Defense and
Combined Defense Conditions [a]

Single	AS	SA	AR	RA
	7.30	8.00	9.40	10.60
Combined	ASR	SAR	RAS	SRA
	11.30	11.50	12.10	13.20

[a] Neither-attack-nor-defense $= 13.75$; attack-only $= 4.70$.

SOURCE: Adapted from Tannenbaum and Norris, 1965, pp. 151–152, with permission of the American Sociological Association.

were somewhat more superior in the immunization than in the restoration sequence, but the effect is not significant. Except for the significant effect of the source attack in the restoration sequence, these results agree with those of Tannenbaum, Macaulay, and Norris (1966).

Each of the double defenses is significantly greater than the attack-only control and, except for the SRA condition, significantly less than the neither-attack-nor-defense control. Analysis of just the four double defense conditions revealed that refutation in the immunization sequence (SRA+RAS) was superior to refutation in the restoration sequence (ASR+SAR) in conferring resistance to persuasion. The similar immunization-restoration difference for the source attack defense is not significant. Considering the data for both double and single defenses, there is a significantly greater effect in the immunization sequence (SA+RA+SRA) than in the restoration sequence (AS+AR+ASR).

In order to check into the assumption that the double defenses represent the additive effects of the single defenses three tests were used. First, it was found that in every case the double defenses were significantly greater than either of the component single defenses (e.g., SRA versus SA and SRA versus RA). Second, it was found that the double defenses did not deviate significantly from expectations based on the simple addition of the relevant component defenses. The effect of each single defense was calculated on the basis of the difference between the particular single defense and the attack-only control relative to the total difference between the attack-only control and the neither-attack-nor-defense control. And third, it was found that there was no significant interaction between the single defenses as they were combined in any of the four double defenses. The interactions were obtained by constructing 2×2 analyses of variance in which, for example, SRA and the attack-only control represented one diagonal, and SA and RA represented the other. As Tannenbaum and Norris point out, none of these three tests proves the additivity hypothesis, but they nonetheless do provide "supportive evidence."

Macaulay (1965) reports evidence indicating that the denial and refutational mechanisms or strategies have additive effects. In addition to the attack-only and neither-attack-nor-defense control conditions there were four single defense conditions (AR, RA, DA, AD) and two double defense conditions (DRA, ADR). Three of the defense conditions were in an immunization sequence (RA, DA, DRA) and three in a restoration sequence (AR, AD, ADR). The denial treatment, unlike Tannenbaum, Macaulay, and Norris (1966), had the source both disclaiming any connection with the attacking arguments and supporting the health practice in question (annual chest X rays). In the double defense conditions the refutation and denial were combined in the same communication and, furthermore, the communication was attributed to the same source as the attack.

An after-only assessment of belief indicated that all of the defenses, including the single denial defenses, conferred significant resistance to persuasion. Tannenbaum, Macaulay, and Norris (1966) failed to find a significant conferral of resistance for their simpler denial treatment. Macaulay did find, however, that the denial defenses conferred less resistance than the other defenses. The results for all three tests of the additivity hypothesis yielded positive results. The double defenses conferred significantly more resistance than either of their component single defenses; the combined defenses did not deviate significantly from the resistance predicted by adding the effects of the two relevant single defenses; and the single defenses did not significantly interact when combined in the double defense.

In addition to assessing belief Macaulay also included some assessments of interest in receiving more information regarding chest X rays, certainty of belief in the advisability of obtaining annual chest X rays, and credibility of the attack. Rating-scale responses revealed essentially no difference among groups for either the interest or certainty assessments. According to inoculation theory the refutational defense operates by stimulating the person to acquire belief bolstering material. There is thus some reason for supposing that the subjects in the refutational condition might have shown more uncertainty regarding their beliefs and more interest in receiving additional information regarding chest X rays. In accordance with the assertion-weakening assumption, however, Macaulay did find that the attack was rated as less credible in the refutational conditions than in all other conditions.

Tannenbaum (*in press*) obtained evidence indicating that some defense combinations (source attack with concept boost and denial with concept boost) have additive effects and some (refutation with concept boost and denial with source attack) do not. The study dealt solely with the X-ray issue and all of the messages occurred in an immunization sequence. Tannenbaum maintains that the source attack and concept boost treatments should have additive effects because they evoke independent mechanisms. Similar reasoning applies to the denial and concept boost mechanisms. However, due to the fact that the denial treatment in the present experiment involved the source's denying responsibility for the attacks as well as expressing agreement with the practice of obtaining X rays, the situation is somewhat ambiguous. Tannenbaum points out that it is quite reasonable to suppose that the source's expression of agreement has much the same effect as the supportive arguments contained in the concept boost message. With regard to the combinations of refutation with concept boost and denial with source attack, Tannenbaum argues that additivity definitely should not obtain. In refuting the attacking arguments the refutational message makes assertions favorable to the concept and thus implicitly contains some concept-boosting assertions. The denial and source attack strategies have contrary or negating effects. The source attack message attempts to disparage or derogate the source, and the source of the denial message denies responsibility for the attack. If, however, the source is regarded unfavorably because of the source attack, then his denial is not as likely to be taken seriously.

The results, by and large, agree with Tannenbaum's theoretical statement. The double source attack and concept boost defense had an effect greater than that of either single defense, and the single defenses did not interact when joined in the double defense. No mention was made either of the third test for additivity or of the results for attack-only and neither-attack-nor-defense controls. The double denial and concept boost defense also had an effect greater than that of either single defense, and there was a suggestion of an interaction ($p = .15$) between the single defenses. The double refutational and concept boost defense was significantly superior to the concept boost defense but not significantly different from the effect produced by the refutational defense. A departure from additivity is further indicated by a significant interaction between the single defenses. Finally, the double denial and source attack defense produced an effect significantly less than that produced by the source attack defense and nonsignificantly less than that produced by the denial defense.

McGuire (1961b) obtained some previously described results which are consistent with Tannenbaum's findings regarding the double refutational and concept boost (supportive) defense. McGuire found a significant main effect indicating that the double refutational (same or different) plus supportive defense was significantly superior to refutational-only defense and a qualifying interaction indicating that the above difference was only apparent for the refutational-different defense. For the refutational-same defense, which is comparable to Tannenbaum's refutational defense, the double refutational and supportive defense was not superior to the refutational-only defense.

Tannenbaum (*in press*) also reports some evidence bearing on the assertion weakening interpretation of the refutational defense. The experiment involved two independent variables: favorability-unfavorability of the attacking source ("Dr. John A. Schmidt, Professor of Clinical Medicine of Johns Hopkins Medical School" or a "Truth and Health" magazine distributed by "health food stores") and presence-absence of an immunizing refutation attributed to a favorable source ("Dr. William J. McGuire"). The messages dealt with one issue, the advisability of obtaining annual chest X rays.

After-scores corrected by analysis of covariance for the before-variance revealed significant effects for both the favorability of the attacking source and the presence or absence of the refutation. (Mean changes for the four conditions were $A+ = -6.00$, $A- = -3.76$, $R+A+ = -1.48$, $R+A- = +.92$.) Tannenbaum interprets the unfavorable source as weakening the attack or assertion just as the refutation weakens the attack or assertion. Thus he reasoned that if the $A-$ condition had essentially the same effect as the $R+A+$ condition, this would constitute support for the postulated assertion weakening mechanism. As a matter of fact, however, the $R+A+$ condition produced significantly greater reduction in persuasion than did the $A-$ condition. Tannenbaum interprets this difference as possibly indicating that the $R+A+$ condition contained something beyond an assertion weakening mechanism—perhaps the threat arousing and defense producing mechanisms postulated by inoculation theory. Such reasoning is hazardous, however, due to the fact that there is no way of knowing if the $A-$ and $R+A+$ conditions were exactly equated in terms of assertion weakening efficacy. There is also a problem regarding the extent to which the $A-$ and $R+A+$ conditions were equated in terms of concept boosting efficacy. In connection with his combinational study Tannenbaum (in press) argues that the refutational defense has concept boosting effects, and, at least under some circumstances, a negative assertion by an unfavorable source theoretically produces increased valuation of the concept.

Manis and Blake (*1963*) tested the hypothesis that relative to immunized subjects attack-only control subjects attempt to maintain their initial attitudes by displacing the perceived position of the attack toward their own positions (assimilation). Each subject served in three conditions: attack-only, refutation-same, and refutation-different. The refutational immunizations were given in an initial session and the attacks 1 week later in a second session. Both the refutations and attacks were purportedly written by reputable physicians associated with major medical centers. Three issues (penicillin, daily toothbrushing, annual physical checkups) were systematically rotated among the three conditions so that for any given subject the attack-only condition involved one issue, the refutation-same condition a second issue, and the refutation-different condition a third issue. Following the attacks the subjects rated each communicator's probable position on the relevant issue and their own positions on the same issues. The results for the belief or opinion data indicated that both immunization conditions were approximately equal in conferring significant resistance to persuasion. While this finding is in good agreement with inoculation theory, the results for the judgment data are not in accord with Manis and Blake's initial hypothesis. Relative to the attack-only condition the two refutation conditions, and particularly the refutation-same condition, assimilated the attacks in the pro direction. This finding is exactly opposite to prediction.

In a second experiment Manis and Blake replicated the initial experiment with the addition of an active as well as a passive immunization condition. The results for the passive condition, in general, replicated the results of the first experiment. The results for the active condition showed no significant judgment distortion and a nonsignificant tendency for refutation to confer some resistance to the attacks. The judgment data for the first experiment and the similar passive condition in the second experiment both showed a tendency for the conditions to be ranked refutational-same, refutational-different, and attack-only in terms of the attacking communicators' perceived favorability toward the health issues. This significant ranking was evident even when the subjects' attitudes were held constant.

Manis and Blake interpret this general pattern of results as indicating that the subjects in the passive immunization conditions acted so as to minimize the perceived discrepancy between the prestigious communicators associated with the attacks and the prestigious communicators associated with the refutations. This tendency would produce the assimilation trend found in both experiments and would not require mediation by the subjects' own attitudes. Furthermore, the lack of any judgmental effect in the active condition of the second experiment can be attributed to the fact that the refutations were not associated with prestigious communicators.

Up to this point we have encountered reference to four defensive mechanisms which are theoretically evoked or supplied by refutational messages. Two of these mechanisms flow from inoculation theory (defense alerting, defense producing), and two flow from congruity theory (assertion weakening, concept boost). Manis and Blake now offer a fifth mechanism, perceptual defense (reduced perceived discrepancy between attacks and refutations). It is apparent, however, that Manis and Blake's perceptual defense mechanism is not specific to just refutational defenses but refers to any situation in which attacks and defenses, of whatever type, are attributed to prestigious sources.

Comment. The research described in this section has made it quite apparent that the process of defensive resistance to persuasion is quite complex. There are apparently many defensive mechanisms other than the ones emphasized by inoculation theory. Denial, source attack, assertion weakening, concept boost, and reduced perceived discrepancy between attacks and refutations may conceivably all be important defensive mechanisms, although the evidence for some mechanisms (e.g., denial in its unadulterated form) is not as compelling as it is for others. As Tannenbaum (in press) points out, however, the existence of additional mechanisms or processes does not mean that inoculation theory is incorrect; the threat reacting and defense producing mechanisms of inoculation theory are not necessarily incompatible with other mechanisms. Inoculation theory may simply prove to be part of a larger and more complex picture.

EVALUATION

It is a credit to McGuire's creativity that while other people were developing theories directly concerned with how to produce attitude change, he was the first to develop a theory concerned with how to produce resistance to attitude change. Although other theories do have implications concerning resistance to persuasion, inoculation theory was the first major formulation that focused directly on the problem.

McGuire's development and testing of inoculation theory is in many ways extremely impressive. He and his associates present experiment after experiment which replicate and extend the basic inoculation theory concepts. One cannot help but be impressed by McGuire's ability to intuit and support unlikely sounding hypotheses.

From an internal consistency point of view the major reservation concerning inoculation theory is the previously expressed one concerning the extent to which the basic biological analogy is forsaken in the development of additional predictions. The theory starts with the assumption that exposure to weakened counterarguments, like exposure to weakened virus, will inoculate the individual against subsequent stronger counterarguments. Understandably, however, McGuire is not content with this simple analogy alone, but attempts to formulate some purely psychological principles which explain why exposure to weakened counterarguments should produce resistance to persuasion. These principles are based on the concepts of motivation and practice. The weakened counterarguments pose a threat that motivates the individual to develop bolstering arguments for his somewhat weakened beliefs. This leads to the obtaining of needed practice in the development of bolstering counterarguments. So far so good. We have the basic analogy and the postulated principles that explain why the analogy is an appropriate one. Apparently, in thinking about his persuasive materials, however, McGuire was led to formulate additional principles which neither follow from the basic analogy nor help to explain the utility of the analogy. Most of these principles or assumptions concern the relative efficacy of active and passive defenses. What McGuire really appears to have is a collection of explicitly and implicitly formulated assumptions and principles. The theory is a coherent one, not because all of the principles follow from the biological analogy, but because the principles appear to have pragmatic value in explaining conferral of resistance to persuasion.

One good example of the extent to which McGuire really forsakes the biological analogy is in connection with one of his sequence hypotheses. McGuire predicts that a restoration (attack then defense) sequence will be more effective than an immunization (defense then attack) sequence. This hypothesis is justified on the basis of the individual's increased motivation to assimilate the defensive material as it follows rather than precedes the attack. And this justification indeed makes at least some degree of sense. However, the biological analogy alone would not lead to such an expectation; i.e., no one would argue that it is better to obtain an inoculation after rather than before being exposed to a virus. Indeed, some of the evidence obtained by Tannenbaum and his associates indicates that it would have been preferable for McGuire to have followed the analogy more closely, at least with regard to his sequence predictions.

An additional theoretical problem relates to the possible existence of defensive mechanisms other than the ones postulated by inoculation theory. From the present point of view it is at least possible to suppose that a complete explanation of resistance to persuasion will depend upon the inoculation theory mechanisms as well as upon some additional mechanisms. There is considerable evidence indicating that this may be the case. However, one can hope that future work will produce a more parsimonious and coherent explanation of defensive resistance to persuasion than is provided by the current combination of inoculation theory, congruity theory, and "perceptual defense" theory.

From an empirical orientation a major shortcoming of inoculation theory has to do with the failure of the sequence or order predictions. Not a single one of these predictions has been upheld, and in some cases effects exactly contrary to prediction have been obtained. It seems likely that the failure of these sequence predictions will force an eventual revision of McGuire's theoretical statement.

One interesting question with regard to which McGuire presents no data has to do with the generalizability of the immunizing effect to non-truism kinds of issues.[9] McGuire specifically predicts that only issues such as truisms which exist in a "germ free" environment can be strengthened through immunization. This important expectation, however, has not been tested. Until some such test is made we will have no knowledge as to the generalizability of inoculation theory principles. Eventually, of course, we hopefully will have some principles that apply generally to the conferral of resistance to persuasion.

[9] The literature on one-sided and two-sided communications is indirectly relevant to this problem (see Lumsdaine and Janis, 1953, and Insko, 1962).

13

Type Theories

INTRODUCTION

There is a small group of theories which is primarily oriented toward types of attitudes. These theories make the assumption that in order to change attitudes it is first necessary to know what type of attitude you are trying to change. This assumption, of course, implies that the construction of an adequate theory of attitude change involves discovering an appropriate basis upon which attitudes may be classified. Three theories have taken this classificatory approach. These are the theories developed by Smith, Bruner, and White (1956), Katz (1960), and Kelman (1961). Each of these theories will be described in turn.

SMITH, BRUNER, AND WHITE'S THEORY

Smith, Bruner, and White's (1956) theory was developed in conjunction with an extremely comprehensive clinical study of the attitudes toward Russia held by ten men. The theory is an attempt to state the functions that opinions and attitudes serve for the personality.

Concept of Attitude

Smith, Bruner, and White (1956) define an attitude as "a predisposition to experience, to be motivated by, and to act toward, a class of objects in a predictable manner" (p. 39). This is a very broad definition encompassing more than is usually implied by the concept of attitude. They explicitly state that they do not wish to be "fussy" about the word used to denote the phenomenon described in their definition and that "opinion" or "sentiment" will do just as well as "attitude." For most contemporary theorists the concept of attitude specifically implies affect or a feeling of pro or con, favorable or unfavorable with regard to a particular object, while the concept of opinion has to do with cognitive beliefs about some aspect of reality. Smith, Bruner, and White (1956), however, prefer to lump these concepts together apparently because they want to emphasize the interrelation of personality and, further, "do not think the time is ripe to be theoretically solemn about the definition of attitude" (p. 34).

For Smith, Bruner, and White, the object of an attitude may be anything that exists within the life space of the individual or more simply anything that exists for the individual. Furthermore, attitude objects have various characteristics such as differentiation, salience, time perspective, informational support, and object value. Differentiation refers to perceived complexity in the attitude object. For example, one individual may perceive Russia as being a social experiment, an aggressor, a land of great musicians, and a land of great agricultural resources, while another individual may simply perceive Russia as a collectivity of ignorant peasants ruled by a small group of radical troublemakers. The salience of an attitude object refers to the extent to which the object is central or marginal to the individual's everyday concerns. An attitude object's time perspective has to do with whether the object is of only transitory interest or whether it is something of more long term interest. Informational support has to do not with the attitude object itself but rather with information or knowledge possessed by the individual which is relevant to the attitude object. Finally, object value refers to the affective tone of an attitude object. This is, of course, what is typically regarded as the defining characteristic of an attitude.

Functional Approach

According to Smith, Bruner, and White, personality is inferred from regularities in behavior. Some of these regularities give rise to the concept of opinion, but all of the regularities together give rise to the concept of personality. Personality thus constitutes the context in which opinions exist and it seems appropriate to regard opinions in terms of the functions that they serve for the personality. What this means is that opinions are regarded primarily in terms of how they help the individual to adapt to and modify his environment so as to best bring about need reduction or the continued functioning of personality.

Typology

Smith, Bruner, and White assert that three types of functions are served by holding an opinion or attitude: object appraisal, social adjustment, and externalization. The object appraisal function refers to an opinion's usefulness in orienting the individual to objects in the environment. Stated another way this function has to do with an opinion's potentiality for classifying objects so that appropriate action may be possible. Object appraisal is thus a cognitive function that aids in what the psychoanalysts refer to as "reality testing."

The social adjustment function refers to an opinion's function in facilitating, maintaining, and disrupting social relationships. When, for example, the individual wishes to be accepted into a group he will tend to express acceptable opinions and withhold unacceptable ones. On the other hand, if the individual wishes to assert his independence from a particular group he may express unacceptable opinions and withhold acceptable ones. Social adjustment is thus a function that aids in the mediation of self-other relationships.

Opinions serve the externalization function when they are formed in such a way as to defend the ego from anxiety generated by inner problems. Race prejudice, for example, may serve the externalization or ego defense function by projecting onto an outgroup some of one's own unacceptable characteristics and impulses. This is the type of function that has been emphasized by Adorno, Frenkel-Brunswik, Levinson, and Sanford (1950) in *The Authoritarian Personality*.

Attitude Change

Why do attitudes change? Smith, Bruner, and White answer this question in terms of a shift in one or more of the three functional purposes served by attitudes. For example, the acquisition of new or different information about some aspect of reality, a modification of social factors, or a shift in anxiety-producing internal problems may all produce attitude change. Attitude change may be precipitated by any one of these factors, but the whole process will involve a change in the balance of all three.

Despite the fact that any one attitude serves all three functions, one determinant may be more important than the other two. To the extent that this is true it is theoretically possible to identify the change procedure that is likely to be most effective. An attitude in which the object appraisal function predominates is most likely to change in response to new information or rational arguments. An attitude in which the social adjustment function predominates is most likely to change in response to prestige suggestion, group pressure, testimonials, or information discrediting the social support for opposing views. And an attitude in which the externalization function predominates is most likely to change in response to "reassurance and permissiveness," presumably like that obtained in psychoanalysis. Knowledge as to the main function underlying a given attitude is thus the key to a successful change manipulation.

Evaluation

Smith, Bruner, and White's main assumption, that in order to change an attitude you have to know its functional basis, seems plausible. Furthermore, the threefold classification of the functions served by attitudes has an eclectic appeal about it. Cognitive psychology, social oriented psychology, and psychoanalytic psychology are all given a slice of the functional pie. Cognitive psychology is represented by the object appraisal function, social oriented psychology by the social adjustment function, and psychoanalytic psychology by the externalization function. The theory, however, is not completely eclectic. Reinforcement psychology, for example, is not given any one category or functional type that is unambiguously all its own.

Unfortunately, the theory is not supported by a body of experimental literature. Smith, Bruner, and White present ten extremely interesting case studies which attempt to illustrate the three functional bases of attitudes toward Russia, but this case history material is not a test of the theory's adequacy. In order to test the theory it would be necessary, first, to establish operational procedures for distinguishing between attitudes supported by different functional bases and, second, to establish whether or not these different attitudes respond in the expected manner to the appropriate change procedures. If the second step is carried through successfully then we can have some faith in the adequacy of the classificatory scheme. The first step, however, is an obvious prerequisite for the second. Smith, Bruner, and White state that ways of accomplishing the first step are possible, but themselves offer no suggestions.

If this analysis of the conditions of attitude change is correct—and it is supported not only by impressions from our cases, but also by the burden of much contemporary work in clinical and social psychology—it becomes important to devise rigorous and objective means of assessing the contribution of the different functional supports to people's opinions on given issues. Ways of doing so seem entirely within the range of feasible attainment. (1956, p. 278)

Unfortunately this "feasible attainment" has not yet been achieved. Certainly until the theory is stated in an empirically testable manner it will not be a serious contender in the field of attitude change.

KATZ'S THEORY

Katz (1960) has developed a theory that is in many respects very similar to that of Smith, Bruner, and White. Katz's theorizing draws heavily upon some earlier work with Sarnoff (Sarnoff and Katz, 1954) and with Stotland (Katz and Stotland, 1959).

Concept of Attitude

According to Katz (1960) "Attitudes include both the affective, or feeling core of liking or disliking, and the cognitive, or belief elements which describe the object of the attitude, its characteristics, and its relations to other objects" (p. 343). Thus it follows that attitudes include beliefs, but beliefs do not include attitudes. This is still a different usage of the terms "attitude" and "belief." Katz goes further and states that when attitudes are organized into a hierarchical structure, they form a value system. He illustrates this with the example of the person who holds not only attitudes against deficit spending and unbalanced budgets but also a systematic organization of attitudes in the form of an economic conservatism value.

Like Smith, Bruner, and White (1956), Katz lists various dimensions of attitudes. He mentions such things as intensity, specificity or generality, differentiation, number and strength of linkages to a related value system, and relation to overt behavior.

Functional Approach

As was the case with Smith, Bruner, and White, Katz also espouses a functional or motivational approach to attitudes. Once again the argument is advanced that without knowledge as to the motivational basis of an attitude it is difficult to accurately predict change. These points are explained as follows:

Stated simply, the functional approach is the attempt to understand the reasons people hold the attitudes they do. The reasons, however, are at the level of psychological motivations and not of the accidents of external events and circumstances. Unless we know the psychological need which is met by the holding of an attitude we are in a poor position to predict when and how it will change. (1960, p. 170)

Typology

Katz lists four functions that attitudes perform for the personality: the instrumental, adjustive, or utilitarian function, the ego-defensive function, the value-expressive function, and the knowledge function. These four functions are described as follows:

1. *The instrumental, adjustive, or utilitarian function* upon which Jeremy Bentham and the utilitarian constructed their model of man. A modern expression of the approach can be found in behavioristic learning theory.

2. *The ego-defensive function* in which the person protects himself from acknowledging the basic truths about himself or the harsh realities in his external world. Freudian psychology and neo-Freudian thinking have been preoccupied with this type of motivation and its outcomes.

3. *The value-expressive function* in which the individual derives satisfactions from expressing attitudes appropriate to his personal values and to his concept of himself. This function is central to doctrines of ego psychology which stress the importance of self-expression, self-importance, self-development, and self-realization.

4. *The knowledge function* based upon the individual's need to give adequate structure to his universe. The search for meaning, the need to understand, the trend toward better organization of perceptions and beliefs to provide clarity and consistency for the individual, are other descriptions of this function. The development of principles about perceptual and cognitive structure have been the contribution of Gestalt psychology. (1960, p. 170)

Attitude Arousal and Change

Attitude arousal generally depends on the excitation of some underlying need or on stimulation by some relevant cue in the environment. Attitude change, on the other hand, generally depends on an attitude no longer fulfilling its old need or function. Katz illustrates these general arousal and change conditions for each of the four functions separately. Attitudes based on the ego-defensive function, for example, may be aroused by frustration or authoritarian suggestion and may be changed through the removal of threats or catharsis. Katz's summary of both the origin and dynamics as well as the arousal and change conditions for each of the four functions is presented in Table 13–1.

Evaluation

Katz's classification of the functions served by attitudes is similar to and yet not identical with Smith, Bruner, and White's classification. The knowledge function roughly corresponds to object appraisal and the ego-defensive function roughly corresponds to externalization. The instrumental, adjustive, or utilitarian function and the value-expressive function, however, do not correspond to social adjustment. Katz's eclecticism seems to be slightly more thoroughgoing than Smith, Bruner, and White's.

Does the disagreement between Katz and Smith, Bruner, and White prove that the concept of differing functional bases for attitudes is incorrect? No, not any more than the disagreement about lists of instincts proved that there were no instincts. Truth is not dependent upon consensus but upon empirical validation. This lack of consensus about func-

TABLE 13–1.   Katz's Determinants of Attitude Formation,
Arousal, and Change in Relation to Type of Function

Function	Origin and Dynamics	Arousal Conditions	Change Conditions
Adjustment	Utility of attitudinal object in need satisfaction. Maximizing external rewards and minimizing punishments	1. Activation of needs 2. Salience of cues associated with need satisfaction	1. Need deprivation 2. Creation of new needs and new levels of aspiration 3. Shifting reward and punishment 4. Emphasis on new and better paths for need satisfaction
Ego defense	Protecting against internal conflicts and external dangers	1. Posing of threats 2. Appeals to hatred and repressed impulses 3. Rise in frustrations 4. Use of authoritarian suggestion	1. Removal of threat 2. Catharsis 3. Development of self-insight
Value expression	Maintaining self-identity; enhancing favorable self-image; self-expression and self-determination	1. Salience of cues associated with values 2. Appeals to individual to reassert self-image 3. Ambiguities which threaten self-concept	1. Some degree of dissatisfaction with self 2. Greater appropriateness of new attitudes for the self 3. Control of all environmental supports to undermine old values
Knowledge	Need for understanding, for meaningful cognitive organization, for consistency and clarity	1. Reinstatement of cues associated with old problem or of old problem itself	1. Ambiguity created by new information or change in environment 2. More meaningful information about problems

SOURCE: Katz, 1960, p. 192.

tions, as well as instincts, is due to the fact that empirical validation procedures have not been carried out. The possibility of adequate empirical validation, however, is dependent upon the theory being stated in testable terms. Thus the main problem with Katz's theory, as with Smith, Bruner, and White's, has to do with an inadequate specification of the means whereby the functional bases of attitudes can be operationally identified.[1] Katz is aware of the problem and does spend some time discussing it. He does not, however recommend any final solution.

KELMAN'S THEORY

Functional Approach

Kelman's type theory, like the two preceding theories, takes a functional approach to attitudes. Kelman (1961) "starts with the assumption that opinions adopted under different conditions of social influence, and based on different motivations, will differ in terms of their qualitative characteristics and their subsequent histories" (p. 60). This assumption that knowledge of functional basis is most important in the understanding of attitudes is the familiar assumption also made by Smith, Bruner, and White (1956) and by Katz (1960). Kelman, however, specifies the functional basis not just in terms of motives but also in terms of antecedent social influence conditions. Approaching attitudes as a function both of motives and of antecedent social influence conditions leads to a distinctively different kind of theory.

Typology

Kelman distinguishes three processes of social influence: compliance, identification, and internalization. Each of these social influence processes theoretically leads to a different type of opinion or attitude. Compliance occurs when an individual accepts influence from another person or group with the hope of gaining some reward or avoiding some punishment controlled by this person or group. In order to join a certain social club, for example, a person may attempt to express only certain "correct" opinions. These opinions are not adopted because the individual believes in their content, but simply in order to gain external incentives.

Identification occurs when an individual adopts another person's or group's opinions because these opinions are associated with a satisfying self-defining relationship with this person or group. A self-defining

---

[1] This is not meant to imply that the theory is either emotionally or cognitively meaningless.

relationship is "a role relationship that forms a part of the person's self-image" (Kelman, 1961, p. 63). This role relationship can either take the form of classical identification in which the individual takes over all or part of the influencing agent's role, or it may take the form of a reciprocal role relationship in which the roles of the two parties are defined with reference to each other. The former type of role relationship is illustrated by brainwashed prisoners who identify with their captors or by socialized children who identify with their parents. The latter type of role relationship is illustrated by two friends or by a doctor and a patient who act in a mutually satisfying way. Since identification involves attitude change in order to gain an external incentive (a satisfying self-defining relationship), the process is in some respects similar to that of compliance. The difference is that attitudes acquired through identification, unlike those acquired through compliance, are actually, and not just outwardly, accepted. Identification-based attitudes, however, are not thoroughly integrated with the individual's value system and are not independent of the external source.

Internalization occurs when an individual accepts an opinion because it is congruent with his value system. In this case the content of the opinion itself is rewarding and external incentives are unimportant. While the whole process appears highly rationalistic Kelman emphasizes that internalization can occur because an opinion is congruent with either a rational or an irrational value system.

Finally, Kelman points out that the three processes are not mutually exclusive and seldom occur in pure form. Most opinions are a function of some combination of these processes.

Antecedents

For each of the three processes Kelman distinguishes a specific set of antecedents and consequents. Kelman's summary of these matters is presented in Table 13–2.

pliance is concern with the social effect of behavior; the motivational basis for identification is concern with the social anchorage of behavior; and the motivational basis for internalization is concerned with the value congruence of behavior. With regard to the power of the influencing agent, compliance is dependent upon the agent controlling the means whereby reward can be achieved, identification is dependent upon the agent possessing the personal qualities that facilitate a satisfying self-defining relationship, and internalization is dependent upon the agent possessing high source credibility. Finally, influence occurs in a compliance situation through a limitation of alternative paths to a goal, in an identification situation through a specification of role requirements,

TABLE 13-2. *Kelman's Summary of the Distinctions Among the Three Social Influence Processes*

	Compliance	Identification	Internalization
Antecedents:			
1. Basis for the *importance of the induction*	Concern with social effect of behavior	Concern with social anchorage of behavior	Concern with value congruence of behavior
2. Source of *power of the influencing agent*	Means control	Attractiveness	Credibility
3. Manner of achieving *prepotency of the induced response*	Limitation of choice behavior	Delineation of role requirements	Reorganization of means-end framework
Consequents:			
1. Conditions of performance of induced response	Surveillance by influencing agent	Salience of relationship to agent	Relevance of values to issue
2. Conditions of change and extinction of induced response	Changed perception of conditions for social rewards	Changed perception of conditions for satisfying self-defining relationships	Changed perception of conditions for value maximization
3. Type of behavior system in which induced response is embedded	External demands of a specific setting	Expectations defining a specific role	Person's value system

SOURCE: Kelman, 1961, p. 67.

Three general classes of antecedents are distinguished: the motivational basis for influence, the power of the influencing agent, and the manner whereby the influence occurs. The motivational basis for com- and in an internalization situation through a reorganization of the individual's conception of the instrumental relations between opinions and values.

Kelman emphasizes that the three processes of compliance, identification, and internalization are in fact determined by the nature of the three antecedents. To the extent that the antecedents take any of the above specified forms then either compliance, or identification, or internalization will occur.

Consequents

Kelman distinguishes three general classes of consequents: the conditions in which the opinion or attitude will be expressed, the conditions in which the opinion or attitude can be changed, and the type of behavior system in which the opinion or attitude exists. An opinion acquired under compliance circumstances will be expressed only when there is surveillance by the influencing agent; an opinion acquired under internalization circumstances will tend to be expressed when the relevance of the opinion to certain values is perceived. The conditions of change for a compliant opinion are the perception that the opinion is no longer the best means of obtaining social rewards; the conditions of change for an identification opinion are the perception that a particular self-defining relationship is no longer the most satisfying; and the conditions of change for an internalization opinion are the perception that the opinion is no longer the best path toward the maximization of important values. Finally, compliant opinions exist in a behavior system of demands characterizing a specific setting; identification opinions exist in a behavior system of expectations defining a specific role; and internalization opinions exist in a behavior system of consistently held inner values. These consequents for compliance, identification, and internalization are regarded as resulting from the above antecedents. According to Kelman if an opinion has certain antecedents it will of necessity have certain consequents.

Research

Kelman has reported a number of studies designed to test the adequacy of his theory. These experimental tests of necessity contain operational translations of some of his theoretical concepts.

Kelman (1958) examined the extent to which the influencing agent's power would determine the conditions under which the newly acquired opinion would be expressed. The experiment was conducted with freshman students in a Negro college just before the announcement of the Supreme Court decision on the desegregation of public schools. Subjects were presented with a taped communication represented as being part of a transcribed radio program and told that the experimenter was interested in obtaining their reactions. The communication argued that even if the Supreme Court decided that segregation was unconstitutional it would still be desirable to keep some of the private Negro colleges segregated in order to preserve Negro culture and tradition. The power of the communicator was manipulated by having the guest speaker described differently by a moderator on the radio program and by having the speaker himself reveal further information concerning his power during the course of the program. In a high means-control condition the speaker was introduced as the president of the National Foundation for Negro colleges. During the course of the program it became evident that he was primarily responsible for the allocation of the Foundation's funds to the college in which the study was being conducted and that he furthermore would not hesitate to withdraw support if the students at any college expressed opinions contrary to his on the issue in question. In a high attractiveness condition the speaker was introduced as a senior and the president of the student council in a leading Negro university and also as the chairman of his university's "Student Poll." The latter organization was reported to have recently done a study on the attitudes of Negro college seniors on issues relating to the impending Supreme Court decision. During the course of the program the speaker made it clear that he was presenting not just his own attitude but the attitudes expressed by the overwhelming majority of seniors represented in his poll. In a high credibility condition the speaker was introduced as a professor of history in a leading university. During the course of the program it became clear that he was a highly respected authority on the history and problems of minority groups and that he had a great concern for the welfare of the American Negro community. He made it clear that his position was based on research and historical evidence. Finally, in a low power condition the speaker was introduced as an "ordinary citizen," and portrayed as a white man with a southern accent who had recently come from Mississippi. At some time after exposure to the communication the subjects filled out three attitude questionnaires which were identical except for manipulations of salience and surveillance. Salience was manipulated by administering two of the questionnaires immediately after exposure to the communication and the other questionnaire 1 to 2 weeks later in an entirely different context. Surveillance was manipulated by telling the subjects that their signed copies of the first questionnaire would be shown to the communicator and by allowing the subjects to turn in their second and third questionnaires unsigned. The first questionnaire was thus high in salience and surveillance, the second high in salience and low in surveillance, and the third low in both salience and surveillance.

Kelman had three predictions, all derived from his theory. First, opinions acquired from an influencing agent having high means control will be expressed only under conditions of high surveillance and salience (i.e., on the first questionnaire). Second, opinions acquired from an influencing agent having high attractiveness will be expressed only under conditions of high salience (i.e., on the first and second questionnaires). And third, opinions acquired from an influencing agent having high credibility will be expressed under conditions of relevance of the issue (i.e., on the first, second, and third questionnaires). The results support the hypotheses to a very high degree. In the high means control group there was more agreement with the communicator on the first than on either the second or third questionnaires. In the high attractiveness group there was more agreement with the communicator on the first and second than on the third questionnaires. And in the high credibility and low power groups there were no significant differences between questionnaires. No other differences between questionnaires were significant for any of the groups. Kelman does not report any significance tests for the comparisons between groups, but in general the low power group did show less agreement than the high power groups on all of those questionnaires in which the high power groups were predicted to show high agreement. A subanalysis of only those subjects who were judged by virtue of their high scores on the first questionnaire to have been influenced revealed even more striking agreement with the theoretical predictions. Kelman argues that his theory makes predictions only for subjects who are in fact influenced.

This very interesting experiment provides striking support for Kelman's theory. Confirmation of the hypothesis regarding increased agreement with the communicator having high means control only under conditions of surveillance is perhaps not too surprising, but confirmation of the second hypothesis relating to increased agreement with the attractive communicator only under conditions of salience is provocative. Kelman appears to have isolated some very important aspects of source power or credibility.

Kelman (*1960*) attempted to relate two antecedents, the motivational basis for the influence and the manner whereby the influence occurs, to one of the consequents, the conditions under which the opinion or attitude is expressed. The experiment was concerned only with identification and internalization. The taped communication was a simulated radio broadcast which supposedly had originated at a Canadian university. The communication advocated a novel program in science education that involved having science students study ethics, political science, and international relations to enable them to make the practical decisions demanded by the contemporary world. Two versions of this communication were presented to different groups of subjects. The versions varied in terms of additional information that was included to produce differing orientations. In the role-orientation or identification condition the additional information related acceptance of the induced opinion to important positive and negative reference groups. This was accomplished by having the main speaker provide information relating to positive reference groups and having other speakers provide information relating to negative reference groups. The main speaker, a physics professor at the fictitious Canadian University, reported that the faculty and students at his university, as well as important science educators, were very much in favor of the program. A second speaker, the president of a superpatriotic women's organization, denounced the education program as a Communist device, and a third speaker, a local school-board member, argued that the program was an attempt by college professors to control educational policy. Kelman's intention was to produce both a concern for the social anchorage of the opinion and a specification of the appropriate opinion necessary to maintain the required role relationships to the positive and negative reference groups. In the value-orientation or internalization condition the additional information specified the implications of the new opinion for maintaining an important value—personal responsibility for the consequences of one's actions. This was done by having the fictitious physics professor argue that if scientists are going to maintain personal responsibility for the consequences of their actions in the contemporary world, they will of necessity have to become better educated in political science, international relations, and ethics. Kelman's intention here was to produce a concern for the value congruence of opinions and a reorganization of the perceived instrumental relationship between the recommended opinion and the personal responsibility value.

In each of the groups half of the subjects filled out an attitude questionnaire immediately after hearing the communication and half a few weeks later. Kelman's theory predicts that the role-orientation communication should produce greater agreement after the presentation when salience is high than a few weeks later when salience is low, but that the value-orientation communication would not be affected by the delay of measurement. This prediction was significantly upheld.

An additional manipulation and test concerned the resistance of the subjects in each of the groups to countercommunications. Kelman predicted that the subjects in the value-orientation group would be influenced to a greater degree by a value-oriented countercommunication than a role-oriented countercommunication, but that the subjects in the role-orientation group would be more influenced by a role-oriented countercommunication than a value-oriented countercommunication. The results revealed the predicted pattern to a nonsignificant degree.

In general the results of this experiment provide encouraging, although not completely unambiguous, support for Kelman's theoretical speculation. In view of the fairly elaborate nature of the manipulations it is perhaps not too surprising that the results were not completely in accord with theoretical expectations.

Evaluation

Kelman's theory is in some respects the most impressive of the type theories discussed in this chapter. Relating the three types of opinions both to differing motives and to differing antecedent conditions makes the theory more readily testable than either Smith, Bruner, and White's theory or Katz's theory. This, however, does not mean that Kelman's position is necessarily any more correct than Smith, Bruner, and White's or Katz's. Empirical examination of the latter two positions could conceivably prove otherwise.

Kelman is the only one of the type theorists who has submitted his theory to direct empirical test. Unique as this testing is, however, it is still rather incomplete. Other than for the two investigations described above and some other work that is only tangentially relevant (e.g., Bailyn and Kelman, 1959; Kelman and Cohler, 1959) the theory is still largely untested. Certainly the initial work has indicated that further empirical investigations would be worthwhile and desirable.

The basic assumption of the type theories is that in order to know how to change attitudes you have to know what type of attitude you are trying to change. This assumption sounds so plausible that it is surprising that more theorists have not been attracted by it. Perhaps one of the difficulties lies in deciding just how attitudes should be classified. It is conceivable that future theorists might find factor analysis of some use in this respect, although from the present vantage point there does not seem to be any compelling reason for supposing that a factor analytic classification would be the most theoretically fruitful one. This, however, is an approach that conceivably might be of value.[2]

[2] Cattell (1957) has made some effort in this direction.

14

Evaluation

RESEARCH

Laboratory studies of attitude change have obviously come a long way since the days of World War II when research was being carried out by Hovland and his colleagues in the Information and Education Division of the War Department. Social psychologists have become very skilled in experimentally investigating problems that a few decades ago would have been considered too complex for laboratory study. Knowledge concerning many problems is still far from complete, but impressive beginnings have been made with regard to such things as source credibility, communicator-communicatee discrepancy, forced compliant and/or role-playing behavior, inoculation against persuasion, and the relation between belief similarity and prejudice.

Despite this impressive beginning, however, it is quite apparent that existing research leaves much to be desired, both from the standpoint of methodological rigor and from the standpoint of neglected problem areas. First of all, despite the uncertainty about pretest interactions the bulk of attitude change research has utilized and continues to utilize before-after rather than after-only designs. Many researchers still appear reluctant to engage in the extra work needed to increase sample sizes to the point where differences based on posttest scores will be statistically reliable. Second, there is a continuing lack of sophistication with regard to demand characteristics and experimenter bias. Certainly these are important problems that need to be considered when any research project is undertaken. Third, much attitude change research has relied and does rely on poorly conceived assessment procedures despite the known availability of many sophisticated psychometric techniques. Perhaps part of the problem in the past has been the labor involved in constructing Thurstone, Likert, or Guttman attitude scales. Now, however, with the development of the easily applicable semantic differential technique there is less reason for using more unsophisticated procedures. Fourth, too much research from the very recent past has been analyzed with multiple t tests rather than with more appropriate analyses of variance and trend analyses. With the current availability of these techniques for both equal and unequal cell frequencies there is no reason for using a multiple t test approach. Fifth, a problem that has been too long neglected relates to the long term attitudinal and opinion effects of various persuasive manipulations. Most researchers have been content to demonstrate that a manipulation has an immediate effect and have simply neglected the equally important long term effects. There are undoubtedly several reasons for this neglect, such as the difficulty of gaining access to subjects for a second time, the problem of repeated measurements on the same subjects, and the belief that long term effects will be minimal or nonsignificant. The first problem can be handled with more work, the second problem can be handled by increasing the sample size and assessing different subgroups at only one point in time, and the third problem is a matter for empirical study. Certainly if most of the manipulations do, in fact, have only transitory effects, this is a serious indictment of attitude change research. Sixth and last, there is the problem of immediate and long term behavioral effects of attitude and opinion change. This neglected problem was brought to attention by Cohen (1964), Festinger (1964a), and Greenwald (1965). Granted that the connection between attitudes and behavior may not be a very direct one, there certainly should be some connection and it is time to thoroughly investigate this whole problem. Perhaps rather than approaching the problem by investigating the effect of attitude change upon behavior change, a more immediately productive approach would be to investigate the effect of behavior change (e.g., through experimentally manipulated role-playing) upon attitude change.

THEORIES

Since the publication of Hovland, Janis, and Kelley's *Communication and Persuasion* in 1953 the field of attitude change has seen an impressive proliferation of different theories. These diverse theoretical orientations tend to be small models concentrating on special problems. It is possible, however, to overemphasize the specificity because there are many common areas in which the theories have different implications. For example, many theories maintain that high credibility sources are more persuasive than low credibility sources; but dissonance theory, at least as Brehm and Cohen (1962) interpret it, makes the opposite prediction in the special case in which the individual chooses to expose himself to the communication. Dissonance theory also predicts that engaging in counterattitudinal advocacy for a small reward will result in more attitude change than doing the same thing for a large reward —a prediction that certainly does not flow from a reinforcement orientation. Both dissonance theory and assimilation-contrast theory make similar predictions with regard to the effect of communicator discrepancy, but assimilation-contrast theory does not include the important variable of source credibility. Congruity theory and belief congruence theory have contradictory predictions with regard to the shift in evaluation that follows the associating of diverse objects of judgment. Certainly contemporary theorizing has not been as active as it should have been in the formulating of alternative predictions, but a step has definitely been made in that direction.

Taking a long look back over the theories presented in the preceding pages it is apparent that many of the theories are characterized by one or both of two emphases, the importance of reward, reinforcement, or need reduction and the importance of consistency. An emphasis on reward or need reduction is seen in reinforcement theory, logical-affective consistency theory, affective-cognitive consistency theory, psychoanalytic theory, and the type theories. An emphasis on consistency is seen in logical-affective consistency theory, congruity theory, belief congruence theory, affective-cognitive consistency theory, and dissonance theory. In addition, many other theories make more minor use of these explanatory concepts. Inoculation theory, for example, deals with threat reduction, and reinforcement theory deals with attitude change as a consequence of opinion change. Threat reduction is a kind of reinforcement, and attitude change following opinion change is a movement toward consistency.

In view of the pervasiveness of these two principles it is not surprising that an attempt has been made to reduce one to the other in the interest of theoretical parsimony. Hovland and Rosenberg (1960) argue that the motivation to reduce inconsistency can be explained on the basis of reinforcement-produced learning. They state that this learning can occur as a consequence either of adaptation to the environment or of deliberate social training. If the individual adapts successfully to the environment he will have to achieve consistent relations between his feelings, beliefs, and behaviors; otherwise conflicts could not be resolved in a manner productive of reinforcement. Eventually consistency may itself become a rewarding state of affairs and thus be a learned incentive. Direct social training for consistency occurs, for example, when individuals are criticized for their grossly inconsistent communications. Hovland and Rosenberg state that all known societies have a norm favoring consistency.

This is an interesting and possibly important point of view. It should be noted, however, that one conceivably could take the opposite approach and argue that reinforcement is a type of inconsistency reduction in which homeostatic imbalance is restored. This would make the tendency toward consistency and not the tendency toward reinforcement the basis and primary explanatory principle. The attempt to reduce either of these two tendencies to the other, however, is undoubtedly subject to criticism.

The survey of the various theoretical orientations in the preceding pages makes it quite evident that the field of attitude change is a long way from having any one theory that is a serious contender as a respectable general theory. From the present vantage point the most glaring weakness of contemporary theorizing is the lack of emphasis upon the relation between attitudes and behavior. The theories seem to have concentrated on the relation between attitudes (affection) and opinions (cognitions) and have almost completely neglected behavior (conation). Common sense seems to suggest that there is some relation between attitudes and behavior, but social psychology has been slow to explore the matter. What are the circumstances under which attitude or opinion change might be expected to produce behavior change? Surely such circumstances need to be theoretically specified.

A different approach to the relation between attitude and behavior is to concentrate not on behavior change following attitude change but on attitude change following behavior change. This is one type of causal sequence upon which dissonance theory has focused. Problems relating to revaluation of the alternatives following the resolution of conflicts and the persuasive impact of counterattitudinal advocacy, in essence, relate to attitude change as a consequence of behavior change. This matter, however, has only begun to be explored. It may indeed turn out that most of the consistency between attitudes and behavior is due not to the effect of attitudes upon behavior but of behavior upon attitudes. Certainly subsequent theorizing and research should look into this problem.

None of the theories presented in the preceding pages is perfect or even near perfect. Subsequent research will undoubtedly make these theoretical orientations appear more and more inadequate. Future theorists, however, will be able to benefit from their predecessors' mistakes and hopefully arrive at increasingly sophisticated formulations. Whatever the ultimate outcome of theoretical advances, these theories are the primitive beginnings which will make greater sophistication possible.

REFERENCES

Abelson, R. Modes of resolution of belief dilemmas. *J. conflict Resol.*, 1959, *3*, 343–352.

Abelson, R., and Rosenberg, M. Symbolic psycho-logic: a model of attitudinal cognition. *Behav. Sci.*, 1958, *3*, 1–13.

Adorno, T., Frenkel-Brunswik, E., Levinson, D., and Sanford, R. *The authoritarian personality*. New York: Harper & Row, 1950.

Allen, V. Cognitive familiarity and dissonance reduction. In L. Festinger (Ed.), *Conflict, decision and dissonance*. Stanford: Stanford Univer. Press, 1964. Pp. 34–42.

Allport, G. Attitudes. In C. Murchison (Ed.), *A handbook of social psychology*. Worcester, Mass.: Clark Univer. Press, 1935. Pp. 798–844.

Allport, G., and Allport, F. *A-S reaction study*. Boston: Houghton Mifflin, 1928.

Anderson, L., and Fishbein, N. Prediction of attitude from the number, strength, and evaluative aspects of beliefs about the attitude object. *J. Pers. soc. Psychol.*, 1965, *2*, 437–443.

Anderson, L., and McGuire, W. Prior reassurance of group consensus as a factor in producing resistance to persuasion. *Sociometry*, 1965, *28*, 44–56.

Anderson, N. Test of a model for opinion change. *J. abnorm. soc. Psychol.*, 1959, *59*, 371–381.

Anderson, N. Averaging versus adding as a stimulus combination rule in impression formation. *J. exp. Psychol.*, 1965a, *70*, 394–400.

Anderson, N. Primacy effects in personality impression formation using a generalized order effects paradigm. *J. Pers. soc. Psychol.*, 1965b, *2*, 1–9.

Anderson, N., and Hovland, C. The representation of order effects in communication research. In C. Hovland, *et al.* (Eds.), *The order of presentation in persuasion*. New Haven: Yale Univer. Press, 1957. Pp. 158–169.

Aronson, E. The effects of effort on the attractiveness of rewarded and unrewarded stimuli. *J. abnorm. soc. Psychol.*, 1961, *63*, 375–380.

Aronson, E., and Carlsmith, J. The effect of severity of threat on the devaluation of forbidden behavior. *J. abnorm. soc. Psychol.*, 1963, *66*, 584–588.

Aronson, E., and Golden, B. The effect of relevant and irrelevant aspects of communicator credibility on opinion change. *J. Pers.*, 1962, *30*, 135–146.

Aronson, E., and Mills, J. The effects of severity of initiation on liking for a group. *J. abnorm. soc. Psychol.*, 1959, *59*, 177–181.

Aronson, E., Turner, J., and Carlsmith, J. Communicator credibility and communication discrepancy as determinants of opinion change. *J. abnorm. soc. Psychol.*, 1963, *67*, 31–36.

Asch, S. Forming impressions of personality. *J. abnorm. soc. Psychol.*, 1946, *41*, 258–290.

Asch, S. The doctrine of suggestion, prestige, and imitation in social psychology. *Psychol. Rev.*, 1948, *55*, 250–276.

Asch, S. *Social psychology*. New York: Prentice-Hall, 1952.

Asch, S., Block, H., and Hertzman, M. Studies in the principles of judgments and attitudes: I. Two basic principles in judgment. *J. Psychol.*, 1938, *5*, 219–251.

Bailyn, L., and Kelman, H. The effects of a year's experience in America on the self-images of Scandinavians: report of research in progress. Paper read at Amer. Psychol. Ass., Cincinnati, 1959.

Ball, J. The influence of background and residual stimuli upon the measurement of attitudes. Unpublished master's thesis, Univer. of Texas, 1953.

Bergin, A. The effect of dissonant persuasive communications upon changes in a self-referring attitude. *J. Pers.*, 1962, *30*, 423–438.

Berkowitz, L., and Cottingham, D. The interest value and relevance of fear arousing communications. *J. abnorm. soc. Psychol.*, 1960, *60*, 37–43.

Birch, H. The effect of socially disapproved labeling upon a well-structured attitude. *J. abnorm. soc. Psychol.*, 1945, *40*, 301–310.

Blake, R., and Brehm, J. The use of tape recordings to simulate a group atmosphere. *J. abnorm. soc. Psychol.*, 1954, *49*, 311–313.

Blake, R., Helson, H., and Mouton, J. The generality of conforming behavior as a function of factual anchorage, difficulty of task, and amount of social pressure. *J. Pers.*, 1957, *25*, 294–305.

Blake, R., Rosenbaum, M., and Duryea, R. Gift-giving as a function of group standards. *Hum. Relat.*, 1955, *8*, 61–73.

Blandford, D., and Sampson, E. Induction of prestige suggestion through classical conditioning. *J. abnorm. soc. Psychol.*, 1964, *69*, 332–337.

Bochner, S., and Insko, C. Communicator discrepancy, source credibility, and influence. *J. Pers. soc. Psychol.*, 1966, *4*, 614–621.

Bostrom, R., Vlandis, J., and Rosenbaum, M. Grades as reinforcing contingencies and attitude change. *J. educ. Psychol.*, 1961, *52*, 112–115.

Brehm, J. Post-decision changes in the desirability of alternatives. *J. abnorm. soc. Psychol.*, 1956, *52*, 384–389.

Brehm, J. Increasing cognitive dissonance by a fait-accompli. *J. abnorm. soc. Psychol.*, 1959, *58*, 379–382.

Brehm, J. Attitudinal consequences of commitment to unpleasant behavior. *J. abnorm. soc. Psychol.*, 1960, *60*, 379–383.

Brehm, J. An experiment on coercion and attitude change. In J. Brehm and A. Cohen, *Explorations in cognitive dissonance*. New York: Wiley, 1962. Pp. 84–88.

Brehm, J. Comment on "counter-norm attitudes induced by consonant versus dissonant conditions of role-playing." *J. exp. Res. Pers.*, 1965, *1*, 61–64.

Brehm, J., and Cohen, A. Choice and chance relative deprivation as determinants of cognitive dissonance. *J. abnorm. soc. Psychol.*, 1959a, *58*, 383–387.

Brehm, J., and Cohen, A. Re-evaluation of choice alternatives as a function of their number and qualitative similarity. *J. abnorm. soc. Psychol.*, 1959b, *58*, 373–378.

Brehm, J., and Cohen, A. *Exploration in cognitive dissonance.* New York: Wiley, 1962.

Brock, T. Cognitive restructuring and attitude change. *J. abnorm. soc. Psychol.,* 1962, *64,* 264–271.

Brock, T. Effects of prior dishonesty on postdecision dissonance. *J. abnorm. soc. Psychol.,* 1963, *66,* 325–331.

Brock, T., and Blackwood, J. Dissonance reduction, social comparison and modification of others' opinions. *J. abnorm. soc. Psychol.,* 1962, *65,* 319–324.

Brock, T., and Buss, A. Dissonance, aggression, and evaluation of pain. *J. abnorm. soc. Psychol.,* 1962, *65,* 197–201.

Brown, R. Models of attitude change. In R. Brown, E. Galanter, E. Hess, and G. Mandler (Contributors), *New directions in psychology.* New York: Holt, Rinehart and Winston, 1962. Pp. 1–85.

Burdick, H., and Burnes, A. A test of "strain toward symmetry" theories. *J. abnorm. soc. Psychol.,* 1958, *57,* 367–370.

Byrne, D., and McGraw, C. Interpersonal attraction toward Negroes. *Hum. Relat.,* 1964, *17,* 201–213.

Byrne, D., and Wong, T. Racial prejudice, interpersonal attraction, and assumed dissimilarity of attitudes. *J. abnorm. soc. Psychol.,* 1962, *65,* 246–253.

Calvin, A. Social reinforcement. *J. soc. Psychol.,* 1962, *56,* 15–19.

Campbell, D. Factors relative to the validity of experiments in social settings. *Psychol. Bull.,* 1957, *54,* 297–312.

Campbell, D., and Fiske, D. Convergent and discriminant validation by the multitrait-multimethod matrix. *Psychol. Bull.,* 1959, *56,* 81–105.

Cantril, H. The intensity of an attitude. *J. abnorm. soc. Psychol.,* 1946, *41,* 129–135.

Carlsmith, J., Collins, B., and Helmreich, R. Studies in forced compliance: I. The effect of pressure for compliance on attitude change produced by face-to-face role playing and anonymous essay writing. *J. Pers. soc. Psychol.,* 1966, *4,* 1–13.

Carlson, E. Attitude change through modification of attitude structure. *J. abnorm. soc. Psychol.,* 1956, *52,* 256–261.

Cartwright, D. Some principles of mass persuasion. *Hum. Relat.,* 1949, *2,* 253–267.

Cartwright, D., and Harary, F. Structural balance: a generalization of Heider's theory. *Psychol. Rev.,* 1956, *63,* 277–293.

Cattell, R. *Personality and motivation structure and measurement.* New York: Harcourt, Brace & World, 1957.

Chapanis, N., and Chapanis, A. Cognitive dissonance: five years later. *Psychol. Bull.,* 1964, *61,* 1–22.

Chen, W. The influence of oral propaganda material upon students' attitudes. *Arch. Psychol.,* 1933, No. 150.

Choo, T. Communicator credibility and communication discrepancy as determinants of opinion change. *J. soc. Psychol.,* 1964, *64,* 1–20.

Cohen, A. Communication discrepancy and attitude change. *J. Pers.*, 1959, *27*, 386–396.

Cohen, A. A dissonance analysis of the boomerang effect. *J. Pers.*, 1962a, *30*, 75–88.

Cohen, A. A "forced-compliance" experiment on repeated dissonances. In J. Brehm and A. Cohen, *Explorations in cognitive dissonance*. New York: Wiley, 1962b. Pp. 97–104.

Cohen, A. An experiment of small rewards for discrepant compliance and attitude change. In J. Brehm and A. Cohen, *Explorations in cognitive dissonance*. New York: Wiley, 1962c. Pp. 73–78.

Cohen, A. *Attitude change and social influence*. New York: Basic Books, 1964.

Cohen, A., and Brehm, J. An experiment on illegitimate coercion, volition, and attitude change. In J. Brehm and A. Cohen, *Explorations in cognitive dissonance*. New York: Wiley, 1962. Pp. 206–210.

Cohen, A., Brehm, J., and Fleming, W. Attitude change and justification for compliance. *J. abnorm. soc. Psychol.*, 1958, *56*, 276–278.

Cohen, A., and Latané, B. An experiment on choice in commitment to counter-attitudinal behavior. In J. Brehm and A. Cohen, *Explorations in cognitive dissonance*. New York: Wiley, 1962. Pp. 88–91.

Cohen, A., Terry, H., and Jones, C. Attitudinal effects of choice in exposure to counterpropaganda. *J. abnorm. soc. Psychol.*, 1959, *58*, 388–391.

Cohen, B. Role of awareness in meaning established by classical conditioning. *J. exp. Psychol.*, 1964, *67*, 373–378.

Cole, D. "Rational argument" and "prestige-suggestion" as factors influencing judgment. *Sociometry*, 1954, *17*, 350–354.

Collins, B., and Helmreich, R. Studies in forced compliance: II. Contrasting mechanisms of attitude change produced by public-persuasive and private-essays. Paper read at East. Psychol. Ass., Philadelphia, 1965.

Cromwell, H. The relative effect on audience attitude of the first versus the second argumentative speech of a series. *Speech Monogr.*, 1950, *17*, 105–122.

Culbertson, F. Modification of an emotionally held attitude through role playing. *J. abnorm. soc. Psychol.*, 1957, *54*, 230–233.

Dabbs, J., and Janis, I. Why does eating while reading facilitate opinion change? An experimental inquiry. *J. exp. soc. Psychol.*, 1965, *1*, 133–144.

Das, J. Prestige effects in body-sway suggestibility. *J. abnorm. soc. Psychol.*, 1960, *61*, 487–488.

Das, J., and Nanda, P. Mediated transfer of attitudes. *J. abnorm. soc. Psychol.*, 1963, *66*, 12–16.

Davidson, J. Cognitive familiarity and dissonance reduction. In L. Festinger (Ed.), *Conflict, decision and dissonance*. Stanford: Stanford Univer. Press, 1964. Pp. 45–49.

Davidson, J., and Kiesler, S. Cognitive behavior before and after decisions. In L. Festinger (Ed.), *Conflict, decision and dissonance*. Stanford: Stanford Univer. Press, 1964. Pp. 10–19.

Davis, K., and Jones, E. Changes in interpersonal perception as a means of reducing cognitive dissonance. *J. abnorm. soc. Psychol.*, 1960, *61*, 402–410.

Deutsch, M., Krauss, R., and Rosenau, N. Dissonance or defensiveness? *J. Pers.*, 1962, *30*, 16–28.

DeWolfe, A., and Governale, C. Fear and attitude change. *J. abnorm. soc. Psychol.*, 1964, *69*, 119–123.

Dillehay, R. Judgmental processes in response to a persuasive communication. *J. Pers. soc. Psychol.*, 1965, *1*, 631–641.

Dillehay, R., Insko, C., and Smith, M. Logical consistency and attitude change. *J. Pers. soc. Psychol.*, 1966, *3*, 646–654.

Di Vesta, F., and Merwin, J. The effects of need-oriented communications on attitude change. *J. abnorm. soc. Psychol.*, 1960, *60*, 80–85.

Doob, L. The behavior of attitudes. *Psychol. Rev.*, 1947, *54*, 135–136.

Droba, D. A scale of militarism-pacificism. *J. educ. Psychol.*, 1931, *22*, 96–111.

Dulany, D. The place of hypotheses and intentions: an analysis of verbal control in verbal conditioning. *J. Pers.* (Supplement), 1962, *30*, 102–129.

Duncker, K. Experimental modification of children's food preferences through social suggestion. *J. abnorm. soc. Psychol.*, 1938, *33*, 489–507.

Ekman, P. A comparison of verbal and nonverbal behavior as reinforcing stimuli of opinion responses. Unpublished doctoral dissertation, Adelphi College, 1958.

Elms, A., and Janis, I. Counter-norm attitudes induced by consonant versus dissonant conditions of role playing. *J. exp. Res. Pers.*, 1965, *1*, 50–60.

Ewing, T. A study of certain factors involved in changes of opinion. *J. soc. Psychol.*, 1942, *16*, 63–88.

Farnsworth, P., and Misumi, I. Further data on suggestion in pictures. *J. abnorm. soc. Psychol.*, 1931, *43*, 632.

Feather, N. A structural balance model of communication effects. *Psychol. Rev.*, 1964, *71*, 291–313.

Ferster, C., and Skinner, B. *Schedules of reinforcement.* New York: Appleton-Century-Crofts, 1957.

Festinger, L. *A theory of cognitive dissonance.* Stanford: Stanford Univer. Press, 1957.

Festinger, L. Behavioral support for opinion change. *Publ. Opin. Quart.*, 1964a, *28*, 404–417.

Festinger, L. (Ed.) *Conflict, decision and dissonance.* Stanford: Stanford Univer. Press, 1964b.

Festinger, L., and Aronson, E. The arousal and reduction of dissonance in social contexts. In D. Cartwright and A. Zander (Eds.), *Group dynamics: research and theory.* (2nd ed.) New York: Harper & Row, 1960. Pp. 214–231.

Festinger, L., and Bramel, D. The reactions of humans to cognitive dissonance. In A. Bachrach (Ed.), *The experimental foundations of clinical psychology.* New York: Basic Books, 1962. Pp. 254–279.

Festinger, L., and Carlsmith, J. Cognitive consequences of forced compliance. *J. abnorm. soc. Psychol.*, 1959, *58*, 203–210.

Festinger, L., Riecken, H., and Schachter, S. *When prophecy fails.* Minneapolis: Univer. of Minnesota Press, 1956.

Festinger, L., and Walster, E. Post-decision regret and decision reversal. In

L. Festinger (Ed.), *Conflict, decision and dissonance*. Stanford: Stanford Univer. Press, 1964. Pp. 100–110.

Fishbein, M. An investigation of the relationships between beliefs about an object and the attitude toward that object. Unpublished Technical Report, Office of Naval Research, Contract Number N6 onr-233(54), 1961.

Fishbein, M. An investigation of the relationships between beliefs about an object and the attitude toward that object. *Hum. Relat.*, 1963, *16*, 233–239.

Fishbein, M., and Hunter, R. Summation versus balance in attitude organization and change. *J. abnorm. soc. Psychol.*, 1964, *69*, 505–510.

Fisher, S., and Lubin, A. Distance as a determinant of influence in a two-person serial interaction situation. *J. abnorm. soc. Psychol.*, 1958, *56*, 230–238.

Fisher, S., Rubenstein, I., and Freeman, R. Intertrial effects of immediate self-committal in a continuous social influence situation. *J. abnorm. soc. Psychol.*, 1956, *49*, 325–329.

Freed, A., Chandler, P., Blake, R., and Mouton, J. Stimulus and background factors in sign violation. *J. Pers.*, 1955, *23*, 499.

Freedman, J. Attitudinal effects of inadequate justification. *J. Pers.*, 1963, *31*, 371–385.

Freedman, J. Involvement, discrepancy, and change. *J. abnorm. soc. Psychol.*, 1964, *69*, 290–295.

Freedman, J. Long-term behavioral effects of cognitive dissonance. *J. exp. soc. Psychol.*, 1965, *1*, 145–155.

Freedman, J., and Sears, D. Selective exposure. In L. Berkowitz (Ed.), *Advances in experimental social psychology*. Vol. 2. New York: Academic Press, 1965. Pp. 58–97.

Freedman, J., and Steinbruner, J. Perceived choice and resistance to persuasion. *J. abnorm. soc. Psychol.*, 1964, *68*, 678–681.

French, J. A formal theory of social power. *Psychol. Rev.*, 1956, *63*, 181–194.

Gerard, H., and Mathewson, G. The effects of severity of initiation on liking for a group: a replication. *J. exp. soc. Psychol.*, 1966, *2*, 278–287.

Goldberg, H., and Iverson, M. Inconsistency in attitude of high status persons and loss of influence: an experimental study. *Psychol. Rep.*, 1965, *16*, 673–683.

Goldberg, S. Three situational determinants of conformity to social norms. *J. abnorm. soc. Psychol.*, 1954, *49*, 325–329.

Goldstein, I., and McGinnies, E. Compliance and attitude change under conditions of differential social reinforcement. *J. abnorm. soc. Psychol.*, 1964, *68*, 567–659.

Goldstein, M. The relationships between coping and avoiding behavior and attitude modification. Unpublished doctoral dissertation, Univer. of Washington, 1957.

Goldstein, M. The relationship between coping and avoiding behavior and response to fear-arousing propaganda. *J. abnorm. soc. Psychol.*, 1959, *58*, 247–252.

Gorfein, D. Methodological considerations in attitude change. *Psychol. Rep.*, 1963, *13*, 475–484.

Greenwald, A. Behavior change following a persuasive communication. *J. Pers.*, 1965, *33*, 370–391.

Haefner, D. Some effects of guilt-arousing and fear-arousing persuasive communications on opinion change. Unpublished Technical Report, Office of Naval Research, Contract Number N6 onr-241, 1956. (Abridgement of unpublished doctoral dissertation, Univer. of Rochester, 1956.)

Hain, J., Grahm, R. Jr., Mouton, J., and Blake, R. Stimulus and background factors in petition signing. *Southwest. soc. sci. Quart.*, 1956, *36*, 385–390.

Hardyck, J., and Braden, M. Prophecy fails again: a report of a failure to replicate. *J. abnorm. soc. Psychol.*, 1962, *65*, 136–141.

Harvey, O., and Beverly, G. Some personality correlates of concept change through role playing. *J. abnorm. soc. Psychol.*, 1961, *63*, 125–130.

Hastorf, A., and Piper, G. A note on the effect of explicit instructions on prestige suggestion. *J. soc. Psychol.*, 1951, *33*, 289–293.

Heider, F. Attitudes and cognitive organization. *J. Psychol.*, 1946, *21*, 107–112.

Heider, F. *The psychology of interpersonal relations.* New York: Wiley, 1958.

Helson, H. Adaptation-level theory. In S. Koch (Ed.), *Psychology: a study of a science.* Vol. 1. New York: McGraw-Hill, 1959. Pp. 565–621.

Helson, H. *Adaptation-level theory.* New York: Harper & Row, 1964.

Helson, H., Blake, R., and Mouton, J. An experimental investigation of the effectiveness of the "big lie" in shifting attitudes. *J. soc. Psychol.*, 1958a, *48*, 51–60.

Helson, H., Blake, R., and Mouton, J. Petition-signing as adjustment to situational and personal factors. *J. soc. Psychol.*, 1958b, *48*, 3–10.

Helson, H., Blake, R., Mouton, J., and Olmstead, J. Attitudes as adjustments to stimulus background and residual factors. *J. abnorm. soc. Psychol.*, 1956, *52*, 314–322.

Hicks, J., and Spaner, F. Attitude change and mental hospital experience. *J. abnorm. soc. Psychol.*, 1962, *65*, 112–120.

Hildum, D., and Brown, R. Verbal reinforcement and interview bias. *J. abnorm. soc. Psychol.*, 1956, *53*, 108–111.

Horowitz, M., and Pastore, N. Relationship of motive to author and statement. *Science*, 1955, *121*, 110–111.

Hovland, C. Summary and implications. In C. Hovland, *et al.* (Eds.), *The order of presentation in persuasion.* New Haven: Yale Univer. Press, 1957.

Hovland, C. Reconciling conflicting results derived from experimental and survey studies of attitude change. *Amer. Psychologist*, 1959, *14*, 8–17.

Hovland, C., Harvey, O., and Sherif, M. Assimilation and contrast effects in reactions to communication and attitude change. *J. abnorm. soc. Psychol.*, 1957, *55*, 244–252.

Hovland, C., Janis, I., and Kelley, H. *Communication and persuasion.* New Haven: Yale Univer. Press, 1953.

Hovland, C., Lumsdaine, A., and Sheffield, F. *Experiments on mass communication.* Princeton: Princeton Univer. Press, 1949.

Hovland, C., and Mandell, W. An experimental comparison of conclusion-drawing by the communicator and by the audience. *J. abnorm. soc. Psychol.*, 1952, *47*, 581–588.

Hovland, C., and Mandell, W. Is there a "Law of Primacy in persuasion"? In

C. Hovland, *et al.* (Eds.), *The order of presentation in persuasion.* New Haven: Yale Univer. Press, 1957.

Hovland, C., Mandell, W., Campbell, E., Brock, T., Luchins, A., Cohen, A., McGuire, W., Janis, I., Feierabend, R., and Anderson, N. *The order of presentation in persuasion.* New Haven: Yale Univer. Press, 1957.

Hovland, C., and Pritzker, H. Extent of opinion change as a function of amount of change advocated. *J. abnorm. soc. Psychol.,* 1957, *54,* 257–261.

Hovland, C., and Rosenberg, M. Summary and further theoretical issues. In C. Hovland and M. Rosenberg (Eds.), *Attitude organization and change.* New Haven: Yale Univer. Press, 1960. Pp. 198–232.

Hovland, C., and Weiss, W. The influence of source credibility on communication effectiveness. *Publ. Opin. Quart.,* 1951, *15,* 635–650.

Hull, C. *Principles of behavior.* New York: Appleton-Century-Crofts, 1943.

Hunt, W., and Volkmann, J. Anchoring effects in judgment. *Amer. J. Psychol.,* 1937, *54,* 395–403.

Insko, C. One-sided versus two-sided communications and counter-communications. *J. abnorm. soc. Psychol.,* 1962, *65,* 203–206.

Insko, C. Primary versus recency in persuasion as a function of the timing of arguments and measures. *J. abnorm. soc. Psychol.,* 1964, *69,* 381–391.

Insko, C. Verbal reinforcement of attitude. *J. Pers. soc. Psychol.,* 1965, *2,* 621–623.

Insko, C., Arkoff, A., and Insko, V. Effects of high and low fear-arousing communications upon opinions toward smoking. *J. exp. soc. Psychol.,* 1965, *1,* 256–266.

Insko, C., Murashima, F., and Saiyadain, M. Communicator discrepancy, stimulus ambiguity, and influence, *J. Pers.,* 1966, *34,* 262–274.

Insko, C., and Oakes, W. Awareness and the "conditioning" of attitudes. *J. Pers. soc. Psychol.,* 1966, *4,* 487–496.

Janis, I. Motivational factors in the resolution of decisional conflicts. In M. R. Jones (Ed.), *Nebraska symposium on motivation.* Vol. 7. Lincoln: Univer. of Nebraska Press, 1959.

Janis, I., and Feshbach, S. Effects of fear-arousing communications. *J. abnorm. soc. Psychol.,* 1953, *48,* 78–92.

Janis, I., and Feshbach, S. Personality differences associated with responsiveness to fear-arousing communications. *J. Pers.,* 1954, *23,* 154–166.

Janis, I., and Gilmore, J. The influence of incentive conditions on the success of role playing in modifying attitudes. *J. Pers. soc. Psychol.,* 1965, *1,* 17–27.

Janis, I., Hovland, C., Field, P., Linton, H., Graham, E., Cohen, A., Rife, D., Abelson, R., Lesser, G., and King, B. *Personality and persuasibility.* New Haven: Yale Univer. Press, 1959.

Janis, I., Kaye, D., and Kirschner, P. Facilitating effects of "eating-while-reading" on responsiveness to persuasive communications. *J. Pers. soc. Psychol.,* 1965, *1,* 181–185.

Janis, I., and King, B. The influence of role-playing on opinion change. *J. abnorm. soc. Psychol.,* 1954, *49,* 211–218.

Janis, I., and Mann, L. Effectiveness of emotional role-playing in modifying smoking habits and attitudes. *J. exp. Res. Pers.,* 1965, *1,* 84–90.

Janis, I., and Terwilliger, R. An experimental study of psychological resistances to fear-arousing communications. *J. abnorm. soc. Psychol.*, 1962, *65*, 403–410.

Jansen, M., and Stolurow, L. An experimental study in role playing. *Psychol. Monogr.*, 1962, *76*, No. 31.

Jecker, J. The cognitive effects of conflict and dissonance. In L. Festinger (Ed.), *Conflict, decision and dissonance*. Stanford: Stanford Univer. Press, 1964. Pp. 21–30.

Johnson, H., and Steiner, I. Effort and subjective probability. *J. Pers. soc. Psychol.*, 1965, *1*, 365–368.

Jones, E., and Cooper, J. Incentive magnitude and time of commitment as determinants of cognitive dissonance. Unpublished paper, 1966.

Jordan, N. Behavioral forces that are a function of attitudes and of cognitive organization. *Hum. Relat.*, 1953, *6*, 273–287.

Katz, D. The functional approach to the study of attitudes. *Publ. Opin. Quart.*, 1960, *24*, 163–204.

Katz, D., McClintock, C., and Sarnoff, I. The measurement of ego defense as related to attitude change. *J. Pers.*, 1957, *25*, 465–474.

Katz, D., Sarnoff, I., and McClintock, C. Ego-defense and attitude change. *Hum. Relat.*, 1956, *9*, 27–45.

Katz, D., and Stotland, E. A preliminary statement to a theory of attitude structure and change. In S. Koch (Ed.), *Psychology: a study of a science*. Vol. 3. New York: McGraw-Hill, 1959. Pp. 423–475.

Kelman, H. Attitude change as a function of response restriction. *Hum. Relat.*, 1953, *6*, 185–214.

Kelman, H. Compliance, identification and internalization: three processes of attitude change. *J. conflict Resol.*, 1958, *2*, 51–60.

Kelman, H. Effects of role-orientation and value-orientation on the nature of attitude change. Paper read at East. Psychol. Ass., New York, 1960.

Kelman, H. Processes of opinion change. *Publ. Opin. Quart.*, 1961, *25*, 57–58.

Kelman, H., and Cohler, J. Reactions to persuasive communication as a function of cognitive needs and styles. Paper read at East. Psychol. Ass., Atlantic City, 1959.

Kelman, H., and Hovland, C. "Reinstatement" of the communicator in delayed measurement of opinion change. *J. abnorm. soc. Psychol.*, 1953, *48*, 327–335.

Kerrick, J. The effect of relevant and non-relevant sources on attitude change. *J. soc. Psychol.*, 1958, *47*, 15–20.

Kerrick, J. News pictures, captions and the point of resolution. *Journ. Quart.*, 1959, *36*, 183–188.

Kerrick, J. The effects of instructional set on the measurement of attitude change through communications. *J. soc. Psychol.*, 1961, *53*, 113–120.

Kimbrell, D., and Blake, R. Motivational factors in the violation of a prohibition. *J. abnorm. soc. Psychol.*, 1958, *56*, 132–137.

King, B., and Janis, I. Comparison of the effectiveness of improvised versus nonimprovised role-playing in producing opinion change. *Hum. Relat.*, 1956, *9*, 177–186.

Knower, R. Experimental studies of changes in attitude: II. A study of the effect of printed argument on changes in attitude. *J. abnorm. soc. Psychol.*, 1936, *30*, 522–532.

Krasner, L., Knowles, J., and Ullmann, L. Effects of verbal conditioning of attitudes on subsequent motor performance. *J. Pers. soc. Psychol.*, 1965, *1*, 407–412.

Krech, D., and Crutchfield, R. *Theory and problems of social psychology.* New York: McGraw-Hill, 1948.

Lana, R. A further investigation of the pretest-treatment interaction effect. *J. appl. Psychol.*, 1959a, *43*, 421–422.

Lana, R. Pretest-treatment interaction effects in attitudinal studies. *Psychol. Bull.*, 1959b, *56*, 293–300.

Lana, R. Familiarity and the order of presentation of persuasive communications. *J. abnorm. soc. Psychol.*, 1961, *63*, 656–659.

Lana, R. Controversy of the topic and the order of presentation of persuasive communications. *Psychol. Rep.*, 1963a, *12*, 163–170.

Lana, R. Interest, media and order effects in persuasive communications. *J. Psychol.*, 1963b, *56*, 9–13.

Lana, R. The influence of the pretest on order effects in persuasive communications. *J. abnorm. soc. Psychol.*, 1964a, *69*, 337–341.

Lana, R. Three theoretical interpretations of order effects in persuasive communications. *Psychol. Bull.*, 1964b, *61*, 314–320.

Lana, R., and Rosnow, R. Subject awareness and order effects in persuasive communications. *Psychol. Rep.*, 1963, *12*, 523–529.

Lefkowitz, M., Blake, R., and Mouton, J. Status factors in pedestrian violation of traffic signals. *J. abnorm. soc. Psychol.*, 1955, *51*, 704–705.

Lerner, M. The effects of preparatory action on beliefs concerning nuclear war. *J. soc. Psychol.*, 1965, *65*, 225–232.

Leventhal, G. Reward magnitude, task attractiveness, and liking for instrumental activity. *J. abnorm. soc. Psychol.*, 1964, *68*, 460–463.

Leventhal, H., and Niles, P. A field experiment on fear arousal with data on the validity of questionnaire measures. *J. Pers.*, 1964, *32*, 459–479.

Leventhal, H., and Niles, P. Persistence of influence for varying durations of exposure to threat stimuli. *Psychol. Rep.*, 1965, *16*, 223–233.

Leventhal, H., Singer, R., and Jones, S. Effects of fear and specificity of recommendation upon attitudes and behavior. *J. Pers. soc. Psychol.*, 1965, *2*, 20–29.

Levin, S. The effect of awareness on verbal conditioning. *J. exp. Psychol.*, 1961, *61*, 67–75.

Lewin, K. *Dynamic theory of personality.* New York: McGraw-Hill, 1935.

Lewis, H. Studies in the principles of judgments and attitudes: IV. The operation of "prestige suggestion." *J. soc. Psychol.*, 1941, *14*, 229–256.

Lorge, I. Prestige suggestion and attitude. *J. soc. Psychol.*, 1936, 7, 386–402.

Lumsdaine, A., and Janis, I. Resistance to counter-propaganda produced by a one-sided versus a two-sided propaganda presentation. *Publ. Opin. Quart.*, 1953, *17*, 311–318.

Lund, F. The psychology of belief: IV. The law of primacy in persuasion. *J. abnorm. soc. Psychol.*, 1925, *20*, 183–191.

Macaulay, J. A study of independent and additive modes of producing resistance to persuasion derived from congruity and inoculation models. Unpublished doctoral dissertation, Univer. of Wisconsin, 1965.

Maccoby, E., Maccoby, N., Romney, A., and Adams, J. Social reinforcement in attitude change. *J. abnorm. soc. Psychol.,* 1961, *63,* 109–115.

McConnell, J., and Blake, R. A methodological study of tape-recorded synthetic group atmospheres. *Amer. Psychologist,* 1953, *8,* 395.

McGuire, W. Order of presentation as a factor in "conditioning" persuasiveness. In C. Hovland, *et al.* (Eds.), *The order of presentation in persuasion.* New Haven: Yale Univer. Press, 1957. Pp. 98–114.

McGuire, W. A syllogistic analysis of cognitive relationships. In C. Hovland and M. Rosenberg (Eds.), *Attitude organization and change.* New Haven: Yale Univer. Press, 1960a. Pp. 65–111.

McGuire, W. Cognitive consistency and attitude change. *J. abnorm. soc. Psychol.* 1960b, *60,* 345–353.

McGuire, W. Direct and indirect effects of dissonance-producing messages. *J. abnorm. soc. Psychol.,* 1960c, *60,* 354–358.

McGuire, W. Resistance to persuasion conferred by active and passive prior refutation of the same and alternative counterarguments. *J. abnorm. soc. Psychol.,* 1961a, *63,* 326–332.

McGuire, W. The effectiveness of supportive and refutational defenses in immunizing and restoring beliefs against persuasion. *Sociometry,* 1961b, *24,* 184–197.

McGuire, W. *Immunization against persuasion.* Unpublished manuscript, 1962a.

McGuire, W. Persistence of the resistance to persuasion induced by various types of prior belief defenses. *J. abnorm. soc. Psychol.,* 1962b, *64,* 241–248.

McGuire, W. Inducing resistance to persuasion. In L. Berkowitz (Ed.), *Advances in experimental social psychology.* Vol. 1. New York: Academic Press, 1964. Pp. 191–229.

McGuire, W. Attitudes and opinions. In P. Farnsworth (Ed.), *Ann. Rev. Psychol.,* 1966, *17,* 475–514.

McGuire, W., and Papageorgis, D. The relative efficacy of various types of prior belief-defense in producing immunity against persuasion. *J. abnorm. soc. Psychol.,* 1961, *62,* 327–337.

McGuire, W., and Papageorgis, D. Effectiveness of forewarning in developing resistance to persuasion. *Publ. Opin. Quart.,* 1962, *26,* 24–34.

Manis, M. The interpretation of opinion statements as a function of recipient attitude. *J. abnorm. soc. Psychol.,* 1960, *60,* 340–344.

Manis, M. The interpretation of opinion statements as a function of message ambiguity and recipient attitude. *J. abnorm. soc. Psychol.,* 1961a, *63,* 76–81.

Manis, M. The interpretation of opinion statements as a function of recipient attitude and source prestige. *J. abnorm. soc. Psychol.,* 1961b, *63,* 82–86.

Manis, M., and Blake, J. Interpretation of persuasive messages as a function of prior immunization. *J. abnorm. soc. Psychol.,* 1963, *66,* 225–230.

Marlowe, D., Frager, R., and Nuttall, R. Commitment to action taking as a consequence of cognitive dissonance. *J. Pers. soc. Psychol.*, 1965, *2*, 864–867.

Meehl, P. On the circularity of the law of effect. *Psychol. Bull.*, 1950, *47*, 52–55.

Michael, W., Rosenthal, B., and DeCamp, M. An experimental investigation of prestige-suggestion for two types of literary material. *J. Psychol.*, 1949, *28*, 303–323.

Miller, N. Involvement and dogmatism as inhibitors of attitude change. *J. exp. soc. Psychol.*, 1965, *1*, 121–132.

Miller, N., and Campbell, D. Recency and primacy in persuasion as a function of the timing of speeches and measurements. *J. abnorm. soc. Psychol.*, 1959, *54*, 1–9.

Miller, N., and Dollard, J. *Social learning and imitation.* New Haven: Yale Univer. Press, 1941.

Mills, J. Changes in moral attitudes following temptation. *J. Pers.*, 1958, *26*, 517–531.

Mitnick, L., and McGinnies, E. Influencing ethnocentrism in small discussion groups through a film communication. *J. abnorm. soc. Psychol.*, 1958, *56*, 82–90.

Moltz, H., and Thistlethwaite, D. Attitude modification and anxiety reduction. *J. abnorm. soc. Psychol.*, 1955, *50*, 231–237.

Morrissette, J. An experimental study of the theory of structural balance. *Hum. Relat.*, 1958, *11*, 239–254.

Mouton, J., Blake, R., and Olmstead, J. The relationship between frequency of yielding and the disclosure of personal identity. *J. Pers.*, 1956, *24*, 339–347.

Murphy, G., Murphy, L., and Newcomb, T. *Experimental social psychology.* New York: Harper & Row, 1937.

Newcomb, T. An approach to the study of communicative acts. *Psychol. Rev.*, 1953, *60*, 393–404.

Newcomb, T. Individual systems of orientation. In S. Koch (Ed.), *Psychology: a study of a science.* Vol. 3. New York: McGraw-Hill, 1959. Pp. 384–422.

Nuttin, J. Attitude change after rewarded dissonant and consonant "forced compliance." *Int. J. Psychol.*, 1966, *1*, 39–57.

Olmstead, J., and Blake, R. The use of simulated groups to produce modification in judgment. *J. Pers.*, 1955, *23*, 335–345.

Orne, M. The nature of hypnosis: artifact and essence. *J. abnorm. soc. Psychol.*, 1959, *58*, 277–299.

Orne, M. On the social psychology of the psychological experiment: with particular reference to demand characteristics and their implication. *Amer. Psychologist*, 1962, *17*, 776–783.

Orne, M., and Evans, F. Social control in the psychological experiment: antisocial behavior and hypnosis. *J. Pers. soc. Psychol.*, 1965, *1*, 189–200.

Orne, M., and Scheibe, K. The contribution of nondeprivation factors in the production of sensory deprivation effects: the psychology of the "panic button." *J. abnorm. soc. Psychol.*, 1964, *68*, 3–12.

Osgood, C. The nature and measurement of meaning. *Psychol. Bull.*, 1952, *49*, 197–237.

Osgood, C. Cognitive dynamics in the conduct of human affairs. *Publ. Opin. Quart.*, 1960, *24*, 341–356.

Osgood, C. On understanding and creating sentences. Paper read at Amer. Psychol. Ass., Philadelphia, September 1, 1963.

Osgood, C., Suci, G., and Tannenbaum, P. *The measurement of meaning*. Urbana: Univer. of Illinois Press, 1958.

Osgood, C., and Tannenbaum, P. The principle of congruity in the prediction of attitude change. *Psychol. Rev.*, 1955, *62*, 42–55.

Papageorgis, D., and McGuire, W. The generality of immunity to persuasion produced by pre-exposure to weakened counterarguments. *J. abnorm. soc. Psychol.*, 1961, *62*, 475–481.

Pastore, N., and Horowitz, M. The influence of attributed motive on the acceptance of statement. *J. abnorm. soc. Psychol.*, 1955, *51*, 331–332.

Peak, H. Attitude and motivation. In M. Jones (Ed.), *Nebraska symposium on motivation*. Lincoln: Univer. of Nebraska Press, 1955, *3*, 149–188.

Peak, H. Psychological structure and psychological activity. *Psychol. Rev.*, 1958, *65*, 325–347.

Perloe, S. Status and judgment of occupational prestige. Unpublished paper, 1960.

Powell, F. Source credibility and behavioral compliance as determinants of attitude change. *J. Pers. soc. Psychol.*, 1965, *2*, 669–676.

Price, K., Harburg, E., and McLeod, J. Positive and negative affect as a function of perceived discrepancy in ABX situations. *Hum. Relat.*, 1965, *18*, 87–100.

Price, K., Harburg, E., and Newcomb, T. Psychological balance in situations of negative interpersonal attitudes. *J. Pers. soc. Psychol.*, 1966, *3*, 265–270.

Rabbie, J., Brehm, J., and Cohen, A. Verbalization and reactions to cognitive dissonance. *J. Pers.*, 1959, *27*, 407–417.

Raven, B., and Fishbein, M. Acceptance of punishment and change in belief. *J. abnorm. soc. Psychol.*, 1961, *63*, 411–416.

Razran, G. Conditioning away social bias by the luncheon technique. *Psychol. Bull.*, 1938, *35*, 693.

Razran, G. Conditioned response changes in rating and appraising sociopolitical slogans. *Psychol. Bull.*, 1940, *37*, 481.

Rogers, S. The anchoring of absolute judgments. *Arch. Psychol.*, 1941, *37*, 261.

Rokeach, M. (Ed.), *The open and closed mind*. New York: Basic Books, 1960.

Rokeach, M. Belief versus race as determinants of social distance: comments on Triandis' paper. *J. abnorm. soc. Psychol.*, 1961, *62*, 187–188.

Rokeach, M., and Mezei, L. Race and shared belief as factors in social choice. *Science*, 1966, *151*, 167–172.

Rokeach, M., and Rothman, G. The principle of belief congruence and the congruity principle as models of cognitive interaction. *Psychol. Rev.*, 1965, *72*, 128–172.

Rokeach, M., Smith, P., and Evans, R. Two kinds of prejudice or one? In M.

Rokeach (Ed.), *The open and closed mind.* New York: Basic Books, 1960. Pp. 132–168.

Rosenbaum, M. The effect of stimulus and background factors on the volunteering response. *J. abnorm. soc. Psychol.,* 1956, *53,* 118–121.

Rosenbaum, M., and Blake, R. Volunteering as a function of field structure. *J. abnorm. soc. Psychol.,* 1955, *50,* 193–196.

Rosenbaum, M., and Franc, D. Opinion change as a function of external commitment and amount of discrepancy from the opinion of another. *J. abnorm. soc. Psychol.,* 1960, *61,* 15–20.

Rosenberg, M. The experimental investigation of a value theory of attitude structure. Unpublished doctoral dissertation, Univer. of Michigan, 1953.

Rosenberg, M. Cognitive structure and attitudinal affect. *J. abnorm. soc. Psychol.,* 1956, *53,* 367–372.

Rosenberg, M. An analysis of affective-cognitive consistency. In C. Hovland and M. Rosenberg (Eds.), *Attitude organization and change.* New Haven: Yale Univer. Press, 1960a. Pp. 15–64.

Rosenberg, M. Cognitive reorganization in response to the hypnotic reversal of attitudinal affect. *J. Pers.,* 1960b, *28,* 39–63.

Rosenberg, M. A structural theory of attitude dynamics. *Publ. Opin. Quart.,* 1960c, *24,* 319–340.

Rosenberg, M. Some content determinants of intolerance for attitudinal inconsistency. In S. Tomkins and C. Izard (Eds.), *Affect, cognition and personality.* New York: Springer Publishing Company, 1965a. Pp. 130–147.

Rosenberg, M. When dissonance fails: on eliminating evaluation apprehension from attitude measurement. *J. Pers. soc. Psychol.,* 1965b, *1,* 28–42.

Rosenberg, M. Some limits of dissonance: toward a differentiated view of counterattitudinal performance. In S. Feldman (Ed.), *The consistency postulate in social attitudes and behavior.* New York: Academic Press, 1966. Pp. 137–170.

Rosenberg, M., and Abelson, R. An analysis of cognitive balancing. In C. Hovland and M. Rosenberg (Eds.), *Attitude organization and change.* New Haven: Yale Univer. Press, 1960. Pp. 112–163.

Rosenberg, M., Hovland, C., McGuire, W., Abelson, R., and Brehm, J. *Attitude organization and change.* New Haven: Yale Univer. Press, 1960.

Rosenblatt, P. Enhancement of persuasion by threat. Paper read at Midwest. Psychol. Ass., Chicago, April, 1965.

Rosenthal, R. On the social psychology of the psychology experiment: the experimenter's hypothesis as unintended determinant of experimental results. *Amer. Scient.,* 1963, *51,* 268–283.

Rosenthal, R. The effects of the experimenter on the results of psychological research. In B. A. Maher (Ed.), *Progress in experimental personality research.* New York: Academic Press, 1964. Pp. 80–114.

Rosenthal, R., and Fode, K. Psychology of the scientists: V. Three experiments in experimenter bias. *Psychol. Rep.,* 1963, *12,* 491–511.

Rosenthal, R., Fode, K., Vikan-Kline, L., and Persinger, G. Verbal conditioning: mediator of experimenter expectancy effects. *Psychol. Rep.,* 1964, *14,* 71–74.

Saadi, M., and Farnsworth, P. The degree of acceptance of dogmatic statements and preferences for their supposed makers. *J. abnorm. soc. Psychol.*, 1934, *29*, 143–150.

Sampson, E., and Insko, C. Cognitive consistency and performance in the autokinetic situation. *J. abnorm. soc. Psychol.*, 1964, *68*, 184–192.

Sarnoff, I. Identification with the aggressor: some personality correlates of anti-Semitism among Jews. *J. Pers.*, 1951, *2*, 199–218.

Sarnoff, I. Psychoanalytic theory and social attitudes. *Publ. Opin. Quart.*, 1960a, *24*, 251–279.

Sarnoff, I. Reaction formation and cynicism. *J. Pers.*, 1960b, *28*, 129–143.

Sarnoff, I. *Personality dynamics and development*. New York: Wiley, 1962.

Sarnoff, I. The experimental evaluation of psychoanalytic hypotheses. *Trans. N. Y. Acad. Sci.*, 1965, *28*, 272–289.

Sarnoff, I. Psychoanalytic theory and cognitive dissonance. Unpublished paper, 1966.

Sarnoff, I., and Corwin, S. Castration anxiety and the fear of death. *J. Pers.*, 1959, *27*, 374–385.

Sarnoff, I., and Katz, D. The motivational bases of attitude change. *J. abnorm. soc. Psychol.*, 1954, *49*, 115–124.

Sarnoff, I., and Zimbardo, P. Anxiety, fear and social affiliation. *J. abnorm. soc. Psychol.*, 1961, *62*, 356–363.

Schopler, J. Social power. In L. Berkowitz (Ed.), *Advances in experimental social psychology*. Vol. 2. New York: Academic Press, 1965.

Schopler, J., and Bateson, N. A dependence interpretation of the effects of a severe initiation. *J. Pers.*, 1962, *30*, 633–649.

Schultz, D. Primacy-recency within a sensory variation framework. *Psychol. Rec.*, 1963a, *13*, 129–139.

Schultz, D. Time, awareness, and order of presentation in opinion change. *J. appl. Psychol.*, 1963b, *47*, 280–283.

Scott, W. Attitude change through reward of verbal behavior. *J. abnorm. soc. Psychol.*, 1957, *55*, 72–75.

Scott, W. Attitude change by response reinforcement: replication and extension. *Sociometry*, 1959, *22*, 328–335.

Sherif, M. An experimental study of stereotypes. *J. abnorm. soc. Psychol.*, 1935a, *29*, 371–375.

Sherif, M. A study of some social factors in perception. *Arch. Psychol.*, 1935b, *27*, 187.

Sherif, M., and Hovland, C. *Social judgment*. New Haven: Yale Univer. Press, 1961.

Sherif, C., Sherif, M., and Nebergall, R. *Attitude and attitude change*. Philadelphia: Saunders, 1965.

Sherif, M., Taub, D., and Hovland, C. Assimilation and contrast effects of anchoring stimuli on judgments. *J. exp. Psychol.*, 1958, *55*, 150–155.

Silverman, I. In defense of dissonance theory: reply to Chapanis and Chapanis. *Psychol. Bull.*, 1964, *62*, 205–209.

Sims, V. Factors influencing attitudes toward T.V.A. *J. abnorm. soc. Psychol.*, 1938, *33*, 34–56.

Singer, R. Verbal conditioning and generalization of prodemocratic responses. *J. abnorm. soc. Psychol.*, 1961, *63*, 43–46.

Smith, E. The power of dissonance techniques to change attitudes. *Publ. Opin. Quart.*, 1961, *25*, 626–639.

Smith, M. Personal values as determinants of a political attitude. *J. Psychol.*, 1949, *28*, 477–486.

Smith, M., Bruner, J., and White, R. *Opinions and personality.* New York: Wiley, 1956.

Solomon, R. An extension of control group design. *Psychol. Bull.*, 1949, *46*, 137–150.

Spielberger, C. The role of awareness in verbal conditioning. *J. Pers.* (Supplement), 1962, *30*, 73–101.

Staats, A., and Staats, C. Attitudes established by classical conditioning. *J. abnorm. soc. Psychol.*, 1958, *57*, 37–40.

Staats, A., Staats, C., and Biggs, D. Meaning of verbal stimuli changed by conditioning. *Amer. J. Psychol.*, 1958, *71*, 429–431.

Staats, A., Staats, C., and Heard, W. Attitude development and ratio of reinforcement. *Sociometry*, 1960, *23*, 338–350.

Staats, C., and Staats, A. Meaning established by classical conditioning. *J. exp. Psychol.*, 1957, *54*, 74–80.

Stachowiak, J., and Moss, C. Hypnotic alterations of social attitudes. *J. Pers. soc. Psychol.*, 1965, *2*, 77–83.

Stagner, R., and Britton, R. The conditioning technique applied to a public opinion problem. *J. soc. Psychol.*, 1949, *29*, 103–111.

Stanley, J., and Klausmeier, H. Opinion constancy after formal role playing. *J. soc. Psychol.*, 1957, *46*, 11–18.

Stein, D. Similarity of belief systems and interpersonal preference: a test of Rokeach's theory of prejudice. Unpublished doctoral dissertation, Univer. of California, 1965.

Stein, D., Hardyck, J., and Smith, M. Race and belief: an open and shut case. *J. Pers. soc. Psychol.*, 1965, *1*, 281–289.

Steiner, I. Sex differences in the resolution of A-B-X conflicts. *J. Pers.*, 1960, *28*, 118–128.

Steiner, I. Receptivity to supportive versus nonsupportive communications. *J. abnorm. soc. Psychol.*, 1962, *65*, 266–267.

Steiner, I., and Johnson, H. Relationships among dissonance reducing responses. *J. abnorm. soc. Psychol.*, 1964, *68*, 38–44.

Steiner, I., and Rogers, E. Alternative responses to dissonance. *J. abnorm. soc. Psychol.*, 1963, *66*, 128–136.

Suchman, E. The intensity component in attitude and opinion research. In S. Stouffer, L. Guttman, E. Suchman, P. Lazarsfeld, S. Star, and J. Clausen, *Measurement and prediction.* Princeton: Princeton Univer. Press, 1950. Pp. 213–276.

Taffel, C. Anxiety and the conditioning of verbal behavior. *J. abnorm. soc. Psychol.*, 1955, *51*, 496–501.

Tannenbaum, P. Attitudes toward source and concept as factors in attitude change through communications. Unpublished doctoral dissertation, Univer. of Illinois, 1953.

Tannenbaum, P. Initial attitude toward source and concept as factors in attitude change through communication. *Publ. Opin. Quart.*, 1956, *20,* 413–425.

Tannenbaum, P. Mediated generalization of attitude change via the principle of congruity. *J. Pers. soc. Psychol.*, 1966, *3,* 493–500.

Tannenbaum, P. The congruity principle revisited: studies in the reduction, induction and generalization of persuasion. In L. Berkowitz (Ed.), *Advances in experimental social psychology.* Vol. 3. New York: Academic Press, in press.

Tannenbaum, P., and Gengel, R. Generalization of attitude change through congruity principle relationships. *J. Pers. soc. Psychol.*, 1966, *3,* 299–304.

Tannenbaum, P., Macaulay, J., and Norris, E. Principle of congruity and reduction of persuasion. *J. Pers. soc. Psychol.*, 1966, *3,* 233–238.

Tannenbaum, P., and Norris, E. Effects of combining congruity principle strategies for the reduction of persuasion. *Sociometry,* 1965, *28,* 145–157.

Thibaut, J., and Kelley, H. *The social psychology of groups.* New York: Wiley, 1959.

Thomas, E., Webb, S., and Tweedie, J. Effects of familiarity with a controversial issue on acceptance of successive persuasive communications. *J. abnorm. soc. Psychol.*, 1961, *63,* 656–659.

Triandis, H. A note on Rokeach's theory of prejudice. *J. abnorm. soc. Psychol.*, 1961, *62,* 184–186.

Triandis, H. Exploratory factor analyses of the behavioral component of social attitudes. *J. abnorm. soc. Psychol.*, 1964, *68,* 420–430.

Triandis, H., and Davis, E. Race and belief as determinants of behavioral intentions. *J. Pers. soc. Psychol.*, 1965, *2,* 715–725.

Triandis, H., and Fishbein, M. Cognitive interaction in person perception. *J. abnorm. soc. Psychol.*, 1963, *67,* 446–453.

Triandis, H., and Triandis, L. Race, social class, religion, and nationality as determinants of social distance. *J. abnorm. soc. Psychol.*, 1960, *61,* 110–118.

Tuddenham, R. *Studies in conformity and yielding: V. The influence upon judgment of a moderately distorted norm.* Unpublished Technical Report No. 6, Office of Naval Research Contract NR 170–159, Univer. of California, 1958a.

Tuddenham, R. The influence of a distorted group norm upon individual judgment. *J. Psychol.*, 1958b, *46,* 227–241.

Underwood, B. Retroactive and proactive inhibition after five and forty-eight hours. *J. exp. Psychol.*, 1948, *38,* 29–38.

Wallace, J. Role reward and dissonance reduction. *J. Pers. soc. Psychol.*, 1966, *3,* 305–312.

Walster, E. The temporal sequence of post-decision processes. In L. Festinger (Ed.), *Conflict, decision and dissonance.* Stanford: Stanford Univer. Press, 1964. Pp. 112–127.

Watts, W. Cognitive reorganization following a disconfirmed expectancy. *J. Pers. soc. Psychol.*, 1965, *2,* 231–241.

Watts, W., and McGuire, W. Persistence of induced opinion change and retention of the inducing message contents. *J. abnorm. soc. Psychol.*, 1964, *68,* 233–241.

Weiss, W. The effects of a communication on attitude change and scale judgments. *J. abnorm. soc. Psychol.*, 1961, *62*, 133–140.

Whittaker, J. Opinion change as a function of communication-attitude discrepancy. *Psychol. Rep.*, 1963, *13*, 763–772.

Woodruff, H., and Di Vesta, F. The relationship between values, concepts, and attitudes. *Educ. psychol. Measmt*, 1948, *8*, 645–660.

Woodworth, R. *Experimental psychology.* New York: Holt, Rinehart and Winston, 1938.

Yaryan, R., and Festinger, L. Preparatory action and belief in the probable occurrence of future events. *J. abnorm. soc. Psychol.*, 1961, *63*, 603–606.

Zajonc, R. Structure of cognitive field. Unpublished doctoral dissertation, Univer. of Michigan, 1954.

Zajonc, R. The concepts of balance, congruity, and dissonance. *Publ. Opin. Quart.*, 1960, *24*, 280–296.

Zimbardo, P. Involvement and communication discrepancy as determinants of opinion conformity. *J. abnorm. soc. Psychol.*, 1960, *60*, 86–94.

Zimbardo, P. The effect of effort and improvisation on self-persuasion produced by role-playing. *J. exp. soc. Psychol.*, 1965, *1*, 103–120.

Zimbardo, P., Weisenberg, M., Firestone, I., and Levy, B. Communicator effectiveness in producing public conformity and private attitude change. *J. Pers.*, 1965, *33*, 233–255.

NAME INDEX

Abelson, R., 1, 140, 155, 177, 180, 181, 182, 183, 190, 191, 196
Adams, J., 20
Adorno, T., 332
Allen, V., 214, 218
Allport, F., 2
Allport, G., 2, 99
Anderson, L., 136, 304, 305, 307
Anderson, N., 1, 53, 61, 137
Arkoff, A., 38, 40, 41
Aronson, E., 42, 47, 48, 78, 81, 82, 83, 85, 246, 247, 248, 251, 252, 271, 278
Asch, S., 60, 121, 123, 124, 139, 189

Bailyn, L., 344
Ball, J., 95
Bateson, N., 248, 250, 252
Bergin, A., 48, 81, 85, 90
Berkowitz, L., 37
Beverly, G., 221, 223
Biggs, D., 26
Birch, H., 125
Blackwood, J., 254
Blake, J., 325
Blake, R., 72, 85, 94, 95, 96, 97, 98, 99, 100
Blandford, D., 26
Block, H., 123, 124
Bochner, S., 48, 82, 85
Bostrom, R., 16, 17
Braden, M., 280
Bramel, D., 295
Brehm, J., 1, 96, 204, 207, 208, 209, 210, 213, 218, 228, 232, 233, 237, 245, 251, 252, 253, 255, 256, 258, 259, 260, 266, 269, 282, 283, 346
Britton, R., 30
Brock, T., 1, 210, 218, 254, 258, 262, 264, 269
Brown, R., 18, 24, 115, 117, 139
Bruner, J., 330, 331, 333, 334, 337
Burdick, H., 173
Burnes, A., 173
Buss, A., 264, 269
Byrne, D., 147, 152

Calvin, A., 20
Campbell, D., 4, 5, 52, 54, 55, 56, 59, 60, 61, 219, 295
Campbell, E., 49, 60
Cantril, H., 70
Carlsmith, J., 42, 48, 78, 81, 82, 83, 85, 227, 234, 238, 239, 241, 242, 243, 246, 247, 251, 278, 288
Carlson, E., 70, 187, 196
Cartwright, D., 164, 167, 175, 185
Cattell, R., 344
Chandler, P., 97
Chapanis, A., 209, 227, 248, 250, 261, 272
Chapanis, N., 209, 227, 248, 250, 261, 272
Chen, W., 70
Choo, T., 47
Cohen, A., 1, 49, 60, 70, 77, 85, 204, 209, 213, 218, 228, 230, 232, 239, 243, 252, 253, 254, 258, 259, 260, 261, 265, 266, 269, 274, 282, 346
Cohen, B., 28
Cohler, J., 344
Cole, D., 126, 127
Collins, B., 238, 240, 241, 243
Cooper, J., 242, 243
Cottingham, D., 37
Cromwell, H., 49
Crutchfield, R., 125
Culbertson, F., 221, 223

Dabbs, J., 32, 33
Das, J., 27, 127
Davidson, J., 211, 218, 270, 283
Davis, E., 151
Davis, K., 262, 269, 270
De Camp, M., 125
Deutsch, M., 208, 217
DeWolfe, A., 38, 41
Dillehay, R., 108, 110
Di Vesta, F., 185, 187, 188, 196
Dollard, J., 12
Doob, L., 12
Droba, D., 95
Dulany, D., 23, 24
Duncker, K., 122, 123, 124
Duryea, R., 95

SUBJECT INDEX

Adaptation-Level theory (Helson), 92–101
  adaptation-level, 92–93
  contextual stimuli, 93
  dimensions, bipolar, 92
  evaluation of, 100–101
  focal stimuli, 93
  research on, 94–100
  residual stimuli, 93
Affective-Cognitive consistency theory (Rosenberg-Abelson), evaluation of, 197
  initial version of, 177–179
    attitude, definition of, 177
    attitude structure, 177–178
    attitudinal homeostasis, 178–179
    two sequences of attitude change, 179
  later version of, 179–184
    cognitive elements, 179
    cognitive relations, 179
    cognitive units, 180
    conceptual arena, 181
    imbalance, resolution of, 182–183
    psycho-logic, 181–182
  research on, 183–197
  (*See also* Balance theories)
After-only design (Campbell), 5–6, 345
Assimilation, relation to summation, 159
  Rokeach and Rothman's evidence for, 156
  Rokeach's theory of, 143–144
  (*See also* Assimilation-Contrast theory)
Assimilation-Contrast theory (Sherif-Hovland), 64–91
  anchors, 65–67
  assimilation, 66–67
  contrast, 66–67
  evaluation of, 90–91
  latitudes of acceptance and rejection, research on, 88–90
    theory of, 68
  reference scales, 64–65
  research on, 69–70
  (*See also* Discrepancy)
Attitude, concept of, 2–3
  Hovland, Janis, and Kelley's definition

Attitude—*continued*
  of, 12
  Katz's definition of, 334
  opinion, 2–3, 330–331
  Osgood and Tannenbaum's definition of, 112–113
  Rosenberg's definition of, 177
  Sarnoff's definition of, 286–287
  Smith, Bruner, and White's definition of, 330–331
Attitude structure, affective-cognitive consistency theory of, 177–178
  research on, 184–187

Balance theories, evaluation of, 174–176
  Heider's theory, 161–165
    balance, 161–164
    graph theory, statement of (Cartwright-Harary), 164–165
    imbalance, results of, 164
    self-sentiment, 164
    sentiment relations, 161
    unit relations, 161
  Newcomb's theory, 165–167
    autism, 166
    communication, 166
    constructs, 165
    strain induction, 166
    strain reduction, 167
  research on, 167–174
  [*See also* Affective-Cognitive consistency theory (Rosenberg-Abelson)]
Before-after design (Campbell-Solomon), 3–6, 345
Belief congruence theory (Rokeach), 141–160
  assertions, 141–142
  belief congruence, principle of, 144
  C and *S*, 142–143
  compared with congruity theory, 144–145
  CS and *C*, 143–144
  evaluation of, 158–160
  relevance comparison, 142
  research on, 145–157
Boomerang (*see* Discrepancy)

371